CW00456732

CONTENTS

AUSTRALIAN MURDERS

127 Killings That Shocked The Nation

JIM MAIN

Publishing

Third reprint.
First published 2004. Reprinted 2005 (twice).

Published by:

Bas Publishing
ABN 30 106 181 542
F16/171 Collins Street
Melbourne Vic. 3000
Tel: (03) 9650 3200
Fax: (03) 9650 5077
Web: www.baspublishing.com.au
Email: mail@baspublishing.com.au

The National Library of Australia Cataloguing-in-Publication entry

Main, Jim, 1943- .
    Australian murder : 127 killings that shocked the nation.

    ISBN 1 920910 31 X.

    1. Crime - Australia. 2. Criminals - Australia. 3. Murder
    - Australia. I. Title.

364.994

Page Layout: exigene.com.au
Cover Design: Selina Low
Printed in Australia by Griffin Press

INTRODUCTION

There is something gruesomely fascinating about murder. Indeed, British author and playwright J.B. Priestley once remarked that one of the great pleasures in life was leaning back in a favourite armchair on a Sunday afternoon and reading newspaper reports of the latest murder sensation. The more lurid the better.

Australians are no different and newspapers with headlines screaming 'Murder Hunt' or 'Mutilated Body Found in River' are sure sellers. Tragically, murder has been part of Australian society almost from the First Fleet and this book refers to several remarkable murders of the nineteenth century colonial era.

My fascination with murder was sparked by one particular subject in a law degree course at the University of Melbourne — Criminal Law and Procedure. The subjects of Public International Law, Principles of Property, Equity and Mercantile Law bored me witless. However, I could not get my hands on enough murder reports and was first to line up for lectures in Forensic Medicine. They were the only law lectures crammed with students from other faculties. Engineering students fascinated with exhumations, commerce students keen on post-mortems.

I started reading a wonderful series titled *Famous Criminal Trials* and other books on notorious British murders, as well as the biographies of criminal barrister Sir Edward Marshall Hall and the remarkable pathologist Sir Bernard Spilsbury.

Murder had grabbed me by the throat and I started reading as much as I could about famous Australians cases. This resulted in my first book on infamous killings, *Murder Australian Style*, followed by *Murder in the First Degree*. Then, about a year ago, Bas Publishing suggested I update and combine the two volumes and add new material from recent cases.

This book, therefore, is the result of many years' work, not to mention an inexplicable fascination with the foulest of crimes. In between collecting as much as possible about Australian murder cases, I have studied overseas killings and several years ago was invited to visit 'The Black Museum' at Scotland Yard in London. This museum is not open to the public, but I visited it as the author of two casebooks of Australian murder. The museum is horrifying yet, at the same time, fascinating. It is this polarity of emotions that attracts us to murder and why there now are so many television dramas based on murder investigations, post-mortems and the psyche of the killer.

However, the killings in this book are chillingly real. This is a book about the killers who have been and are among us. Do not read alone at night.

JIM MAIN

THE BACKPACKER MURDERS

Australians recoil with horror at the very mention of Ivan Milat's name and with good reason. He will forever be remembered as one of the nation's worst mass murderers, with seven known victims. The word 'known' has special significance as there are many who believe the number of victims could be well into double figures. Yet Milat, the Backpacker Murderer, could have been apprehended much earlier in his bloodthirsty spree around the Belanglo State Forest area south of Sydney.

It probably will never be known when Milat turned to murder, but his first known victims were British backpackers Caroline Clarke and Joanne Walters. Both 22 years of age, their bodies were discovered in the Belanglo State Forest on September 19, 1992, five months after being reported missing after leaving Sydney for Melbourne.

Both women had been stabbed, but Clarke also had been shot numerous times in the head. In fact, forensic examination revealed that Clarke had been shot from different angles, suggesting she had been used as target practice. Indeed, the wounds of both young women were horrific, with Walters slashed to the neck, chest and head with a large hunting knife. Clarke also had been stabbed.

NSW police were horrified but, despite a number of clues, were unable to determine a suspect. Then, just three weeks after the bodies of Clarke and Walters were discovered, English tourist Paul Onions accepted the offer of a lift by a man driving a silver four-wheel drive vehicle. The young Englishman was on the Hume Highway when approached and was on his way to work at the fruit orchards in Mildura.

The four-wheel driver, who had a large, bushy moustache and introduced himself as 'Bill', slowed down just outside Mittagong and then pulled over to remove some item. 'Bill' by now had started to act aggressively, so the concerned Onions got out of the vehicle on the pretence of stretching his legs. However, 'Bill' barked at him to get back into the car. Onions obliged, but then had a black revolver pointed at his head.

Terrified, Onions immediately jumped out of the vehicle and ran down the road. A shot was fired while the Englishman tried to flag down a passing car. 'Bill' eventually caught up with Onions and grabbed him, only for the young man to again break free. Onions waved down a car carrying two women and five children, jumped into the vehicle, locked the door and told the woman behind the wheel to drive off as the man who had been attacking him had a gun.

The driver, Mrs Joanne Berry, dropped Onions off at the Bowral Police Station where an officer took down details. Then, incredibly, Onions was given directions to the railway station. He caught a train back to Sydney and stayed in Australia another six months, his near escape never far from his mind, although seemingly far from the minds of Bowral police.

Back in England two years later, Onions read in a newspaper about bodies being found in the Belanglo State Forest. Perturbed, he went to his local police station and then was advised to contact the Australian Embassy. Onions eventually reached the task force investigating the Backpacker Murders.

Police by now were dealing with the appalling fact that seven bodies had been discovered and, despite every effort, they seemed no closer to solving the murders. They accumulated files on dozens of suspects, including Milat. He once had owned a silver four-wheel drive vehicle, had a bushy moustache and sometimes was known as 'Bill'.

Police decided to have a closer look at Milat's background, especially after learning that he had a long criminal record and once had been charged with rape after picking up two female hitchhikers along the Hume Highway in New South Wales. The two girls alleged that Milat had threatened to kill then, but he was found not guilty. However, his profile both alarmed and appalled the police investigating the Backpacker Murders.

Finally, police read Onions' claim that he had been threatened when hitchhiking along the Hume Highway. His description was too much of a coincidence so, after being flown to Australia, Onions was asked to pick out his attacker from photographs of a dozen other suspects. He picked out Milat without hesitation.

This was just the break the police needed, so they raided Milat's home at Eaglevale, near Liverpool. Significantly, the house was close to the Hume Highway, the road to death for so many. Milat was arrested on May 22, 1994, and when police searched his home they had no doubt they finally had nabbed the Backpacker Murderer. The evidence they gathered was overwhelming and, for example, they found the .22 rifle that had been used to kill Caroline Clarke, as well as the dead woman's camera.

Milat was charged with the murder of seven backpackers and the attempted murder of Onions. His trial started in March, 1996, and lasted more than three months. Jurors heard from more than 100 prosecution witnesses and had to deal with more than 300 exhibits and photographs, many of them gruesome in the extreme.

Justice David Hunt in his summary said: 'It is sufficient here to record that each of his (Milat's) victims was attacked savagely and cruelly, with force which was unusual and vastly more than was necessary to cause death, and for some form of gratification.

'Each of two of the victims was shot a number of times in the head. A third was decapitated in circumstances which establish that she (German backpacker Anja Habschied) would have been alive at the time. The stab wounds to each of the other three would have caused paralysis, two of them having their spinal cords completely severed.

'The multiple stab wounds to three of the seven victims would have been likely to have penetrated their hearts. There are signs that two of them were strangled. All but one appear to have been sexually interfered with before or after death.'

The jury deliberated for three days before returning on July 27, 1996, for their verdict of guilty on all charges. Milat was sentenced to life imprisonment on the seven counts of murder and to seven years' jail on the charge of attempted murder. Then, in 1998, the NSW Court of Criminal Appeal rejected a Milat appeal and declared that he was to spend the rest of his life behind bars.

However, several questions remain, with many police convinced that Milat did not act alone in at least some of his murders. Also, were there other victims of the Backpacker Murderer? It is doubtful whether these mysteries will ever be solved.

THE 'DISGUSTING' MONSTER

Theresa Crowe, to say the least, had a most unusual lifestyle. And, tragically, this led to a most unusual death. The twenty-two-year-old former student teacher was a regular on the Melbourne disco scene and lived almost hermit-like in a tiny room measuring no more than four metres by three metres. This room, which was really a loft above and behind a boat building factory, was off Chapel Street, Prahran, an inner Melbourne suburb.

Crowe's meagre possessions were crammed into this minute living area, jostling for space with a swing seat which hung from the rafters. Crowe would climb into her room from a staircase and enter through a trapdoor. It might have been ever so humble, but it was home, sweet home to Theresa Crowe. Few people ever received an invitation.

Theresa, who had attended Strathmore High School and Toorak Teachers' College before accepting, and abandoning a number of jobs, loved the nightlife and was a regulat at Chaser's Nighclub, not far from her 'home'. In fact, she was there six nights a week and was such a familiar face there that she was a gold pass member, giving her free admittance.

She almost always wore black and, because of this and her surname, her nickname was 'Blackbird'. If Theresa was not at Chaser's there usually was a good reason, and that was why her friends started asking questions after they had not seen her for several days from June 19, 1980.

Theresa's 'disappearance' was still the subject of discussion at Chaser's when, on June 25, two Prahran men, Simon Greig and Hugo Ottoway, went to her room and made an horrific discovery. They found Theresa's naked body wrapped in a blanket. Police later said that Theresa had been dead several days and that her body had been mutilated.

There were numerous cuts on her face and a sharp instrument had been used to slash her body from throat to vagina. Although the initial post-mortem failed to disclose the cause of death, there were bruise marks on Theresa's neck and it was later proven that she had died of asphyxiation.

Police were mystified at first and even suggested that Thereas might have been held captive for several days before being killed. They also considered the possibility that the unfortunate young woman had been killed in some weird satanic rite. They based this theory on the fact that medical evidence pointed to Theresa being killed on June 24, which was a Beltane—one of four Sabbaths on the Satanists calendar. However, police later indicated they had a suspect, but not enough evidence to press charges.

The Blackbird Case, as it was dubbed by the Melbourne media, faded from the headlines for three years. Police then charged Malcolm Joseph Thomas Clarke, a twenty-eight-year-old assistant projectionist from the inner western suburb of Brunswick, with manslaughter.

Clarke had seen Theresa Crowe at Chaser's on the night of her death three years earlier and had later walked with her to her loft. She went upstairs and Clarke left, only to return later. By this time Theresa had stripped for sleep, and when she rejected his overtures, Clarke got angry.

However, Clarke insisted that Theresa's death had been accidental and that she had died of asphyxiation when her neck pressed against a rope on her swinging chair. Medical evidence suggested that this could well have been the case.

On the other hand, government pathologist Dr James McNamara told the Criminal Court that he had found a bite mark on Theresa's back, apart from the throat-to-vagina mutilation. Clarke was found guilty of manslaughter and Mr Justice Nathan, in passing sentence of fifteen years' imprisonment, said a 'joyful and pleasant' young woman had died because of Clarke's 'bests of motives ... sexual gratification'. He added: 'You committed this crime in the most horrific and depraved circumstances because not only did you cause her death, but after death you defiled her body ... in the most disgusting of all defilements.'

Clarke was ordered to serve twelve years before being eligible for parole but, two years before he was jailed, he had committed a far worse crime, the killing of six-year-old Bonny Clarke (no relation) at her home in the inner Melbourne suburb of Northcote.

Clarke, who was released from jail in 1994 for Theresa Crowe's death and the stabbing and raping of a woman at Brunswick in August, 1983, boarded with Bonnie's mother Marion for eight months at the Westbourne Grove house in 1982.

Bonnie Melissa Clarke was asphyxiated and stabbed on the night of December 21, 1982, but, despite an inquest and intensive police efforts, the crime remained unsolved for 22 years. However, when police re-examined the case in 2001, Clarke eventually became the chief suspect.

In a video-taped interview he said the little girl woke when he sexually abused her. He then put a pillow over her face to quieten her. He said: 'I was extraordinarily drunk ... and when I come to my senses (after pressing a pillow to the girl's face), I realised that Bonnie was deceased. When I took the pillow off ... she didn't struggle. I just held it down with one hand 'cause she had one hand up.

'She was lying down and one hand came up when I put it over her face. Her hand came up, then it just dropped. It just dropped. It was like, lifeless. I gave her a bit of a shake, whatever, I realised there was something wrong and I maybe, as I said, in panic did it with the knife.'

The Supreme Court of Victoria jury in June, 2004, took just seven hours to find Clarke guilty of murdering little Bonnie. Clarke burst into tears, but others in the court cheered the verdict.

THE RAMPAGING RUMANIAN

Zora Kusic had the face of a woman who had seen the seamier side of life. She was, in fact, a slut. Zora Kusic frequented Adelaide's darker salons and bars, selling her body virtually to anyone who would buy her a day's drinking. She lived with a Bulgarian named Ivan Nankintseff in a tiny tin shanty hut behind a house in North Parade, Torrensville, an Adelaide suburb. She sometimes took men to this hut. On the night of December 5, 1952, Nankintseff returned to the hut after a drinking session and discovered Zora Kusic on their bed. Nankintseff did not realise at first that his live-in companion was dead. In fact, Zora Kusic had been killed in the most revolting circumstances and Nankintseff soon realised that he had come across a dead and mutilated body. He fled in terror and police immediately launched a murder investigation.

Zora Kusic's throat had been cut almost from ear to ear and her stomach ripped open. Her chest was slashed and there was blood everywhere in the little tin shanty. In fact, there was a dish containing blood-stained water, and a knife was found on the floor.

Nankintseff had last seen Kusic alive at seven o'clock that morning when he left for work. He had arranged to meet Kusic at 4 p.m. but the appointment was not kept. Nankintseff discovered the body at 6.30 p.m., police estimating that Kusic had been dead two to three hours before Nankintseff had returned home. Police were convinced Kusic had been killed by a psychopath and no stone was left unturned in the search for the killer. Because Kusic frequented New Australian clubs and bars, police called in a team of translators to help them in their investigations. Hundreds of New Australians were interviewed in migrant clubs around Adelaide.

Police started moving in on their man. Their prime suspect became a 28-year-old Rumanian migrant who was seen with the dead woman shortly before her death. However, the man denied that he was with the woman and police were told that their suspect led a quiet, respectable life. Then, however, discrepancies appeared in the man's statements. Police finally charged John (real name Joan, pronounced Jo-anne) Balaban with the murder of Kusic.

The charge against Balaban was dismissed in sensational circumstances. After a five-day hearing in the Adelaide City Court, the Crown, with Mr E.B. Scarfe prosecuting, told Mr Clarke, P.M., that there was not enough substantial evidence against Balaban. Mr Scarfe said, 'The evidence puts him (Balaban) fairly and squarely inside that room (the tin hut)… but… suspicion itself is not enough. The evidence does not establish a prima facie case of murder. There is nothing concrete against Balaban apart from the fact that he was the last person seen with Kusic.' Mr Clarke, P.M., discharged Balaban. Balaban, an industrial chemist with qualifications from a Rumanian university, kissed his counsel, Mr L. McLean Wright, and embraced friends. His nightmare seemed over.

Balaban later told the Adelaide Truth newspaper, 'I am arrested and charged with a murder which revolted me as soon as I heard the details. For many seemingly endless days I hear the prosecution try to build a case against me. The public read the reports and hate me. Then finally I am discharged, though I have been innocent all through. The scars against me remain. Where can I go? What can I do? How can I make people forget I was once branded a killer?'

Balaban even told Truth of his meeting with Kusic. He said he had been drinking with a friend in the lounge of the Royal Admiral

Hotel, Hindley Street, Adelaide, when he saw Kusic at a nearby table. He said, 'I had £20 made of four £5 notes in my wallet and I paid for my friend's drink and my own with one of the £5 notes. I am sure Kusic saw me with the money. Shortly after my friend and I had been served with our drinks, Kusic came over to our table and asked if she could join us. We said she could. She still had a glass of beer with her and I did not have to buy her one. My friend left us and I stayed talking with Kusic for a while. She told me if I had £5 I could go to her place. I knew what she meant and I agreed. We caught a taxi and I remember saying to her on the way to Torrensville how poorly she spoke English. She told me she was not interested in speaking English because Australians did not give enough money. New Australians, she said, always paid well, so why should she bother to learn English.

'When we arrived outside her shack I knew I could not go through with it. I put my hand on the gate to enter and I decided suddenly to get away. She was not just dirty; she was filthy. I suggested we go to another hotel and she agreed. The hotel was not so very far away from her place and when we arrived I went into the bottle department. I had an appointment to meet another New Australian in the Southern Cross Hotel at four o'clock. It was four o'clock then and I told Kusic I was leaving. That was the last time I saw her. I arrived in the city but I could not find my friend and the two girls in the Southern Cross. I went looking for them down Hindley Street. I called into the Beograd Cafe but they were not there. Then I went to the Continental Cafe and had something to eat. That was about 5 o'clock. I returned to the Southern Cross about 5.20 but I still could not find them. I left the hotel a little after 5.30. I walked to North Adelaide, where I was living, and bought a piece of sausage from a delicatessen. Then I went to the park nearby and ate the sausage without bread. I then walked back to the city and saw the show at the Theatre Royal by myself. I was visited by the police about three o'clock the following afternoon.'

Balaban then said he had suffered terrible mental anguish in the days he stood in the dock. He said, 'I think I experienced every emotion possible, from fear to laughter. Fear for what might happen to me if I was committed and laughter for many of the silly things that were said against me. When they described how Kusic was mutilated I could sense the weapon at my own throat. I must have felt everything she felt.'

It wasn't the knife Balaban felt at his throat but the threat of the hangman's noose. A committal could have meant anything from an acquittal to a death sentence. No wonder Balaban was worried. Balaban's account in the Adelaide Truth was printed in the January 24, 1953, edition. A week earlier, in the January 17 edition, Truth stated, in reporting Balaban's discharge, 'So ended one of the most sordid stories heard in a South Australian Court.' The writer of that sentence could hardly have known that the Balaban saga was only in its infancy. There was much more, and much worse, to follow. Adelaide was to hear a lot more of Balaban, the man freed on a murder charge. In fact, Balaban's story reached Paris, where police took extreme interest in the happenings in the otherwise quiet city of churches.

John Balaban was big news in Adelaide at the time of his discharge in January, 1953. However, his name had hardly had time to fade from public memory when it appeared in print again just three months later. And the circumstances were even more sensational than the Zora Kusic killing.

Balaban went on a rampage of death and destruction for about an hour soon after 1.30 a.m. on April 12, 1953. Passers-by heard screams from Balaban's Sunshine Cafe in Gouger Street, Adelaide. The passers-by could not have guessed the horror that had erupted upstairs in the unfashionable cafe and snack bar. They then saw a woman fall 20 feet from an upper cafe window. The woman, Verna Manie, a waitress at the cafe, was critically injured, suffering back and head injuries. She lapsed into unconsciousness, although later recovering in hospital. Meanwhile, police forced their way into the cafe and discovered some of the most blood-curdling sights in South Australian criminal history. Balaban's wife Thelma, 30, was dead in bed, her face smashed to a pulp. Her mother, 66-year-old Mrs Susan Ackland, was critically injured in another bedroom. Mrs Ackland later died in hospital. But even more tragically, police discovered the mortally wounded six-year-old son of Mrs Balaban by a previous marriage. Little Phillip Cadd died 11 days later in hospital. Police were stunned. It undoubtedly was one of Adelaide's worst murder cases.

The search was on for the missing Balaban, the man discharged only three months earlier. The rampaging Rumanian was found outside the cafe shortly after police started their search. Balaban was charged with the murder of Kusic and Mrs Balaban.

Balaban stood trial at the Criminal Court in July, 1953. He pleaded insanity. The most interesting aspect of Balaban's trial was that he was charged with the murder of a woman (Kusic) for which he had already been in the dock. However, Balaban was not acquitted of murder at the Adelaide City Court but discharged instead.

Balaban's murder trial was a sensation from start to finish, virtually the whole of Adelaide taking enormous interest in the proceedings. Newspapers carried column after column on the trial and Balaban's name was as well known as any in Adelaide. But although sensation followed sensation, the most incredible was Balaban's own statement. It was an incredible document, although Balaban did not strictly adhere to the typed statement. He told the court, in a halting, often emotional voice of not one, not even four but five killings - including one in Paris.

Before mentioning the deaths of Kusic and his family, Balaban gave details of his early life. He also spoke of the killing in Paris. Part of his statement read:

> I am to give you the effect of what I feel, not because I am afraid to die, but because I think I am not guilty. I have made a very big mistake and I think I am not responsible. It is very hard to explain what I did feel at this time and I will read as I can from this paper.
>
> When I was young my mother with me left my father because of his cruelty. He used to drink. I became very depressed and because he hanged himself I can go to die. I did think that what I did was right and I am the person who had suffered. I am sure of this and I tell again that I am not frightened.

When I was 19 years of age… I was having a fight with myself as to whether or not God exists. I have been previously a religious man and attended the Greek Orthodox Church and believed in prayer.

After my reading I came to the conclusion that there was no God. Soon after this conclusion I was lying in my bed in my bedroom. At seven o'clock in the morning - I know I was awake - God came.

A bright light came and lit the room and God appeared. He had a great beard and long white hair. He was kind and quiet and smiled.

God had four or six angels with him. He said, 'John, it is all right if you don't believe in me any more. You can do anything your conscience dictates to you and you will be happy.' He then disappeared. This was not a dream.

Afterwards I thought I could do anything and I was not frightened of the law.

I used to have fantasies about scientific things and imagined queer shapes. I always imagine I was in Russia and I could hear a Russian plane in the air.

After a fight I was in a mental hospital at Cluj. I was bound up in sheets and I have some scars. I was released after three weeks and ordered to take a holiday … .

I arrived in France in October, 1947. My sister was admitted to a mental hospital in Rumania for treatment. She is mentally deficient and is not quite normal.

When in France I became depressed and could not control my thoughts. As a result of this I was ordered a month's holiday. After this I improved.

On February 10 I met a woman called Riva Kwas in a subway tram. She worked at a chemistry laboratory. We were talking and I walked home with her. We sat up so late talking that I missed the last tram. She showed me a couch to sleep on. I went to her bedroom and made love to her.

After about an hour I became furious with her. I felt very powerful and strong. I put my hands around her neck and strangled her.

I did not have any intention of killing her but I had a feeling I had to. I had not been drinking beforehand. I stayed in her room until about 5 o'clock in the morning and then I decided to come to Australia.

Part of Balaban's statement, referring specifically to the deaths of Kusic and the Balaban family read:

> On December 5, 1952, I was drinking with my friends in the hotel in Hindley St., and Zora Kusic came over to our table. She was not drunk and apart from this she asked me to come home to her place to have some fun.
>
> Going down in the taxi she told me that she lived with a man and she was a prostitute. I became very disgusted with her, because I thought she was married to the man and she was being unfaithful. I intended to leave her and not to enter the shed with her because she was so dirty and immoral.
>
> However, she enticed me into the shed. I took off all my clothes except my underwear; she pulled her clothes off. She sat on my knee and held my glass while I drink the beer.
>
> I say again I am not afraid to die. I put her on the bed, and she ask me for £5. I then looked at her and saw how dirty and common she was.
>
> I became very disgusted and angry with her and put my hand on her neck and started to strangle her. She struggled for a minute and then lay still. I continued to strangle her.
>
> I then took a knife off the dressing table and cut her throat. I then cut her up and down the body and across her chest …
>
> I did not feel sorry for killing Kusic. I thought I was quite justified for doing so because anybody could tell she was a low woman and deserved to die.
>
> I told the police lies about not killing Kusic because it was the only way to look after my wife and Phillip and escape.
>
> On April 11 I left the Sunshine Cafe in the morning, and my wife complained as I was leaving that I never came home for lunch. I met some friends and had a few schooners of beer in the morning …
>
> At night I went down by the Torrens and fought a girl in the ladies' toilet. Then I went to the University bridge and drank some wine liqueur. I found a bar of iron and put it in my pocket because somebody attacked me and I am afraid he hurt me. I think I hit a man sleeping on the ground behind the Adelaide oval but I do not know.

I went to the Morphett St. bridge near some reeds, where I saw a black-fellow and a white girl. With them I drank and then I hit them, I think, with the iron bar.

Going on, I turned at the Torrens near the back of the tennis court. A man chased me and I hit him with the iron bar. This man had been lying on the ground with a woman. I do not know why I hit him with the iron bar but I disapproved of him, as I do of people lying on the banks of the Torrens and making love. Everyone knows that that is a very bad thing to do.

I met a man in Frome Rd. who was drunk. I walk with him into the oval and I trip him up and beat him. I kicked his face many times with my right foot …

I then went home to the Sunshine Cafe. I was tired and dirty and had blood on me and I wondered what my wife would say when she saw me dirty, bruised and cut as I was. I was very unhappy and I thought everyone was against me. I thought if my family cannot understand me, who will?

Balaban then said that he decided 'instantly' to kill his wife because she was the cause of his condition. He continued:

I went into her (his wife's) bedroom. I did not switch on the light. I hit her on the head. I don't know how many times. Then I thought I would kill Mrs Ackland.

Mrs Ackland had made my wife's first husband, Mr Cadd, unhappy, and I thought she would also make us unhappy. Phillip sat up and cried and I hit him. I thought it better that he die too. I would like to die, too, myself.

I went out to the sleepout where Verna Manie slept. I went out to kill her because she had been stealing money from the shop, and she had been siding with my wife against me.

She had been insolent. I hit her on the head and told Verna that I wanted her, and put her on the bed. I had intercourse with her. I went back and had a look at the bodies and hit them again and then came back to the sleepout and saw that Verna was on the ground.

I took some money and climbed over some roofs into Thomas St.

I only killed the people from the Sunshine Cafe because they deserved to be killed.

It was an incredible rampage of destruction, and witnesses told the court of the incidents leading up to the cafe deaths. Dorothy Rowan, 16, told the court how Balaban tried to kiss her and then punched her in the face. Miss Rowan was the girl Balaban 'fought' in the ladies' toilet. The defence later called three police officers, who all took part in Balaban's arrest, to give evidence. The officers, Sergeant Bert Lucas and Constables Earl Dougherty and Kevin Moran deposed that Balaban expressed no regret for the attacks on the three people in the cafe. They said that Balaban's demeanour was calm and unemotional.

The defence also called Adelaide psychiatrist Dr Harold Southwood, who told the court that he had two interviews with Balaban at Adelaide jail on May 26 and June 6, 1953. Dr Southwood said, 'I formed the impression he is suffering from a mental disorder which I diagnosed as a form of schizophrenia... The sufferer may have delusions and hallucinations. He may respond abnormally to situations. Paranoia is especially characterised by delusions that there are enemies who are trying to injure the sufferer in some way. In the case of Balaban I found evidence of persecutory delusions and also hallucination disorders in his thinking process... In my opinion, Balaban is certifiable. As a result of my experiences I would be prepared to certify him as mentally defective. I would not expect him to recover from his condition. He said that sometimes he finds himself thinking that he did not kill Kusic at all but that his enemies did it and made things look as if he were guilty. But most of the time he knows this is not true. I do not know of anyone feigning insanity who could produce a statement like this.'

However, the prosecution called Dr H.M. Birch, superintendent of Government Mental Institutions in South Australia. He told the court that he did not agree with Dr Southwood. He said, 'Summing up I would say that Balaban is not mentally disordered but he has a very abnormal personality. He comes within the category of a psychopathic personality; that is, a person who is not insane, not mentally disordered but who, on account of abnormality in his personality or character, has been unable or unwilling to conform to the normal standards of society.'

Balaban was unmoved when the jury foreman announced the verdict 'guilty'. Balaban turned to Mr Justice Abbott and said, 'According to the law, I want to obey the law, and I think I am not guilty.' Mr Justice Abbott then sentenced Balaban to death, saying, '… and may God have mercy on your soul.' Balaban replied, 'God, I think, have mercy.' Balaban appealed to the State Full Court against the death sentence but this appeal was dismissed by the Chief Justice, Sir Mellis Napier, sitting with Mr Justice Ligertwood and Mr Justice Ross.

Balaban spent his last few days playing chess and cards. He spent the last half hour of his life with a Church of England padre and was taken from his cell only two minutes before his execution on August 26, 1953.

Police in two countries closed files on separate murders. Adelaide police closed their files on the Kusic and Mrs Balaban killings, while Paris police, on Balaban's confession, closed their files on the death of Riva Kwas in 1948.

THE SICK KILLER

A young married man used to sit with his wife by an open fire during the 1930s and stare into the glowing embers. Arnold Karl Sodeman, a quiet family man, would be lost in his own thoughts. Mrs Dolly Sodeman did not think twice about her husband's quiet moods. She knew that Arnold was a good husband, an adoring father and a good worker. She also knew that although her husband liked to have a drink, and even came home worse for wear because of beer, he never laid a hand on her. Sodeman's quiet moods were typical of her husband, a quietly spoken labourer who kept very much to himself. However, Mrs Soderman could not have guessed the cause of her husband's reflective moods. Sodeman was brooding over murders he had committed. The guilt of the murders was bottled up inside him, tearing him to pieces. But worse was Sodeman's self-knowledge that there could be more murders, unless he could control himself after a few glasses of beer.

Sodeman's trail of human destruction started on the afternoon of November 9, 1930. The young labourer had been drinking in the Orrong Hotel, Armadale, before deciding on a walk. That walk took Sodeman through Fawkner Park, a beautiful area in Melbourne's inner suburb of South Yarra. There, Sodeman saw a group of girls playing and chasing each other in the green park-land. Sodeman's mind clicked into one of its moods and the 30-year-old labourer asked one of the girls, 12-year-old Mena Griffiths, to run a message for him. Sodeman went with the girl on the message, later suggesting that they go somewhere. The girl agreed and they caught a tram and a bus to the southern suburb of Ormond, Sodeman buying the girl some chips to eat on the way.

Sodeman's own account of what followed was that he then spotted an empty house in Wheatley Road. He said, 'I took her in there. The back door was open. We walked in and as soon as we got in I seized her by the throat. I then let her go and she fell on the ground. Looking down on her my memory came back, and I said, "My God, she's dead. I have killed her."

'I stood there wondering what I could do and I must have remembered or read of something being done about tying people up. So I stripped her, bound her and gagged her with her own clothing, and dragged her into the bathroom and left her. I have no recollection of getting an erection and an emission of semen. I did not interfere with the child. How can I remember one thing and forget the rest? I am positive I did not interfere with the child. I can't see why I should forget a point such as this.'

In cross-examination at Sodeman's trial, Coroner's Surgeon Dr Crawford Mollison said that in his opinion Mena Griffiths had had sexual intercourse on the day of her death.

After the killing of Mena Griffiths, Sodeman made his way home to his wife and two-year-old daughter Joan, whom he idolised. Sodeman had murdered for the first time and the thought chilled him to the marrow. He later told how he had been close to killing before he chanced upon Mena Griffiths but circumstances prevented him.

Strangely, Sodeman did not show any thought for a man arrested for Mena Griffith's murder shortly after the killing. Mena Griffith's body was discovered the day after her death and police later charged a young man with the murder. Sodeman must have believed that the arrest would have meant the perfect escape for his own crime. He also must have known that an innocent man could have been tried, or even hanged, for the Mena Griffiths killing. However, the unlucky man had a perfect alibi. In fact, the innocent man was not even in Melbourne the day Mena Griffiths was killed. Police investigations then led nowhere, Sodeman not being suspected in any way, the killer vanishing into the anonymity of a big city.

Police were still trying to make headway in the case when Sodeman struck again. This time the victim was 16-year-old Hazel Wilson. Sodeman again struck in the suburb of Ormond, Hazel Wilson's body being discovered in a vacant allotment in Oakleigh Road. The girl was last seen on the night of January 9, 1931—two months after the Mena Griffiths murder—heading for a local dance. The girl's brother discovered the body the next morning, the allotment not being far from the Wilson house in Mellon Avenue. Police could not help but notice the similarities in the deaths of Mena Griffiths and Hazel Wilson. The strangler had struck again and police were horrified. They immediately launched a massive investigation, worried that the killer would strike again. However, there were precious few clues and senior police knew that they were looking for a needle in a haystack.

The whole of Melbourne was alarmed but fears subsided with each passing month and year. The mysterious strangler was all but forgotten by the general public. Police files on the Griffiths and Wilson deaths were not closed but at least the killings had stopped. Sodeman, meanwhile, had shifted his small family to the eastern Victoria area of Gippsland in search of peace of mind and work.

He killed again on New Year's Day, 1935, almost four years after his previous murder. The victim was 12-year-old Ethel Belshaw, who was just one of thousands who had attended a huge picnic at the beach resort of Inverloch. Sodeman, who again had been drinking, said that Ethel Belshaw had wanted to walk with him. Sodeman told her that he didn't want her to accompany him on his walk, but then relented. Then, according to Sodeman, 'While walking up a narrow track towards the back beach something came over me and I took her by the throat. When I released her she sank to the ground. I thought she was dead. I thereupon bound her as in previous cases and went to the hotel and had a drink.'

Ethel Belshaw was quickly missed, a search was launched, and her body was discovered the next day, trussed in the manner Sodeman later described.

Police were stunned. The killer they had so desperately tried to nail four years previously, had struck again, in a totally different part of the state. Incredibly, police questioned Sodeman as one of the picnickers. The killer told them he knew little or nothing, and they believed him. After all, who would suspect Sodeman, a quietly-spoken family man with the reputation of being kind-hearted and gentle? In fact, police later said that Sodeman's behaviour and general manner would have made him one of the least likely suspects imaginable.

Sodeman, who attended Miss Belshaw's funeral, was still a free man. Police arrested a youth in connection with Miss Belshaw's death but lack of evidence forced them to release the innocent youth. But yet again, Sodeman made no confession, even though he must have known that an innocent man was in danger of his life over a crime Sodeman himself had committed.

The next, and final, murder in the Sodeman tragedy was in Leongatha on December 1, 1935, eleven months after Miss Belshaw's death. Sodeman, who was working at a road camp near Dumbalk, strangled 6-year-old Jane Rushmer, a friend of his own daughter Joan. Little Jane Rushmer, who knew Sodeman well, had asked the kindly man to give her a dink on his bike. Sodeman, who again had been drinking, agreed and took the little girl to her death. The body was dumped and a huge police and civilian search was launched when it was discovered that the strangler had struck yet again. However, this time police had several leads, including sightings of the little girl being dinked on a bike. It was just the lead police needed, although the final breakthrough came from Sodeman himself.

Sodeman returned to his work camp after the murder, and naturally, his workmates later got around to discussing the murder. One workmate jokingly mentioned that Sodeman was riding his bike on the night of the murder. Sodeman immediately flew into a rage and stalked off. The workmate thought Sodeman's behaviour was strange and after a night of thinking the matter over, the worker contacted police the next day and told them of his suspicions. Sodeman was questioned and almost immediately confessed to murdering little Jane Rushmer. Sodeman had tried to form an alibi but when police proved that the alibi was false Sodeman broke down.

Sodeman told police, 'After tea I went out and rode down Roughhead Street. Did not know where I was going. I saw the little kid. She asked me for a ride. I said, "Where to?" and she said, "Oh anywhere." We rode down the road. Just past the scrub she said, "Oh this is far enough." She got off the bike and I got off and turned it around. I made a playful pass at her. She screamed and ran into the bush. I caught her. The same happened.' The last sentence was pregnant with meaning. Police would have been more than happy to have solved one murder but Sodeman added, 'There were three others'. He then told of the murders of Mena Grifiths, Hazel Wilson and Ethel Belshaw.

The police had their man but it was only the start of the Sodeman saga. Sodeman was charged with the murder of Jane Rushmer, his fourth victim.

The trial, before Mr Justice Gavan Duffy and jury, opened at the Melbourne Criminal Court on February 17, 1936. The case created enormous public interest, virtually the whole of Melbourne wanting to know the outcome of the trial. Sodeman pleaded insanity, and it was because of that plea that his defence did not object to the Crown making reference to the three earlier killings by Sodeman.

During his stay in Pentridge awaiting trial, Sodeman wrote to his wife and made specific mention of his mania. He wrote, 'I have confessed my mania, and will pay for my sins. Please try and forget me.' His wife replied, pleading with him to tell the truth. Sodeman's reply is poignant, to say the least. It read,

'Dear Dolly,

I was pleased to receive your letter, you seem to be able to look at this dreadful business now in the proper light. I am convinced in my own mind that I did them, and that the drink is the primary cause. The drink seems to affect my brain in some way, unknown to me, and this dreadful craze to destroy comes over me. I realize when it is too late what I have done, and then naturally try to cover it up to protect my home. I have tried and tried, as you know, to give up drink altogether but through some weakness would give up to the drink again. Dear Doll, you know now why I used to sit, hour after hour, by the fire, apparently dreaming; I was fighting against this thing, afraid to confide in you and afraid that it would eventually turn my brain. I think that there is something wrong inside, and when I take drink, I am then unable to get it under control. I am very pleased to be able to tell you, that never have I had any desire to outrage my poor victims. With regard to the child Griffiths, the police say that this child was interfered with. I cannot explain this but I feel sure - I am positive - that I did not interfere with this child. Dear Doll, be brave for mine and Joan's sake; my only regrets and sorrow, are for all those who have suffered through my maniacal madness. Well dear, I don't feel that I am able to write any more at present so will close with love to Joan and you.'

Sodeman himself sensed that he was mentally ill. He refers to his maniacal madness. Yet the letter does not reflect the attitude of a man faking madness for the sake of escaping the hangman's noose. The letter is painfull honest, a statement of a man's feelings. The fact that the writer was a sick murderer makes the letter all the more heartrending.

Sodeman's life virtually hinged on the question of insanity and Sodeman's appalling family history of mental illness was recalled at the trial. The court was told that Sodeman's father and paternal grand-father had died in the same asylum and that his mother had suffered bouts of amnesia for many years. It also was obvious that Sodeman had had a miserable childhood and youth. He was beaten by his father and young Sodeman then drifted into a life of petty crime. In fact, Sodeman served sentences for forging, larceny, robbery and escaping from custody. To his credit, Sodeman settled down after being released from jail in 1926, his marriage to Dolly no doubt having a settling influence on him. The birth of his daughter also helped quell his earlier tendencies to live a life of petty crime by stealing and robbing.

Two government prison doctors who had examined Sodeman in Pentridge while he was awaiting trial testified that Sodeman was insane when he killed. This evidence was supported by a psychiatrist in private practice. Government medical officer Dr Albert Philpott told the court that when Sodeman killed Jan Rushmer, he was not conscious of what he was doing. Questioned by Mr Bourke about the influence of liquor on Sodeman's mental state at the time of the killings, Dr Philpott replied, 'I would say that in my opinion that there often is then what I call an obsessional impulse all the time but which does not affect him when he has no liquor. That is an idea in the mind which is always obtruding itself, more or less, but which can be controlled under some circumstances but not under others.' The Crown did not call any medical evidence in rebuttal of the claim of insanity but relied largely on Sodeman's confession.

The jury found Sodeman guilty of murder and Mr Justice Duffy sentenced him to death. Sodeman appealed to the High Court and the Privy Council but to no avail. He was hanged at Pentridge on June 1, 1936. A post-mortem examination showed that Sodeman had been suffering from a brain disease known as leptomeningitis. This disease helped explain the murders. Sodeman, simply, was unable to account for his action after a few glasses of beer, delicate brain tissues becoming inflamed. There now seems little doubt that Sodeman should not have been hanged. The post-mortem was poor consolation for Sodeman or any of his four victims. But at least Sodeman's anguish was over. His letters show that he lived in mental torment, sickened by the knowledge that he had killed during his moods.

THE
WOMAN-HATING
KILLER

Triple murderer Paul Charles Denyer added insult to injury for Victorians in 2004 when he announced that he wanted to change his sex to become a woman and was seeking details on government policy. Earlier, Denyer had been refused permission to wear make-up at the Barwon prison, where he was serving a life sentence, with a minimum of 30 years.

Yet Denyer, when asked to explain why he killed three women in Melbourne's bayside suburbs in 1993, had replied: 'I just hate them'. When pressed by a police interviewer as to whether he hated his particular victims or women in general, Denyer said chillingly 'General'.

Denyer had gone on a murder frenzy over seven weeks from June to July, 1993, stabbing and slashing three women, with another just managing to escape with her life at the hands of the monster.

Denyer was born in 1972 in Sydney, but moved to Melbourne with his family when he was just nine years of age. A lazy, indolent boy, he had few interests and, on leaving school, drifted from job to job with long periods of unemployment. However, he struck up a relationship with a girl named Sharon Johnson and moved in with her at her Frankston flat in 1992.

Then, on June 12, 1993, Denyer struck for the first time, killing 18-year-old student Elizabeth Stevens, whose body was found in Lloyd Park, Langwarrin. Her throat had been cut, she had been stabbed several times in the chest and her torso slashed. Significantly, however, she had not been sexually assaulted.

Police launched a massive hunt for the killer but, less than four weeks later, on July 8, their attention turned to two attacks, one in which the victim survived and the other not so fortunate.

The first attack occurred after bank clerk Roszsa Toth stepped from a train at Seaford. Dragged into bushes by a man she believed was carrying a gun, she eventually managed to fight off her assailant and then called police.

However, that very night another woman was attacked, with fatal consequences. Young mother Debbie Fream, 22, had driven to a store in Seaford to buy some milk but never returned home. Her body was found four days later in a paddock at Carrum. She had been stabled 24 times but, again, there had been no sexual assault.

Then, 12 days later (on July30), the killer struck in broad daylight after carefully planning his third murder. Denyer, after cutting wire alone a fence at a reserve, waited for a victim to drag her through the gap and into bushes.

Schoolgirl Natalie Russell, just 17, was Denyer's third victim. She was riding her bike home from school when the monster struck and her body later was found in bushland. She had been stabbed and her throat cut.

However, police soon were onto their man as they discovered a piece of skin on the neck of the dead girl. Also, a policeman had taken down the registration number of a yellow motor vehicle sighted near the bike track earlier in the day. Police soon discovered that the car was registered to Denyer.

Police called at the flat where he lived with Johnson, but Denyer was not home. Police told Johnson that they merely were making 'routine inquiries' and asked if her partner could call them when he returned home. Johnson called them two hours later and police returned to the flat, where they noticed Denyer had cuts on his hand. He explained these had been caused by trying to fix a motor fan, but the police knew they had their man.

Denyer was taken to the Frankston police station where he confessed after intitially pleading his innocence. After asking about what DNA tests would prove, he blurted out: 'OK, I killed all three of them.'

In his statement, Denyer said of killing his first victim, Stevens, that he followed her and then grabbed her from behind before marching her into Lloyd Park. He then said he reached a particular area and then started strangling her. The statement said: 'She passed out after a while. You know, the oxygen got cut off to her head and she just stopped breathing.' Denyer then stabbed her repeatedly and admitted 'I stuck my foot over her neck to finish her off'.

Asked why he had killed the teenage student, Denyer callously replied: 'I just wanted … just wanted to kill. Just wanted to take a life because I felt my life had been taken many times.'

Denyer admitted attacking Toth and said he was 'gunna drag her in the park and kill her'. When Toth escaped, Denyer went in search of another victim and saw Fream get out of a car outside a milk bar. He then let himself into the back of the car and waited for his intended victim to return.

He said in his statement: 'I startled her … and she kept going into the wall of the milk bar, which caused a dent in the bonnet. I told her to, you know, shut up, or I'd blow her head off and all that shit.'

Debbie Fream drove herself to her death and, after Denyer told her to stop the car, pulled out a length of cord and started strangling her. Then, just as she was passing out, he stabbed her repeatedly before dragging her body into bushes and then covering it with branches.

When police asked why he had killed the young mother, who had given birth to a son less than a fortnight earlier, Denyer said: 'Same reason I killed Elizabeth Stevens. I just wanted to.'

Of the killing of schoolgirl Russell, Denyer said in his statement that he grabbed her from behind and held a knife to her throat. Russell, obviously fearing for her life, offered Denyer sex in exchange for letting her go, but he kept telling her to 'shut up'. In the most appalling part of his statement, he said: 'I cut a small cut (in her throat) at first and then she was bleeding. And then I stuck my fingers into her throat ... and grabbed her cords and twisted them.'

When police asked him why he did this, he replied: 'Stop hear from breathing ... so she sort of started to faint and then, when she was weak, a bit weaker, I grabbed the opportunity of throwing her head back and one big large cut which sort of cut almost her whole head off. And then she slowly died.'

But, to make sure his victim was dead, the callous killer kicked the body before slashing Russell's face.

Denyer pleased guilty to the murders of Stevens, Fream and Russell and the attempted murder of Toth. His trial opened at the Supreme Court of Victoria before Justice Frank Vincent on December 15, 1993. Just five days later, Justice Vincent sentenced Denyer to three terms of life imprisonment with no fixed non-parole period.

Denyer appealed to the Full Court of the Supreme Court against the severity of the sentence and subsequently was granted a 30-year non-parole period. This outraged the victims' families and, of course, there was further outrage a decade later when the woman-hating killer declared he wanted to become a woman.

THE INFERIORITY COMPLEX KILLER

Good-looking Ronald Cribbin seemed to have everything going for him. He had a pleasant face, was well-spoken and had a good education at one of Melbourne's best Roman Catholic colleges. He was the sort of young man who would be expected to become one of Melbourne's solid citizens. It all turned out wrong for Ronald Newman Cribbin, however. He ended up a cold-blooded killer. He killed for profit and his crimes shocked New South Wales.

Young Cribbin started his criminal career as a hold-up man, robbing taxi drivers of their hard-earned fares. His technique was to hail a cab and then bail up the driver with an imitation or toy pistol. Cribbin got away with this for some time but eventually got his just deserts when taxi drivers, in a sort of vigilante squad, caught him red-handed and handed him over to police. Cribbin, whose mother died when he was only eight, was sentenced to eighteen months jail, serving his sentence at Melbourne's Pentridge. That was the beginning of the end of Cribbin as a man capable of taking his place in society as a young man.

Cribbin wanted revenge and left jail with an enormous chip on his shoulder. The 21-year-old Cribbin, who already had an inferiority complex, soon showed an extreme tendency to believe that everyone considered him worthless. He always had the impression that people were laughing at him. It wasn't true but Cribbin nurtured his feelings until they festered inside him. Those feelings helped turn him into a killer.

Cribbin's short-lived career as a killer started in Sydney on December 14, 1950. After being released from Pentridge, Cribbins headed for New South Wales, obviously intent on leading a life of crime. He struck pay dirt almost immediately. Cribbin robbed 72-year-old widow Mrs Edith Hill of $30,000 worth of jewels. However, Cribbin killed the unfortunate old widow in the process. Mrs Hill, who lived alone in a flat in Macquarie Street, Sydney, was bashed to death. Mrs Hill was not discovered until that evening, her daughter, Mrs Sibella Brooker, making a visit. Mrs Brooker found her mother in a pool of blood, alive but dreadfully wounded. The police were called and an investigation was launched immediately. That investigation soon became a case of murder, Mrs Hill dying of her wounds.

New South Wales police were baffled. There did not appear to be a motive and the pieces only fell together when it was realised that many of Mrs Hill's most precious gems were missing. Police now understood the motive but still had few leads. However, Cribbin struck again, in completely different circumstances. He killed a taxi driver in an extension of his old modus operandi.

Just two days after killing Mrs Hill, Cribbin hailed a taxi driven by 36-year-old father of five, Norman Cecil Dickson. Cribbin told Dickson to stop after a short journey and immediately produced a gun. Dickson resisted and was shot for his trouble. Cribbin later claimed that the gun 'went off', but he also admitted that he then 'shot at his head to put him out of pain'. In a statement, he said, 'When we started I was in the front seat with the driver. After going over the bridge at Penrith I told him to stop and got into the back seat to hold him up. I produced a gun and said, "This is a stick-up". The driver turned and knocked the gun. It went off. I jumped over to the front seat and he started kicking me and I shot him in the head. He started to gurgle. I fired another shot at his head to put him out of pain. Before I fired the last shot I drove the cab up another lane.'

Cribbin then drove the taxi, with Dickson's body in the back seat, due west. He was only a few miles out of Bathurst when a motorcycle policeman stopped the taxi because he could not notice any passengers. Senior Constable Reg Lowe then dodged a bullet as Cribbin fired at him from the driver's seat. Lowe fired back but Cribbin was able to escape in the taxi.

Cribbin later crashed the taxi but immediately sped off on foot, leaving Dickson's body in the back of the crashed taxi. It was a frantic rush for freedom, Cribbin even swimming a river in his bid to escape his pursuers. However, his efforts were futile, police arresting him at gunpoint. Police, of course, had nabbed Cribbin for the death of Dickson but were shocked when the 21-year-old confessed to the murder of Mrs Hill. Cribbin was taken back to Sydney and was charged with the murders of Mrs Hill and Norm Dickson.

The charge of murdering Mrs Hill went ahead and Cribbin was found guilty as charged. In a statement to police after his arrest, he told how he planned the break-in of Mrs Hill's flat. In a statement, he said, 'When I was leaving Mrs Hill came out of her bedroom. I told her to stand back but she grabbed the rifle and it went off. She held onto the rifle with one hand and scratched my face with the other. I pulled the rifle from her and belted her over the head with it several times. She wouldn't go down but kept fighting me, so I swung the rifle at the side of her head. I think that was the one that killed her, because that brought the blood.'

Cribbin pleaded insanity at his trial but it was obvious that he planned the burglary in minute detail. Finally, Cribbin sent the jewels to the Adelaide GPO, to be picked up by an 'R.S. Newman'. Significantly, Newman was Cribbin's middle name. Cribbin, the cold-blooded killer, was sentenced to death. However, that sentence was commuted to one of life imprisonment.

THE CHALK-PIT
MURDER

'Connoisseurs' of murder might be puzzled by the above title, for the 'Chalk-pit Murder' is one of England's most infamous murder cases. However, it deserves mention in this book of Australian murders because one of the accused once was a leading identity in Australian politics. Indeed, Thomas John Ley was a former New South Wales Minister for Justice, a controversial character in the world of political intrigue during the 1920s. Ley, known as 'Lemonade Ley' because of his temperance beliefs, left Australia at the end of his political career and took up residence in England.

He lived a life of semi-retirement, with his long-standing mistress Mrs Maggie Brook, who was considerably fitter than the grossly overweight Ley, joining him in England. Both were aged 66 but Mrs Brook was still a relatively attractive woman, while Ley was a mountain of fat and aging rapidly. This caused Ley much heartache and he became insanely jealous, regarding Mrs Brook as something of a personal possession. It might have been due to Ley's eventual impotence but, whatever the cause, the obsession led to murder.

Ley believed that several young men were interested in Mrs Brook but particularly accused 35-year-old barman John Mudie, who had the gross misfortune to share the same lodging house with Mrs Brook at one stage in 1946. Mudie had left the lodgings by the time Ley's jealousy had developed into maniacal rage. However, Ley traced the young, harmless barman to his new working place at a hotel in Reigate, Surrey. Ley then set a trap for Mudie, luring him to a 'party' in London on November 28, 1946. Mudie, unsuspecting, attended the 'party' only to find that he was the only guest. Ley and two paid thugs, John Smith and John Buckingham, attacked Mudie. Smith and Buckingham tied Mudie up for Ley, covering Mudie's head with a blanket and then handing the poor victim over to Ley. Buckingham left and Mudie was left to his fate.

A rope around Mudie's neck apparently killed him but there could be no certainty whether this was by accident or by design, or whether the 'hanging' was done with such care as to make it look like a case of suicide. Pathologist Dr Keith Simpson, in his excellent book 'Forty Years of Murder' told the jury at Ley and Smith's trial (Buckingham turning King's evidence) that he could not be certain how Mudie had been 'hanged'. Dr Simpson said, 'There was no mark of jerking or pulling, merely of tightening and suspension.' In his book, Dr Simpson wrote, 'I added that there was nothing to indicate whether death was due to accident, suicide or murder.' Interrupted by trial judge Lord Goddard, Dr Simpson said, 'One could imagine a great deal but there was nothing to show.'

The sensation of the trial was a startling confession by known criminal Robert Cruikshank, who claimed that he had gone to Ley's house on the night Mudie was attacked and noticed a bundle in a chair. Cruikshank, who said his original intention in visiting the house was burglary, said he pulled the rope around the bundle and was now wondering whether this had caused Mudie's death. Judge and jury discounted this, almost certainly seeing it as an attempt to clear Ley and Smith of the charge of murder. And Ley and Smith were, in fact, convicted.

Evidence was overwhelmingly against them, even though no one could say exactly how the rope around Mudie's neck had killed him. Mudie's body was placed in a shallow trench in a chalk-pit near

Woldingham, Surrey, soon after Mudie's death. The body was discovered two nights later. Smith had been seen at the chalk-pit the day before the murder in a car with a registration ending in the number 101. It was exactly the tie-in police needed, the car being traced to Smith, who had hired a car registered number FGP 101 a few days before Mudie's death. He was almost-certainly seeking a 'last resting place' for the man about to be murdered.

Ley, who had condemned men to the gallows in his capacity as NSW Minister for Justice, was sentenced to death, along with Smith. However, Ley, a desperately ill man, was declared insane and he died a few months after his trial. Smith's sentence was commuted to life imprisonment.

MY CONSCIENCE IS CLEAR

Many killers, when brought to justice, cling to the claim of innocence. Many drop this mask when a jury finds them guilty. Some still insist on their innocence, a few going to the gallows still proclaiming innocence. Undoubtedly, some convicted killers are innocent, despite evidence and even eventual hanging. Convicted Queensland murderer Reginald Spence Wingfield Brown died insisting that he was not a killer. However, he did not die at the gallows. Brown hanged himself in Brisbane's Boggo Road jail, just nine days after being sentenced to life imprisonment. Brown hanged himself with a belt from a window grille in the cell in which he would have spent years for the killing of 19-year-old Bronia Armstrong.

The Armstrong case was notorious in Brisbane and it was known as the Brisbane Arcade Murder. The murder was infamous for a number of reasons but mainly because Miss Armstrong was killed during working hours in an arcade office in the middle of the city. The fact that a murder could take place during the hustle and bustle of a city's working day, with passers-by and others hearing the victim's screams, was almost too much for the solid citizens of

Brisbane, the Armstrong case therefore attracting enormous attention and interest.

Pretty Bronia Armstrong worked as a stenographer for the Brisbane Associated Friendly Societies Medical Institute, Brown being the Institute's secretary. Brown, 49 and married with three grown-up children, was hardly a typical killer. He was hard-working, devoted to his job and a typical white-collar worker of his generation. Bronia Armstrong was hardly a likely murder victim, either. A typical teenager, Bronia liked outings, sport and generally enjoyed life as much as any 19-year-old girl. She had no real problems and she came from a good family. In fact, Bronia knew the Brown family quite well, being a former schoolfriend of Brown's daughter.

Brown obviously became infatuated with Miss Armstrong, his interest causing her some discomfort. Brown did not push himself onto the attractive teenager but Bronia told friends that she suspected Brown had not passed on messages from boyfriends. Miss Armstrong could not tolerate the uncomfortable situation any longer and resigned from her position. She was due to leave her position on January 17, 1946, but Bronia did not live that long. She was murdered a week before that date.

Bronia Armstrong went to work as normal on Friday, January 10, and was seen by a number of people. However, she did not return home from work that night and her worried family contacted Brown, who told them that his stenographer had received a telephone call from a boyfriend. However, Miss Armstrong already was dead. Her body was discovered in a Brisbane Associated Friendly Societies' waiting room first thing on the Saturday morning, Brown being called in almost immediately. Police noticed that the girl was wearing only a brassiere and slip and the body was bruised and bloodied. Cause of death later was given as asphyxiation.

Incredibly, Brown tried to make the murder look like a case of suicide. He even told police that Bronia was unhappy at home and that he had told her that suicide would be foolish. He claimed that

Miss Armstrong talked of jumping off a bridge. Brown said he advised her, 'I told her that if she did that the prawns and the crabs would pick her eyes out.' Police suspected that suicide was doubtful and several clues pointed to Brown.

Firstly, screams could hardly come from someone committing suicide, although it was first thought that the screams came from a child in a nearby dental surgery. Secondly, an empty anaesthetic bottle was found near the body. Yet the post mortem showed that Miss Armstrong died of asphyxiation, and not from any overdose or poison. Thirdly, Brown's office appeared to have been cleaned and scrubbed, presumably to get rid of blood. Blood stains, in fact, were found in the office, Brown claiming that this was from a cut finger. And that cut finger was one of the most damning aspects of Brown's account.

Brown said that he cut his finger on the night of Miss Armstrong's death. He told police that he was assaulted in a side street and that one of his attackers bit him on the left hand, causing bleeding. The Brown story just did not make sense, police concluding that Brown received his injuries in the struggle with Miss Armstrong.

Because Miss Armstrong's body was not found in Brown's office but in the nearby waiting room, police concluded that Brown had murdered the girl in his office and then dragged her body into the surgery when the offices were otherwise empty. Police discovered a long scratch running from Brown's office to the waiting room, strongly suggesting that Miss Armstrong's body was dragged from one room to the other, leaving the scratch mark. The evidence seemed conclusive.

Brown stood trial in the Queensland Supreme Court, the public waiting on every word of evidence. The case had created enormous interest and the public wanted to know what would happen to Brown, who vehemently stuck to his claims of innocence. In fact, Brown insisted that he had been framed. However, he was found guilty of murder and sentenced to life imprisonment. Brown went to jail still declaring his innocence, and tragically, his suicide note read 'I did not kill Bronia Armstrong. My conscience is clear.'

THE MAD GENERAL

Sydney had rarely seen a funeral like it. It was a double funeral, two police officers being honoured by a city. It was January, 1931, and both police officers had been killed by a madman known as 'The Mad General'. The funeral procession drew thousands of onlookers, men removing their hats and women weeping as two flower-laden hearses moved slowly through Sydney's streets.

The dead policemen were Constable Norman Allan and Constable Ernest Andrews. Their killer was a wild man named John Kennedy, who was also killed on that bloody summer's day of January 3, 1931.

Kennedy, who had been rejected by the army for service during World War I, had developed a neurosis over his rejection and brooded over it for many years. He lived by himself in a rented cottage at Waverley, a Sydney suburb. There he practised rifle shooting, marched up and down the street singing military songs and generally became known as the shell-shocked 'Mad General'. Unfortunately, neighbours did not know of Kennedy's military rejection and believed he was a victim of the war.

Kennedy's condition worsened each year and on the fateful day of the killings he picked up his .22 rifle and a sharp hunting knife and headed for Bondi Junction. There, he bought a packet of cigarettes, then refused to pay for them. He told the female shop assistant to charge them to the Governor-General. The girl and the shopkeeper called in Constable Allan and he took after the mad Kennedy.

Allan eventually overtook the long-haired and maniacal looking Kennedy and spoke to him about the cigarettes. Kennedy's answer was to shoot Allan three times in the chest from close range.

Kennedy started marching to his cottage and was pursued by other police officers and at least one civilian. Constable Andrews, who was off duty, joined the chase and he and other police officers raced to Kennedy's cottage, only to find that Kennedy had bolted himself inside. Andrews banged on the cottage door and Kennedy had an answer for him, too—three shots to the body and a slashed throat with the hunting knife. Kennedy then headed back inside.

The police, now much more cautious, broke the windows in the front door and a Constable Johnson fired a shot from his revolver. It hit Kennedy in the stomach, mortally wounding him. Kennedy was taken to St Vincent's Hospital, Darlinghurst, but died a few hours later.

Police later discovered that Kennedy had been mentally ill for years, his mind snapping soon after being rejected by the army. He stuck to himself and his condition deteriorated when his mother died after the war. Kennedy's obsession with the military which rejected him cost New South Wales the lives of two young police officers. Sydney mourned the tragedy of Bondi.

THE FIRST STEP TO
THE WEDDING

The quiet city of Adelaide was shocked in September, 1957, when three members of a Greek family were shot dead in their own home. The Greek community was outraged when one of their own community members was later charged with murder. Community members felt that the killings had brought shame on their community. Dead were Mr Tom Galantomos, his wife Anna and daughter Ploheria (Ritsa). A 24-year-old Greek, Stalianos Athanasiadis, was later charged with murder. The Galantomos killings created enormous interest in Adelaide, with a Romeo and Juliet type of drama being unfolded before the courts.

Stalianos Athanasiadis had migrated to Australia from the Greek island of Rhodes three years earlier and worked in Adelaide as an electrician. The Galantomos family also came from Rhodes and Athanasiadis started courting 17-year-old Ritsa. Athanasiadis fell in love and decided to ask the Galantomos family for the hand of their daughter. Mr and Mrs Galantomos agreed and everyone seemed more than happy about the whole situation. Police later alleged in the Adelaide Police Court that Athanasiadis had written a 14-page statement, entitled 'The First Step to the Wedding', about the whole

Galantomos affair. The alleged document read, in reference to the engagement:

> I tell them, 'I am a man and I would like to do things right and I come to ask you for the hand of your daughter. Well I plead to you if you are good enough to give me an answer yes or no on that matter.'
>
> He said, 'With pleasure I'll tell you. My daughter, I don't know if she do like you or if she don't, and for that reason I think it would have been a lot better to give us one day so I can ask my daughter to see what she will answer, but from what I can see and understand from the look of my daughter's face, she is fond of you, and I can see that you are fond of her.
>
> 'Also my wife is sympathetic to you and you have my consent now.' I got off my seat and I tell them, 'Thanks very much.'
>
> At the same time I ask permission of her parents to let me speak to their daughter privately. They told me I could do it with pleasure.
>
> I said to her, 'Now, Miss Ritsa, our dream has come true. Happiness has come into our hands. We had better not let it go.'
>
> Her parents could hear what we were saying, and they were crying. I asked the girl, 'What you say, Ritsa.' The girl answered, 'Yes, the same as you say. I agree.'
>
> Then I got up and shake hands with them and kissed her hand at the same time, and the father winked his eye at me that I could kiss the girl. I did not lose any time.
>
> Then I said to the girl, 'Now, Miss Ritsa, we have consent of parents. I must kiss you.' The girl blushed and she knew she could not avoid it. She put her hands out and we kissed one another.

Indeed, everything seemed perfect for the young couple. They were married in a registry office on April 27, 1957, and in the eyes of the law they were man and wife. However, they did not live as man and wife because they were awaiting the Greek religious ceremony. Athanasiadis described the registry office wedding as a 'political' wedding 'as is required in this country'. The Galantomos family bought their new 'son-in-law' a Ford Mainline car, valued at £2200 as a wedding present.

Athanasiadis was delighted and took the family for drives. However, he was far from pleased when he discovered that the car had been bought for him on hire purchase. Athanasidis claimed he received an account stating that £1800 was owed on the car, with payments of £44/12/6 per month. According to the statement, 'from that day on things automatically changed'. The statement referred to 'grizzling and complaints'.

Athanasiadis claimed that his in-laws were arranging for their daughter to travel to Greece with them so that she could be married to a young student doctor. This, naturally, infuriated Athaniasidis. The statement produced in court told of a conspiracy to blacken his name and how the family turned against him. The religious wedding was due to be held on November 3, 1957. However, the Galantomos family were preparing for a visit to Greece. Athanasiadis could not take anymore from Mr and Mrs Galantomos, the young Greek feeling he was being thwarted in his love for their daughter, his own legal wife. He was told to leave the Galantomos home in the suburb of Southwark on September 22.

According to the statement produced by police at Athanasiadis' trial, the young Greek then decided he had to do something to save his marriage. The alleged statement read:

I went to my room and I sat down and started thinking and I was talking to myself. I saw that they were hard-hearted parents and would not give their child her happiness.

After that I started thinking who the devil is the young student doctor. Thinking of that drove me silly and I lost my mind. I don't know what I was thinking or what I was doing.

The next morning I got up. I went to town with a friend of mine and we went to the women police.

It was useless. They couldn't help us.

I went back home again, worried, thinking and sorry. I started thinking how I could help my wife.

That's what happened. Here it is.

Without thinking I took the gun with the intention of frightening her parents. Correct.

At 12.30 at dinner time I spoke to her father on the phone and told him, 'I will call you a father once again for the last time and let's forget all that's happened up till now and let's take the good road to happiness and to the wedding and so we will stop all the troubles and the gossip.

'I want to get married and go into our own house and be happy with my beloved.'

He told me, 'Now listen here. I will be leaving in a little while to go to Greece and I will take my daughter with me to marry the young student doctor.'

I heard another voice call out over the phone, 'No.' I understand that it was the voice of Ritsa.

After that he said, 'It's worried me and my family and my home.' He told me to pass outside his house again and he would take desperate measures to stop me.

I told him, 'Thank you!' and I shut the phone. I was silly and my blood was boiling and my temper.

I didn't lose any time. I took the gun. I was in a silly and desperate condition, and I went to their house and opened the door and sang out, 'Hands up.'

When I asked the mother, 'Where is Ritsa?' she told me, 'I don't know.' As soon as I walked in her father jumped up from the room and hit me automatically on the chest and hands to make me drop the gun.

At the same time he used the same language he used over the phone.

At that moment Ritsa came out and she said, 'Now I understand that you are a man and that you love me.'

At the same time the gun was spreading death everywhere. I was silly. I lost my sense and I did not know what I was doing.

I heard a voice saying, 'Steve, Steve. Do you love me? Come and kiss me, I am dying.' I went more silly. It was the angel voice of my beloved Ritsa.

How she got hit God only knows. She must have stepped into the path from one door to the other. What was the good of life to me? My beloved was dying and I would have to die too.

When she was injured before she died she said, 'Sorry, I know the instigators were my parents. Kiss me, Steve.'

She was crying and her eyes were running. She appeared to be in pain and suffering.

The parents had destroyed the future life of their child.

She said, 'Steve, come and kiss me because I am dying.'

I was kissing her all the time and then she told me with low words, 'Steve, do you love me? Kiss me and hug me and kill yourself, too.'

I said to her, 'Yes,' and I put up the gun and shoot myself. When she heard the noise and my movement of pain, I said, 'Ritsa, we are dying for our love.' She answer 'Yes, kiss and hug me.' I tried all I could.

I turn around, we hug one another, and she opened her eyes and she said quietly, 'Steve, kiss me, kiss me.'

I said, 'We will kiss one another for the last time. Let's die for our honor and our oath and our love.'

'Yes,' she answered, 'Kiss me. Kiss me.' I kissed her and she said, 'I die smiling. Yes, let's die.'

On the last kiss I lost consciousness. I was shaking, but my unforgettable died happy, but I am still suffering, I want to die for my love.

Ritsa and her parents were dead. Athaniasidis had pumped eleven bullets into his wife. Athaniasidis was critically wounded and was rushed to the Royal Adelaide Hospital. Athanadiadis had his arm around his wife when discovered by police. The woman was still alive and the rifle was lying across them. The mother was dead on arrival at hospital, while the girl and her father died in hospital later on September 23.

Athanaisidis was tried twice, being found guilty of murder both times. He was sentenced to death at his first trial, but an appeal to the High Court resulted in a new trial. Athanasiadis again was found guilty and again was sentenced to death. He was reprieved five days before he was due to hang. Athaniasidis, who pleaded insanity at both trials, told the second jury, 'I never at any time wanted to harm my darling wife or her parents. I wanted my wife to live and not to die: I wanted her more than anything else in the world'. Athaniasidis' sentence was commuted to one of life imprisonment.

THE VIET CONG BUNKER

There have been few Australian murder cases as bizarre, or as tragic, as the Viet Cong Bunker case. The death of two little sisters in December, 1978, shocked Western Australia and created headlines around the rest of Australia. The case had a number of incredible aspects, none the least being that the bodies of the two little girls were found entombed more than thirty-six hours after their mother was held captive in a Viet Cong style bunker. The girls' father later was charged with murder.

The drama started on December 14, 1978, when Brian Raymond Altham, a major in the Australian Army, abducted his two daughters, Samantha, 6, and Cherand, 4, both pretty little blondes. Altham, who had been married to his wife Elizabeth for ten years, had been separated from his wife for a year before the night of the tragedy. That night he waited at his wife's Perth home, hitting her over the head with a sand-filled sock when she returned from shopping. He bound and gagged her and then pushed her into his car. Altham drove his wife to his own flat, where the two girls were staying on a visit. He then brought the two girls out to the car and drove off into bushland. He told his wife to keep her head down or he would kill her.

Altham eventually pulled up, took his wife out of the car and tied her to a tree. He drove off with the children and disappeared into the bush. Altham returned on foot about twenty minutes later, untied his wife and led her into the Viet Cong-style bunker. The bunker was about three metres long, a metre deep and less than a metre wide. It was supported by poles and sheets of iron. Altham closed the entrance with bricks and offered his wife a knife so that she could slash her wrists. She refused and Altham told her that she would suffocate. She was bound tightly and left to die, Altham taking an overdose of sleeping pills. The terrified Mrs Altham almost certainly would have died with her husband in the bunker if she had not been able to wriggle herself free of the binding ropes. She then took the bricks out and escaped while her husband was unconscious from the effects of the sleeping pills. Mrs Altham also tied up her husband's hands, 'just in case he came to'.

Mrs Altham eventually flagged down a passing car and was taken to the Brentwood police station. Police did not waste any time and an immediate search for Altham and the two girls was launched. More than two hundred police officers and volunteers eventually became involved in the search for the girls. Altham was found in a coma and was rushed to hospital. Police found three other bunkers in the vicinity and reasoned that these were decoys. They also found what appeared to be a boobytrap at the entrance to the main bunker. Bomb disposal experts were called in but the boobytrap was a dummy and the bunker was declared safe.

The first day's search failed to find the little girls and police, under Detective Sergeant Frank Zanetti, intensified their efforts. Mounted police, trackers, dogs and even a light aircraft joined in the search, which lasted more than thirty-six hours. Mounted police eventually found the bodies of the two girls in a bush grave, realising the public's worst fears. The tiny bodies were wrapped in a blanket and buried in a two-metre hole near a group of trees about two miles from the bunker. The girls had been hit on the head by a hammer.

Altham was charged with the murder of his daughters, and pleaded insanity. At the start of the trial, in May, 1979, Altham's counsel accepted that Altham had killed Samantha and Cherand, and that the only issue to be decided was that of the accused's sanity. Altham's counsel, Mr R. W. Cannon, told the Perth Supreme Court that Altham's crime was so bizarre that the jury must believe it was dealing with a very sick man. Mr Cannon said, 'The major is mad, not bad.' However, the jury did not see it that way and Major Altham was found guilty and sentenced to death. The major, who had served in Papua-New Guinea and in Vietnam, was reprieved the next month, his sentence being commuted to one of life imprisonment. Altham's reprieve was expected, the last man to be hanged in Western Australia being Eric Edgar Cook, in October, 1964. However, Altham almost died by the noose. He was found hanging in his cell at Fremantle prison in March, 1979, before his trial. A warder found Altham unconscious, hanging from strips of sheeting. Of course, Altham recovered to face trial for murder.

TWO LUCKY DIGGERS

Although hundreds of British and Commonwealth servicemen were executed for desertion, cowardice or other military offences during World War I, only one Australian paid the ultimate penalty. Yet Private John King was an Australian serving in a New Zealand uniform, with the Canterbury Infantry Regiment. King, who was found guilty, not of desertion, but of being absent without leave, was executed on August 19, 1917.

King's sentence of death was confirmed by General Sir Douglas Haig, who had made strong representations that Australian soldiers also should be subject to the extreme penalty. However, the Australian government decreed that none of its servicemen would be executed, regardless of the circumstances, mainly because all its soldiers were volunteers.

Yet two Diggers could have considered themselves fortunate to have escaped the hangman's noose in wartime England. Privates Ernie Sharp and Tom Maguire were absent without leave on the evening of August 21, 1917, when they went drinking at the Rising Sun Hotel off the Waterloo Road in south-east London. Ironically, this watering hole now is just a few hundred metres from the Imperial War Museum.

Sharp and Maguire started drinking with a petty English crook named Joe Jones and, late in the night, the three of them followed two cashed-up Canadian soldiers, Oliver Imley and John McKinley, into the dark, narrow Valentine Place. The Canadians, to use an Australian expression, were 'rolled'. McKinley recovered from the injuries he received in the bashing and robbery, but Imley died four days later. Jones, Sharp and Maguire faced possible murder charges.

Sharp, who recognised the gravity of his situation, turned King's evidence and, for stepping forward had a murder charge against him dropped and, instead, was handed a seven-year penal sentence. Sharp also insisted that it was English civilian Jones, who had been discharged from the army after twice being wounded on the Western Front, who was responsible for bashing the two Canadians and therefore killing Imley.

Both Sharp and Maguire claimed that Jones had laid into the two Canadians with a police truncheon. Jones denied he had a truncheon and even claimed that the Australians had done all the bashing, but other witnesses said they had seen him with a weapon earlier in the night. Jones' fate was sealed and he was sentenced to death. Maguire, for his part in the robbery that led to Imley's death, was sentenced to eight years' jail.

Jones' execution was set for dawn on February 20, 1918, and as executioner John Ellis slipped the noose over his head, he mumbled: 'God forgive them.' It is presumed that Jones was referring either to the jury that had found him guilty or to the execution party, including hangman Ellis.

Or could he have been referring to the two Australian Diggers, Sharp and Maguire, his partners in crime, if not in murder, that night near Waterloo Road?

THE BODY IN THE BARWON

Tall and elegant, Mr H.A. Winneke QC (later Sir Henry Winneke, Governor of Victoria) chose his words carefully. Mr Winneke was making an opening address in one of the most sensational murder trials in Victorian criminal history. Mr Winneke said, 'Someone has committed a foul and ghastly murder. On May 13 (1953) the dead man left his home after his evening meal, giving no indication he was not returning. Nothing more was heard of him until a diver recovered the decapitated body from the Barwon River, Geelong, on August 1. When the body was recovered the head was sawn off the trunk, and each hand had been sawn off above the wrist. The trunk was in two sacks wired to a 126 pound stone, and the head and hands in a kerosene tin punctured with holes. A post-mortem examination showed the body to be very, very extensively damaged. The trunk had been mutilated – there were six main wounds on the skull and there were underlying fractures beneath three of them caused by extremely heavy blows.'

On trial before Mr Justice Martin in the Supreme Court at Geelong were Andrew Gordon Kilpatrick, 33, and Russell William Hill, 22, both of Colac, a prosperous rural city in Victoria's Western District. Both had pleaded not guilty to a charge of murdering

Donald Brooke Maxfield, also of Colac, on or about May 13. The case was widely known as 'The Body in the Barwon' murder and it captured headlines in Victoria for years. Yet, incredibly, only a determined policeman's hunch led to a murder investigation.

The tough policeman was Detective Sergeant Fred Adam, a well-known member of Victoria's Homicide Squad. Detective Adam was sent to Colac to investigate a number of mysterious break-ins in the district. It was not a murder investigation and there was not even a hint of murder, at first. Detective Adam's job was to prosecute Andrew Kilpatrick and Russell Hill on a charge of assaulting a local constable with a weapon. That case alone drew considerable publicity, the Melbourne Truth giving the case a great deal of space in its issues of June 13 and July 11, 1953. Kilpatrick and Hill were found guilty of assaulting Constable George Ross Chester and sentenced to a year's jail. They gave notice of appeal and were released on bail.

The appeals could have been heard and that might have been the last anyone heard of Kilpatrick and Hill. However, Detective Adam felt that there was something wrong. He could not put his finger on the very cause of his anxiety but he felt strongly about his nagging suspicions and he decided to act. He filed a report to police headquarters suggesting that there was a conspiracy of crime in Colac which needed investigation by local detectives. The file was returned to Detective Adam with an order to investigate the matter himself. Detective Adam, in a newspaper interview in 1967, described his hunch about Kilpatrick and Hill. He said, 'It all started with a hunch I had in Colac ... I don't believe in hunches as a rule, they're no substitute for hard leg-work, no matter what the detective stories say'. Detective Adam remarked to another policeman, 'There's something heavy here, not just hoodlums and break-ins' . Detective Adam was so right, and he did not have to wait long to prove his hunch right.

Detective Adam believed that by putting pressure on the younger Hill he would get further than he would by questioning Kilpatrick. Hill was young, impressionable and not as smart as

Kilpatrick, who had been educated at the exclusive Geelong Grammar School. Detective Adam had studied the police file on a break-in case involving Hill and Donald Maxfield, and noted that Maxfield had 'opened his mouth' quite a bit. Detective Adam was hoping that Hill would talk freely about what was happening in Colac. He lined up an interview with Hill but his man did not turn up. Hill had fled. Detective Adam then heard that Maxfield had 'shot through' in similar circumstances a couple of months earlier.

Detective Adam looked up the file on Maxfield's disappearance and for the first time suspected murder. Detective Adam said later, 'I had a look at the Missing Friend report on Maxfield and it had "murder" written all over it'. Detective Adam's first step was to see Maxfield's father, who confirmed Adam's worst fears. The father, Charles Maxfield, told Detective Adam that he was convinced his son was dead. Mr Maxfield's suspicions were justified. Young Donald Maxfield, just 22 years of age, had simply vanished, leaving a trail of mysteries behind. Why had he left behind his beloved motor cycle? Why had he not collected his wages? Why had he left money on his dressing table? It just didn't add up and Mr Maxwell told Detective Adam, 'Donald's dead. I walk around the lake (Colac is situated on a large lake) every morning waiting for his body to come up'. It certainly appeared that Donald Maxfield was dead and Detective Adam now believed he was investigating a case of murder.

Police sent out an all stations alert for the missing Hill, who was picked up on a holding vagrancy charge at Hamilton, another Western District town. Detective Adam arrived at Hamilton the following day, July 30, and immediately questioned Hill, who started confessing about break-ins. Detective Adam was angling for bigger fish and he already had made a file marked 'The Murder of Donald Brooke Maxfield'. Hill kept babbling on about robberies in the Colac district. Detective Adam stopped him dead in his tracks when he said, 'It wasn't exactly what I came up to see you about. It's about Donald Brooke Maxfield. We've reason to believe he's been murdered'. Hill broke down immediately and allegedly blurted out 'That's right. It's no good denying it. He's dead. He's in the river. We cut him up'. Detective Adam then took down a confession.

The alleged confession, which Hill signed, told an amazing story. It claimed that Maxfield had been killed because he had told police too much about what had been happening in Colac. Maxfield, the confession said, had been executed. Kilpatrick had decided that the 'squealer' was not going to get away with telling stories to police and he arranged for Maxfield to meet him in a garage on the night of May 13, 1953. Kilpatrick worked at the garage as a panel beater and Maxfield's suspicions would not have been aroused by going to the garage.

Hill was supposed to kill Maxfield but could not go through with it. Hill said that Kilpatrick hit Maxfield on the back of the head with an iron bar and threw him into the back of a Pontiac car owned by Elliminyt farmer Mr George Leary, who had left the car at the garage for repairs. Maxfield was still alive as Kilpatrick and Hill headed for the Barwon River in the big Pontiac, registration number LB306.

Hill's alleged statement read: 'Kilpatrick said to me "Maxfield had got to come here tonight with a .22 rifle. Now is our chance to get rid of him". I was a bit dubious of doing it … We had a few beers and then Maxfield arrived … We had a general conversation, and then Andy picked up an iron bar about 18 inches long and hit Maxfield on the side of the head with it. He hit him on the head four or five times and he went on his back … He was unconscious and groaning, and we both lifted him into the back of the car. We then mopped up the blood on the floor with water. Andy put a hacksaw in the car. We went out to Queen's Park. There is a waterfall up there. It would be a good place to put him. I stopped the car and we got out … Andy opened the door to get him out … Maxfield was still alive, and he said "You … " Andy pulled him out of the car and hit him with the butt of a .45 pistol. I think that was where he died. We carried him along a track and got some of the way up. The going was too rough and we decided to turn back.'

The statement then said that the two drove to the Barwon River. It said: 'I stopped the car and Andy pulled him (Maxfield) out. We both carried him down the river bank. Andy said, "Now we will cut off his hands and then his head, and they won't be able to identify him". He got out a hacksaw and cut off his hands and then his head. Andy said, "You put the head and hands in a tin".' The statement added that the body then was thrown into the Barwon River near the Princes Bridge.

The alleged statement was an incredible document. It told of a killing as brutal as any in Victorian criminal history. Detective Adam asked Hill to sign his confession and Hill wrote 'This statement is true. I was hoping that Maxfield wouldn't come around to the garage that night. Russell William Hill'. Hill was taken to Geelong and was charged with murder. Police then apprehended Kilpatrick, who at first decided not to say anything. However, when tackled with Hill's alleged statement, Kilpatrick said, 'He's a liar, he had as much to do with it as I did ...'. Kilpatrick did not make a statement.

Meanwhile, police had to find the body of the unfortunate Maxfield. Detective Adam had already charged Kilpatrick and Hill with murder, before a body had been found. Detective Adam said later, 'If we hadn't found Maxfield's body I could have been back on a pushbike'. Police divers eventually found Maxfield's body in about thirty feet of water. An hour later a diver found a kerosene tin containing Maxfield's hands and head. The other tin, containing Maxfield's clothes, was not found until after Kilpatrick and Hill had been convicted.

The inquest created enormous interest but the trial was the real star turn. Hill stuck to his statement at the inquest but changed his account at the trial before Mr Justice Martin. He blamed Kilpatrick for Maxfield's murder, and that added enormously to the mounting interest in the case. The trial at Geelong created headlines in Melbourne newspapers, one report even suggesting that teenage girls flocked to the trial when Kilpatrick and Hill took the stand.

Naturally, a number of gruesome details came to light at the trial in October, 1953. The court was told that Maxfield's death was caused by head injuries and drowning. Senior government pathologist Dr Keith Bowden told the court that he examined Maxfield's body on August 2. Dr Bowden said the head and hands could have been removed with a hacksaw. There were wounds on the right arm and on both thighs and three deep wounds on the stomach. Three of the six wounds on the head had fractures beneath them which could have been caused by iron bars produced in court. Dr Bowden said that a man with such head wounds would have died fairly quickly—in about twenty minutes. Dr Bowden said he could find no evidence that decapitation and dismemberment occurred while Maxfield was alive. Dr Bowden said he believed the head injuries followed by drowning had caused death. The water in the lungs had been taken into the body before decapitation. Dr Bowden said this was his opinion after experiments with three freshly killed heifers whose headless bodies were immersed in a running stream for a month. A post-mortem on the animals showed there was no water in the lungs. Dr Bowden said that in his opinion the head and hands were severed after death.

Victorian government analyst Mr Douglas William Wilson said that he had examined two bars taken from the Colac garage. Mr Wilson said the bars had no bloodstains. He had found no bloodstains on the hacksaw handed to him by police but had found stains on a .45 Webley Scott revolver, on the butt and near the trigger guard. Chemical tests revealed blood on a rug taken from the Pontiac car.

The Crown based its case on a combination of a number of factors, including the forensic evidence, the statement alleged to have been made by Hill, and evidenced by a number of witnesses. One of the most important witnesses was taxi driver Maxwell George Benson, of Colac. Benson told the court that on the morning of June 3, about three weeks after Maxfield's disappearance, he drove Hill, Kilpatrick and two others to Melbourne. Kilpatrick asked Benson to turn off near the Princes Bridge. Benson said Kilpatrick and Hill then got out of the car for about five to ten minutes and went under the bridge.

This evidence was particularly relevant because in the statement allegedly made by Hill, reference was made to a visit to the Barwon River near the Princes Bridge. The statement read: 'About a fortnight later Andy and I were going to Melbourne and we went to the spot where we put the body and saw that it had floated down-stream. We went on to Melbourne, and on the way back in the dark we got the body and wired a big rock to it and sunk it. I didn't like the idea of doing it and I didn't want to say to Andy that I wouldn't do it'.

Colin Thomas, a grader driver of Colac, told the court that he was with Kilpatrick and Hill on the day that they caught a taxi to Melbourne. Thomas said he saw them go down under the Princes Bridge. George Leary, who owned the Pontiac car used by Kilpatrick and Hill, told the court that he recognised a rug left in the car. Leary said he had left the brown car in the garage on May 8 for repairs. A bran bag and a chaff bag, similar to those produced in court, were in the boot when he left the car but were not there when the car had been returned on May 22. The petrol tank, which was almost full when he left the car at the garage, was almost empty when the car was returned. Leary said no one had permission to use the car.

Edward Goodall, of Goodall's Garage, Colac, said he employed Kilpatrick as a welder for about four years and worked in a rear shed known as 'Andy's shop'. Shown two iron bars, Goodall said they had been kept in 'Andy's shop'. Maxfield's father, Mr Charles Maxfield, also gave evidence that his son left home at about 7 p.m. on May 13 and appeared to be worried. That was the last time Mr Maxfield saw his son alive.

Kilpatrick and Hill both went into the witness box and put the blame on each other. Each said he was in bed at the time Maxfield was killed. Each denied dismembering the body and dumping the torso and the head and hands in the Barwon River. Asked by his counsel, Mr J.F. Moloney, if he killed Maxfield, Kilpatrick replied 'No'. Asked if he had taken any part, Kilpatrick again said 'No'. Mr Moloney asked Kilpatrick 'Do you know where you were on the evening of May 13?' Kilpatrick replied, 'In my bed at home, at my mother's place in Colac'. Kilpatrick said he asked Benson to turn off the Geelong-Colac road at Princes Bridge because it was a short cut to his sister's home. However, Detective Adam told the court that Kilpatrick made a verbal admission.

Hill told the court that he did not go to the garage on the night of May 13. He said that after looking in shop windows and sitting in the park he went to bed. Hill said he went to the Union Club Hotel, Colac, the next day and Kilpatrick 'roasted me for not going around at night'. Hill added, 'He said that Maxfield came around with the rifle, that they had a few beers and that he hit him with the iron bar'. Hill said that Kilpatrick told him 'I took him in the car to Queen's Park. He was still alive and called me a b ... The going was rough, so near a bridge I cut off his hands and head with a hacksaw'. Hill said that about a fortnight later, on a trip to Melbourne on a motor cycle, Kilpatrick pointed out to him where he had put the body, looked over the bridge and said, '"The damn thing's floating. We'll have to do something about that on the way back". We got some wire off a fence between Werribee and Geelong. Just before dark we got to the bridge. Kilpatrick said that I would have to give him a hand. I did not want to. He got a big rock and tied it to the bag with the wire. He pointed out where he had put the tins and told me to keep quiet about it. He told me that he put the body in the bag and wired them together. On the trip to Melbourne with the taxi driver he told the driver to stop at the bridge. We got out and went below the bridge. Kilpatrick wanted to see if the bag was still there.'

Hill then claimed that when he was interviewed by police at Hamilton they told him that they believed Kilpatrick and he had put Maxfield out of the way. Hill then claimed that his shoes and socks were taken off and he was hit on the feet with a rubber hose. Hill alleged in court: 'McLeod (Detective Don McLeod) pulled me on to the floor by the hair and slapped me. I then made a statement. The only part of the statement that was true is the part about the sinking the body with the stone. Kilpatrick told me the rest. I made the statement because I was frightened. I knew Kilpatrick did not like squealers. After the inquest I decided not to stick to the statement because of what I saw and heard. I went with the police and pointed out the spots near the bridge'.

Mr S. Cohen, for Hill, said it was highly unbelievable that a young man like Hill could have planned and committed such a callous and cold-blooded murder. Mr Cohen said, 'Hill has sworn he was subjected to physical persuasion before making his statement. Isn't it rather improbable that he should make such an incriminating admission by his own will.'

Mr Moloney, for Kilpatrick, told the jury that Kilpatrick had no motive in killing Maxfield. Mr Moloney said, 'Before this trial began most of you read newspaper reports and heard rumours about the murder. Probably some of you instantly condemned Kilpatrick but you must judge him solely on evidence given in court. Hill has done much damage to Kilpatrick by his incriminating accusations. In Hill, you have a man clutching at a last straw by blaming Kilpatrick. Hill's unfortunate lying is in strict contrast to Kilpatrick's straightforward evidence. Do you think Kilpatrick, a reserved, quietly-spoken man, would have committed such a crime and confided in Hill about it? Surely the weakest person would protest, if according to Hill, Kilpatrick had suggested that they murder Maxfield, Hill's close friend. The case against Kilpatrick is one of alleged verbal admissions … There was absolutely no motive for Kilpatrick to do the slightest harm to Maxfield'.

Mr Winneke, for the Crown, said in his sixty-four minute address to the jury that both men had denied any part in Maxfield's murder. Mr Winneke said, 'But how could police have recovered Maxfield's body on August 1 if either accused had not made admissions the day before? It has been suggested that police used force to obtain a statement from Hill but this has been strongly denied on oath by detectives. Hill has admitted he did not complain to Detective-Inspector Donnelly or the magistrate at the inquest that he had been ill-treated. Kilpatrick's story that he was framed by detectives is hard to believe. Would three detectives conspire to fabricate evidence to convict a man of murder?'

Mr Justice Martin, in summing up on Thursday, October 22, said, 'No one could hear this trial or see the Court's exhibits without a deep feeling of horror or indignation. However, horror and indignation must not influence you in arriving at your verdict of the accuseds' guilt or innocence'. Mr Justice Martin said that vital features of the case were the alleged admissions by both accused. Mr Justice Martin said, 'Hill ... had incriminated himself in a written statement which he said was forced from him by detectives. If you think it was made entirely freely you must regard it seriously'. However, Mr Justice Martin indicated that the firmness of Hill's notes and signature on the statement suggested that he had not been subjected to violence. Mr Justice Martin also referred to Kilpatrick's claim that he had been framed.

The jury considered its verdict.

The jury was out for almost three hours, and Kilpatrick and Hill rose slowly to their feet as the jury returned. Kilpatrick was as composed as he had ever been during the three day trial, while Hill looked nervous. Both Kilpatrick and Hill were found guilty of murder. Mr Justice Martin sentenced both men to death and told them, 'You have been found guilty of a horrible and cruel murder, of a crime planned in cold blood and completed in circumstances of the utmost barbarity.' Asked by the judge if they had anything to say, Hill replied, 'No sir', while Kilpatrick replied, 'I am not guilty, sir'.

The death sentences were never carried out. Hill had his death sentence commuted to 20 years' jail, while Kilpatrick's sentence was commuted to life imprisonment. Kilpatrick's name became synonymous with the crime and he became a notorious figure in Pentridge jail. He was known there as 'The King' during the early years of his sentence, although he later became an ideal prisoner. Kilpatrick was released from jail in August, 1976, on parole. He was a sick man, suffering from an enlarged heart. His release created a great deal of public interest, although there was no outrage at his release after twenty-three years in prison.

Nine months after his release, Kilpatrick gave a Melbourne newspaper an interview. Kilpatrick said, 'To go to jail is a terrible thing. It's twenty-odd years out of a man's life. If I had my time over it is an act I wouldn't do again'. Kilpatrick then told how his early years in jail were difficult, self-discipline helping him pull through the difficult years. Kilpatrick learned to be a radio and television technician while in jail, and helped repair watches and clocks. On his release, he went for a holiday in Queensland and sent cards to his pals 'inside'. Kilpatrick said that one of his greatest pleasures was taking a 'nice and quiet' walk in the country.

THE INSCRUTABLE ORIENTAL

Melbourne newspaper reporters had never seen anyone like Chang Gook Kong in court before. Chang, a Chinese seaman from the docked British freighter Fort Abitibi, was charged with the murder of 23-year-old labourer Douglas Vivian Alcock outside a Fitzroy hotel on March 29, 1947. Chang, who did not speak much English, sat almost motionless throughout his trial two months later and the press were treated to the near-perfect example of the inscrutable Oriental. Chang appeared to have little idea about the proceedings of the court and spoke only rarely, through an interpreter. Even when the Criminal Court jury gave its verdict Chang showed little or no sign of emotion.

Chang found himself in court as a result of an incident outside the Perseverance Hotel, Brunswick St, Fitzroy. Alcock was stabbed twice in the stomach, medical evidence stating that either wound would have proven fatal. Alcock died an hour later in the nearby St Vincent's Hospital. Chang claimed, through the interpreter, that he was attacked and knocked down by three men, including Alcock. He defended himself with his knife, which had a spring-blade operated by a brass stud, striking at one of the men (Alcock) as they closed in on him. Chang said he believed the men were going to rob him. He also told police, 'Three men fight me, knock me down. I don't want fight. I say, "I do not want fight". I have knife. I kill.' Chang then ran away from the fight scene.

The jury obviously believed Chang's self-defence account of the incident and the inscrutable Oriental was acquitted of both murder and manslaughter. Chang did have a cut lip when interviewed by police after Alcock's death and this must have gone in his favour, heavily suggesting that the three men had fought with Chang. When discharged by Mr Justice O'Bryan, Chang walked from the dock as if he had never been in danger of swinging from the hangman's noose. He was as inscrutable as ever.

THE SEALED ROOM MURDER

Young Salvatore Tabone left his home in Malta in 1916, determined to make his fortune in Australia. Tabone, who later changed his name to Borg, did not make a fortune but he did build up a profitable business after years of hard work. Sam Borg worked in Queensland's canefields soon after arriving in Australia but later built up a cafe business in Melbourne's Little Lonsdale Street. It was not a fancy cafe but Borg seemed reasonably happy with his lot. He made a small amount of money and was able to indulge in his favourite pastime—card gambling.

Borg was hooked on cards and often played with migrant friends in Maltese clubs. He also made money by renting a room in his cafe for gambling purposes. Card games were everything to Borg and he was able to build up substantial bank rolls through his gambling activities. In fact, Borg was regarded as an expert gambler. The only trouble was that Borg, like many elderly people of his generation, did not trust banks. Borg would prefer to hide his money in his bedroom. It was a dangerous habit as Borg eventually was killed, with robbery the probable motive.

Borg, 67, was seen flashing £1000 in notes shortly before he was murdered in May, 1960. That was most unlike Borg, who usually was smart enough to keep his winnings to himself. However, friends told police that Borg was seen with £1000 on the Saturday night before his death. That was the last anyone saw of Borg alive. He was seen leaving a Maltese club in North Melbourne just before 10 p.m. and his body was discovered the following Monday night, May 30.

Police were called to Borg's cafe when a local Maltese identity told them that he had not seen Borg for a few days. Police immediately went to the cafe and Constables J. Kane and J. Charles had to smash in a cafe door. Borg's battered and bloodied body was found in a bedroom but, incredibly, the door to that bedroom had been nailed—from the inside. Melbourne newspapers immediately named the case the 'Sealed Room Murder'. The headline in the Melbourne Sun of May 31 read 'Slain Man Found In Nailed Up Room.'

Police, in reconstructing the crime, reasoned that Borg had been battered to death with the leg of a heavy wooden table, the body then being dragged into a spare bedroom where it was pushed under a bed. The killer, or killers, then climbed out of the room through a skylight which adjoined another room. The killer(s) then left the building by the front door. Borg's pyjama-clad body was wrapped shroud-like in sheets and blankets and bound by strips of rag.

The most puzzling aspect for police was that, despite the claims that Borg had been seen with £1000 on the Saturday night, £450 was found in the bedroom and cafe.

There was £400 in notes in a pillowslip and £50 in silver on a window shelf in the cafe. If the killing was committed primarily for robbery, why overlook the £400 in notes? Besides, Borg was attacked and killed while he slept, ruling out the possibility that the killer(s) was disturbed. The killer(s) did not panic, either. Police said that the killer obviously knew his way around the cafe and 'coldly went around wrapping the body up, nailing the door and then padlocking it from the outside'. Police had a real puzzle on their hands.

Melbourne newspapers seized on the mysterious aspects of the murder and it created headlines for some weeks. Police interviewed more than four hundred people in a desperate effort to get the breakthrough they so badly needed. But although they often seemed close to solving the murder mystery, the trail eventually grew cold.

Police then had what they considered their best lead yet when it was reported that a hatless man, wearing a dark overcoat, had been seen lurking outside Borg's cafe on the Saturday night he was last seen alive. A taxi driver told police that he had dropped Borg off at the cafe shortly before 10 p.m. and had noticed a hatless man standing near Borg's front door in the otherwise deserted street. Police tried everything to discover the identity of the mysterious hatless man but their efforts proved futile. The mysterious hatless man never came forward to answer police questions.

Police then had three telephone calls from a man Melbourne newspapers dubbed Mr X. Police arranged to meet the mysterious Mr X on the beach front at Brighton just after midnight on June 10. Mr X then told police to investigate the movements of people he thought were associated with the crime. Mr X, who was described as a New Australian, told police, 'I have been in trouble myself and the only reason I have done this is because violence worries me. If it was an ordinary crime it would not have worried me but a murder like this has.' Homicide Squad head Detective Inspector Jack Matthews said that it was not possible to reveal Mr X's disclosures but said that police would check the information. 'He could be wrong but we don't think so,' Inspector Matthews said.

Members of the Homicide Squad later interviewed two men in Queanbeyan and Sydney but were satisfied that the men had nothing to do with the murder. The police investigation had run into a deadend. Inspector Matthews said he was still hopeful of solving the mystery but despite further massive attempts to find the killer(s), the murder mystery remains unsolved.

'THE THREE LITTLE ANGELS'

Unfortunately, Australia has had more than its share of pathetic murder cases. However, few cases have been as sad as the murder of three innocent little girls in Sydney in 1924. The case shocked, revolted and then saddened almost everyone in Sydney, and indeed, the whole of Australia. When the bodies of the three little innocents were discovered there was an enormous outcry. However, when the files were closed on the case, the public were to shed tears for the accused as well as the three little angels.

The murders occurred in the Sydney suburb of Paddington, now trendy and fashionable. However, Paddington was a slum suburb in 1924. Edward Williams, a 52-year-old piano teacher, struggled interminably to raise his three daughters, Rosalie, 5, Mary, 3, and Cecilia, 2, by himself. Williams' wife was an inmate at the Callan Park asylum, Williams and the three girls visiting the deranged Mrs Williams almost every weekend. Williams often had to leave his daughters in the care of neighbors while he went about his business. He lived frugally, often borrowing money from friends to make ends meet. It was a tough, difficult life and Williams eventually cracked under the strain. On the night of February 4, 1924, he told his little Rosalie, the eldest of the innocents, that he would help her get to heaven. Rosalie earlier had told her father that she would like to go to heaven one day, and that was one of the contributing factors to the steps Williams took that night while his daughters were asleep.

The distraught Williams, broke, without hopes and wearied by the eternal struggle to maintain his three daughters, sought a happy release for the three children he loved. He cut their throats with a razor while they were asleep. He bundled the bodies together on top of their double bed and placed newspapers under the bed to catch and mop up the dripping blood. He then left Sydney but not before he told a local furniture dealer that he could take the furniture and sell it for what he could get.

The dealer turned up at Williams' rented room and took a piano. He noticed a lump of bedding but did not remove it from the room. The bodies of the three little angels were not discovered until half an hour later when landlady Mrs Florence Mahon went to the rooms to see what was going on. She threw back the bed clothes and got the shock of her life. The sight was pathetic, the dead little girls all bundled together, blood everywhere from the gaping wounds. Police were called immediately and the hunt was on for Williams.

Incredibly, Williams got as far as Newcastle before handing himself in to police. He claimed later that he waited five days before handing himself in so that he could ensure his daughters had a decent burial. Naturally, Williams was charged with murder and, also naturally, public sympathy was violently against him. Williams was advised to plead insanity at his trial but steadfastly refused, obviously knowing his own mind and wanting to carry out his intentions to the end.

Williams, a pathetic figure in Sydney Central Court, made an extraordinary statement to the court, outlining in detail his reasons for murdering the children he loved so dearly. The speech is as poignant as any in Australian court records, Williams indicating beyond doubt that the murders were committed as 'acts of love'. Williams reasoned that he wanted his daughters to go to heaven rather than risk their souls in a life of struggle and possible degradation if they had been sent to live in an institution.

Williams referred to a conversation he had had with the Mahons (Mrs Mahon being his deranged wife's sister) about the possibility of the girls being placed in an institution. That horrified Williams, for several reasons. Firstly, he would have been deprived of the children he loved. Secondly, he believed that most of Sydney's prostitutes had been institution girls and, as a devout Roman Catholic, that turned his blood cold. The final straws were little Rosalie's ambition to live in heaven, and a truly tragic similarity Williams saw in his eldest daughter and her mother.

Williams, on the night of the tragedy, believed he saw his wife's crooked eyes in his daughter. That turned his head completely. He could not let his daughter go the same way as the mother. However, Williams reasoned that if Rosalie was to die the others had to die as well. Williams therefore killed the three of them. Williams, in his incredible courtroom speech, said, 'That night, February 4, Mahon suggested that I should send my children to an institution, and I asked him whether he thought anybody could love, or that he could love, my children better than I ...

'I was agitated in my mind about the morrow. Tuesday was my busy day, and I could not go out and leave the children alone. I had no one to care for them. But I could not neglect my pupils. I had to teach to buy food for the children. It was then I decided to do as I did. I was not insane, gentlemen. I told the government medical officer that I would have nothing to do with a plea of insanity, for I do not want to escape the consequences of my crime.

'I saw if my girls went to an institution they would be separated. They would not be able to sit at the same table together, and when they came out they would be tools for the first smooth-tongued person who came along. I know, and you know, gentlemen, that the majority of prostitutes are the women who were raised in public institutions such as my girls would have been sent to had I been agreeable. I saw it all, and saw beyond it.

'All who have seen my wife in Callan Park must notice that the eyes are out of alignment. The right eye is not in line with the left one which is much higher than the other. I saw that in my little Rosalie too the same unevenness as in her mother, who went insane. I don't know but I feared that she would go as her mother went. I could not kill her and leave the other two, so I decided to murder all three. I say murder because it was murder. When I did it I pictured them happy in heaven. They went to God with untarnished souls. I was not the callous man they pictured me here today, for when I killed my three children, that was the moment that I loved them most intensely …

'I did not want to see them after I killed them. That was why I covered them up so heavily. I did not want to see them again. I had seen them last happy in sleep. What happened after that I am not quite clear. I put paper under the bed so that the blood would not drip through. I did it because I could not bear to see their blood. It was not done to hide my crime.

'I think I lay down about two in the morning but was up sitting in my chair again at three o'clock. At seven in the morning I went to Mass and asked God's pardon for what I had done. I knew then, as I had before I murdered my children, that I would be hanged, or imprisoned for life, for my crime.

'So, far from bring a callous act, it was to me an act of great love. I intended to give myself up but decided not to do so until the Monday, in order that I might learn that my children were properly buried …

'I seek neither favour nor mercy. I only ask for justice. I am entitled to a fair trial, and I know I shall receive it from you. If I am to be hanged, then let me be hanged. Take no notice of the plea of insanity. I myself do not raise it. As for it being temporary insanity, I can't say myself.'

The court was stunned. However, it seems certain Williams knew what he was doing. He specifically mentioned that he 'murdered' the girls. He virtually was asking for the death sentence, refusing to plea insanity. Most men who kill their families usually suicide almost immediately, wiping out the entire family. Williams did not do this, presumably because of his religion. As a Catholic, Williams knew that one of the most serious sins in the church's teachings was suicide. Williams would have been condemned to the eternal fires of hell had he suicided. However, he elected to stand trial for his murders, resisting chances to escape the hangman's noose.

It is quite plausible, therefore, to suggest that Williams wanted to be hanged to save himself the grave sin of suicide. If that was the case, Williams got his wish. He was found guilty of murder and was hanged on April 29, 1924. Presumably, he was reunited with his three little angels.

A BONZER KID

Charles Louis Havelock le Gallion, 52, ran a successful motor engineering business in the Sydney suburb of Crow's Nest. A big, burly man, Charles le Gallion was separated from his wife and family of four sons. However, the successful engineer still paid his family's living expenses, even paying for their grocery bills. The father went his way but the sons, especially young Charles, 17, took the mother's side in the domestic rift. Young Charles and his father often had rows about the family split, the son accusing the father of neglecting Mrs Heather le Gallion. Young Charles at one time was apprenticed to his father but there was one row too many and the boy ceased to work in the family business.

Young Charles le Gallion found the whole situation intolerable. He firmly believed that his father should have been providing much more money to the family and decided to tackle his father about it. The boy went to his father's engineering works on the night of September 30, 1948, to see what he could do about the situation. Mrs le Gallion had not received any money from her husband for two weeks and young Charles was not going to tolerate that. He told his father that he had come for money for the house, and the father replied, 'It's no business of mine'.

Mr le Gallion then answered a telephone call. Young Charles tackled his father as soon as the telephone conversation ended and the father replied, 'That's nothing to do with me'. Mr le Gallion then opened a drawer, pulled out a bundle of bills and said, 'Have a look at those'. The son argued with his father about the regularity of household bills and the father then worked out some figures relating to household expenses. Young Charles told his father, 'Mum is sick, you should provide for her ... Mum's people started you off. Mr le Gallion replied, 'Mind your own business. I'm after a divorce. I've made a will and left everything to Betty de Groen.'

The conversation lasted a considerable time and was punctuated by telephone calls made to the le Gallion office. Miss Edith de Groen, who once had worked as a typist in le Gallion's office, later said she had been ringing the le Gallion office on le Gallion's instructions. Miss de Groen made the last telephone call at 9 p.m., the telephone giving an engaged signal. Miss de Groen tried to get the le Gallion number for ten minutes but could not get through. She then rang North Sydney police.

Police discovered le Gallion's body later that night. The engineering wizard had been stabbed and was slumped against a table in the office. Detective Alan Clark later told a Coroner's Court that 'the body was dressed in trousers, shirt with the sleeves rolled up, collar and tie, shoes and socks.' There were blood smears and splashes on the walls and floor of the office. The post mortem revealed that le Gallion had been drinking before he was killed. There was a blood alcohol reading of . 107 per cent. Dr C.E. Percy, government medical officer, told the Coroner's Court that death was caused by a wound on the left side of the chest, about half an inch long, which had penetrated the chest wall and into the front of the heart.

The Sydney press gave the murder considerable coverage. The Sydney Daily Mirror of October 1, 1948, headlined the case 'Strange Telephone Calls Before Vicious Stabbing—Wide Hunt for Killer'. The report said, 'So far police have formed no definite theory about the actual manner in which le Gallion was attacked.' The Daily Mirror the following day headlined the murder: 'Missing Coat Vital - Lead in Stabbing Mystery—Intense Hunt by Detectives'.

That report said that police were searching for a blue-grey single-breasted coat missing from le Gallion's office. Le Gallion was seen wearing the coat only hours before his death. The report also said that police had interviewed more than fifty friends, relatives and business colleagues of the dead man. More importantly, the report said that Mrs Heather le Gallion had told police that she could not suggest a motive for her husband's death.

Police finally arrested young Charles le Gallion on October 4, 1948. Detectives Whiteman and Gilmore, of North Sydney police, arrested le Gallion on a bus at Wynyard Square. The arrest followed the discovery of a blood-stained jacket and a knife, found in a culvert between North Sydney and Lindfleld. The boy was remanded to October 20, the date set for the le Gallion inquest, which proved to be sensational.

The case created enormous interest and the public waited on just about every word. Detective Inspector Joseph Ramus told the court that he interviewed le Gallion just after midnight on October 5 and told the boy, 'We have reasonable cause to suspect that you were implicated in your father's death and we have no alternative but to charge you with the murder of your father.' Detective Inspector Ramus said le Gallion then asked to see his mother.

The boy saw both his mother and his brother Richard, and Detective Inspector Ramus told the court that le Gallion later said, 'I want to tell you the truth. I don't want a solicitor. I did see my father that day. I met him outside his office at 6.30 p.m. I spoke to him for about five minutes and the phone rang, and he went inside and asked me to come in with him. I went inside with him and spoke to him for about an hour. I asked him for some money for Mum. He was writing figures on a piece of paper and told me how much it cost to keep Mum and us. The phone rang a couple of times and he answered it. He said, "Ten minutes. Five minutes. Ten minutes." All of a sudden he got wild and struck me across the face. I pulled out my pocket knife. I struggled with him and stabbed him. He fell down and was crawling about the floor. I got him a glass of water and gave him a drink. He told me he was all right and to go home. I took his coat and ran outside. I stood outside for about a minute and then ran down the lane and up a back street to Baden Street. I put the knife in my back pocket, and at the Suspension Bridge I put them down the drain. I half walked, and half ran across the bridge, up past the Northbridge pictures. I threw the wallet into a hollow. I ran across the golf links to Archbold Road and I threw my father's coat and a sweater into the bush. I then ran home, had a wash, and went to bed at 8 p.m.'

At the conclusion of police evidence, Mr J.J.B. Kinkead (for le Gallion) said, 'On my advice, my client will not give evidence before this inquiry.' The Coroner, Mr J.D. Austin, then committed le Gallion for trial.

Charles Ivan le Gallion pleaded not guilty at his trial for murder in November, 1948. The boy told the Central Criminal Court that he visited his father at the Crow's Nest engineering works on September 30 because of the row about household payments. The seventeen-year-old told the court that his father pulled out a drawer and showed him some bills. The boy told his father that these bills did not come in all the time, to which the father replied, 'I'm not going to send her (Mrs Heather le Gallion) any money because I hate everyone at home. I would rather live with Betty de Groen.' Young Charles answered back, 'Mum's sick and you should provide for her.' He later told the court that his father rushed at him. The boy, who claimed he was sitting in a chair, told the court that he defended himself with a pen knife. Charles le Gallion claimed that his father had him by the throat and said, 'I'll kill you, you little …' The boy said that after the scuffle, in which the father was stabbed, he helped his father and gave him a safari jacket to wipe away the blood. The father told the boy to go home and not to worry about a doctor, the court was told. Young le Gallion broke down in court when shown the pen knife that killed his father.

Mr Kinkead, for le Gallion, told the jury that his client was ill-prepared for murder. He said, 'There was no attempt to hide himself. In fact, the evidence shows he made it plain that he was there—pretty rotten preparations for a murder! The fact that the boy only had a pen knife on him shows that he was ill-equipped for a murder'. Mr Kinkead also argued that examination of the clothes belonging to the son and the father showed that the boy had taken off his safari jacket to staunch his father's wounds, which proved that he did not want him to die.

Mr Kinkead described the father as an 'unnatural father', but added, 'Yet nobody at home wanted the father to die, if for no other reason they thought that everything would go to somebody else … they would be killing the goose that laid the golden egg.' He also claimed ' … when Charles went to see him (the father) at his office for his mother's house money that night he so taunted the boy that he did not even tell him that he had already posted the money to her. If he had told the boy that, that would have been the end of it. He would have gone away and le Gallion senior would have been alive today.'

The jury deliberated for 105 minutes before handing down its verdict. That verdict was 'guilty'. Mrs le Gallion was in the court as Mr Justice Herron passed sentence on le Gallion. Mr Justice Herron said, 'You have been ably defended and in my view you have had a fair trial. In the circumstances I have no alternative but to sentence you to life imprisonment. Sydney appears to be besieged by juvenile gangsters. They must be deterred.'

To the jury, Mr Justice Herron said, 'You have had a very trying experience but you have done your duty to the State under what, I am sure, were trying circumstances.'

Mrs le Gallion gave a cry of anguish as sentence was passed on her son.

Mrs le Gallion, in a newspaper interview soon after her son's trial, told a reporter that she had received six hundred letters from sympathisers. She said, 'Charles was a bonzer kid. I will miss him frightfully … He never fought with his brothers at home and would always kiss me when he came inside the house. I wish he had obeyed me and not gone to see his father that night. When the police came and told me my husband was dead, I told Chickie (young Charles) that he would have to tell them everything. I told him that he simply had to tell, and he said he thought he would commit suicide. I told him to be a man and face it ... I told Detective Inspector Ramus that I lied to him because I would never tell on my son, and he said that I would not be much of a mother if I didn't try to protect Chickie.'

Charles le Gallion senior might have told his seventeen-year-old son that he intended to leave his money to someone else, but in fact, an estate of £20,580 was left to Mrs Heather le Gallion. The will, which consisted of a mere ten lines, was made in September, 1941, seven years before the fatal stabbing. Le Gallion spent most of his sentence in Goulburn jail and was released in August, 1960, almost twelve years after being sentenced.

However, the le Gallion tragedy did not end there. Mrs Heather le Gallion died in a petrol blaze in a Melbourne milk bar she was running as a business. Mrs le Gallion had bought the milk bar, in the suburb of Malvern, only two weeks before her death in August, 1965. A notice in a Melbourne newspaper after her death read: 'Le Gallion – Heather, on July 30 (suddenly), widow of Charles (dec.), mother of Richard (dec.), Robert (dec.), Harvey, Charles, Michel. Sadly missed. R.I.P.'.

THE CASE OF THE WALKING CORPSE

There have been few more shocking murders than the ones committed by a man known initially as 'The Mutilator' and then as 'The Walking Corpse'. William MacDonald's gruesome crimes horrified Australia yet, incredibly, his blood-saturated spree could have continued indefinitely if he had not panicked after killing his final victim.

Born Allan Ginsberg in England in 1924, he served in the British army before changing his name to William MacDonald and migrating to Canada and then to Australia. Unable to hold down a job for any length of time, he moved from city to city before settling in Sydney.

Then, on the night of June 4, 1961, the lonely MacDonald started a conversation with vagrant Alfred Greenfield as they sat on a bench in a Darlinghurst park. MacDonald, who was working as a letter sorter with the Post Master General (now Australia Post), suggested to Greenfield that they move on to a more secluded spot to drink some beer. Then, after a walk to a spot near the Domain Baths, MacDonald repeatedly stabbed his unsuspecting victim.

It was a frenzied and premeditated attack as MacDonald had slipped into a plastic raincoat before he slashed and slashed

Greenfield, severing the arteries in the vagrant's neck. But there was worse to follow. MacDonald removed Greenfield's trousers and sliced off the dead man's penis and testicles. The Mutilator had struck. Yet the man whose deeds shocked the nation walked calmly away. MacDonald slipped his bood-stained knife into a plastic bag and threw Greenfield's genitals into Sydney Harbour.

The discovery of Greenfield's body created uproar. The horrific murder, naturally, was splashed all over the front pages of Sydney's newspapers, with the term 'The Mutilator' used for the first time to describe the killer. The police, despite every effort, were baffled and the NSW government eventually offered a reward of 1000 pounds ($2000) for any information leading to the arrest of the mutilation killer.

Every police inquiry led to a dead-end and, six months later, MacDonald struck again. The body of Ernest William Cobbin was found in a blood-splattered public toilet in Moore Park. MacDonald again had used the lure of drinking beer together. The Mutilator slashed Cobbin to the neck, severed his jugular vein and inflicted many other wounds. He then sliced off his victim's penis and testicles. The seemingly cool, calm and collected MacDonald washed himself on the way home and again threw his victim's genitals into the harbour. The media again referred to 'The Mutilator' and the police, despite staking out public toilets in the area and issuing warnings, again were baffled.

Another five months passed and, with the police fearing The Mutilator could strike again at any time, MacDonald made their worst nightmares come true. He struck again in Darlinghurst after striking up a conversation with a man named Frank McLean. Again, MacDonald invited his intended victim for a drink but, for the first time, ran into difficulties in carrying out his murderous intention.

McLean resisted after being stabbed in the neck and tried to fend off MacDonald's thrusts with the sheath-knife. Despite being much taller than his attacker, McLean was unable to ward off the many blows and was stabbed in the neck, chest and face. MacDonald then cut off McLean's penis and testicles. However, the mutilation killer was far from cool, calm and collected this time and almost panicked. He fled the scene as quickly as he could and not long after his frenzied attack, McLean's body was discovered.

Although police were on the scene almost immediately, MacDonald had made it safely home. Sydney, of course, was in a frenzy over The Mutilator's killing. Police formed a special task force and the State Government increased its offer of a reward to 5000 pounds ($10,000).

Meanwhile, MacDonald, who had been working at the PMG under the alias of Allan Brennan, had decided in a change of career and took over a mixed business in the Sydney suburb of Burwood. However, the urge to kill remained and, on the night of June 2, 1962, The Mutilator struck again.

MacDonald's next victim was Irish derelict Patrick Hackett, who has just been released from jail for a minor offence. This time MacDonald took his victim back to his own home and, when Hackett had passed out from drinking too much, The Mutilator stabbed him in the neck. The Irishman quickly came to his senses and shielded himself from the blows MacDonald rained on him with his knife. In the process, MacDonald slashed his own hand. Finally, however, the multiple killer stabbed Hackett in the heart.

MacDonald tried to remove Hackett's genitals, but the knife by now was too blunt for the task. Exhausted, the killer fell asleep, but next morning took himself to hospital to have stitches inserted in his wounded hand. He then set about cleaning up his shop, wiping away pools of blood and tearing up the linoleum on the floor.

His final task was to drag Hackett's body under the shop. Realising he would find it almost impossible to dispose of the body, MacDonald decided to flee the scene. He caught a train to Brisbane and prayed he could change his identity and melt into the background.

Although MacDonald daily expected to read headlines about the discovery of Hackett's body, there was no mention in any newspaper or on any radio news service. Then, several weeks after Hackett's murder, neighbours noticed a terrible odour from MacDonald's shop on Burwood Road. Police discovered Hackett's body, but it was so decomposed that identification was impossible. In fact, police believed the body was that of MacDonald and it was buried under MacDonald's assumed name of Allan Brennan.

Coroner F.E. Cox, who returned an open verdict, was not convinced it was the body of the man known as Brennan and said:

'It seems extraordinary that the body of Mr Brennan should have been found in the position and the condition in which it was found. According to the evidence, the deceased had neither trousers on, nor his boots or shoes, or singlet. He was clad only in his socks, with his coat and trousers alongside him.

'Nothing was found to indicate to any degree of certainty that the deceased had taken his own life, even if it were his intention to do so. It seems to me an extraordinary thing that the deceased should have gone under the house to commit an act that would result in his death.'

The astute coroner then added that the dead man could have been 'the victim of foul play'. Although he stressed that he had no evidence of this, he noted: 'I cannot exclude that possibility.'

MacDonald breathed easier in the belief that he was a dead man walking. No one knew he was still alive and he believed the police would never be able to charge him with even one of the murders he had committed. However, he had not counted on fate, in the form of a former workmate.

MacDonald was walking down a Sydney street one day when he bumped into an old work mate who expressed great surprise that 'Allan Brennan' was still alive. The work mate, who even had attended the funeral service, could not believe his eyes. The stunned MacDonald fled down the street and almost immediately caught a train to Melbourne.

The work mate contacted a Sydney crime reporter with his remarkable near-collision with a ghost and the following day the Mirror newspaper ran Morris' account under the headline CASE OF THE WALKING CORPSE.

Police, stunned by the report, re-examined the case of the body under the shop and finally realised they had made a mistake and, in fact, that the body was that of Irishman Hackett. The body was exhumed and this time stab and cut marks were found on the body's genitals. The police believed they finally were onto the trail of The Mutilator, albeit almost by accident.

The police released an identikit description of MacDonald, and it paid dividends when workers at Melbourne's Spencer Street railway station thought the portrait resembled a new work mate. They notified the Victoria Police who arrested the man who had moved from Sydney as The Mutilator.

MacDonald confessed to his crimes and was brought to trial in Sydney in September, 1963. However, he pleaded not guilty on the grounds of insanity. After all, what sane man would kill for the thrill of it and then remove his victim's genitals? Yet the jury did not see it that way and found MacDonald guilty on four count of murder. He was sentenced to life imprisonment. However, after bashing an inmate at Long Bay jail, he was removed to the Morriset Pyschiatric Centre for the criminally insane before eventually being returned to protective custody.

THE AMOROUS BARBER

The area surrounding the Victoria Market in Melbourne is known as 'Little Italy'. The suburbs of North Melbourne, West Melbourne and Carlton are 'home' to many thousands of Italian migrants. The area has countless coffee bars, migrant clubs, bistros and continental grocery shops. Gregario Marazita and his brothers ran a flourishing licensed grocery business opposite the Victoria Market and Marazita was highly regarded in the Italian community. Marazita had a number of friends in the vicinity, and these included Salvatore Manusco, who worked as a barber in Victoria Street, North Melbourne, opposite Marazita's grocery shop. Marazita, 37, treated Manusco, 25, like a brother and the two got on well together. Marazita even took Manusco to his home in West Brunswick, where Manusco used to cut the children's hair. Manusco and Marazita had been friends for about four years in 1962, when the friendship started cooling. Marazita had heard that Manusco had tried to kiss his wife. The situation exploded into violence on the night of June 18, 1962.

Marazita had left the grocery shop in Victoria Street and was walking to his parked car nearby. However, the two tangled and a scuffle developed. Shots were heard and Marazita was found badly wounded. He was rushed to the nearby Royal Melbourne Hospital with bullet wounds, but died soon after arrival at hospital. Manusco later walked into the Swan Hill police station in northern Victoria and he was charged at the City Watchhouse on June 19. At the Coroner's Inquest in August 1962, Mr H.W. Pascoe, SM, committed Manusco for trial on a charge of murder.

The Crown alleged at Manusco's trial in the Criminal Court in November, 1962, that Manusco fired four shots from a revolver at Marazita in Little Cobden Street, North Melbourne, at about 5.40 pm on June 18. The Crown also claimed that the shooting was after alleged advances by Manusco to Marazita's wife. Mrs Rita Marazita told the court that Manusco had repeatedly tried to kiss her and that only five weeks before the shooting her husband had slapped Manusco on the face. She said that Marazita had told Manusco over the tea table in West Brunswick, 'I have treated you like a brother and you are trying to upset my home.'

Manusco said, 'There is nothing in it.'

Mrs Marazita said, 'Tell him the truth, that you tried to kiss me.'

Her husband then slapped Manusco across the face and said to him, 'You can come here any time you like as long as you do not try to upset my home.' The Crown Prosecutor, Mr G. Byrne, told Mr Justice O'Bryan that Marazita had been shot four times. The Crown claimed that Marazita left his grocer's shop at the usual time and stopped to talk to a friend in Little Cobden Street. Manusco went up to where the two men were talking and waited for Marazita. Three shots were fired a few minutes later. Marazita ran around a corner and was followed by Manusco. A witness, Stephen Chiodo, said he saw Manusco run up behind Marazita, lift a revolver and fire a fourth and final shot in Marazita's back. Manusco then ran up Little Cobden Street.

Manusco's account was altogether different. He told the court that he had never tried to kiss Marazita's wife, and had not made advances to her. He said that he left the hairdressing salon where he worked and saw Marazita leaving his shop across the road. Manusco said he set out to walk to his car, but Marazita ran after him, caught him and spat in his face, saying, 'If you think this is all finished you are wrong.' Manusco said that Marazita held him by the overcoat with one hand and punched him with the other. As they struggled into Little Cobden Street, Marazita drew a revolver from a pocket. Manusco said he grabbed Marazita's arm and the gun went off. He said he did not think Marazita had been hit because Marazita still kept a grip on the gun. Manusco said, 'We struggled for some time, during which some shots were fired, and then I got the revolver from him and ran towards my car. As I ran away I saw Marazita fall to the ground.'

The jury took an hour and a quarter to reach its verdict—guilty. Manusco stood motionless in the dock as Mr Justice O'Bryan sentenced him to death for the murder of Gregario Marazita. Manusco's death sentence was commuted to forty years imprisonment by the State Executive Council in May, 1963.

THE NARROMINE
BONES MYSTERY

The Western Plains district of New South Wales is wild, wonderful country; the place where a man could get lost for months. It is the home of a great deal of Australian folklore, thanks largely to the type of men who settled in the area. It is rugged country and those who know it love its quiet beauty. Men still hump their swag in the area but the sight of a swagman humping his belongings along a dusty track or road is nowhere near as common as it used to be. During the Great Depression of the early 1930s and just after, men often roamed the district looking for any work they could get. They would sleep under the stars and drift from town to town, homestead to homestead. It was among these men in the Western Plains district that the New South Wales police stumbled across one of their most puzzling cases. It was known as the Narromine Bones Mystery, although police cleared up a great deal of the mystery. However, some mysterious circumstances still remain in one of the State's most gruesome crimes.

In 1939 a drover named Charles Carpenter started a whole investigation which created headlines throughout Australia. Carpenter came across a drifter named Albert Andrew Moss near Narromine and noticed a chestnut horse in Moss's possession.

Carpenter recognised the horse immediately. It had belonged to a friend of his, an old local identity named Tom Robinson. Carpenter tackled Moss about the horse and there was a row. Moss insisted that he had raised the horse from a foal, while Carpenter was equally adamant that it was his mate's horse. Moss got angry and made threats, so Carpenter beat a hasty retreat. However, the incident rankled with Carpenter, who decided that there was something most peculiar about Moss having old Tom's horse. Carpenter did a little snooping and discovered that old Tom Robinson had not collected his old age pension for some time.

The incident with Moss took place in April, 1939, yet Robinson's pension had been untouched since January. It was most unlike Robinson to leave his pension untouched and Carpenter became extremely worried about his old mate. Carpenter told his story to police, who decided that they had better investigate. Robinson might have sold or traded his horse to Moss but the pension was a real worry to the police as well as Carpenter.

Two police officers went to Moss's camp but there was no sign of their man. Moss had done a moonlight flit, taking all his 'possessions' with him. What worried police most was that Carpenter told them that he had seen Robinson, 68, sharing camp with Moss in January and hadn't been seen since, even though Moss had Carpenter's horse.

Before setting out after Moss, police decided to investigate their man's background. They discovered that Moss had been in and out of asylums and had been in serious police trouble before. He had a long criminal record, with his first offence at 17 for forgery. Moss's first spell in an asylum followed custody for attempted rape at Pymble. There was no doubt that Moss was an unsavoury character, locals finding hardly a good word for the man who drifted around the plains. Police moved in on Moss and made an arrest so as to hold him. Moss was in possession of some mutton and a few pumpkins when police apprehended him and charged him with having 'goods in possession'. The police did not want Moss to slip though their fingers and they were just making sure they knew where he was.

Apart from the Robinson mystery, there was added mystery because of other goods in Moss's possession. Moss, when confronted by police, had a spare horse, a great deal of clothing and even a bicycle. Moss had never had many possessions and police were determined to discover who really owned all these goods. They knew that one of the horses was old Tom Robinson's but where did Moss get the other goods, and did he get them legally? Police were so worried by now that they called in extra detectives from Sydney to help them in their investigation, which finally spread to Sydney itself.

The police got their first lead in the case through sheer luck. Moss's possessions included a piece of blotting paper which had been used extensively. The police held the paper to a mirror and were able to read the name T. O'Shea. They asked locals if they knew anyone by this name and the whole of Narromine answered that it must be Tim O'Shea, who had not been seen for quite some time. The police had to trace O'Shea's movements in an effort to see whether he was still alive. However, they could trace the missing O'Shea only as far as Moss, the last man seen with O'Shea.

The police now believed they had a murder investigation on their hands, with possibly two victims. They worked deeper into the mystery and found a laundry mark on a pair of trousers. They went from laundry to laundry in an effort to identify the owner of the trousers. That search led police back to Lidcombe, in Sydney, where a laundry proprietor remembered cleaning the trousers for a man named Bartley. That information stunned police, as a man named Bartley also had been reported missing from the Narromine district. Worse was information received in Sydney that Bartley owned a Nivon brand bicycle and was seen with Moss at a camp on the banks of the Macquarie River in February.

Police now were looking for Robinson, O'Shea and William Henry Bartley. The Melbourne Argus even suggested that police were looking for six missing men. A report of the issue of April 11 read: 'Police who have been inquiring into supposed murders in the

Narromine district are now attempting to trace six men, all of whom disappeared mysteriously.'

The police knew that finding bodies would be difficult but they made a massive search. They raked over every camp fire they could find, no matter how cold the ashes. They sent boats up and down the Macquarie River, looking into every nook and cranny of the riverway. They even exploded gelignite in efforts to reach into deep holes along the river. Civilians joined the search with the police convinced that at least one man, but probably three, was dead.

Police eventually made a discovery on April 23. A report in the Sydney Truth of that day headlined: 'Bones Found at Narromine May Lead to Solution of Mystery' read 'A dramatic development today in the search for the missing pensioner, Thomas Robinson, 68, who disappeared in January, was the discovery of what are believed to be human bones in an old fire, three miles north of Narromine. In the ashes were discovered what are believed to be pieces of a broken skull and also two vertebra bones. Buttons and buckles were also recovered from the ashes. A short distance from the fire, hidden under some debris, was a travelling rug, and farther away some old shirts. The bones were submitted to Dr Sutherland, Government Medical Officer, of Narromine, but as he was unable to say whether they were human or animal, they will be despatched to the Government Analyst in Sydney. The discovery was made on what is known as Mack's Reserve, three miles north of Narromine, and about ten miles from Brummagem Creek. The Reserve adjoins the Macquarie River. If the bones are human, detectives are faced with the possibility that a body was dismembered and portions burned at various places over a wide area. In addition to Robinson, for whom a search has been in progress for eleven days, police have been endeavouring to trace two other men.'

The Government Medical Officer, Dr Percy, confirmed in Sydney that the fragments were human. A report in the Melbourne Argus of April 28 read 'Part of a backbone found at Narromine was from a human body, the Government Medical Officer (Dr Percy) told detectives today. With other bones, it had been found close to the ashes of a fire at Narromine, near where three men are believed to have been murdered ... Investigating detectives hold the theory that after Robinson was murdered his body was placed on a large fire, which several people say they saw burning, As the bones were discovered about fifteen yards from the remains of the fire, they think that after the fire the bones were placed in a rug, which was found nearby, to be thrown into the Macquarie River. On the way to the river it is believed that several of the bones were dropped from the rug.'

Moss was charged with the murders of Robinson, O'Shea and Bartley but was tried at Dubbo before Mr Justice Owen only on the charge of having murdered O'Shea. The trial was sensational, apart from being a murder trial without the discovery of a full body.

The magisterial inquiry in the Dubbo Police Court was even more sensational. Moss, 61, stripped to the waist and shouted obscenities during the hearing. Moss went berserk when the third murder charge was preferred against him. He shouted obscene remarks at the magistrate, court officials and police.

He kept saying, 'You are ... liar ...' when Dr Gordon Fitzhill, government medical officer at Dubbo, was giving evidence on Moss's sanity. Dr Fitzhill said, 'I examined him this morning. He was acting in an insane manner but I am not prepared to certify that he is insane. I have seen him six times since April, and on every occasion I found him perfectly sane and rational. All reports from jailers at Dubbo say he was exceptionally well-behaved and has acted reasonably throughout.' Dr Fitzhill gave evidence on oath that Moss was 'definitely not insane.'

Moss had attempted earlier to convince police officers that he was mad. He would pick thistles and pretend they were lettuces, and point in the opposite direction to the Macquarie River and exclaim, 'There's the river, the river'.

Much depended on a police claim that Moss had confessed to them. Asked if the bones found at the camp site belonged to O'Shea, Moss told police, 'Yes, I burnt him there.' Asked if he would tell how O'Shea lost his life, Moss said, 'Yes, I will make a full confession later. I don't want to do it now. Before I went to Dargondale I killed him and burnt him there.' However, Moss denied this at his trial. He told the court in a statement from the dock, 'Detectives Calman and Sherringham took me all over the Dubbo district, and one night, after being out all day, they came into my cell at Dubbo and kept me awake. Sherringham stayed for two hours questioning me, and I said, "Go away and leave me alone." He went away, and Calman came in and questioned me. They took turn about at this all night, and next day took me out again. That night they carried out the same procedure and when I would drop off to sleep, Sherringham would tap me on the chest with his fist. I said, "If I say I killed O'Shea will you leave me alone?" They said "yes" and I said, "I killed O'Shea!" Next morning, Sherringham and Calman came into the cell and Calman said, "He did it, all right. We will get the brute hanged. We will make the jury believe that he really did it."'

The detectives were called back and both denied Moss's accusations from the dock.

The jury took two and three-quarter hours to reach its verdict. Their decision was 'guilty'. Mr Justice Owen then sentenced Moss to death. After passing sentence, Mr Justice Owen praised police officers in charge of the investigation, saying that their efforts had been responsible for having a daring criminal brought to justice.

But how had Moss killed O'Shea? No one will ever know, except that the evidence of one man at the police court could go a long way in telling the tale. Pensioner John Neville told how he was drinking wine with Moss one night when Moss 'knocked me on the head and started to punch me and put the boot in. I later hit Moss with a bottle and he came back at me. He hit at me again, and I went for the lick of my life to a farm. My face was covered with blood and I still have scars on my arm.' It seems that Moss killed his drifter companions for the small gain of their possessions. Old Tom Robinson's chestnut horse eventually led to Moss's death sentence. However, the death sentence was never carried out. The sentence was commuted to one of life imprisonment and Moss died in Long Bay jail in January, 1958, after serving eighteen years for murder.

THE BOMB GENIUS

Residents in and around Paterson Avenue, Kingsgrove, a Sydney suburb, were preparing for a quiet night on August 14, 1956, when the peace of the neighbourhood was shattered by a tremendous explosion. Residents ran from their houses as windows rattled and rooms rocked. Residents in the avenue itself could not believe their eyes when they saw a bomb-wrecked car in their quiet, suburban street. The car was a dreadful sight. Its bonnet was fifty yards down the street, all four doors had been blown out and windscreen glass was spread for yards. People crowded the scene and police and firemen had to link arms to clear the area before a detailed investigation could be launched into the bombing.

The explosion occurred when Dr Edward Brotchie, 50, turned on the car's ignition. Dr Brotchie died in hospital shortly after the explosion and his passenger, his sister Mrs Elsie Foster, 45, died instantly. They were the victims of an expertly planned car bombing. Police knew that whoever planted the bomb knew exactly what he was doing. In fact, Mr S.W.E. Parsons, technical officer of the Explosives Department, said soon after examining the wrecked car, 'To make a bomb of the strength and type, and to be able to place and connect it, would require considerable knowledge of explosives.'

Mr Parsons was perfectly correct in his judgment. The bomb was the work of an expert. It was planted by Mrs Foster's brother, Henry Foster, who shot himself through the head soon after the bombing.

Police did not discover Foster's body, in Dr Brotchie's surgery only one hundred yards from the bombing scene, until the next morning. Incredibly, Foster left behind a swag of notes which painstakingly described the bomb's mechanism. Foster wanted the experts to know exactly how the bomb worked so that there would be no confusion after his own death. Foster's death bomb was made of piping fifteen inches long and two and a half inches in diameter. It was fitted with two spark plugs adapted so that they would heat two wires Foster soldered to them. The bomb, filled with a mixture of carbon, saltpetre and sulphur, would be ignited by the hot wires and would instantaneously generate carbon dioxide gas which would expand and explode.

Foster's notes explained everything, down to the last detail. It seemed he disliked his brother-in-law for failing to treat him to his satisfaction for a back complaint. But strangely, it seemed Foster loved the wife he killed in the home-made explosion. Foster, a consulting and designing engineer, even directed that his body be taken to hospital so that the corneas could be removed for some blind person's sight to be restored. That part of Foster's plan backfired but not because of the lack of detail in his planning. Foster, incredibly, shot himself through the head at such an angle that his eyes would not be damaged. However, his body was not discovered in time for the corneas to be donated for surgery. For that to be successful, his corneas would have had to be removed within five hours of death. It was just about the one wish Foster did not realise. The rest of his carefully planned killings succeeded in detail. Foster, the inventive genius, killed and died with the efficiency of an analytical scientist.

THE TAXI MURDER MYSTERY

Melbourne has often been described as the graveyard city of Australia, with nightlife non-existent. This, of course, is a gross misrepresentation. The problem is that visitors often find it difficult to find any night activity in Melbourne. However, ask any Melbourne taxi driver and he will be able to tell any visitor where the action is in the city. That applied particularly in the period from 1942-5, when Melbourne was crowded with servicemen. Taxi drivers usually were the best go-betweens in the business. They knew the brothels, sly-grog shops and gambling houses of Melbourne. Servicemen and taxi drivers got on well together, and a taxi driver was not worth his salt if he could not direct a serviceman to a party.

Francis John Phelan was a driver with Red Top taxis and knew the ropes well. In fact, it was rumoured that Phelan had contacts in the black market and sly-grog rackets. Phelan, a former wharf laborer, was 32 and married with four children. He worked hard at his job and knew Melbourne better than most taxi drivers. Phelan usually worked the early night shift, often ferrying servicemen to parties.

He was on duty on February 6, 1943, and seemed to be doing well early in the evening. He was seen driving two American servicemen and at least one woman at about 8.30 p.m. Phelan's cab later was seen in St Edmund's Road, Prahran, an inner Melbourne suburb. The cab was stationary. Shots were fired and several residents heard what they described as 'loud bangs'. The taxi sped off but stopped in Izett Street, Prahran, where Francis Phelan's body was dumped. The cab then stopped at the corner of Commercial and Punt Roads, a distance of about half a mile. The cab was abandoned and a solid man was seen getting out.

Phelan had been shot three times from behind. One shot went through his left shoulder, while the other two shots went through his chest, one passing through his heart as well. A newspaper report of the time said, 'Phelan's body was first seen about 9.30 p.m. by a passer-by, who told Prahran police that a drunken man was lying in the street. When two constables went to Izett Street they lifted the body and found Phelan's clothing saturated with blood. His body was still warm. There was no sign of a struggle and nothing to indicate that Phelan had been shot where his body was found.' Phelan's abandoned cab was noticed by another taxi driver, who 'directed a passing patrol to it'. Police found empty shells, from a heavy calibre service-type firearm, on the front floor of the cab.

Police investigating the shooting were struck by one incredible coincidence. The sign 'L. Phelan' had been painted in white on a fence opposite to where Francis Phelan's body was discovered. However, the sign proved to be nothing more than a macabre coincidence, having nothing to do with Phelan's shooting. Police were baffled, with robbery a highly unlikely motive. Police found £11/15/5 in the dead man's pockets, a more than tidy sum in those days. Police were forced to follow other lines, and that led to the twilight world of sly-grogging and black market tobacco. One police theory was that Phelan had been 'executed'. Phelan's car often was seen parked outside 'houses of ill-fame' in Prahran and police left no stone unturned in their investigations.

Police believed their best clue was an American service cap found in the back of the murder cab. Police even had two names to work on, the cap bearing the two names. The names were Sergeant Robert

Willard French and Sergeant John Freeman Martin, who were both in Camp Murphy, Melbourne.

French told police that he had sold the cap to Martin in 1941, and Martin said he had lost the cap in America. French said he had not seen Martin wearing the cap for more than twelve months. Martin and French were asked only a few questions at the inquest on Phelan's killing. Both Americans had alibis and police were forced to abandon that line of investigation.

Phelan's widow, Mrs Joyce Phelan, told the City Coroner, Mr Tingate, that her husband did not carry a gun and did not own one. Mrs Phelan also said that her husband sometimes had trouble with his customers. She said that in these cases he did not hesitate in going to the police. Asked if her husband would defend himself if attacked, Mrs Phelan replied, 'Yes, he would'.

Detective-Sergeant S.H. McGuffie, who was in charge of the investigation, did not give evidence at the inquest. However, Detective Charles Petty, of Prahran police, told the inquest that 'up to the present we have been unable to discover who caused Phelan's death'. Recording his finding, Mr Tingate found that Phelan had been wilfully and maliciously murdered by some person unknown. The taxi murder mystery is still unsolved.

THE RICHMOND BORGIA

A sensible family always will make sure that members of the family, especially the breadwinner, are covered by insurance and that all insurance policies are paid promptly. No family wants to be left without its source of income. Even families in the Victorian era thought along these lines, and most middle and upper class families had insurance cover. The Needle family in the Melbourne suburb of Richmond was no exception, members of the family having numerous insurance policies. The only trouble was that there were just as many claims on the policies.

Martha Needle, an extremely attractive young woman, was 'unfortunate' enough to lose her entire family through 'serious illnesses'. She won enormous sympathy from friends and neighbours, who could not believe that one delightful, frail, intelligent young woman could have so much bad luck. What the friends and neighbors did not know, until years later, was that Martha Needle was a mass poisoner. In fact, she was so adept in arsenic poisoning that she was dubbed the 'Richmond Borgia'. It was an apt nickname.

Pretty Martha was raised in Adelaide but moved to Melbourne soon after her marriage to carpenter Henry Needle in 1881. Martha was just 17 and Henry Needle was regarded as an extremely lucky man. It seemed an ideal marriage and the couple was blessed with the birth of daughter Mabel. Henry Needle was an adoring husband and father but Martha was not satisfied with the family income. She dreamed of running a boarding house but did not have the capital.

That problem was solved by the death of Mabel, who was just three years of age when poisoned by her mother in 1885. Martha had laced her little daughter's food with a preparation called Rough on Rats. Naturally, no one suspected the attractive young mother of killing her own daughter and a death certificate was issued. Martha collected £200 from little Mabel's insurance policy. However, Martha Needle's trail of death was just starting, with her husband next on the death list.

Martha, despite her husband's willingness to work hard for his beloved wife, still was not satisfied with the family income. She had given birth to two more daughters, Elsie and May, and decided that the boarding house was the only answer to her financial desires. She spiced her husband's food with Rough on Rats, and watched him die in agony. Martha even nursed her husband and neighbours commented on her 'absolute devotion'. Yet the only time that Martha was really happy was when Henry Needle finally succumbed, in October, 1889. Martha Needle was a widow, doctors certifying that Henry Needle had died of 'inflammation of the stomach'.

Poisoning was not suspected, and Martha again collected £200 insurance money.

This time Martha was able to set up her boarding house business. However, it did not flourish as she would have hoped, and the pretty killer decided to cash in on her other assets—her daughters. Both were insured, and both were killed. First to die was little Elsie, just four years of age. Elsie's mother laced the little girl's food with Rough on Rats and Elsie became seriously ill. Doctors were puzzled but Martha Needle was so impressive in her grief that poison again was not suspected. Elsie died of a 'wasting disease' in

November, 1890, Mrs Needle collecting the £100 insurance money. And that left only little May, who was only three years of age.

Pretty little May also fell ill and died in October, 1891. Mrs Needle, careful not to arouse suspicion, collected only £66 this time, taking her total insurance 'income' to £566, a large amount of money in those days. But to get that sum, Martha Needle had to wipe out her entire family. The fact that she managed to do this over a number of years without raising the slightest suspicion was a credit to her acting ability, the grief-stricken widow being pitied by everyone who knew her. And those who took pity on the young widow were in danger themselves, Mrs Needle not content to let her career in poison grind to a standstill.

Widow's garb did not suit Mrs Needle, who now realised that she was free to do and act as she pleased, her entire family being buried. She renewed an old friendship with former Adelaide saddlers Louis and Otto Juncken and became attached to handsome Otto. This caused Louis to be jealous and he tried everything in his power to stop his brother from becoming 'involved' with the widow. Martha Needle resented that and decided that the best way to stop Louis was to feed him Rough on Rats. Louis became ill in April, 1894 and had to be nursed back to health by his sister. Poison was not directly suspected. Martha Needle 'got at' Louis again and the unfortunate young man died in May, 1894.

Mrs Needle escaped suspicion yet again but the Juncken family was far from happy with Louis' death. Otto was still determined to marry Mrs Needle, his mother and brother Herman being violently against any such marriage. Mrs Juncken stuck to her guns and advised her son not to have anything to do with Mrs Needle. However, Herman became infatuated with the widow and took her side … for a while. He visited Mrs Needle and became violently ill after drinking a cup of tea. He recovered but still had no idea that Mrs Needle was a poisoner. He again visited the 27-year-old widow and again became violently ill. He saw a doctor and arsenic was at long last suspected. Herman Juncken took his suspicions to police and a trap was set for the Richmond Borgia.

Herman Juncken visited Mrs Needle and was offered a cup of tea. Herman accepted and called to the police immediately he was handed his cup of tea. The police, waiting nearby, took the cup of tea and had it analysed. It contained arsenic and Mrs Needle's career as a poisoner was over. Police, now fully aware of Mrs Needle's tragic family history, ordered the bodies of her husband and daughters to be exhumed. All bodies showed substantial traces of arsenic poisoning. Louis Juncken's body also was exhumed and that also showed arsenic poisoning. Mrs Needle was charged with Louis Juncken's murder and was found guilty.

Mrs Needle went to the gallows in Melbourne on October 22, 1894. She refused help on her way to the gallows and told the hangman that she wanted to die quickly and with dignity. Martha Needle, killer of five innocent people, died quickly but no execution has dignity.

AUSTRALIA'S 'CHARLES MANSON'

The British public was outraged late in January, 2004, when serial killer Archie McCafferty was fined just 50 pounds for striking a police officer and sentenced to a 12-month community order. It was nothing more than a slap on the wrist for the man known as 'Mad Dog' for his murderous spree and infamous behaviour as a prisoner on the other side of the world in Australia.

McCafferty was born in Scotland, but migrated to Australia with his family when he was just 10 years of age. The McCafferty family first settled in Melbourne, but then moved to Sydney, where young Archie soon found himself in trouble with the police. The tough young Scot's family believed Archie would settle down after his marriage to Janice Redington in 1972, especially when the couple announced they were going to be parents.

Son Craig was born in February, 1973, only for the McCafferty joy to be short-lived. Little Craig lived just six weeks, dying on March 17 in truly tragic circumstances when his mother rolled on top of him after falling asleep while breastfeeding him. An inquest exonerated the young mother, but McCafferty accused his wife of killing their son.

The death of baby Craig appeared to tip McCafferty over the edge and although he admitted himself to a psychiatric institute, he checked out again a few days later. McCafferty threatened violence against his family, but no one could have known the extent to which he was prepared to go in his lust for blood.

McCafferty's brief but dreadful reign of terror started on August 24, 1973, when he teamed up with girlfriend Carol Howes, 16-year-old psychiatric patient Julie Todd and teenagers Michael Meredith, Richard Whittington and Rick Webster to kill World War II veteran George Anson.

The gang had been looking for someone to 'roll' for easy money, and the drink-affected Anson appeared to be the perfect victim. However, the assault went way beyond a robbery with violence. McCafferty kicked Anson several times to the head and chest before repeatedly plunging a knife into the 50-year-old's chest and neck.

Most of McCafferty's young gang were too shocked to make any comment, but Webster asked the heavily-tattooed Scot why he had gone berserk. McCafferty replied that he had reacted to Anson swearing at him.

Just three nights later, on August 27, McCafferty took his gang to the Leppington Cemetery to show them his little son's grave. The gang then retreated to a nearby pub, only for McCafferty to insist on returning to the grave site. Todd and Meredith went their own way, but McCafferty, Howes, Whittington and Webster went back to the cemetery.

Then, at the cemetery, a car pulled over near Craig McCafferty's grave. Todd and Meredith had returned to the group with a victim, 42-year-old Ronald Cox, at gunpoint. They had been hitchhiking in the rain when the miner — on his way home from work — gave them a lift. McCafferty ran over to where Todd and Meredith were holding Cox and ordered Meredith to kill the terrified father of seven. Both Meredith and McCafferty shot Cox to the back of the head.

McCafferty, who later claimed he had heard voices in his head telling him to kill seven people, the following day ordered his gang members to find him another victim. Todd and Whittington went hitchhiking and were given a ride by young driving instructor Evangelos Kollias. However, Whittington then produced a rifle from under his coat and ordered Kollias to lie on the floor while Todd drove back to McCafferty's unit.

McCafferty then drove away and ordered Whittington to kill Kollias. The youth did as he was told and shot the driving instructor through the head. Then when ordered to shoot again, Whittington fired into Kollias' head again. The body was dumped in a nearby street.

Meanwhile, McCafferty seemed determined to do what the voices had instructed — 'kill seven' — and high on his hit list was his wife, her mother and one of his gang members, 17-year-old Webster, who had questioned him over the brutal killing of Anson. However, a gang member alerted Webster to McCafferty's plans and he decided to act to save his own life.

Webster, an apprentice compositor with the Sydney Morning Herald, called the police from his workplace. Detectives arrived to interview him, but Webster had spotted McCafferty and his gang in a car outside and was too terrified to leave the building. Armed police therefore surrounded the car and arrested McCafferty and Whittington.

Although McCafferty admitted to police that he had killed Anson, Cox and Kollias, he pleaded not guilty at a committal hearing, as did Howes, Meredith, Whittington and Webster.

The gang was sent to trial, with newspapers referring to McCafferty as 'Australia's Charles Manson', the American hippie leader who organised a gang to commit multiple murders in the late 1960s.

Everything revolved around the question of whether McCafferty was insane or not and, near the end of the trial, he read a statement from the dock which, in part, stated: 'I would like to say that at the time of these crimes I was completely insane. The reason why I done (sic) this is for the revenge of my son's death. Before this, I had stated to a doctor that I felt like killing people, but up until my son's death I had not killed anyone.

'My son's death was the biggest thing that ever happened to me because I loved him so much and he meant the world to me. And after his death I just seemed to go to the pack. I feel no wrong for what I have done because, at the time that I did it, I didn't think it was wrong.

'I think, if given the chance, I will kill again for the simple reason that I have to kill seven people and I have only killed three, which means I have four to go. And this is how I feel in my mind, and I just can't say that I am not going to kill anyone else, because in my mind I am.'

The jury rejected the insanity plea and found McCafferty guilty as charged on all counts. He was sentenced to be imprisoned for life, with Meredith and Whittington sentenced to 18 years in prison and Todd for 10 years for the murders of Cox and Kallios. Webster was given four years for the manslaughter of Cox. Howes, who was pregnant with McCafferty's child when the verdicts were announced, was found not guilty.

McCafferty, who married and then divorced a woman named Mandy Queen while in jail, proved to be one of the most difficult prisoners in NSW penal history and was transferred from one jail to another until, to the horror of NSW police and public, he was given parole. He was deported to his native Scotland in 1997.

However, McCafferty could not stay out of trouble and was involved in a number of incidents, including threatening police officers. He settled in Hampshire and remarried Mandy Queen, but then fled to New Zealand when he faced a charge of assaulting a police officer.

McCafferty was arrested immediately as he returned to the United Kingdom but, to the amazement of the British public, escaped with that 'slap on the wrist' fine and community order. The court had been told that the man known as 'Australia's Charles Manson' was a changed man and had even taken up painting to 'calm him down'. Indeed, lawyer Simon Moger said his client's work was 'of a very high standard which could sell commercially'.

McCafferty, who once had threatened to kill seven people, therefore was left to continue family life, despite once being told he would never be released from jail for the three murders he committed.

DEATH ON A TRAIN

According to many experts, the first recorded railway murder was in 1864. The murder of Thomas Briggs by Franz Muller was on a train in London, Muller being hanged for his crime. The motive, quite clearly, was robbery. And that same motive of robbery has been evident in most train murders ever since.

Australia has had more than its share of rail murders and Sydney was shocked by a particularly senseless killing on a train in 1966. Mrs Pamela Irene Blair was bashed and left to die on a Sydney suburban train on November 29. She died without regaining consciousness two days later, on December 1. The motive could have been robbery, Mrs Blair's handbag being missing and never being recovered. However, Mrs Blair had little more than $2 in her handbag and she could have been the victim of a sadist.

Mrs Blair, 24, lived with her husband in the Sydney suburb of St Peters. She worked as a sales demonstrator and was returning home from work the night she was murdered. Mrs Blair caught a train at Hurstville station at 8.1I p.m., intending to leave the train at the Sydnenham station twenty-two minutes later. However, Mrs Blair was attacked on the last leg of her journey home. She was bashed about the head with a heavy brass door lever, wrenched from a carriage, and left to die. Mrs Blair suffered terrible head injuries and was discovered by fellow passenger Mr Cecil Johnson, who tried to help the woman by putting a handkerchief to her head wounds. Mrs Blair was partly conscious but largely incoherent, unable to give Mr Johnson or the train guard any vital information on her attacker. Mrs Blair was rushed to hospital but did not recover from her head wounds, despite emergency surgery.

It seemed incongruous that she could be attacked so openly and yet the attacker be able to flee without hindrance. This, as much as anything, alarmed Sydney- siders used to travelling to and from work by train.

A mysterious young man was seen on the train on the night of the murder and one witness said that the 'aggressive' young man made a 'sort of growling noise' as he moved around on the train. But whether this 'aggressive' young man was the murderer remains a mystery. Mrs Blair's killer has never been brought to justice, despite massive police efforts. The New South Wales government offered a reward for information leading to the arrest of Mrs. Blair's attacker but the reward money has never been claimed.

MURDER AT THE MILL

'Paddy' O'Leary was a tough customer, and he knew it. Charles Patrick O'Leary had spent time in the merchant navy and the army during World War Two and took a job as a sawmill hand after the war. In 1946 O'Leary was working at a government forest at Nangwarry, in south-eastern South Australia. It was a tough life and the men who worked with O'Leary were a mixed lot, tough in their ways and often rough in their manners. O'Leary liked a drink and a weekend spree eventually led to the death of 58-year-old Walter Edward Ballard on July 6, 1946.

O'Leary and some of his work mates went on the drinking spree on the Saturday morning, drinking well into the night. O'Leary, 34, was involved in a number of scuffles but no one could have guessed that the night would end in death for the inoffensive Ballard. O'Leary, well after Ballard had gone 'merry' to bed, bashed Ballard and killed him, according to the Crown at O'Leary's trial at the Mt Gambier Criminal Circuit Court. The Crown Prosecutor, Mr R.R. Chamberlain, alleged that O'Leary visited Cubicle J, occupied by Ballard, bashed him, dumped him on a bunk, poured inflammable liquid (kerosene) over him and set a light to Ballard and the bunk. Ballard died about two hours later in hospital.

Medical evidence was given that Ballard had been bashed eight times across the head with a beer bottle, a broken end of the bottle being smashed into his face, piercing the cheek and entering the cavity of the head. Ballard was pulled out of the cubicle by O'Leary and a worker named Francis O'Toole. Smoke from Ballard's cubicle warned O'Toole of danger and he called O'Leary, who was walking by a nearby bathroom, to help. Ballard had been exposed to flames for about fifteen minutes and the body was charred. Other workers later claimed that they heard O'Leary say, 'Give me an axe and I'll put the poor man out of his misery … let me finish him off.'

O'Leary, in an unsworn statement at his trial, denied that he had killed, or even assaulted, Ballard. He told the court, 'I am not guilty of this charge. I started work at Nangwarry in the last week of June. At the time of my arrest I knew only a few of the men working there because we work at different places on different shifts.

'Walter Ballard had not quarrelled with me at any time. He did nothing to me to cause me to be annoyed with him. I did not at any time have any intention of doing harm to Ballard.

'On the Saturday morning, with other men from the camp, I went to Penola. I had a number of drinks at the hotel and returned to the camp for lunch. Before leaving Penola I purchased two bottles of wine, and a man named Kelly and I drank one bottle at lunch time at the camp.

'In the afternoon I went with others to Kalangadoo, where I again had a number of drinks. I had about nine drinks at Penola and about twenty at Kalangadoo.

'Before I left Kalangadoo I bought four bottles of wine and O'Toole bought three bottles of wine.

'Although I was under the influence of liquor I remember going to my own room. I did not pass Ballard's room.

'Some time early in the morning, when it was still dark O'Toole came into my room and said, "Get up. Shorty's room is on fire." I knew "Shorty" was the deceased Ballard.

'I left my room with O'Toole and went to Ballard's hut. Ballard was lying on his bed and his bed and clothes were smouldering.

There were no flames and little smoke in the room. Ballard was moaning, but I could not distinguish what he was saying. There were a couple of bottles of beer and a bottle of wine on the bed.

'O'Toole and I carried Ballard out of his hut to the roadway. I was at his head and carried him by putting my arms under his shoulders.

'I got a considerable amount of blood on my clothes and arms while carrying Ballard out of the room.

'After we got Ballard outside, I asked O'Toole to get somebody to help us and some time later a number of men came. I tried to cut the clothing off Ballard with a pair of scissors.

'I could see Ballard was in pain and all I wanted to do was to get his clothes off so he would not suffer so much.

'I don't remember saying anything about getting an axe or using the scissors to finish Ballard off, and even if somebody had given me an axe I certainly would not have touched him with it.

'I did all in my power to ease his suffering. I don't know how long I was with Ballard, but after I had done all I could for him and other assistance came I went back to my room. I then noticed blood on my hands and clothing.

'I was not wearing a pullover that morning, but was dressed in khaki trousers, khaki shirt, white gaiters and military boots. The pullovers produced in court are not mine.

'After I returned to my room I drank more wine. O'Toole, who was asleep, awoke and he drank some wine with me. I was drinking wine most of the morning until lunch, but I don't remember how much I had.

'I have no recollection of picking up a pullover in front of Ballard's hut and hiding it.

'When I was questioned by police officers at the camp I was muddled with drink and I don't remember what I told them.

'I did not know which room was Ballard's as we did not work together. I had never been in Ballard's room until O'Toole took me there when I helped to carry Ballard from his room.

'I did not possess a glass and I don't know how the broken glass found by police got into my suitcase. On the morning of July 7, I went to my suitcase to get some cigarettes and nothing appeared to be out of place.

'On the Sunday morning there was a beer bottle in my bedroom. Several of the men came to my room that morning and some of them had drinks there.

'I had a lot of drink on the Saturday and early Sunday morning and I was not sober, but I am not guilty of murdering Ballard. I did not assault him, nor was I present when he received his injuries. Ballard was only a little man and had I wished to hurt him I would have used my fist.'

Despite O'Leary's denials about evidence like the pullover and broken glass found by police, O'Leary was found guilty of murder. Chief Justice Sir Mellis Napier then sentenced O'Leary to death. O'Leary's reply was one of the most incredibly calm in the history of South Australian courts. O'Leary replied, 'Thank you, sir. Your Honour need not do anything about the matter, and I am quite prepared to pay the full penalty. I do not want concessions, thank you.' O'Leary thanked his counsel, Adelaide barrister Mr C.J. Philcox, turned to the body of the court, waved cheerily and called 'good-bye.'

O'Leary might have said that he was prepared to pay for his crime but the legal fight to save his life was only just beginning. O'Leary appealed unsuccessfully to the South Australian Supreme Court and to the Full Bench of the High Court. The South Australian Cabinet refused a reprieve. O'Leary was hanged less than forty-eight hours after the High Court refused his application to appeal against the death sentence. O'Leary walked calmly to the gallows, nodded his head in the direction of four guards and said, 'Thank you gentlemen.' O'Leary was sentenced to death on October 18, 1946, and was executed on November 14 that year.

THE MERCY
KILLING

When middle-aged Max Enkhardt heard the squeal of a car tyres early one night in 1968, he had no idea that the motor accident he had heard from a couple of blocks away would turn his life into a nightmare. Max Enkhardt's wife was seriously injured in that accident and spent the following forty-five days in hospital, recovering from head injuries and a broken pelvis. Indirectly, the accident led to Anna Lena Maria Enkhardt's death, Max Enkhardt being charged with the murder of his wife.

Max Enkhardt arrived in Australia as a cabin boy on a German freighter in 1928. Max liked Australia and decided to stay. He met Anna, dark and beautiful, less than a year after settling in Australia. They met at a Lutheran church in Melbourne and Max Enkhardt later described the meeting as 'love at first sight'. They were married in 1936 and although life had provided the couple with its usual ups and downs, the Enkhardts generally were blessed with happiness. Max worked as a journalist, syndicating a pet column, and his wife worked as a cashier in a Melbourne store. Their lives changed after that accident in 1968.

Anna Enkhardt was racked by pain and her condition slipped dramatically. She was suffering from stomach upsets and she was convinced she had cancer. There was no doubt that she was in considerable pain and it tore Max's heart to pieces to hear his wife moaning in agony. Max gave up work to attend his wife night and day, and he became a devoted nurse to his beloved Anna. The couple were renting a house in the south-eastern suburb of Bentleigh but the Enkhradts were about $500 in arrears on the rent. Anna's condition seemed to be worsening and the future looked grim.

Then, sixteen months after Anna's accident, Max acted. On the afternoon of November 3, 1969, Max shot Anna dead. Max said later that he killed because he loved his wife and he only wanted to end her days of pain. It was, he claimed, a mercy killing.

Enkhardt, 59 when he shot his wife, who was 69, was charged with murder and tried in Melbourne's Criminal Court the following year. The case attracted a great deal of public interest, with one newspaper headline reading 'Man Kissed Wife Then Shot Her—Court Told'. The Crown Prosecutor, Mr J.L. Morrissey, told the all-male jury that Anna Enkhardt was in bed suffering from a gastric attack when she was shot in the head. Enkhardt, who pleaded not guilty before Mr Justice McInerney, said he was convinced his wife was going to die. He also told the jury that he tried to shoot himself. However, the pistol jammed.

Enkhardt went shopping soon after midday on November 3 and bought himself a large quantity of brandy, as well as having a prescription prepared for his wife. Enkhardt drank some of the brandy on the way home and shot his wife soon after 3 p.m. Senior government pathologist Dr J.H. McNamara told the Criminal Court that he examined three gunshot wounds in Anna Enkhardt's head. He said that two bullets had entered the left side of the head and one had gone through from the right side of the head. The jury were even shown a film re-enactment of the killing. The film, made by a police photographer soon after Anna Enkhardt's death, ran for three minutes, with Enkhardt himself (followed by a detective) illustrating the killing.

Enkhardt said that his wife used to say that she wished she could 'end it all'. He also said that he kissed his wife before shooting her. 'I kissed her before I shot, and she didn't show any response to my kiss. I loved her. I only did it for her. Believe me, I didn't come here to grovel for anything. She was my love ... my only love for 35 years ... she didn't nag me, she loved me. I couldn't bear to see her suffer.'

Enkhardt, in his unsworn statement in the dock, earlier said, 'My wife was badly mangled in a car accident in 1968. She was very ill. She needed my help ... My wife was convinced she had incurable cancer. In 1968 she was in great pain and losing weight ... In 1969 we got behind in our rent and my wife was getting sicker and sicker. I felt helpless. I worked at many things but they offered no success. I was marked for failure. I drank sometimes but I could not control my drinking. We talked a lot. The weekend before she died I picked her up, carried her to the bathroom and put her on the scales. She weighed six stone. She was very ill. She had some sort of convulsive fit. I thought she was going to die on the Monday night. She was certain she had cancer. On Monday morning I got a ring from the agent to say we would have to get out of the house that day ... I couldn't tell her. The doctor came and I went down the street to the chemist. I got some brandy. I drank some on the way home. Shortly after I came home I got her a tablet ... she was very ill ... she said it was the end. I drank the rest of the brandy. I couldn't stand it. I went outside and got the pistol which had been in a trunk since we were married.'

Anna Enkhardt's sister, Lillian Zoller, said she went to the Bentleigh house at 4.20 p.m. and thought at first that her sister had a black eye. 'I leaned over to talk to her and could see the blood all over her. I shouted out several times but could get no answer. I called outside a few times. Suddenly Max approached from the garage. I said, "What have you done to Anna?" and he said, "Nothing." I went into the kitchen and he followed and I said again, "What have you done to Anna?" and he replied, "I killed her ..." He didn't say whether he was going to kill himself first or after shooting his wife.'

The jury found Enkhardt guilty of murder and Mr Justice McInerney sentenced him to death. Enkhardt then said, 'Your Honour, I believe Anna Enkhardt was dead when I shot her.' The

Victorian Executive Council later commuted the death sentence to twenty years imprisonment, with a minimum of fifteen years to be served to be eligible for parole.

Enkhardt, the mercy killer, became a model prisoner. In fact, he won several art and public speaking awards while serving his sentence in Melbourne's Pentridge Prison. Enkhardt said after serving his sentence that he was determined to make the most of his time in prison. His art awards included the 1972, 1974 and 1975 Robin Hood art prize for prisoners. Enkhardt was released in August, 1978, after serving eight years and eight months of his sentence.

Enkhardt was a lost man when he left prison, admitting that he seemed out of place. 'I have got no one, no family—nothing, except my paintings. Where do I go?', Enkhardt said after his release. Enkhardt was a minor Melbourne identity, known as a 'gentle old man'. The convicted killer exhibited his paintings, looked up old friends and gave press interviews. In all those interviews he insisted that he was right in killing his wife. 'She begged me to do it,' he said.

Ironically, Enkhardt died from injuries he received when hit by a car in Elsternwick in September, 1979. Not long before his death Enkhardt said, 'All that's left to say is my conscience is clear. I can face my Maker. He knows.'

THE PYJAMA GIRL

Most countries have one or more murder cases that criminologists—
as well as the general public—regard as classic cases. Britain has had
many outstanding murder cases, including the Dr Buck Ruxton,
John George Haigh (the acid-bath murderer) and Neville Heath
cases. The United States of America had the Lizzie Borden case (she
was acquitted of charges of murdering her father and stepmother),
France had the incredible mass murderer Henri Desire Landru
(executed in 1922) and Germany had the infamous monster of
Dusseldorf, Peter Kurten. Australia's most notorious murder case
was the Pyjama Girl case. However, it generally is forgotten that this
case, which attracted world-wide interest over a number of years,
ended in a conviction of manslaughter, and not murder.

The Pyjama Girl case burst into public prominence in 1934,
reached its climax in 1944 and even now manages to create headlines
from time to time.

Young farmer Tom Griffiths was walking along the
Albury-Howlong Road in the Riverina, on a crisp, sunny Saturday
morning in 1934. It was September 1 and young Griffiths was
leading an expensive prize bull along the grass verge of the highway
when the bull became restless. Griffiths and the bull were
approaching a culvert and the bull backed away. Griffiths did not
know what was wrong but soon noticed a bundle under the culvert.

He investigated and what he saw turned his stomach. It was a body, damaged by fire. Griffiths immediately contacted police in Albury, about four miles away, and returned to the culvert to wait for them.

The body, of a woman, had been pushed into the entrance of a water pipe. The woman had been terribly wounded and police even then believed that identification would not be easy. However, they had a number of clues. The woman had been badly battered about the head and there was a bullet wound near the right eye. Of course, there were also the burns, the body obviously being exposed to naked flame. The clues included a burnt bag and towel used to cover the body, a skid mark from a car possibly used by the killer to dump the body, and most importantly, a charred pair of pyjamas. Those pyjamas gave the case its name, and police believed at the time that it was the best clue of them all. However, investigating police soon discovered that the cream and green pyjamas, which had been partly burnt, were available in almost every large town in Australia. Although the pyjama jacket had a large dragon motif, this proved to be of little use to police in the identification of the body.

In fact, idenfication of the body became the first, and most important, job for police in their investigations. The dead woman was in her mid-twenties, was well-developed and well-nourished, had had considerable dental work on her teeth, an unusually shaped nose and slightly malformed ears.

A number of people who saw the body within forty-eight hours of its discovery made identification. However, each identification proved wrong. Police worked painstakingly to investigate all these early identifications, fully aware that the sooner the identity of the woman was known, the easier it would be to solve the murder riddle. However, all leads proved fruitless. Police worked on every available clue, including the bag thrown over the body and the towel wrapped around its head.

The towel, which had a blue and red border, was common enough in New South Wales and Victoria and identification along these lines would have proved impossible. The bag, which had been badly charred, was identified as a bag used in potato packing in

Victoria. Again, it was a common enough bag and police could not expect any developments in the case in regard to the bag. That left the pyjamas, and as already mentioned, these were common in Australia, even though they had been made in Japan or China and imported.

With clues found at the discovery site proving little more than useless it became more and more obvious that the body itself held the key to identification, despite its gruesome wounds. The head had been badly battered and the lower part of the body had been damaged by the fire in the culvert. Whoever had dumped the body had obviously tried to burn it in the culvert. The killer had only partly succeeded. The body was preserved in the Albury Hospital and was available for identification purposes to anyone who believed they could help police. Leads were followed but no trail proved positive.

Police notified forces overseas and every police station in Australia and New Zealand had a description of the body. It seemed incredible that a woman's body could be discovered and that no one could positively identify her. Police worked overtime on the case and no stone was left unturned in the immediate question of investigation. Police even had X-rays of the teeth taken, a dental chart then prepared for dental surgeries throughout Australasia. Again, this failed to identify the dead woman. Police were baffled. They had tried every possible line of investigation but the Pyjama Girl mystery still was unsolved.

Six weeks of painstaking investigation had led virtually nowhere when it was decided to remove the body to Sydney University, where it was placed in a specially prepared formalin bath for preservation. Hundreds of visitors inspected the body in an effort to identify it. Meanwhile, police followed further lines of investigation, tracing the movements of a number of women. Again, there were no leads.

The best hope police had was that one of the many people who viewed the body at Sydney University would make an identification that would prove fruitful with follow-up work. A number of 'positive identifications' were made but none of them stood up to thorough police investigation. Several people who saw the body told police that it looked like a woman named Linda Agostini, nee Platt.

This sounded promising and a detective in Melbourne went to speak with Linda Agostini's husband, an Italian migrant named Antonio (Tony) Agostini. That was in July, 1935, almost a year after the discovery of the Pyjama Girl's body. Agostini was helpful and co-operative but police obviously did not believe that the little Italian immigrant had anything to do with the Pyjama Girl. Agostini told police that his wife was missing but that she had left him in August, 1934, and had been working as a hairdresser on a cruise ship. Shown a photograph of the Pyjama Girl, Agostini said that it was not his missing wife. Although asked to go to police headquarters the following day, Agostini was not suspected. Police obviously believed his claim that his wife had left him and that the dead woman was not Linda Agostini. Police did not even bother to speak to Agostini the following day, even though he turned up at Russell Street headquarters. All police leads fizzled out.

They seemed no closer to solving the riddle, and more than three years after the discovery of the body, a coroner's inquest was held. This took place in Albury, in January, 1938.

The inquest created headlines throughout Australia. It seemed the whole nation had taken an interest in the Pyjama Girl case. It already had been established as one of Australia's greatest mysteries and Australians everywhere wanted to know the outcome of the inquest.

The best information anyone had on the dead woman was information previously given by Professor A. N. Burkitt, professor of anatomy at Sydney University, who said that the woman was probably English or European and aged about 25. Professor Burkitt had examined the body and police were grateful for his conclusions. But to the time of the coroner's inquest Professor Burkitt's information still had not identified the dead woman. However, his information later was to prove remarkably accurate, especially in relation to the woman's nationality. Meanwhile, the inquest went ahead.

After hearing the evidence, the Albury coroner, Mr C. W. Swiney, delivered his finding. Mr Swiney obviously had listened intently to all the evidence but must have paid particular attention to that given by acting Government Medical Officer, Dr Leslie Woods. The body had been discovered with terrible head wounds, including a bullet wound from a .25 calibre Webley Scott automatic pistol. But although Dr Woods referred to the bullet wound, he said that the woman had died of a fractured skull. Mr Swiney's finding was 'I find that between August 28, 1934, and August 31, 1934, a woman whose name is unknown, aged about 25 years, of slight build, height around 5 ft. 11 in., with brown hair and bluish-grey eyes, whose partly-burned body was found at a culvert on the Albury-Corowa Road, about four miles from Albury on September 1, 1934, died from injuries to the skull and brain apparently maliciously and feloniously inflicted upon her, but where and by whom such injuries were inflicted the evidence does not enable me to say'.

The mystery was as deep as ever and police almost seemed to be back at square one. In fact, the mystery was to remain for some years, with many an odd twist and turn—some of them dramatic.

Despite the coroner's findings, some people were convinced that they knew the dead woman. More 'positive' identifications were made, the body still being kept in its formalin bath. Most of these so-called 'positive' identifications were made genuinely but none of them proved really worthwhile.

The case always seemed to be in the headlines. For example, a report in the Melbourne Herald of July 15, 1938, was given the following headline: 'Another Pyjama Girl Search To Be Made'. The report said, 'Scotland Yard, and all interstate police forces will be asked by the New South Wales Criminal Investigation Branch to assist in tracing an English girl, said to have been missing for four years, and who, it has been suggested, may be the Albury "Pyjama girl" murder victim. A constable was surprised a few days ago when a woman rushed up to him in the street with a note she had found in a rest room at the Central Railway Station (Sydney). The note indicated that the missing English girl was identical with the "pyjama girl", whose body was found on September I, 1934, in a culvert in Howlong Road, four miles from Albury. The note was signed "North Shore". Detective Wilks wishes to interview the writer of the note. He seeks further details of the girl named ... Scotland Yard will be asked to supply details of the girl's movements in England. Rewards of £1000 for information leading to the murderer's conviction, and £500 for the identification of the body have been offered by the New South Wales Government.' This was typical of reports involving the Pyjama Girl mystery.

One of the strangest twists to the case was the claim by a Dr T.A. Palmer Benbow and others that the dead woman was a missing woman named Anna Philomena Morgan. A woman, Mrs Jeanette Rutledge, claimed that the body was that of her missing daughter, Anna Morgan. The woman was supported by Dr Benbow, who insisted that there were seventeen points of anatomical identification to support the contention that the body in the formalin bath was that of Anna Morgan. Mrs Rutledge issued a writ against the Department of Justice for possession of the Pyjama Girl's body. That issue went to court when the department refused to hand over the body. Police maintained that the Pyjama Girl was not Anna Morgan. In December, 1942, Mrs Rutledge asked Mr Justice Nicholas to grant her an order making her administrator of her daughter's estate. Dr Benbow told an incredible tale of how the woman Morgan had been bashed and throttled in a shack near Albury. However, Mr Justice Nicholas referred the evidence to the Crown Solicitor, with NSW Attorney-General Martin announcing four months later that police believed that a girl had not been attacked in a shack. The matter rested there, for the time being.

The break in the Pyjama Girl case came an incredible ten years after the discovery of the body. It came when Police Commissioner W.J. Mackay assigned a new team of detectives to re-examine the files on the murder mystery. The Pyjama Girl files had never been closed and police still worked for the breakthrough they so desperately needed to solve the riddle that had puzzled Australia for ten long years. The new police team consisted of Detective-Sergeants H.W. Latrobe and J.V. Ramus, and Detective Stackpole.

An old photograph of a group of women led directly to the name of Linda Agostini. One of the women in the photograph identified the woman in the formalin bath as Linda Agostini, who had not been seen for ten years. Again, it was time to question the Italian migrant Tony Agostini. At this time, in March, 1944, Agostini was working as a waiter at the fashionable Romano's restaurant in Sydney. One of the regular patrons at Romano's was the police commissioner, Mr William Mackay. On Saturday, March 4, Agostini received a telephone call to contact Mr Mackay, who now had strong evidence to suggest that the dead woman was Linda Agostini. The body had been identified by a number of people and dental work corresponded almost perfectly with work done by a Sydney dentist on Mrs Agostini some years previously. Agostini went to police headquarters straight from his job.

Agostini's appointment with Mr Mackay was to prove the turning point in the mystery. Mr Mackay told Agostini about certain police inquiries and then told the Italian waiter, 'Now look here, Tony, you appear to be worried. You don't appear to be the same smiling Tony you were back in 1930 at Romano's.' Agostini replied 'Well, Mr Mckay, the thing that makes the difference in my demeanour and my looks is the death of Linda, which has been worrying me. I hid the facts for ten years and now I am not going to worry no matter what happens to me. I am going to tell you the truth.' Agostini then made a statement. However, it now is appropriate to look at the background to what Agostini had to say in that statement.

Agostini had migrated to Australia in 1927 on the Italian liner Regina d'Italia and soon took a lease on the cloakroom at Romano's restaurant. Agostini worked hard at his job and three years later met an English girl—Linda Platt. Linda had migrated to Australia, via New Zealand, after an unhappy love affair in Bromley, Kent, where she had run a small business. Linda Plan sold her business after the break-up of her love affair and sailed south. She worked in Sydney as an usherette at a picture theatre and fell in love with Agostini. They married, after she had made a return visit to England, in a registry office on April 22, 1930.

The young couple lived in Sydney during the early part of the marriage, Linda doing a course in hairdressing. She took a job on the liner Aorangi as a hairdresser and the couple moved to Melbourne in 1933. At this time Agostini was worried about his wife's drinking habits and he claimed that he could not bring friends home because of this. Agostini by now was working as a journalist for an Italian language newspaper, the couple living in the inner Melbourne suburb of Carlton. Agostini, aged 31 in 1933, believed his marriage was in real danger.

His alleged statement, which took three closely typed pages, read in part:

> I married Linda Platt on April 22, 1930. After the first two or three years our relations became more and more unhappy, mainly through my wife drinking too much.
>
> My friends had to be asked not to call any longer at my house because my wife showed that she could not welcome them, as they proved to be an obstacle to her habits.
>
> In 1933 I left my employment and, following her desire, I got a position in Melbourne, because there she thought she would be away from the evil influence and temptation of the circle of friends that she had in Sydney. After a very short while her ways in Melbourne became the same as in Sydney.
>
> On several occasions she left me, saying that she was trying to separate permanently from me, because she understood the harm she was doing to me by her conduct, and was hindering me in my success in business.
>
> My connection with the Italian Club and ceremonies there, at which I had to be present as a reporter, were no longer possible, because to leave home it meant coming back to find her waiting for me drunk and threatening and arguing and accusing me of having been out with women. On several occasions she threatened my life, saying I'll kill you some day, but I could never take these threats seriously.

One Sunday evening I said that on the following morning I would have to go to Shepparton on business, I asked her if she would like the journey, as I used to take her with me whenever she desired.

She refused to join me, and said that I would never go to Shepparton, but declined to give me any reason for her statement.

To prevent me from keeping my appointments in the morning she used to make it impossible for me to sleep, thus I thought that when she said I would never go to Shepparton she intended to prevent me getting my proper sleep and rest, and to argue with me and misbehave herself so that I would not be in a proper state to go.

She went to bed and I joined her later after preparing myself for the journey, but before going to bed I set the alarm clock for 7 a.m.

I had a restless night, as I had on many nights previously but towards the break of day I fell into a sound sleep and wakened with a start when the alarm went off at 7 o'clock, and felt something hard pressing into my head behind the left ear.

I realised it was a gun she was holding against my head and I quickly turned my head on the cushion and grasping her hand in my hand, I commenced to struggle with her for possession of the revolver, intending to disarm her. In doing so, we rolled over on the bed.

She struggled bitterly and was very determined. She surprised me at her strength. We rolled over in the bed and I thought she was going to let go of the revolver because her hand relaxed.

The next thing I heard was a shot going off. She gave a long gasp and ceased to struggle.

The realisation that she was dead gave me a terrible shock and unbalanced my mentality. For a long while I was staring at her, failing to put my thoughts together. It was long after the full realisation of what had happened, and of its consequences, came fully in my mind.

My first thought was of going to report to the police, and I was making myself presentable for going out. While doing so I could not dress for thinking of what had happened, and I would sit down in the middle of dressing to think of what I could do and what had caused the trouble.

By the time that I got dressed and downstairs I started to see what would happen to my friends, my relations, and the firm with whom I was employed when the big headings would come out in the paper about the shooting. In the work I was doing I had made a lot of friends in the Italian and Australian communities in Melbourne, and I felt that I was highly regarded by them all. The thought of what they would think of me swayed my better judgment of going and telling the police straight away, particularly that my action would ruin the enterprise I was connected with, and which I was keenly interested in and had started to build up to a strong newspaper of Italian thought.

I sat down in my office, and after what may have been hours I came out of the confusion and I felt that I could not let my action be a blot on the Italian community, although I had nothing to do with the firing of the weapon. I felt there would be suspicion on me.

By this time so much time had passed by that I felt that if I went to the police and told the truth they would look on me with suspicion and would not believe me. Then I came to my decision to do my utmost to hide traces of the happening and the death of my wife, and I decided to dispose of the body by taking it out into some part of the country.

At 8 p.m. on the day of the accident to my wife at 7 p.m. I left Melbourne with the body and took the highway to Albury. I had no plans. I was just running.

I continued on, and I realised by the lights I saw that I was nearing Albury, because it was a large town, so I took the first branch road I met and, after travelling for some time, I stopped the car at a quiet part of the road where there is a little bridge or culvert.

I had taken with me some extra petrol in a tin because I knew that it was late at night and I might have difficulty in waking anyone up at a garage to get a fresh supply.

So I poured some of the petrol from the tin on to a bag in which the body was enclosed and placed the body under the bridge and set fire to it by lighting it with a match.

Light rain was falling at the time, and I immediately got into my car, put the balance of the petrol into the tank of my car and drove back the same road to Melbourne. I garaged my car in front of my house, where I was in the habit of leaving it.

As soon as I arrived back in Melbourne I went into the home and grocer's shop of Mr Castellano, who had a grocer's shop two doors away in Swanston Street, Carlton. I remember he asked me how I got a scratch that was on the side of my head. It was a cut which I received in the struggle with my wife the previous morning and which had dried black on my cheek.

The cut was inflicted by the sight of the revolver when I was struggling to get possession of it from my wife on the bed. I told him that the cut had been caused by the door on my car, and he remarked on how dreadful I looked and sick.

Mrs Castellano got the coffee prepared and I had coffee and some biscuits or bread. I then returned to my own home and I was in a dreadfully nervous state. I did no work but just lay about for two days.

A couple of days afterward Castellano came to see me as he was worried because I did not call at his place, as I used to do practically every day. He remarked that I was looking not my old self and asked me if I would have liked to go out for a short run with the car. I said I would like to go and I got my car.

While in the car he asked me about where my wife was and he told me that the photographs of the Albury victim looked remarkably like my wife Linda. I then confessed to him that she had been accidentally killed while she and I were struggling for a revolver.

I told him all that I have put into this statement. He then told me that my wife was a whisky fiend and that she had developed into taking cheap wine from some sly grog shop around Swanston Street, and that he had noticed a change in her outlook by her conduct; that she was going downhill through drink.

I told him of what I had done and my reason for so doing as set out in this statement that I am making now and I said, 'I think it is better that I go to the police because I can't carry on as I have been doing during the last couple of days.' He insisted that I should confide in him, and that he would help me in every possible way, but that I must not go to the police or confide in any other person.

He invited me to come to his place every day and have my meals there and build myself up, meet people and get confidence and to deny any knowledge of what happened to my wife, if anyone should ask me.

I had my weak moments, which he noticed, and he would talk and try to get my mind away from what he knew I was thinking about. I afterward realised that he had an object in so advising me when something occurred in 1938, which I will state later in this statement.

Sometime after that when I was in Melbourne a detective called at my place and showed me the photographs of the Albury victim, my wife, and asked me if I recognised them.

I looked at them and I was very nervous at the time, but the detective did not appear to take much notice of my state and I said that I did not recognise her.

I received instructions from him to call at Russell Street Police Station next day to see if there was anything else they could show me by which I could recognise her, I called there two or three times and they would say nothing had come through, so I stopped going there.

In 1936 and 1937 I was working in Western Australia and about January 1938 I had come to Sydney and there I met some of my wife's friends. I had been asked my wife's whereabouts several times by them and had explained that she had gone away. I was either approached by Mr Wilks, of the Police Force or at the request of some of my wife's friends I saw Mr Wilks by calling on him at the Detective Office and went with him to see the body of my wife at the University.

I saw the body. I could not recognise it as my wife's body in such a state. I knew it must be her body because it had been found where I left it. I think I said to Mr Wilks, 'I cannot recognise her as my wife.'

This alleged statement went only half-way in explaining the Pyjama Girl mystery, and one huge question remained. Agostini, in the statement, referred to the shooting of his wife. However, the Pyjama Girl suffered dreadful head injuries, apart from the bullet wound. What had caused these injuries? Police continued their investigations and Agostini was taken to the country spot where the Pyjama Girl's body was discovered. Further questioned by police, Agostini told them that as he was carrying his wife's body to the car, he tripped on the stairs at his home and dropped the body, which fell downstairs and hit a flatiron at the bottom. Agostini was charged on March 6, 1944, with the murder of his wife. He was remanded to appear before a coroner's inquest, which opened in Melbourne on March 23 before Mr A. C. Tingate, PM.

The second coroner's inquest on the Pyjama Girl was even more sensational than the first inquest, held years previously in Albury. Apart from anything else, the coroner had the problem of deciding the identity of the mysterious Pyjama Girl. There was, of course, still the claim of Dr Benbow and Mrs Rutledge that the dead woman was Anna Morgan. Mr Tingate rejected that claim after listening to sixty-two witnesses over twenty-three days. Mr Tingate found that the body was that of Linda Agostini and committed Antonio Agostini for trial.

Agostini's trial opened before Mr Justice Lowe in the Supreme Court in Melbourne on June 19, 1944. Agostini's defence was that he did not intend killing his wife but that she died accidentally. However, a great deal hinged on the statement Agostini was alleged to have made. There was no mention in that statement of the head injuries received by the dead woman. The trial opened with a legal argument over the admissibility of the statement. Agostini's counsel Mr Fazio claimed that the statement was questionable on the grounds of voluntariness. The statement was admitted as evidence and was read to the jury. Sub-Inspector William Edward Davis later told the court that in an interview with Agostini the accused told him that Linda Agostini received the injuries to her head when the body fell downstairs. Dr Crawford Mollison, the coroner's surgeon, told the court that in conjunction with another medical expert he had made a post-mortem examination of the body on April 17 and 18, 1944. Dr Crawford said they had found that vital parts that would have caused death had not been struck by the bullet.

Naturally, a great deal hinged on the evidence given by Agostini himself. Agostini insisted that his wife already was dead when he carried the body downstairs and dropped it. Yet earlier the court had heard from Dr Crawford that the bullet had missed vital parts that would have caused death. Agostini was cross-examined at length on this particular point, Agostini saying that he knew his wife already was dead because 'I bent down to her chest and there was no sign that I could detect of her breathing'.

After counsel had addressed the jury and Mr Justice Lowe had summed up, the jury retired to consider its verdict. It returned just under two hours later. The verdict was not guilty of murder, but guilty of manslaughter. Mr Justice Lowe sentenced Agostini to six years' jail, and commented 'I think the jury were merciful to you'.

The Pyjama Girl, now fully identified as Linda Agostini, was buried, after a Church of England service, at the Preston Cemetery on July 13, 1944—exactly thirteen days after Agostini was sentenced to prison. Agostini served three years and nine months of his sentence and was then deported to Italy. He left for Italy in a first-class two-berth cabin on the promenade deck of the liner Strathnaver on August 22, 1948. Interviewed through his cabin door, Agostini said he probably would live with relatives in Genoa. However, he refused to answer all other questions. The Pyjama Girl mystery was closed.

THE BABES IN THE CAVE

Little John Ward and Albert Speirs, like all young boys, liked carnivals. They were looking forward to a day at the Portland, New South Wales, carnival on October 30, 1950. There they expected to enjoy all the fun of the fair and the two seven-year-old playmates were as excited about the carnival as any children in Portland. The two little boys did not return home from the carnival, their day ending in murder.

When the boys failed to return home at a reasonable time after the carnival, John Ward's father, John Alfred Ward, notified police. A huge search was launched and thousands of miners and quarrymen joined police and other volunteers. It was to become one of the biggest searches in Australian criminal history, searchers even carrying torches at night to investigate the possibility of the boys being lost in a quarry cave. Unbeknown to the searchers, they went within less than one hundred yards of a gruesome sight on the first night of the search.

Hopes faded quickly of finding the boys alive and the search dragged on into its fifth day. Then, on the morning of November 4, 23-year-old Herbert Hutchinson, acting on a hunch, decided to search a cave where he had looked for pigeon eggs as a boy. Hutchinson was horrified in finding two small bodies.

Police were shocked. The huddled bodies were a tragic sight, partly because of their very youth, but also because the bodies had been partly eaten by rats. Police appeared to have a case of murder on their hands, although there were initial suggestions that the boys had been lost and died of exhaustion. However, expert medical examination later showed that the boys had died of suffocation, with evidence that shock was a contributing factor.

The man police wanted to interview was John Kevin Seach, a 26-year-old quarryman with the reputation of being a heavy drinker. Seach had left the town of Portland soon after the boys were reported missing. Seach had been talking to the two boys shortly before their disappearance and John Ward's elder brother, Richard, 9, also identified Seach as the man he had seen walking away from the sports ground with his brother and Albert Speirs on October 30.

Seach had headed for Tamworth, taking a job under the assumed name of John Larsen for the short time that he was missing. Police questioned him at Tamworth police station on November 22 and Seach immediately confessed to killing the two boys. Evidence was given later that Seach cried when questioned about the deaths. Detective Raymond Kelly, who questioned Seach at Tamworth, told the Portland Coroner's Court that Seach told him he was leaving the sports carnival when he noticed the two small boys, one of whom was crying.

Seach told the boys he would take them home but took them to a quarry cave instead. He interfered with the boys and immediately panicked. A statement by Seach read, 'I grabbed the little bloke and smothered him by putting a handkerchief over his nose and mouth. As soon as he went limp I just let him fall back. I grabbed the other one and did the same to him… Next morning I went to work. I saw a lot of people searching the top of the quarry and one of the blokes down the bottom where I was working said they were looking for the two boys. I got frightened and went home and changed my clothes and told Mum that I was going to help look for the two boys.'

Seach, of course, killed to cover up his interference of the boys. His statement read, 'I was frightened to let them go because they would have told what I had done.'

The two boys died because they could identify Seach as the man who interfered with them in the quarry cave. Even more tragic was the fact that one of the boys watched as Seach killed the first boy. The second victim was probably too terrified to even attempt an escape.

Seach stood trial at the Central Criminal Court in March, 1951, pleading not guilty to murder on the grounds of insanity. The confession was not disputed by the defence but evidence was given that Seach was certifiably insane at the time of the killings. Dr Sylvester Minogue, a Macquarie Street specialist, said that in his opinion Seach suffered from schizophrenia and was insane when he killed the boys. However, another Macquarie Street specialist, Dr John McGeorge, said he had been unable to find any evidence of gross mental disorder. The jury took only half an hour to find Seach guilty of the murder of John Frederick Ward, the Crown also alleging that Seach murdered Albert Speirs.

Seach was sentenced to death, Mr Justice Street saying, 'It needs no words of mine to speak of the abhorrent and detestable crime of which you have been so rightly convicted. There is only one possible sentence. You are sentenced to death.' Seach, a pathetic looking character was regarded with horror in New South Wales, society considering child-killing to be the most abominable of crimes.

THE LAST WOMAN HANGED

Attractive Jean Lee was not alone in the murder of old, overweight starting-price bookmaker Bill Kent in Carlton, an inner Melbourne suburb, in November, 1949. Robert Clayton, her lover, and another accomplice, Norman Andrews, also were found guilty of murdering Kent. But Lee's name stands out because she was the last woman hanged in Victoria. In fact, Jean Lee believed her sex would save her from the gallows. However, the murder of old Kent was so terrible that even the Victorian State Cabinet turned down a mercy plea. Lee was hanged on February 19, 1951, only fifteen months after Kent was tortured to death.

Jean Lee's early life was to give little hint of the life of crime she was to lead soon after leaving school in Sydney aged 16. She was brought up with a regard for law and order but Jean Lee knew what she wanted—and that was the good life. However, she married when aged 18 and that temporarily ended her life as one of Sydney's Depression butterflies. Jean Lee had a daughter but drifted away from her family and into prostitution during the Second World War.

It was during her 'busy' days entertaining American and Australian troops that she met Clayton, who was to become her pimp. Lee and Clayton also worked a racket in which Lee was found by Clayton in a compromising position with 'another man'. Clayton then threatened violence if the 'other man' did not compensate for luring his 'wife' off to have sex.

This racket worked so successfully over several years that Lee and Clayton decided to branch out in Victoria and headed south in quest of new 'suckers'. That was in 1949 and that was when they met up with the rugged Andrews. The three hit it off almost immediately and they worked their racket in Melbourne, with the bigger Andrews now threatening the violence, generally as Lee's 'husband' or Clayton's 'brother'.

Pickings were good but not as good as when the unholy trio came across old Bill Kent in a Lygon Street, Carlton, hotel. Kent, well known throughout Carlton, had a fistful of notes and Lee, Clayton and Andrews devised a plan to get that bankroll. Lee was to be the attractive bait.

She sidled up to Kent, plied him with drinks and she and her two friends and old Kent then headed off to Old Bill's in nearby Dorritt Street. Lee told her friends that she would 'entertain' Kent, so Clayton headed off temporarily.

However, Kent, drunk as he was, was certainly no fool. He had his money tucked into his fob pocket and Lee, no matter how hard she tried, could not get it. When Andrews and Clayton returned she gave them the bad news, and declared that she would have to get the old SP to take his trousers down. But this only made Kent more aware of Lee's real passion, and that was when the going got violent.

Lee smashed Kent over the head with a bottle, battered him with a piece of wood and then tied him up with sheet strippings. The terrible trio then cut Kent's fob pocket from his trousers but were convinced that the bookie had much more money hidden away. They bashed, cut and jabbed at Kent with several weapons, including the broken bottle, and left him for dead.

Kent's body was found within an hour when a neighbour grew suspicious about the 'quietness after the party'. Police were called immediately and it did not take them long to track down the three killers.

Police already had an idea of their game in Melbourne and were keeping a wary eye on them. Now they fitted the descriptions given to the police. It was only a matter of time in rounding them up. Incredibly, Lee, Andrews and Clayton celebrated that night.

However, there were no celebrations when police fronted them at 4 a.m. at their Spencer Street hotel less than twelve hours after their brutal and greedy murder of Kent. Their arrest came less than three hours before they were due to fly back to Sydney on the proceeds of their murder.

On March 25, 1950, all three were sentenced to death after being convicted of murder. Lee broke down and had to be helped from court. On appeal to the Court of Criminal Appeal two months later a new trial was ordered but that did not save Kent's killers. The Australian High Court reversed that decision and the Privy Council in England turned down a further appeal.

Lee, Clayton and Andrews could only hope that the State Cabinet would show leniency. Lee was convinced that the government would not allow a woman to be hanged and held out hope for herself, at least. But she was wrong. All three were hanged on February 19, 1951.

THE GUN ALLEY MURDER

When 75-year-old Ivy Irene Matthews (alias Ivy Cholet) died in October, 1964, in an East Melbourne hospital, one of Australia's most sensational murder cases hit the headlines yet again. Ivy Matthews was a key witness at the trial of Colin Campbell Ross in 1922. Ivy Matthews was the last surviving witness and the mystery of the Gun Alley murder almost certainly went to the grave with her. Ross was hanged for murder but he swore to his dying breath that he was innocent—and many prominent men were convinced that he was telling the truth. The Gun Alley Murder, as it was known, was one of Melbourne's most publicised crimes, creating headlines for years. Even now the case draws intense academic interest.

The murder investigation started after bottle collector Harry Errington stumbled across the naked body of a young girl at about 5 a.m. on the morning of December 31, 1921. The body lay across a grate in tiny Gun Alley, Melbourne. Gun Alley, a lane running off Little Collins Street, was an unsavoury part of the city in those days, with the notorious Eastern Market nearby. The site later was occupied by the plush Southern Cross Hotel, one of Melbourne's most famous international hotels. The dead girl was Alma Tirtschke, who was just twelve years of age. She had been reported missing the previous afternoon, police launching a search at 8 p.m. on December 30. Alma Tirtschke lived in the city with her grandmother and had disappeared while running a message. Her aunt had sent her to the butcher shop of Bennett and Woolcock's in Swanston Street, in the heart of the city.

Alma was wearing a navy blue box-pleated tunic, a white blouse with blue spots and a school hat bearing the badge of Hawthorn West High School. Alma Tirtschke left the butcher shop at about 1 p.m. and then 'disappeared', although witnesses later gave various accounts of seeing her in the neighbourhood. Significantly, Alma's body was naked when discovered by Harry Errington and, even more significantly, the body had been washed down before being dumped in Gun Alley. Alma Tirtschke had been raped and strangled and the New Year's Eve murder captured the imagination of the whole of Melbourne.

Because Alma Tirtschke was aged only 12, there were terrible rumours circulating about her injuries. All sorts of fantastic stories were told and the public was only too willing to believe them. But although Alma Tirtschke had been strangled, there was no mutilation nor any wounds of a horrific nature. The girl had a number of wounds but these were minor. Government pathologist Dr Crawford Mollison, who performed the post mortem, later outlined these injuries at Ross's trial. The post mortem revealed an abrasion on the left side of the jaw, another on the left side of the neck, a small abrasion on the outer side of the right eye, a small abrasion on the upper lip and a slight graze on the elbow. There was bruising on the right side of the neck and haemorrhages in the scalp and on the surface of the eyes. Dr Mollison's expert view was that the girl had died of strangulation by throttling. The post mortem was held within a few hours of the discovery of the body and Dr Mollison estimated that the girl had died between 7 and 8 p.m. on December 30. Police were left with the unenviable task of trying to trace the dead girl's last hours alive. What happened between 1 p.m., when the girl left the butcher shop, and 5 a.m. the next morning when the body was discovered?

The case was handed to two experienced police officers in Senior Detectives John Brophy and Fred Piggott, who immediately started interviewing residents and habituees of the Eastern Arcade area. Several witnesses helped the two detectives in their investigations. The trail eventually pointed to Colin Ross, who operated a wine bar, the Australian Wine Shop, in the Eastern Arcade. Ross, 26, bought the wine shop business for £400 but, ironically, the licence on the saloon was due to expire on December 31, 1922, the very day that Alma Tirtschke's body was discovered.

The two detectives worked on the theory that whoever killed the girl must have had access to a room in the near vicinity. They struck this theory because the girl's clothes had been removed and because the body had been washed and dried. The police theorised that the killer must have been able to do this without being disturbed, probably in his own premises. Lodging house proprietor George Arthur Ellis also told police that he was sitting outside his lodging house on Friday night, December 30. He said he saw a man at the back gate of the Eastern Arcade look up and down between 9 and 10 p.m. Ellis later identified Ross as the man he had seen.

Police interviewed Ross on December 31 and again on January 5. When first questioned, Ross told police that he had seen a girl answering the description of Alma Tirtschke. However, Ross insisted that he knew nothing of the girl's death. Police on January 5 detained Ross for eight hours and he made a fairly lengthy statement, which read:

> I am at present out of business. I was the holder of the Australian Wine Shop licence in the Eastern Arcade for about nine months past. The licence expired on the 31st December, 1921. I reside at 'Glenross,' Ballarat Road, Footscray. On Friday, the 30th December, I came into the shop about 2 p.m. It was a very quiet day. Between 2 and 3 p.m. I was standing in front of my shop, and looking about I saw a girl about 14 or 15 years of age in the Arcade. She was walking towards Bourke Street, and stopped and looked in a fancy dress costume window. I later saw her walking back, and she appeared to have nothing to do. She wore a dark blue dress, pleated, the pleats were large, light blouse, white straw hat with a colour on it (looked like a college hat), wore dark stockings

and boots—she may have had shoes on. I went back into the cafe. I cannot say where she went. I was about the cafe all the afternoon.

About 4 o'clock, a friend of mine, Miss Gladys Linderman, came to the saloon front. I spoke to her for about an hour. She came into the private room, and we had a talk in the room off the bar, the one in which the cellar is unused. She and I went into the Arcade at 4.45; remained talking for about 10 minutes. I then saw her out into Little Collins Street. I made an appointment to meet her again at 9 p.m. at the place I left her. I went back into the cafe, and remained until 6 p.m., when I left for home, got home about 7 p.m., had tea, left home at 8 p.m., came into the city, waited at the corner of the Arcade in Little Collins Street. Miss Linderman came to me at 9 p.m., and we went straight into the cafe. We remained in there till 10.45, then left, locked the place up, went to King Street. She went to her home, 276 King Street. After leaving her I went to Spencer Street Station, took a train, arrived home at 11.50 p.m., and remained there all night.

I know the shop opposite, No. 33. It is occupied by a man named McKenzie. Several men visit there. I have seen a stout, foreign man go there. I don't know his name—I never spoke to him in my life. I am sure he has not visited the saloon. He has come to my door and spoken to me. On one occasion, about four months ago, I went over to that shop by his invitation. He desired to explain a certain signalling patent. He unlocked the door, and I went inside with him. I saw a box affair, a couch, and nine or twelve chairs. I did not see the patent—it was locked. I have never possessed a key of that shop, and no person has ever loaned me one. I have two keys of my wine saloon. I had one, and my brother Stan had the other. On Friday I possessed one, and my brother had the other. These keys are Yale keys. No person could enter that wine shop unless let in by my brother or myself. I think my brother was in the city that night with his friends. I can't say where he was.

On the Saturday I was again in the saloon. It was the last day of the licence. I saw Mr. Clark, manager of the Arcade, about 11 a.m., and arranged with him to get me a key of the back gate of the Arcade, which is locked by means of a chain and padlock. He gave me a key about noon, and I left there about 6.15 p.m. I came back to the Arcade at 6.50 a.m., Monday, and a van came at 7 a.m., and then took my effects from the saloon, which consisted of 26 chairs, 6 tables, a small couch, a counter, 2 wooden partitions, shelves, and linoleum off the floor, about 20 bottles of wine, and 9 flagons of wine. There were two dozen glasses, and about 18 pictures. My brothers Stanley and Tom were with me. I left there at 8.30 a.m., and went home. I handed the keys to the caretaker.

I cannot say what goes on inside No. 33 in the Arcade, but I have seen several women going in and out, and in company of McKenzie. I have never seen the other man, who looks like an engineer, take women in there. The ages of the women would range from about 20 years and upwards.

I cannot say if any person saw me with Gladys Linderman while at the Arcade. I was not in the company of any other woman that afternoon or evening at the saloon. Close to the saloon, and about 36 feet distant, is a man's lavatory, the door of which is generally locked. At night time it is occasionally left open. I had a key of that lavatory. The water used in my saloon was obtained from a tap in a recess adjoining the cafe.

Ross's mention of the shop opposite—number 33—intrigued police, and especially Senior Detective Piggott, who believed Ross might have been trying to shift suspicion from himself. In fact, in a supplementary statement, Ross described number 33 as a brothel. He said, 'In my opinion No. 33 is a brothel. Several men have keys to the room.'

Police might have suspected Ross and they might have collected some evidence against him but they did not get a substantial lead in their investigations until January 10. A 20-year-old prostitute named Olive Maddox was overheard saying that she had seen the dead girl in Ross's saloon on the fateful Friday afternoon, not too long before the murder. Maddox later said at Ross's trial that Alma Thirtschke had a glass in front of her on a table 'but you couldn't tell whether the contents were white or whether it was empty.' She commented to Ross at the time, 'Hello Col, she is a young kid to be drinking', with Ross replying, 'Oh, if she wants it she can have it.' Olive Maddox admitted that she went to the police only after a conversation with Ivy Matthews, who once had worked for Ross in his wine bar.

Significantly, Matthews gave evidence at the Coroner's inquest on January 26, even though she told police on January 5 that she knew nothing about the crime. Matthews told the inquest:

I was in the Eastern Arcade at 3 o'clock on the afternoon of December 30, 1922, and I saw Ross in the little room. I heard Colin laugh, and immediately afterwards he walked into the bar and passed through without speaking to me.

When he came out of the small room he parted the beaded curtains across the door and I saw a little girl sitting inside.

I noticed that she was only a child and that her hair was not exactly red. She wore a white straw hat of mushroom shape pushed well back, and I had a good look at her face.

When Ross went back to the room the girl parted the curtains and looked out.

She appeared to be a prettier girl than the one in the photograph.

She had a fresher complexion, but the general features resembled those of Alma Tirtschke. She was a little college girl about 13 or 14.

Meanwhile, police had been busy gathering other evidence. They later visited the Ross family home in Footscray, a western Melbourne suburb, later taking Ross to police headquarters. That was on January 12, a significant day in police investigations. The detectives asked Ross for two blankets that had been removed from the wine saloon after Ross vacated the premises. Ross handed the blankets over and police discovered twenty seven golden-red hairs on them. The hairs later proved to be vital evidence against Ross.

Police arrested Ross and he was taken to Melbourne jail. It was there that Ross met Sydney John Harding, who was waiting trial on a shopbreaking charge. Harding had skipped bail in Sydney and was arrested in Melbourne on January 9, just five days after his arrival in Melbourne. Harding told police an incredible story, which he repeated at the inquest on January 26 and at Ross's trial. Harding declared that he struck up a conversation with Ross while walking in the remand yard. Harding said Ross told him about the girl's death, how he created an alibi and how he got rid of the girl's clothing. It was vital evidence and a great deal of interest centred on Harding at Ross's trial before Mr Justice Schutt from February 20-25.

Ross's counsel, Mr G.A. Maxwell, KC, and Mr T.C. Brennan, KC, tried to shake Harding's evidence but Harding stood firm on what he had told police. His evidence was vital. He said:

> When Ross had the girl in the cubicle, he said, he spoke to her for a few moments, and then offered her a drink of sweet wine. She at first refused it, but eventually accepted it and sipped it, and appeared to like it. He said he gave her a second glass, and gave her in all three glasses. He said about this time a woman whom he knew came to the door of the cafe, and he went and spoke to her for about three-quarters of an hour, that when she left he went back to the cubicle and the girl was asleep. About this time his own girl came to the door of the cafe, and he went and spoke to her until nearly 6 o'clock. I asked him who served his customers while he was talking to the girl. He said his brother did. I said 'Could not your brother see the girl in the cubicle when he went behind the counter to get the drinks? He said 'No, the screen was down, and when the screen was down no one dared to go into the cubicle.'

> At 6 o'clock, or a few seconds afterwards, he closed the wine cafe and went back into the cubicle. The little girl was still asleep, and he could not resist the temptation. I asked him did she call out, and he said: 'Yes, she moaned and sang out,' but he put his hand over her mouth, and she stopped and appeared to faint. After a little time she commenced again to call out, and he went in to stop her, and in endeavoring to stop her from singing out, he said, he must have choked her. He further added that 'you will hear them saying that she was choked with a piece of wire or a piece of rope, but that was not so.' He said he picked up her hand, and it appeared to be like a dead person's hand, because it fell just like a dead person's hand would do. I said to him 'I suppose you got very excited when you realised what had happened?' He said 'No; I got suddenly cool, and commenced to think.' There was a great deal of blood about he said, and he got a bucket and got some water from the tap, and washed the cubicle and around the cubicle, but seeing that, by comparison, the rest of the bar looked dirtier than the cubicle, he washed the whole lot. I asked him 'What time was this - 7 or 8?' and he said 'Yes about that time.' I said 'Was it before you met your girl?' He said 'Yes,' that he had time to clean himself and go for a walk around the town before meeting his girl. I asked him

did he meet his girl, and he said he did. I said 'You took a risk, didn't you, in meeting her?' He said 'No, I would have taken a bigger risk had I not met her, because I would have had a job to prove my whereabouts.' I said 'Could not she see the girl when she went into the wine cafe?' He said 'No, we had our drink in the parlour.'

He said he took his girl home at half-past 10, and caught the twenty to 11 train to Footscray. When he got to Footscray he got on to the electric tram for his home. Whilst on the tram he created a diversion so as to attract the attention of the passengers and conductor, so that he could have them as witnesses to prove an alibi. I asked him if he went home, and he said 'Yes.' I said 'Did you come back to Melbourne by car?' He said 'No,' that he had a bike. I said 'Have you a push bike of your own?' He said 'No, but a man I know, who lives near us, had a push bike, and I know where it is kept.' I said 'Did you go straight into the Arcade?' He said 'Yes.' I said 'But the gates are locked there at night.' He said 'Yes, but I have a key.' I said 'When you went to the Arcade did you go straight in and remove the body? He said 'No. I went in and took the girl's clothes off,' that he went out and walked around the block to see if there was anybody about, that he came back and rolled the body in a coat or an overcoat—I don't know which—and carried it to the lane. I asked him was he going to put it in the sewer, and he said he did not know. I said 'Did you not know there was a sewer there?' He said he did, but he heard somebody coming, and he went from the lane into Little Collins Street, and saw a man coming down from the Adam and Eve Hotel.

He added that, if they tried to put that over him, he would ask what the old bastard was doing there at 1 o'clock in the morning. I said 'Where did you go then?' He said he went back to the cafe. I asked him what he did with the clothes. He said he made a bundle of them, put them on his bicycle, and rode to Footscray, that when he got to the first hotel on the Footscray Road he got off the bicycle and sat on the side of the road and tore the clothing into strips and bits. He went round with the bicycle and distributed the strips and bits along the road, and when he came to the bridge crossing the river he threw one shoe and some of the strips into the river, and then distributed more strips, and went down the road and down Nicholson street to the Ammunition Works, to the river, and threw the other shoe and some more strips in. He then went back and got his bicycle and rode home to bed.

It was an astonishing account, doubly important because Harding had been in Sydney at the time of the murder and could not have read a great deal about the crime. He could not have read the Melbourne newspapers in great detail because he was detained at Melbourne jail. The reference to Ross strewing the dead girl's clothes around Footscray proved vital. Ross's defence would have liked nothing better than to be able to prove that no clothing was discovered in the area, strongly suggesting that the strewing of the clothes around Footscray was little more than a story. However, some clothing was found, and it was positively identified.

The clothing was found by Mrs Violet May Sullivan as she was walking down Footscray Road on January 26. Mrs Sullivan later read about Harding's account and decided to go back the next day and get the piece of blue serge she spotted on the road. She handed the serge over to local police and the dead girl's aunt identified the material in court. The evidence was not particularly convincing but it was more than enough.

However, the most damaging evidence against Ross was the discovery of the twenty-seven hairs on the two blankets police took from Footscray. Government analyst Mr Charles Price told the court at Ross's trial that the hairs discovered on the blankets were identical to those taken from the dead girl. Asked by defence counsel if he believed the hairs came from the same head, Mr Price replied, 'I am'. Defence then suggested that the hair could have come from Ross' sister or Gladys Linderman, Ross' friend. However, Mr Price disagreed with this, but his evidence was guarded.

The evidence, although largely circumstantial, seemed overwhelming. Ross did not help his own case by suggesting, against his counsel's wishes, that he had been framed by police. Mr Maxwell and Mr Brennan produced twelve witnesses supporting Ross' alibi. Ross' mother, Mrs Elizabeth Campbell Ross, even said that Ross left home after lunch on December 30, returning to Footscray at 7 p.m. for tea. Yet Alma Tirtschke died between 7 and 8 p.m. that day, according to medical evidence. Ross took the witness stand himself, subjecting himself to cross-examination. He did not waiver from his claim that he knew nothing of the girl's death.

Ross was found guilty of murder at the end of his trial on February 25. Asked if he wanted to say anything before sentence was passed, Ross replied, 'Yes sir. I still maintain that I am an innocent man, and that my evidence is correct. My life has been sworn away by desperate people.' Mr Justice Schutt then sentenced Ross to death. Ross immediately declared, 'I am an innocent man.'

Appeals to the State Full Court and the High Court of Australia failed. Ross was due to hang on April 24, State Cabinet turning down a request for time to appeal to the Privy Council. Ross was hanged shortly before 10 a.m. on April 24, spending his last hours in the company of two ministers of religion.

Ross was able to make one final statement as he waited for the noose to be pulled tight around his neck. He said, 'I am now face to face with my Maker. I swear by Almighty God that I am an innocent man. I never saw the child. I never commited the crime and I don't know who did it. I never confessed to anyone. I ask God to forgive those who swore my life away, and I pray God to have mercy on my poor, darling mother and my family.' Ross also wrote his mother a note from the death cell. It read, 'Goodbye, my darling mother and brothers. On this, the last night of my life, I want to tell you that I love you all more than ever. Do not fear for tomorrow, for I know God will be with me. Try to forgive my enemies—let God deal with them. I want you, dear mother, and Ronald, to thank all the friends who have been so kind to you and me during our trouble. I have received nothing but kindness since I have been in jail. Say goodbye to Gladdie for me, and I wish her a happy life. Dear ones, do not fret too much for me. The day is coming when my innocence will be proved. Goodbye, all my dear ones. Some day you will meet again your loving son and brother. COLIN.'

Mr T.C. Brennan (later Dr Brennan) was so convinced of Ross's innocence that he wrote a book about the case. Significantly, it was titled 'The Gun Alley Tragedy', Brennan leaving no doubt that he believed Ross to be as tragic a figure as poor Alma Tirtschke. The book was subtitled 'A Critical Examination of the Crown Case, with A Summary of the New Evidence'. The book was published not long after Ross was executed. The book has an incredible appendix, telling of a letter Ross received while waiting for death. The letter read:

'Colin C. Ross, Melbourne Gaol.

You have been condemned for a crime which you have never committed, and are to suffer for another's fault. Since your conviction you have, no doubt, wondered what manner of man the real murderer is who could not only encompass the girl's death, but allow you to suffer in his stead.

My dear Ross, if it is any satisfaction for you to know it, believe me that you die but once, but he will continue to die for the rest of his life. Honoured and fawned upon by those who know him, the smile upon his lips but hides the canker eating into his soul. Day and night his life is a hell without the hope of reprieve. Gladly would he take your place on Monday next if he had himself alone to consider. His reason, then, briefly stated, is this: A devoted and loving mother is ill a shock would be fatal. Three loving married sisters, whose whole life would be wrecked, to say nothing of brothers who have been accustomed to take him as a pattern. He cannot sacrifice these. Himself he will sacrifice when his mother passes away. He will do it by his own hand. He will board the ferry across the Styx with a lie on his lips, with the only hope that religion is a myth and death annihilation.

It is too painful for him to go into the details of the crime. It is simply a Jekyll and Hyde existence. By a freak of nature, he was not made as other men ... This girl was not the first ... With a procuress all things are possible ... In this case there was no intention of murder—the victim unexpectedly collapsed. The hands of the woman, in her frenzy, did the rest.

May it be some satisfaction to yourself, your devoted mother, and the members of your family to know that at least one of the legion of the damned, who is the cause of your death, is suffering the pangs of hell. He may not ask your forgiveness or sympathy, but he asks your understanding.'

Brennan commented, '(The letter) bore on its face some suggestion of genuineness. No one, of course, can say definitely but the letter may perhaps be given as possessing some public interest.'

Dr Brennan died convinced of Ross' innocence. It is not the purpose of this book to suggest one way or the other as to Ross' guilt.

However, there was a £1000 government reward, with a pro rata £250 offer from the Melbourne Herald, for information on the murder. That £1000 was distributed as follows,

> Ivy Matthews, £350; Sydney John Harding, £200; Olive Maddox, £170; George Arthur Ellis, £50; Joseph Dunstan, £50; David Alberts, £30; Madame Ghurka, £25; Maisie Russell, £25; Blanche Edmonds, £20; Muriel Edmonds, £20; Violet Sullivan, £20; Michaluscki Nicoli, £20; Francisco Anselmi, £20.

Ross might well have been referring to the reward money when he mentioned that his life had been 'sworn away by desperate people.' Who knows?

A BIRTHDAY IN COURT

Young Michael Anthony Curran, just 15, was so unhappy at home that he wanted to join the navy. The boy had had frequent rows with his policeman father, sometimes suffering physically for his trouble. Michael's father, 38-year-old Clifford James Curran, wanted his son to stay at school. They argued about the boy's career on the night of April 14, 1969, also arguing about the boy eating his food too fast. It was all too much for Michael, who later went to his parents' bedroom, stabbed his father with a bread knife and later slashed his mother with the same knife. Clifford Curran died in the kitchen of the police house in the Launceston suburb of Mayfield. Mrs Doris Curran was found with stab wounds to the throat and face. She was rushed to Launceston General Hospital and later recovered from her wounds.

Michael Curran was charged with the murder of his father and stood trial at the Launceston Supreme Court in July, 1969. Michael, who turned 16 on the second day of his trial, admitted stabbing both his father and mother, although he made an original statement to police claiming that his mother had stabbed his father. A second alleged statement, read to the court by Detective Sergeant B.J. Morgan said Curran intended killing his father. Curran allegedly wrote, 'He was always hitting me and growling at me, and often hit Mum, too.'

Mrs Curran told the court that her son and husband 'did not get on'. She told of an argument on the night of her husband's death and how her husband had been brutal to the children. She said Clifford Curran kicked or punched Michael almost every day, was almost as violent to daughter Julie, 13, but not so violent towards Michelle, 5. Mrs Curran said that after her husband was stabbed in bed he staggered to the kitchen. She said, 'He took two or three steps into the kitchen and collapsed and then I saw blood everywhere … he said nothing after that. I put something under his head and went across to the public telephone to ring for help.' Mrs Jennings then said that she was stabbed while in the telephone box but did not see who stabbed her. 'I never saw Michael with a knife at any time', she said.

Mrs Curran said she and Michael went back to the house. She said, 'I started to talk to him, and he calmed down. When he saw his father lying on the kitchen floor he said, "Oh God, what have I done?" Then Julie opened the kitchen door and screamed when she saw her father, and Michael took her to his room so she would not wake up Michelle.' Mrs Curran said Michael then rang for police and an ambulance.

Michael Curran, who pleaded not guilty, told the court from the witness box that his father threatened to kill him several times a year. He also said that his father often punched and kicked him. He also said that on the night of his father's death his father had held a bread knife at his throat and threatened to kill him if he did not do well in examinations. Questioned by Solicitor-General Mr R.C. Jennings prosecuting, Michael said that the look on his father's face made him believe the threat would be carried out. Mr Jennings asked, 'Did you decide the only thing to do was stab your father?', and Michael Curran replied, 'I didn't know what to do. I was so mixed up and worried'.

The professor of psychiatry at the University of Tasmania, Professor A.S. Henderson, told the court that Curran was suffering from a psycho-mental illness called depression and an abnormal personality which had its origin in the defective model of his father. Professor Henderson said the illnesses led Michael to the impluse to kill his father, being psychotic at the time of the stabbings. Mrs Curran had told the court that her son had fractured his skull in an accident three years earlier. Michael had suffered headaches and dizziness since then, and had been unable to concentrate.

Mr Justice Neasey told the jury that they had three alternatives —guilty, not guilty or not guilty but insane. The jury retired for almost four hours and then returned the verdict—not guilty on the grounds of insanity. Mr Justice Neasey told Michael Curran, 'Having regard to the jury's verdict and the provisions of the criminal code, I order that you be kept in strict custody in Her Majesty's jail at Risdon until Her Majesty's pleasure be known'. Michael Curran embraced his mother as he was led away.

THE TAMAM SHUD RIDDLE

A simple headstone in the West Terrace cemetery, Adelaide, says simply, 'Here Lies The Unknown Man Who Was Found At Somerton Beach—1st Dec 1948'. The body of a middle aged man was buried in the grave in June, 1949, more than six months after the body was discovered on the Somerton sands. The body had been embalmed and this more than anything else suggested that South Australian police were not willing to give up easily on the mystery, known either as the Somerton Sands Mystery or The Tamam Shud Riddle. The body was embalmed so that it could be examined on exhumation at some future date, if necessary. It was said at the time the body was buried that the body would be well preserved for many years. However, there has been no lead in police investigations to warrant an exhumation. The mystery remains. Police do not know who the man was, exactly how he died, or even very much about the mystery man. It is one of Australia's most baffling mysteries. In fact, the Somerton man might not have been murdered at all. However, the mystery surrounding his death and findings at the Coroner's inquest suggest that the case would not be strictly out of place in a book on murder.

The mystery developed on December 1, 1948, when Adelaide jeweller Mr John Lyons was walking along Somerton beach. Mr Lyons had been on the beach the previous night and had noticed a man slumped against the esplanade steps. Mr Lyons was shocked to see the man still there the next morning. In fact, the man was dead and police were called. Mysterious circumstances arose almost immediately, police failing to find any marks on the body, no scuffle signs or anything to suggest a crime. The man could easily have sat down and died of a heart attack. However, police were baffled by another aspect of the body's discovery. There was nothing to identify the dead man—no letters, no passport, no note. There were only one or two clues. One, discovered later, was a tiny scrap of paper bearing the words 'Tamam Shud'. Police had no idea what this meant and originally believed it was part of a foreign language. However, police were more concerned at that stage with the cause of death and one peculiar aspect—name tags had been removed from the clothes, presumably by the man himself before death.

The body was examined at the Adelaide morgue by Dr John Dwyer, a vastly experienced pathologist. Dr Dwyer was struck by the man's superb physical condition. The victim was about 45, 5 ft. 11 in., strongly built and apparently in perfect health before death. All organs were normal and Dr Dwyer concluded that death was caused by heart failure but that itself presented another mystery.

What caused a healthy man's heart to fail? Deputy Government Analyst Robert Cowan made tests to trace poison but could not produce any positive results. Dr Dwyer told the inquest in June, 1949, 'I believe that poison caused death, although it could not be found on analysis.' Cowan said, 'If any of the poisons for which I tested were the cause of death, they would not be absent from the body if they were taken by mouth ... I do not think common poison was responsible for death. Offhand I am not aware of poisons which can cause death but decompose in the body so that they are not discoverable on analysis. I think death is more likely to have been due to natural causes than to poisoning.'

Police seemed to run into dead-ends wherever they turned. There was no scar on the body (which was highly unusual for a man of about 45) and there were absolutely no clues as to the man's identification—except for the scrap of paper and police were left with the words 'Tamam Shud'. Meanwhile, police sent the following description to every police station in Australia, 'Seeking identity of man, about 40-50, 5 ft. 11 in., well built, clean shaven, fair hair, slightly grey at temples, hazel eyes, wearing grey and brown double-breasted coat, brown trousers, socks and shoes, brown knitted pullover, white shirt, red, white and blue tie.'

Meanwhile, police concentrated on their Tamam Shud clue, police being told that the words were from Omar Khayyam's 'Rubaiyat'. The words meant 'The End', having macabre significance for the Somerton man. The translation of the words led to one of the very few police breakthroughs in the case.

An Adelaide doctor contacted police to tell them that he had found a copy of the 'Rubaiyat' on the back seat of his car after he had parked near Somerton beach on the night of November 30. Police examined the book and careful study showed that the piece of paper taken from the Somerton man fitted perfectly in a gap torn from a page in the book found in the doctor's car. This strongly suggested that the man knew he was going to die. Why else would he place the words meaning 'The End' in his pocket? Police reasoned that this was the man's way of saying that death was near. However, the book found by the doctor held one other vitally significant clue. A series of capital letters was pencilled on the last page of the book, possibly signifying a code. The letters were,

MRGOADARD

MTBIMPANETP

MLIABOAIAQC

ITTMTSAMSTGAB

There was a cross over the capital O in the third line. What did it all mean? Police called in code experts and even the public had an attempt at cracking the code. One man suggested that the last line was the name of an Indian ship. Another suggested the following,

'Wm. Regrets. Going off alone. B.A.B. deceived me, too. But I've made peace and now expect to pay. My life is a bitter cross over nothing. Also I am quite confident this time I've made Tamam Shud a mystery.

St. G.A.B. (or signature G.A.B.)'

None of the suggestions helped police identify the Somerton man and police were left with two paths of investigation.

Firstly, police were told by a tailoring expert that the man's clothes had been made in America, strongly suggesting that the Somerton man was American. The expert said the clothes were not imported and was adamant that they were American. He said that the stitching was uniquely American. This narrowed investigations only slightly but even American police could not help. Secondly, police discovered a suitcase at the Adelaide railway station. It contained clothes matching the Somerton man's clothes in size. The suitcase also contained a dressing gown, scissors and a dry cleaning mark on a pair of trousers. Police thought the dry cleaning marks would help end their search but even investigations in other states led nowhere.

The suitcase also contained a laundry bag and police discovered the name 'Keane' printed on it. Other clothing bore the name T. Keane, or Kean. This strongly suggested that the man's name was Keane, or Kean, but again police ran into a dead-end. Members of the public tried to help police in their investigations and a number of 'positive identifications' were made. However, none proved accurate. Police at various times were told that the Somerton man came from Darwin, or that he was a missing husband. Superintendant W.O. Sheridan told the inquest that he had received a letter from a Mrs P. Bailey in Mildura saying that she believed the body to be that of her husband, who left Mildura the previous October for eye treatment. None of the identifications or leads proved positive.

Coroner T.E. Cleland concluded that murder could not be ruled out, and commented that (1) The identity of the man was unknown, (2) Death was not natural, (3) Death was probably caused by poison, and (4) It was almost certain death was not accidental. Coroner Cleland concluded that there was not sufficient evidence to warrant a finding. The riddle was no closer to solution, despite massive police investigations and an exhaustive coroner's inquest. The man's body was buried, along with the mystery. The South Australian Grandstand Bookmakers' Association paid for the funeral and an Adelaide mason provided the headstone. However, police later noticed that a 'woman in black' placed flowers on the grave in the first week of December each year. The woman placed the flowers at dead of night, knelt, prayed and disappeared. Police thought they might have at last a real lead but after interviewing the woman, who claimed to have known the Somerton man, police were convinced she was mistaken. So, the riddle remains. Who was the Somerton man, and how did he die?

THE BABY FARMER

Australia has had more than its share of revolting murders, enough to turn the stomach of the average man in the street. However, undoubtedly one of the most horrifying Australian murder cases surely must be the case of the 'baby farmer', Frances Knorr, whose victims could not defend themselves. Mrs Knorr, who must have been a true ghoul, was hanged in 1894 after being found guilty on three counts of murder. However, newspaper and other reports of the time suggest that Frances Knorr might have been responsible for the death of thirteen babies.

To understand the Frances Knorr case it is vital to understand the morals of the late Victorian era. It was a truly hypocritical era, with the family and mother all but sanctified. Nothing wrong with that, except that underneath that pious sanctity was a powerful and extensive flow of immorality. Men had their mistresses, young women could be bought for a couple of quid and brothels and bordellos flourished. It seemed that the moral ethic of the period was to look and sound highly moral but get away with what you could on the sly. Certainly, one of the greatest sins of the late Victorian era was to be an unmarried mother. This brought disgrace on the mother and her family. It was to be avoided at all cost, even if it meant having the baby and then disowning it.

These moral conditions helped a number of women establish homes for unwanted babies and children. Unmarried mothers (or their embarrassed families) would pay for the care and attention of the unwanted babies. Most of these homes for unwanted children were well above suspicion, sticking to the letter of the law. However, Frances Knorr saw the opportunity to make easy money. She took control of the babies but, to save costs, she also got rid of them. That was what led to her hanging. Frances Knorr (nee Thwaites) was born and bred in London, her father sending her to the Australian colonies after trouble at home. Frances established a police record for larceny soon after her arrival in the colonies and later married another petty criminal, Rudolph Knorr. The baby farming was about to start.

The Knorrs had had their share of marital problems, including the jailing of Rudolph Knorr and Frances' affair with a young man. However, these 'upsets' were soon forgotten in a reconciliation and Frances Knorr started taking in young children for care and lodging. Frances Knorr had joined the Victorian racket of taking money from innocent young mothers and pretending to look after the babies. At this stage the Knorrs lived in a small house in the inner Melbourne suburb of Brunswick. However, Frances Knorr had to be smart and stayed one step ahead of the mothers. It was necessary to shift house frequently. Frances Knorr did this but she did not shift far enough quick enough.

Soon after moving out of a house in Moreland Road, Brunswick, the new tenant decided to pursue his hobby of gardening. He took his spade into the garden and started to dig. Tragically, Frances Knorr had been doing her own digging several months beforehand. The tenant's spade unearthed a baby's body, the tiny victim having been battered to death. Police were called immediately and another two bodies were discovered in shallow graves in the garden. Meanwhile, Frances Knorr and her husband had fled to Sydney. However, police soon traced the missing couple to a rented house in the suburb of Surry Hills. Frances Knorr, now beside herself with worry and anxiety, was taken back to Melbourne to stand trial for murder.

Frances Knorr at first insisted that she had not killed the babies. She even wrote a letter to her lover, a man named Edward Thompson, telling him what to say in evidence. She implored, 'For God's sake be careful, think of me and my two little ones.' Frances Knorr, the mother of two little children, was desperately worried that she would get a death sentence. She believed that at 26 she was far too young to die, especially at the end of the hangman's rope. Frances Knorr's trial was a sensation. Crowds fought to get a glimpse of the accused woman and newspapers gave her a terrible time. In fact, Frances Knorr must have known that public opinion was violently against her well before the jury's verdict was handed down.

Frances Knorr insisted at the trial that she had not killed any babies. She told the court that she knew nothing of killing the babies but hinted that a mysterious man referred to as the 'dark man' knew far more than she did. Frances Knorr also tried to implicate Thompson but to no avail. Frances Knorr was sentenced to death and was due to hang at the Old Melbourne jail on January 15, 1894. And that was sensation enough in the colony of Victoria. No woman had hanged for more than thirty years, Elizabeth Scott being executed in November, 1863. Late Victorian morality led to public demonstrations against the Knorr sentence and it was widely expected that the sentence would be commuted. However, the sentence stood and even Frances Knorr started to believe that she would hang after all. Demonstrations continued but the colonial Cabinet could not be moved.

Frances Knorr, knowing that she would die, eventually confessed to killing three babies. She said she suffocated two of the babies and strangled the other. She said, 'I express a strong desire that ... my fate will not only be a warning to others but also act as a deterrent to those who are perhaps carrying on the same practice.' That last sentence must have sent shivers up and down the spine of everyone in Melbourne. The question was raised, 'How many other woman are killing babies and children placed in their care?' No one would ever know.

Frances Knorr quietly prepared herself for death but the hangman could not accept that he would have to pull the switch on a woman. The hangman, Thomas Jones, was typical of many men of his era. He believed that a woman, and especially a mother, was above such things as execution. He just could not face the fact that he would play the final part in the execution of a woman and a mother. Jones drowned his anguish in liquor and went on an absolute 'bender' a few days before the execution date of Monday, January 15, 1894. Jones was found on the Saturday morning with his throat slit from ear to ear. He had suicided, dreading the thought of sending Mrs Knorr to her death. Jones preferred death himself. However, Jones' last act did not save Frances Knorr, sensation after sensation following her along every step to the gallows.

It was reported after Frances Knorr's hanging, on time with an assistant hangman, that she had sang a popular ditty as she walked along death row. Nothing was further from the truth. Frances Knorr, now fully repentant, sang hymns as she went to her death. However, her public image was so low that most people wanted to think of her as an unfeeling monster. Frances Knorr's crimes might have been terrible in the extreme but she at least made full repentance for these crimes.

THE SWIMMER WHO DROWNED

When Tattslotto agent Ian Freeman drowned at the Cairn Curran Reservoir, near Bendigo, in November, 1996, his adult children reacted with disbelief. Son Paul and daughter Claire kept asking themselves how their father could have drowned in water less than a metre deep. After all, he was a strong swimmer and a proficient and experienced windsurfer.

Despite problems Paul and Claire had with their stepmother, an autopsy at the Bendigo Hospital revealed that Freeman indeed had drowned and that seemed the end of the matter. Sue Freeman had arranged for her husband's body to be cremated, without even discussing it with her stepchildren. Then, to compound problems, Sue Freeman told Paul and Claire that there would be a small private funeral with only a handful of guests.

This horrified Paul and Claire, who eventually discovered their father's most recent will, made three months before his death. This will named them as his beneficiaries and they eventually had their own way, with a well-attended funeral service. Sue Freeman was furious, but there was nothing she could do about it.

Then, the day after Freeman's funeral, a woman contacted Bendigo police with the amazing claim that Sue Freeman had been asking local identities whether they could have her husband killed. The woman even gave police a name — Ian Richard Brown — and said he knew something about Freeman's death.

Police launched an immediate investigation, but were partly stymied by Freeman's cremation the previous day and had to rely on the original pathology report that death was caused by asphyxia, or drowning. To make matters worse, there were no photographs of Freeman's body at the hospital as the mortuary camera had been sent away for repairs.

However, police did have a photograph of Freeman's Mitsubishi Colt car hanging over a ledge above shallow water and another photograph of the body immediately after it was discovered on the morning of November 29. These photographs, in conjunction with the telephone call they had received, finally made police extremely suspicious that a murder had been committed.

Police therefore contacted Brown, who told them Sue Freeman once had told him she wanted her husband killed. She even asked if he knew anyone who would murder her husband. She wanted rid of him because, she told Brown, he no longer showed interest in her and, besides, she suspected him of giving Paul and Claire Tattslotto 'scratchy' tickets.

Brown told police he then came into contact with Greek motor mechanic Emmanuel Chatzidimitriou, who was known as Max Chatz, and told him about Sue Freeman's determination to have her husband killed. Chatz was interested, for a $10,000 down-payment and another $40,000 on completion of the job.

Chatz and Sue Freeman met to discuss 'business' and, on the night of November 28, he launched his murderous plan. Ian Freeman, who also worked at the Adult, Community and Further Education Regional Council, left this job at close of business and arrived at the Tattslotto agency to relieve his wife just before 7pm.

Freeman, according to security records, left the shop at 9.39pm and was not seen alive again. Chatz, it later was argued in court, abducted Freeman at gunpoint and forced him to drive his Mitsubishi to the reservoir. Chatz then tied his victim's hands behind his back, pushed him into the back of the car and drove it into the water. It also was claimed in court that Chatz told a prisoner while on remand that he pulled Freeman out of the car and then held his head under water until he was dead. Freeman's hands then were untied and the body floated on top of the water.

Meanwhile, police had to prove their case and their whistle-blower was a self-confessed drug addict — hardly an auspicious start to their case in proving murder. Police therefore interviewed Brown and after he gave them details of the Freeman-Chatz pay-for-murder arrangement, launched an under-cover operation.

Brown subsequently had several meetings with Sue Freeman, all taped. Finally, Brown met up with Chatz and, despite the motor mechanic frisking him, Brown managed to hide a bugging device. Police arrested Chatz on February 14, 1970, and four days later, Sue Freeman and her solicitor went to the police.

Neither Chatz nor Sue Freeman made any admissions, but police were able to build a strong case, especially as they found money in a drawer at Chatz's home. However, Chatz insisted that, in fact, Brown had killed Ian Freeman. Eventually, Chatz and Freeman went to trial separately for murder, Chatz in Bendigo and Freeman in Melbourne. Both were found guilty of murder.

Freeman, at her plea hearing, was portrayed as a hard-working woman whose husband had been violent towards her. However, Justice Hempel said: 'This is not a case of a desperate, trapped woman or a case of highly emotionally charged circumstances in which some people react and kill ... This is a case of a plan to kill, when each of you had ample time to realise and reconsider what you were about to do.'

Chatz and Freeman each were sentenced to 22 years' jail, with a minimum parole period of 17 years.

THE SKATING GIRL MURDER

Michelle Allport was no ordinary roller skater. When Michelle, 13, pulled on her white skating boots a transformation came over her. She concentrated on her skating and was oblivious to everything around her. Michelle was so good at her sports hobby that she became the New South Wales Under 13 roller skating champion. However, little Michelle was never able to prove her self in senior company. She was strangled and buried in a bush grave after disappearing from a roller-skating rink at Mittagong on November 1, 1974.

Michelle had gone to the rink in a shopping centre, with her brother Philip already waiting for her inside the centre. Philip saw Michelle briefly, the 13 year-old Bowral High School girl telling her brother that she would be back soon. That was 8 p.m. and Michelle was not seen alive again. She did not return home that night and her father, Mr William Allport, reported to police that his daughter was missing. Police interviewed children and others who were at the skating centre that night but Michelle had simply disappeared. Police intensified their search the next day, a Saturday, but did not have immediate luck.

The first break came on the Sunday when Michelle's brother-in-law found part of Michelle's yellow slacks near a road outside Mittagong. Police, sensing that they were close to solving the mystery disappearance, checked out a bush track about three miles from Mittagong. Their worst fears were realised when they discovered a bush grave about two miles along the track. The grave had been concealed by heavy timber. A post mortem showed that Michelle had been strangled. Police working on the case said they had been lucky in tracing Michelle's body so quickly, and said that they believed the killer had virtually left signs telling them where to find the body. Police said that a chainsaw had been used to cut down several trees which had been used to cover the bush grave. The killer also threw three logs and branches over the grave before trying to set them alight. The grave virtually was 'marked' for police, who otherwise might have had difficulty in making their gruesome discovery. Michelle's battered body was partly burnt in the blaze.

Michelle was buried at the Bowral cemetery on November 7, on the same day that police charged Bowral laborer Kenneth William Johnstone with murder. At the commital hearing at Moss Vale Court, Detective-Sergeant A. McDonald alleged that Johnstone, 36, had admitted strangling Michelle. Detective-Sergeant McDonald told the court that Johnstone had said to him, 'I did kill Michelle. I have been having an affair with her for eighteen or nineteen months. Last Friday she told me she was pregnant and I could not face that at her age or mine. So I strangled her with a bit of rope and tried to burn her. But she would not burn so I buried her.'

Johnstone, who knew the Allport family well, having holidayed with them in several parts of New South Wales at various times, pleaded not guilty at the Central Criminal Court. However, the 12-man jury took only one and a half hours to find Johnstone guilty after a seven-day trial. Johnstone was sentenced to life imprisonment.

THE BODY BEHIND
THE FIREPLACE

A Melbourne newspaper report of mid-1979 stated that the occupiers of a cottage in Andrew Street, Windsor, believed it was haunted. The cottage was the site of one of Australia's most sensational early murders and this could have accounted for any haunting, either by the murderer or the victim. The little weatherboard cottage had had a grim reputation for more than eighty years and residents of Melbourne at the end of the nineteenth century often went out of their way to get a glimpse of the cottage.

The murderer was Frederick Deeming, an English con-man and adventurer. His victim was his 'wife', a Miss Emily Mather. However, there were other murders, although several of the murders alleged against Deeming were never proven. Certainly, he murdered his family in England, and that eventually convinced colonial Melburnians that Deeming was a 'monster'. Allegations of murders in South Africa remain allegations only, although bodies were discovered in houses Deeming occupied.

Deeming was one of those characters who could never settle into an ordinary lifestyle. He was a wanderer, always on the move and always on the alert for a quick return for minimal effort. He swindled banks and businesses and always seemed most reluctant to earn an honest living. He was a liar and had several aliases, moving between several countries on several continents. However, there seemed nothing in Deeming's early life to suggest that he would swing from the gallows.

After more than thirty years of a wanderer's life, Deeming settled into a cottage at Rainhill, Merseyside, with his wife and children. However, Deeming started leading a double life and courted Miss Mather. It was obvious that he was heading for matrimonial trouble. His solution was to rid himself of his family—by murdering them and burying their bodies under the kitchen floor. Miss Mather, who did not know that Deeming was married, agreed to marry the scoundrel and settle with him in Australia.

The two sailed for Australia in 1891 and arrived in the summer of 1891-92. They settled into the cottage at Windsor but it was obvious to neighbours that the 'new chums' were far from being a happy couple. 'Mrs Drewen', as she was known to neighbours, always looked miserable. Suddenly, she disappeared. Deeming and Miss Mather had stayed at the cottage only a couple of weeks. Deeming left in early January and no one saw Miss Mather after his departure.

Deeming headed for Sydney and lived there under several names. It was under one of his assumed names that he met another woman who was willing to marry him. However, fate intervened. The new occupiers of the Windsor cottage complained about the smell, which seemed to come from behind the fireplace. This was kicked in and Miss Mather's decaying body was revealed.

Police did not take long to grab Deeming. He was inexpert at covering his tracks and even left a calling card bearing his old Rainhill address. The bodies in the Rainhill cottage were discovered but Deeming was charged only with the murder of Miss Mather and faced trial in Melbourne.

His appearance at the trial was sensational. Crowds fought to see the 'monster' and Melbourne had its very own villain to boo and hiss. Deeming was extremely unpopular and was expected to swing for his crime. He was found guilty of murder, despite pleading insanity, and was sentenced to death. Deeming clung to his insanity plea right to the end, hoping that this would save him from the gallows. However, his 'act' found little sympathy and he was hanged on May 23, 1892.

THE HUMAN GLOVE

There have been few more gruesome murder cases in Australia than the notorious 'Human Glove' case, which was a sensation during the Depression years. The case at first looked almost impossible to solve but pieces then fell into place for police to close their files on a particularly horrible murder.

The drama unfolded on Christmas Day, 1933, the date of the body discovery alone making the case an immediate headline-catcher. The body of a middle-aged man was discovered in the Murrumbidgee River at Wagga and police immediately ran into an enormous stumbling block. The body, which had been in the water for several weeks, was so badly decomposed that facial identification was virtually impossible. The only other hope of early identification also seemed blocked when it was discovered that the skin was missing from both hands, making fingerprints impossible. Police were still trying to solve that problem when they had the luckiest possible breakthrough. They discovered a 'human glove' in the same river and immediately concluded that the 'glove' was the missing skin from the decomposed body. They were right! A policeman volunteered to use the 'glove' over his own hand for a set of fingerprints to be made, police then identifying the body.

The dead man was bushman Percy Smith, who lived with another river identity named Edward Morey. Police charged Morey

169

with murder and the whole case was expected to reach an uncomplicated conclusion. However, during Morey's trial, at which evidence was given that Smith was killed with an axe found in Morey's possession, one of the key prosecution witnesses was shot dead. The victim was Moncrieff Anderson, who was the husband of a woman in love with Morey.

Morey was found guilty of murdering Smith and although sentenced to death, the penalty was not carried out. Mrs Anderson, who claimed that her husband had killed Smith, later was convicted of manslaughter and sentenced to twenty years' jail. Mrs Anderson was trying to protect Morey by claiming that her husband was the real murderer. Her bid to clear Morey only added to an already tragic case.

THE BROWN-OUT KILLINGS

No Australian city, fortunately, has known the blind, black terror of having a crazed multiple killer roaming the streets for months, perhaps years. Other large cities have known this terror. London, of course, had Jack the Ripper, probably the most infamous killer of them all. Jack the Ripper, who was never caught, terrorised London for a few months in 1888. The Ripper was responsible for the mutilation deaths of at least four women. Then there was the horrific Dusseldorf monster, Peter Kurten, who was one of the most sadistic killers in criminal history. Kurten terrorised the German city of Dusseldorf between 1925 and 1928, killing several women and attacking numerous others. Then, there was the Boston Strangler and the Axe Man of New Orleans, among others. The closest Australia went to experiencing the trauma of a mass murderer in its midst was during World War Two in Melbourne. The cases were known as the Brown-out Killings. Melbourne experienced a few weeks of wild terror in 1942. Fortunately, the killer was apprehended.

To understand the environment which spawned the Brown-out Killings it is necessary to look at life in Melbourne during the war years. Melbourne, so often described as the quietest city in the world, still could not shed its reputation of Victorian wowserism even during the years when Allied troops and servicemen poured into the city.

There were many thousands of American servicemen, easy with their money and with their ways. The Americans became enormously popular with some sections of Melbourne's female population because of their comparative wealth, easy-going nature and willingness to have a good time. The Yanks, as they were known, were willing to splash their money around. Melbourne might have been a quiet city, but the Americans knew how to liven it up. It was a time of sly grog shops, prostitution and generally relaxed moral standards. Many Australian men were overseas fighting a war and it was only natural that the girls left behind sought some form of attachment to the men left in town. The Americans were popular, nobody could deny that. They were everywhere and it was difficult for a girl not to come in contact with Americans at some time or another. The Americans, on the whole, were polite, well-behaved and sociable. There was some resentment by members of Australia's armed forces but trouble between the Australians and Americans was kept to a minimum.

Apart from the number of servicemen in the city, Melbourne was experiencing a traumatic period in its history. The war was not faring as well as everyone would have hoped and there was even talk of Japanese invasions. Melbourne was subjected to a less drastic form of the British black-outs and this became known as the 'brown- out'.

Melbourne was a dark city in the autumn of 1942, the city's residents preparing for what they believed would be a long, cold winter. It was during the autumn of 1942 that the whole brown-out killings saga unfolded. It started on the morning of May 3, 1942. The body of a middle-aged women was found in the doorway of a house in Victoria Avenue, Albert Park, a beach suburb only three miles from the heart of the city. The woman had been bashed and strangled. Part-time barman Henry Billings, who discovered the body, later said, 'At about 3 a. m. I saw an American soldier stooping in the doorway of a shop next to the hotel. He might have heard me because he got up and walked towards the corner, turning into Beaconsfield Parade. When I came to the doorway I saw what I thought was a woman lying there. I struck a match. It was a woman. She was naked. Clothes had been ripped from her body and her legs folded back. I then roused the hotel and telephoned the police.'

The police were horrified. The body was a pitiful sight, the poor woman being terribly wounded. Her legs were bruised and her left temple had been fractured. The dead woman was identified as Mrs Ivy McLeod, 40, a woman described by friends as easy-going and happy. Mrs McLeod had been visiting friends in Albert Park and was on her way home to East Melbourne, on the other side of the city. She was waiting for an all-night bus in Victoria Avenue when the killer struck. Poor Mrs McLeod did not have a chance. Police reckoned that the killer was strong, as evidenced by Mrs McKay's injuries, and possibly charming.

Police immediately launched a murder investigation and, surprisingly, had an early tip-off. Detective F.J. (Fred) Adam, in a newspaper interview many years later, said that the U.S. Army headquarters in Melbourne received a telephone call about the murder. The caller said, 'About the dame who was murdered the other night; look for a guy who walks on his hands.' The call was passed on to the investigating police but of course, the cryptic message did not make sense—at first. However, police were soon to learn a lot more about the man who 'walks on his hands'. He was Melbourne's notorious brown-out killer. And he did not take too long to strike again. In fact, he waited only another six days before taking another victim.

Police were struck by one curious aspect of Mrs McLeod's killing. The dead woman's clothing had been ripped in some sort of maniacal frenzy. Whoever had killed Mrs McLeod had done so in some sort of rage of frenzy. Police were still puzzling over the murder, pursuing their inquiries as best they could, when they were confronted with the second killing. This time the body was found almost in the heart of the city. The body, in fact, was discovered in the doorway of a residential building in Spring Street, Melbourne, on the morning of May 9. Night watchman Henry McGowan noticed a bundle in the doorway at about 5.30 a.m. and immediately investigated. His horror can be imagined as he realised that the bundle was the corpse of a woman.

Police were called and medical examination showed that the woman had been dead for about three hours. The case almost immediately reminded police officers of the Mrs McLeod killing six days earlier. The Melbourne press did not take long to make a great deal of the two murders and the public was warned to be on the lookout for the mysterious killer. One newspaper ran the story of the second body's discovery under the following headlines 'Murdered Woman Found in Doorway—Spring Street Crime is Second in Week'. Melbourne buzzed with horrified excitement. Women took greater care at night and rumours swept Melbourne that a mad killer was at large and that the two killings would be just the tip of the iceberg.

Naturally, police were worried. They noticed more than one similarity in the two killings. As in the killing of Mrs McLeod's, the second victim's clothing had been ripped. At least the killer had left a trade mark. The dead woman was identified as Mrs Pauling Coral Thompson, 32, the wife of a Bendigo police constable. Mrs Thompson had seen her husband off to Bendigo on the Friday night and later was seen in the company of an American serviceman.

Police investigating the killings now had a real lead. The only problem was that finding the killer was still a matter of searching the proverbial haystack for the proverbial needle. There were thousands of American servicemen in Melbourne, many hundreds of them on leave in the city on the Friday night. The best police lead was that the American was 'baby-faced' in a handsome sort of way. If the killer was the 'baby-faced' American, he was no baby when it came to handling women. Mrs Thompson had been brutally murdered. She had been bashed and strangled, her face a mass of bruises. Again, it appeared the killer had struck in a frenzy. Police now had to work fast to nab the killer before he could strike again and the case now became a question of time as much as anything else.

Police worked overtime in an effort to solve the brown-out-killings. The pathologist's report said of Mrs Thompson's death: 'Her death was due to pressure on each side of the neck. Considerable force was used in that pressure, probably by hands. Death was due more to nervous paralysis, because of pressure on the nerves, than suffocation or strangulation'.

A report in a Melbourne newspaper of May 15 said that every available police officer was involved in the hunt for the brown-out killer. Police left no stone unturned. Scores of American servicemen were interviewed and police called on prostitutes to report any 'clients' showing odd or peculiar behaviour. Police had several leads but nothing definite. They appeared to be on the right trail but that trail threatened to be a long, painstaking one.

But incredibly, police could have nabbed their man before he could strike again. However, that revelation was made in hindsight. Detective Adam, who was part of the investigating team, later told of a strange coincidence in the Royal Park Hotel, Queensberry Street, North Melbourne, an inner Melbourne suburb. Detective Adam was in the hotel having a beer with a couple of friends when he noticed an American serviceman 'making quite an exhibition of himself'. The American was mixing whisky, beer, aspirins and tomato sauce and gulping it down to the amusement of bar patrons. The 'baby-faced' American then started walking around the bar on his hands. Of course, the mysterious phone call to U.S. Army headquarters about 'the guy who walks on his hands' rang a bell with Detective Adam, who revealed later that he remarked, 'If this is not the bloke, I'll walk to Bourke. Let's pick him up'. Detective Adam, as he recalled later, was 'low man on the totem pole' and was overruled. The turning point probably was a spot identification by a police officer who saw the murder suspect in Albert Park the night before Ivy McLeod's body was discovered. The police officer looked at the American in the North Melbourne hotel and said, 'No, that's definitely not him'. The fact that the American walked on his hands would have been thin grounds for a police interview, so the young American was not questioned.

The killer struck for the third, and last, time on the night of May 18, nine days after his previous killing. The body of 40 year-old Gladys Hosking was discovered in Royal Park, just outside the city proper. Again, the dead woman's clothing had been ripped. The victim, who worked at the University of Melbourne as a secretary with the School of Chemistry, had been strangled.

It appeared that Gladys Hosking was on her way home to a guest house in nearby Parkville when attacked. In fact, Gladys Hosking was less than a quarter of a mile from home when her life was snuffed out. The night of Monday, May 18, was a wet, miserable night, warning Melbourne that winter was just around the corner. It appeared that Gladys Hosking was attacked early in the evening on May 18, although her body was not discovered until about 7 the next morning. A driver noticed a hat on the ground a short distance from the road. He went to investigate and discovered the body. He asked a nearby Australian serviceman to take a look and they soon realised that the woman had been murdered. They at first thought the body had been dug up from a slit trench. However, the body was too fresh and the clothes had recently been torn. Besides, the hat was on the ground not far from the body.

Police rushed to the area, realising almost immediately that the brown-out killer had struck yet again. The body was lying on its face, which was half-buried in a yellow mud slush produced by the rain on heavy clay-like soil. This lead looked highly promising, and it was, in fact, to lead directly to the brown-out killer. Because the victim's face was half-buried in the yellow slush, it was fair enough to assume that the killer would have been splattered by the mud. Again, the dead woman's clothing had been torn to the waist. There was absolutely no doubt that the woman had been the victim of the killer who had terrorised Melbourne for two and a half weeks.

Police were more desperate than ever to nail their man. Each day that passed without an arrest meant that there could be further killings. Police definitely did not want a fourth brown-out killing. However, leads kept pouring in and police were now confident that they were close to their man.

The best lead came directly from the yellow slush at Royal Park. Police were told that an Australian soldier on patrol duty at the entrance to Royal Park had intercepted an American serviceman covered in yellow mud. The American told the Australian soldier that he had fallen in a pool of mud 'across the park'. The American also said that he was with his girl. He said, 'I thought I could drink but she drank me under the table'. Police rushed to U.S. Army base Camp Pell, near the Melbourne zoo. They were armed with a swag of information and were convinced that they only had to reach out to grab their man. They were about to find the proverbial needle in the proverbial haystack. An American serviceman had provided police with exactly the information they needed and police left no doubt on their visit to Camp Pell on May 21 that they knew what they were doing and who they were after. Their prime suspect—in fact, their only suspect—was Private Edward Joseph Leonski, aged 24.

Private Leonski was an unusual character, to say the least. He was big, strong, good-looking and fairly popular. However, it appeared he had two different personalities. When sober, Leonski was quiet, unassuming and a bit of a loner. When he had been drinking he believed he was the life of the party. He was everyone's buddy and would perform at the drop of a hat. His favourite trick, as Detective Adam had seen, was to gulp down his strange concoction of whisky, beer and sauce and walk on his hands. Some of Leonski's soldier buddies found him strange and one of his friends suspected Leonski almost from the start of the killings. Leonski, baby-faced and handsome, had had an unhappy youth. His father was an alcoholic who died during a drinking bout and young Eddie became something of a mother's boy. The Leonski family had a history of trouble, both criminal and mental. A brother had been in a mental institution, while another had served time in jail. Leonski's own youth was not without incident. He had been charged in San Antonio, Texas, with rape. It was an extremely serious charge but Leonski was found not guilty. That acquittal could have meant a death sentence for three women halfway across the world.

Leonski had worked at a number of labouring jobs, including one as an assistant at a grocery store in New York. He had no plans of joining the army but fate again took a hand. He was drafted and was sent to Australia as part of a signals battalion. Leonski was an unknown in the United States but he was to become infamous in Australia, a country he had barely heard of before he was shipped across the seas. In Australia Leonski felt separated from his family, and withdrew deeper into himself. The only times he emerged from his cocoon was when he had been drinking. Then, he became loquacious, insisted on buying drinks and tried everything in his power to attract attention. Sadly, Leonski attracted the wrong type of attention in the worst possible way. He became a brown-out killer.

When detectives walked through the American camp on May 21, they strode straight to Leonski's tent. There, they found yellow mud smears. They also found the yellow mud on Leonski's clothes, even though Leonski had washed them. The yellow mud in itself proved nothing. Leonski quite rightly could have claimed that he had, indeed, fallen in the mud on the way back to camp on the night of May 18. However, police inquiries led further. The mud samples were taken to the government analyst, who proved that the mud from Leonski's tent and the mud from the trench in Royal Park were identical. Leonski already had his head in a noose, and it was about to be tightened from all directions.

At this stage Leonski tried to kid himself that he had nothing to worry about. The police had not arrested him, so he convinced himself that they just did not have enough evidence. However, the police had two trump cards and they played them expertly. Firstly, a tent mate told police that Leonski seemed to have fixations about the brown-out killings. Police were told that Leonski had read every report of the murders he could lay his hands on. He cried about the murders and even confessed. The tent mate thought Leonski's behaviour was strange, to say the least, but decided that his tent mate was a strange fellow anyway. The American tent mate did not report Leonski's antics until after the third killing. Secondly, the Australian soldier on guard duty positively identified Leonski as the young American seen covered in mud at Royal Park on the night of Gladys Hosking's murder. The identification took place at the American camp on May 22 and detectives almost immediately charged

Leonski with murder. Police were more than confident that Melbourne could relax after three terrible killings. The reign of terror was over.

Leonski's arrest created a ticklish problem for the Australian and American allies. As an American serviceman, Leonski did not appear in the criminal courts. He was claimed by the Americans and tried by court martial under an obscure agreement made in Canberra. This created legal history, in more ways than one. It was the first time that a person had been tried in Australia by military tribunal for an offence under civil law. Secondly, it was the first time that a citizen of another country had been tried in Australia under the law of his own country. Leonski's court martial was held at a building in Russell Street, Melbourne. There was enormous interest in the case, naturally, and Private First Class Eddie Leonski was something of a celebrity. He didn't have to stand on his hands to attract attention now.

There was little doubt that Leonski was guilty when police charged him with murder but that was for the court martial to decide. The young American G.I. was subjected to medical and psychiatric examinations. The medical report was that Leonski was sane. Leonski pleaded not guilty to murder. However, even Leonski must have known that he would need every bit of luck on his side to avoid conviction, and a death sentence. For one thing, Leonski had confessed to police. Leonski told them about the three killings in minute detail, even though he had been drinking quite heavily when each of the women had been murdered. Leonski's accounts of the killings make interesting even if gruesome, reading.

Leonski said he had been drinking on the night of the first killing. He met Mrs McLeod in the street. He noticed her because she had a pleasant face. Leonski spoke to Mrs McLeod and commented on her handbag, which he described as unusual. He said, 'It was a funny-looking handbag. I walked over and felt it. It was very soft. I handed it back and we talked about something. She stepped back into the doorway and I grabbed her. I grabbed her by the neck. I changed the position of my hand so that my thumbs were at her throat and I choked her. She fell and I fell on top of her. Her head hit the wall as she was falling. I started to rip her clothes. I ripped them and ripped them, but could not rip her belt, so I left it and came back to it. Then I got mad and thought "I've got to rip it" and I ripped at it and ripped at it'. Leonski then heard footsteps and ran into the darkness, his first victim dead. Leonski said he cried over that first killing, but if he did, it did not take him long to get over his fit of remorse.

Six days later Mrs Pauline Thompson, who had just seen her policeman husband off to duty in Bendigo, was seen drinking with an American serviceman in the Astoria Hotel in the city. Mrs Thompson and the serviceman (Leonski) were drinking there (illegally) until late at night. The couple left the hotel and walked towards Spring Street, only a couple of hundred yards away. Leonski said, 'She was singing in my ear. It sounded as if she was singing for me. She had a nice voice. We turned a corner. There was nobody around. I just heard her voice. Then we came to the steps. They were long steps. I grabbed her. I grabbed her—I don't know why. I grabbed her around the neck. She stopped singing. I said, "Keep singing, keep singing". She fell down. I got mad then and tore at her. I tore her apart. There was somebody coming across the street. I hid behind a stone wall. I was terrified. My heart was pounding a mile a minute. I couldn't bear to look at her'.

Leonski said he again cried, one of his friends noticing his anguish. The friend took Leonski into the city to ease his worries and anxiety, totally unaware that he was helping a killer overcome feelings of remorse. Leonski told his friend the next day that he had killed but, although the friend was almost convinced, he decided not to act. After all, Leonski was always raving on about Dr Jekyll and Mr Hyde, as well as werewolves and other horror creatures. Asked at Leonski's trial if he believed the tale of killings, the soldier replied, 'I wasn't sure, sir … murder is such an awful thing, how could I be sure?'

Leonski could not have had too much remorse for either of his first two victims because he took a third victim. Leonski had been drinking yet again, Detective Adam seeing the walking on the hands routine by the then unknown Leonski in a North Melbourne hotel. Leonski was on his way back to camp on Monday, May 18, when he came across Gladys Hosking, who was sheltering from the rain. Leonski asked if he could walk with her and the unsuspecting woman said yes. Gladys Hosking reached the point in Royal Park where Leonski could find his own way. She was near home and intended heading straight for the guest house. Leonski said, in his confession, 'She had a lovely voice. I wanted that voice. She was leaving to go to her house. I did not want her to go. I grabbed her by the throat. I choked her. She did not even make a sound. She was so soft. I thought "What have I done?" I got her to a fence and pushed her underneath and then climbed over. I pulled her by her armpits and carried her a short distance and fell in the mud. She made funny noises—a sort of gurgling noise. I thought "I must stop that sound". So I tried to pull her dress over her face'. It was lucky for the entire female population of Melbourne that Leonski fell in the mud that night.

Leonski's court martial was not as dramatic as might be imagined. There were no histrionics and only the press and invited guests were allowed to attend. However, that did not stop the case from being talked about the length and breadth of Melbourne. The name Leonski was on everyone's lips. Melbourne newspapers dutifully carried details of the court martial. When evidence that Leonski had admitted the killings was presented to the court martial, a headline read 'Leonski's Alleged Murder Admission Told—Tells of Split Personality—"Wanted" Voices.' Leonski's defence swung to one of insanity at the time of the murders, his defence counsel arguing that Leonski was perfectly behaved when sober but almost the opposite when drunk. The argument was that there was a grave doubt about Leonski's sanity and that a verdict of guilty would be a serious miscarriage of justice. It certainly was a problem and the trial was suspended for a month while three army psychiatrists, one of them Australian, determined whether Leonski was sane. The tests lasted thirty days but failed to save Leonski, who was found guilty and sentenced to death. However, there still was no certainty that

Leonski would be executed. The final decision rested with the President of the United States, President Franklin D. Roosevelt. The case was referred to the President, who confirmed that the execution was to take place.

Leonski was sentenced on August 20, 1942, but was not executed until November 9, by fellow Americans at Pentridge jail, Melbourne. A report of his execution appeared in the Melbourne Herald that day. The report read 'Edward Joseph Leonski, 24 year-old, American private and triple murderer, was hanged early this morning. Brought from his cell in the City Watchhouse in a black maria, he was driven non-stop to Pentridge Prison and taken direct to a room adjoining the scaffold in D Division. The hangman was waiting on the bridge where the drop is placed. Nearby were two U.S. doctors and a priest. The usual procedure with civil execution was carried out. Leonski came onto the scaffold and a black cap was put over his head, while his legs and hands were shackled. He maintained such an attitude of calm indifference to the end as to leave everyone associated with him aghast and amazed. Certainly no other murderer in the memory of Australian students of criminology was so obviously uninterested in his own fate.'

The Melbourne Truth carried a more bizarre account of Leonski's final moments. That report read 'Leonski was an enigma whose name will be constantly referred to by succeeding generations of psychologists. Seemingly indifferent to his own fate, always polite to his guards and visitors, he nevertheless constantly erupted with grisly humor. An official who visited Leonski at the city watchhouse where he was held awaiting execution at Pentridge prison, was greeted by Leonski with a saucy grin. "We are planning to hold a party", he was told. "Hope you can come along". "A party?" the official questioned in amazement. "Sure", Leonski said, highly amused. "A necktie party". Another official was asked by Leonski if he liked swing. The unsuspecting official answered in the affirmative. "Good", he was told. "We've got a real swing session coming up. I've been given top billing".' Leonski's body was shipped back to the United States for burial.

There are a couple of interesting footnotes to the Leonski case, one of them in relation to another murder case referred to in this book. There were suggestions after Leonski's death that he suffered from leptomeningitis, the same disease that afflicted Arnold Sodeman (See 'The Sick Killer'). This disease was suggested as the root cause of Leonski's strange urges to kill innocent women. However, Leonski was thoroughly examined by a team of medical experts, although it was true that only an autopsy would have been conclusive proof of the disease. Leonski was given various tests for organic illnesses, with a Kline test being made in case of venereal disease. The tests proved negative.

The other footnote to the Leonski case concerns one of the main characters at Leonski's trial. The man who prosecuted Leonski was 36 year-old Hayford Enwall, who, until pulled off the reserve list by the U.S. Army, had been assistant district attorney for the southern district of the State of California. Major Enwall was posted to Australia and had no sooner settled in than he was assigned the Leonski case. Major Enwall returned to the United States in 1944, with a Melbourne war-bride. As Professor Enwall, Professor of Law at Florida University, he returned to Australia for a visit in 1973 and spoke to a newspaper reporter about the Leonski case. Professor Enwall said he had doubts at first about Leonski's guilt because Leonski had always been drinking 'for a good many hours' before the killings. However, Professor Enwall said these doubts were swept aside when he interviewed the killer. Professor Enwall said, 'He (Leonski) was so clear and detailed in his answers'. Professor Enwall also said, 'It was the most vicious case I've ever been connected with. It was all so senseless and so sensational because it involved a trilogy of murders in fifteen days. The people of Melbourne were looking pretty closely at the U.S. Army. From a point of view of good relations it was necessary that the case be proved beyond doubt.'

THE SOCIETY MURDERS

Although Melbourne newspapers, particularly the Herald Sun, tagged the slaying of Margaret Wales-King and husband Paul King 'The Society Murders', it was a misleading label and, in fact, had nothing to do with cocktail parties, opening nights or even champagne.

Rather, it earned this slightly misleading tag because Mrs Wales-King was a wealthy woman who was worth more than $5 million and drove a Mercedes Benz. Also, the slain couple lived in the expensive and leafy eastern Melbourne suburb of Armadale.

Yet Mrs Wales-King and her second husband led quiet, exemplary lives. Indeed, Paul King had had two strokes and their daily lives were far from boisterous or glamorous. Indeed, family events took precedence as they settled into their golden years.

It was at one of these family gatherings that they were killed, by Mrs Wales-King's youngest son, Matthew. To all intents and purposes, it was just a normal family dinner, with Matthew and his wife Maritza as hosts at their townhouse in Glen Iris.

The evening meal was a simple affair — a first course of vegetable soup and a main course of risotto. However, there was a special ingredient, provided by Matthew Wales. He had crushed powerful painkiller and blood pressure tablets to make his guests feel drowsy.

Then, as they left the townhouse, he bludgeoned his mother and stepfather to death with a piece of pine. It was alleged at his trial that Wales first hit his mother over the back of the head and then struck his stepfather. Supreme Court Justice Coldrey told Wales: 'You followed them out the front door. Paul King was walking in front of your mother. You switched off the veranda downlight, picked up a length of wood and, wielding it with both hands, you struck your mother on the back of the neck. She was immediately rendered unconscious and fell forward onto the paved concrete surface.

'You then struck Paul King on the back of the neck because you knew it would be quick. Your purpose was to break their necks and your intention was to kill each of them.' The motive? Dissatisfaction over what Wales perceived to be her dominance in financial matters and the proposed sale of a Surfers Paradise unit.

Mrs Wales-King, who owned her Armadale home, the Mercedes Benz, antiques and jewellery, and also had substantial superannuation and shareholdings, also had made a will — with her five children (Sally, Damian, Emma, Prudence and Matthew) and husband Paul getting one-sixth each on her death.

Paul King was the elegant Margaret Wales-King's second husband. Born in 1933, Margaret Lord, had married airline pilot Brian Wales and bore him five children before moving in with King.

Matthew Wales, born in 1968, and his mother long had had rows over financial matters and it all came to a head in the lead-up to that fatal dinner on April 4. However, it all went pear-shaped for Wales as soon as he wielded that one-metre length of pine. He might have planned the killings, but his movements from there were clumsy at best.

Although the Chile-born Maritza Wales had no involvement whatsoever in the deaths of her in-laws, she saw her husband drag the bodies across the front lawn and cover them with their two-year-old son Dominik's deflated plastic pool.

That seemed to be the extent of Wales' planning and the disposal of the bodies was both ad hoc and poorly enacted, starting with the disposal of his mother's Mercedes. Wales drove the car to the seaside suburb of Middle Park, locked it and then caught a taxi. To help cover his tracks, he dropped the car keys down a drain.

But what to do with the bodies? First, he used sheets to cover his victims' faces, so he could not see their seemingly accusing expressions, placed the pool cover back over the bodies and generally made everything look like a pile of rubbish ready for removal.

On the Friday after the killings, Wales put his body disposal plan into action, starting with the rental of a motor trailer. He hitched the trailer to the back of his own vehicle and drove home. There, he wrapped each of the bodies in a doona and then bought a mattock and ordered mulch for his garden.

The following morning he loaded the doona-wrapped bodies into the trailer and headed through Melbourne's outer eastern suburbs towards the picturesque mountain resort of Marysville. Wales drove on to a track more than 20 kilometres past Marysville and started his gruesome task of burying the bodies.

He dug a grave no more than a metre deep about 20 metres away from the track, and placed his mother's body face down and his step-father's body on top. Wales then drove back to Melbourne, more hopeful than convinced the secret grave would never be discovered.

Wales, in fact, was so concerned that he returned to the grave the following Monday and not only bought and then placed rocks on the site, but added soil and the newly-delivered mulch. It was a desperate but futile attempt to prevent the grave being detected. Then, on the way back home, he pulled into a car wash and thoroughly cleaned the trailer before returning it to the hire company.

Meanwhile, other family members had tried to contact Mrs Wales-King and were becoming increasingly concerned. Wales' sister Emma on April 8 reported to police that Mrs Wales-King and her husband were missing.

The disappearance of the wealthy couple made the television news and, within the hour, Mrs Wales-King's missing Mercedes was found where Matthew Wales had left it. The mystery deepened, but police already were suspicious of Wales, especially after they noticed a distinct odour of cleaning fluid at his Glen Iris home. Also, they found traces of blood on the garage floor.

The bodies finally were discovered on April 29, almost four weeks after the killings. Bush rangers had noticed that a vehicle had been driven in a protected area and that there was a mysterious mound — the hastily-dug grave.

Police that night recovered the bodies and an autopsy revealed that both the dead had been asphyxiated and that Mrs Wales-King had suffered facial injuries. Police recovered the trailer used in the disposal of the bodies, but no charges were laid by May 8 when Wales wept at a private funeral service in Toorak, at the church where his mother had worshipped. The public memorial service was held the following day and Wales offered prayers on behalf of the mourners.

Finally, on Sunday, May 11, Wales was arrested and taken for interview by the Homicide Squad in St Kilda Road. Wales soon after confessed to the killings and was charged with murder. Wife Maritza, meanwhile, was charged with attempting to pervert the course of justice by making a false statement.

Wales was sentenced to 30 years' jail, with a minimum of 24 years. Wife Maritza was handed a two-year, wholly-suspended sentence.

DEATH OF A BEAUTY QUEEN

Frank Wilkinson could not help but be attracted to vivacious Dorothy Denzil, a slim, elegant brunette. The attraction seemed mutual and anyone who saw them together in early 1932 would have said they made an ideal young couple. Frank, 26, was very fond of 21-year-old Dorothy and he made a date with her for April 5, 1932. Frank, a printer, called for Dorothy in the Sydney suburb of Burwood and immediately headed for a picnic site in his bright red Alvis motor car. It was fine weather and the young couple expected to be back well before dark.

They did not return that night and their disappearance sparked a huge hunt in the bush area around Bankstown. Frank Wilkinson and Dorothy Denzil both came from good families and there was no suggestion that they had run away together. There seemed no need for that. Police suspected the worst, even though Frank's car could have broken down, stranding the couple somewhere in the bush. However, nagging suspicion turned to desperation for police involved when reports came in that a man in a red Alvis had been buying petrol in the area. Witnesses did not get good sightings of the man but if it had been Frank Wilkinson he would have notified someone that something was wrong. But what worried police most was that in the first sighting there was a large bundle in the back of the red Alvis. However, when the second petrol purchase was made five hours later there was no bundle. This could have meant that Dorothy Denzil had been murdered and her body dumped. But Frank Wilkinson was no killer and this police suspicion of the killing of Dorothy would have meant that Wilkinson also was dead. Police stepped up the search.

Bad weather hampered police, heavy rain washing out tyre tracks in bush roads and turning the area into a quagmire. The hunt dragged on and on, and as each day passed hope faded of anyone seeing the young couple alive again. No trace of either Frank Wilkinson or Dorothy Denzil was found for six days, Wilkinson's body eventually being discovered on April 11.

A policeman involved in the search stumbled across an old bush path and noticed blood in a clearing. To his horror, he also saw three fingers reaching grotesquely out of a dirt mound. Police swarmed to the lonely spot and Frank Wilkinson's body was soon unearthed from its shallow grave. It was a gruesome sight, even allowing for the six days in which putrefaction developed. It was obvious that Wilkinson had been bashed in the face with a heavy object and the back of his head blown apart with a shotgun round fired from point-blank range. His wounds were terrible and angered those who saw the body. Police were determined to nail the killer. But the worse fear for police was that Dorothy Denzil was still missing. There seemed little hope of finding her alive unless the killer had her bailed up in a shack in the bush.

Police combed the entire bush area but could come up with no clue of Dorothy's disappearance for another four days. Then, one of the searchers spotted a suspicious mound of freshly turned earth in a bush clearing. His suspicions were aroused because leaves placed over the mound strongly suggested they had been placed there deliberately to camouflage newly turned soil. And that, of course, could have meant a newly dug grave. Police were rushed to the scene but because the discovery of the mound was not made until late afternoon, police had to wait until the morning before examining the grave. A police guard was placed over the mound. This surely must have been one of the eeriest duties in the history of the New South Wales police force. Careful digging started in the morning and Dorothy Denzil's body was found in the shallow grave. Again, her head had been bashed in with a blunt weapon, presumably a shotgun, with the back of her head being shot away. Medical evidence showed that Dorothy, who had won a beauty contest only a few weeks before her death, had been raped.

By now police had a number of clues. The killer had been seen by a number of people in the district, the red Alvis had been found in pieces in a local garage rented by the killer (the obvious intention being to sell parts of the Alvis) and, frighteningly, the police had found a hessian mask in the garage housing the Alvis. The mask, with slits cut for the eyes, was obviously used when the killer bailed up the unfortunate couple as they were picnicking.

Surprisingly, the discovery of the mask encouraged police. It strongly suggested that the killer was a known criminal, who wore the mask to avoid identification through police files. A robbery, at least, had been planned and police were able to go to their files for identification of the man seen in Wilkinson's car. They were able to do this with a couple of trump leads. Firstly, they knew that the killer had an injured right hand, witnesses all mentioning this fact. Secondly, and more importantly, police were told that a man known as William Fletcher called to see an acquaintance on April 6, Fletcher having an injured right hand. The name William Fletcher was just the lead police had been waiting for because it was an alias used by a well-known petty criminal named William Moxley. Police now knew the identity of the man they wanted for questioning. A massive police hunt was launched, police certain that Moxley was responsible after they visited his home in Burwood. There, they found a hessian bag with a square piece missing. The mask found with the Alvis matched the hole in the bag.

Police dogs, black trackers and volunteers joined hundreds of police officers in one of the biggest manhunts in Australian history. The whole of New South Wales wanted the killer captured or killed on sight. The murders had revolted Australia and police vowed that Moxley would be captured alive so that he would stand trial for murder. A huge dragnet was thrown over the Bankstown district and police were confident that no fugitive could break through. Moxley was eventually flushed out.

Several sightings were reported and Moxley even bailed up a young woman so that he could have a meal. However, Moxley was disturbed by a caller and was forced to flee. He was desperately hungry, police and their volunteers getting closer to their man with each passing hour. The killer then stole a bicycle and boldly rode through the police net and into the heart of Sydney itself. Incredibly, Moxley got as far as Balgowlah, on the other side of Sydney. Police tracked him down and confronted him in the bush. Moxley, as desperate as ever, jumped into a gorge, a police officer jumping after him. They fought but the weakened Moxley was no match for the determined and courageous policeman. The fugitive was in the net.

Moxley stood trial in Sydney two months later and pleaded insanity. He insisted that although he had gone into the bush with the intention to rob someone, he had not planned murder or rape. He claimed that Wilkinson rushed him during the robbery and was flattened for his courage. Moxley said he then tied Wilkinson up and took the couple to a shack, Moxley claimed that when he released Wilkinson the young printer made another attack, Moxley fighting him. Moxley claimed that from that point his memory was blank. The police reconstruction of the crime was that Moxley tied Wilkinson up, bashed his face in with the shotgun and then leaned him against a tree for an execution. Dorothy Denzil's face also had been bashed in, presumably to prevent identification. Moxley's plea of insanity failed and he was hanged on August 18, 1932. There were precious few tears for William Cyril Moxley.

THE HURSTBRIDGE TORTURE MURDER

The area around Hurstbridge, north of Melbourne, has undergone a number of changes over the past quarter of a century. The area has become fashionable recently and the population is larger than it once was. The area is serviced by trains to Melbourne and many commuters now live in Hurstbridge, considered to be an outer suburb of Melbourne rather than a rural community. There are still many farms in the district but once there were only farms. One of the farmers was William John Pill who was no ordinary farmer. He lived alone hoarded money and was a man of frugal standards. Pill's money hoarding habits led to a gruesome death, described by police officers as one of the most horrible they had encountered. Pill was virtually tortured to death.

Pill, 64, was a hard-working market farmer, renowned in the Hurstbridge area for his excellent tomato crops. Pill worked hard on his land and reaped the harvest of that hard work. However, Pill had one great advantage over most other tomato growers. He had an ingenious invention that enabled him to harvest tomatoes well into autumn, much later than most farmers. Pill had perfected an alarm system from a thermometer in his tomato crop, straight to his bedroom. When the thermometer dropped to freezing point an alarm woke Pill, who would rush outside and turn over an engine which rotated an old aeroplane propellor. This in turn cleared the air of frost, enabling the tomatoes to survive almost into winter. The invention helped Pill make a great deal of money. It could have led to his death in 1958. However, there were other aspects to Pill's death.

Only a few weeks before his death he decided to sell thirteen acres of land near where he lived. Pill had been in ill-health and had decided to live with his sister-in-law Mrs Ada Pill. The old man had lived all his life in two shacks. He used one of these shacks as a kitchen, while he slept and lived in the other shack. It was a momentous decision by Pill, mainly because had had been born in one of these shacks and a shift would have meant restructuring his entire life. Pill was paid £800 for the thirteen acres, and that could have been one of the reasons he was tortured to death. However, although the sale of the land was well-known, it was not generally known that Pill's agents had received only an £80 deposit for the land, with the rest to be paid later. Pill had not seen one penny on the land deal when he was brutally killed on December 21, 1958. Whoever killed Pill obviously was after money, and plenty of it.

Pill was seen working with his tomatoes during December 21 but was not seen the following day. A neighbour, Mr Herbert Funnell, became suspicious when he noticed that a newspaper delivered to Pill was untouched. Mr Funnell, who was delivering bread, mail and another newspaper to Pill, also noticed that bread delivered to the Pill shacks was untouched. Mr Funnell said, 'The fly-wire door was closed. The inside door was wide open. I peered in and from the state of the shack I knew that something terrible had happened.' Mr Funnell ran home as fast as his legs could carry him and he telephoned Hurstbridge police. The first person to realise that Pill had been murdered was First Constable Leonard Dugdale, of Hurstbridge police. The Pill shacks were only about two miles out of Hurstbridge, on the main Kinglake Highway and it did not take long for Constable Dugdale to arrive on the scene. The main shack was in total darkness, with the blinds pulled, when Constable Dugdale entered. Pill was dead, tied to the foot of his iron bed. Clothed only in a shirt, he was bound and gagged in a kneeling position at the foot of the bed, with his head on the mattress. Constable Dugdale immediately contacted police headquarters in Russell Street and Detective-Inspector Jack Ford, from the Homicide Squad, rushed to Hurstbridge to investigate the murder.

Police were shocked by the brutality of the Pill killing. The poor old man had been viciously tortured, his killer(s) obviously seeking the hiding place for Pill's money. Pill's wounds were horrific. In fact, he had two hundred and eighty seven separate wounds or bruises on his body, a post-mortem revealed. This was no ordinary murder and police insisted that whoever killed Pill had done so in cold-blood. A police reconstruction of the murder suggested that the killers (and police believed that two men were involved) knocked on Pill's door during the night of December 21. Pill answered the door and was immediately struck by a heavy piece of wood. Police later found a broken piece of wood, one foot long and about two and a half inches wide, outside the front door. The killers had dragged the old man into the shack proper and tied and gagged him with sheets from the bed. When Pill regained consciousness, they had tortured him with incredible barbarity. The killers had obviously prepared themselves for their session of torture, Pill being lashed with a razor strop and burnt with strips of lighted sheeting. Pill must have suffered terribly, although it could not have done his torturers much good. Police later found a large cache of money hidden in the shack.

Police investigated Pill's financial standing and discovered that the old man had approximately £1700 in the Commercial Bank at Hurstbridge, with other valuable assets. These included land, a rotary hoe, tractor, utility and trailer and the engine for keeping frost off the tomatoes. In addition, Pill was to receive the £800 for the sale of his land. Police also discovered that Pill regularly banked between £50 and £120 between April and June of that year, clear evidence that Pill's ingenious anti-frost device was a money-spinner. However, police also received information that there was money hidden in the main shack. Police went to the shack on Christmas Eve and thoroughly searched every nook and cranny. They pulled out a sheet of iron at the back of the fireplace in the living room and removed two old handmade bricks. They found a cavity behind the fireplace, and it contained a flat biscuit tin, a screw-top jar and four old cocoa tins. Police found a total of £870 in these containers. This was made up of 380 £1 notes, 80 £5 notes, two 10 shilling notes, 880 florin pieces and four 5 shilling pieces. The coins contained several interesting items. Some of the florins were minted in 1927 to commemorate the opening of Parliament House in Canberra, while four of the five shilling pieces were minted in 1937. It was obvious that Pill had been a hoarder for some time. Police also believed that the cache probably was the root cause of Pill's death.

Police, in reconstructing the murder, had two theories on why the money's hiding place was not revealed. Pill had been savagely tortured and most men would have broken down in the early stages of the long torture session. However, Pill had had his larynx broken, possibly when struck on the head by the wood. This might have meant he just was not able to tell his killers where the money was hidden. He might not have been able to utter a single word, the killers not realising this and beating him all the more. Alternatively, Pill might have been bravely stubborn, resisting to the end. Whatever the case, Pill's killers eventually gave up and throttled the life out of the old man by strangling him.

Police discovered several clues, one of which was a large torch found at the front of Pill's shack. Police at first did not know whether the torch was used by the killers, or by Pill when he answered the front door on the night of December 21. However, it was later discovered that it was Pill's torch, police losing what at first appeared to be an excellent lead. Police also tried to trace a 1936 Oldsmobile or Pontiac car seen parked near the shack on the night of the murder. This clue did not help police charge anyone with murder, either. Finally, a left-foot shoe, with an unusual waffle sole, was found near the shack. Newspapers ran photographs of the shoe but again the clue proved fruitless.

Police interviewed a number of people in an effort to solve the murder mystery. However, they were never able to make a formal charge. Officially, the murder remains unsolved, although there were rumours that police had strong suspicions about the case. The entry in the police file read, 'At 10 a.m. (23-12-1958) Herbert Funnell of Cottles Bridge reported the death of Pill. He was found bound and gagged and in a kneeling position beside his bed. Pill lived alone on his farm and was reported to have large sums of money hidden in the house. He had apparently been tortured with a metal-ended razor strop and a stick to force him to disclose the whereabouts of the money. It is not known how successful the killer was, because £870 was found hidden in the fireplace.' The mysteries remain, apart from who killed Pill. Did the killer(s) find any money? Were they after the £870 cache, or were they after the £800 from the land sale.

AXED TO DEATH

When Miss Dulcie Sommerlad left her New South Wales farm home to visit her mother in January, 1939, she had no idea that she would return a few days later to a scene of absolute horror. Miss Sommerlad returned to her orchard property home on the morning of February 4 and was surprised when no one approached her with the usual family greetings. It was deathly quiet. Miss Sommerlad lived with her brother Eric, 26, and sister Marjorie, 33. Eric ran the property, while Miss Marjorie Sommerlad acted as her brother's housekeeper.

Dulcie Sommerlad opened the front door of the Tenterfield farmhouse and stepped inside. She immediately saw the blood-spattered body of her sister, and in horror and fear started calling for her brother. There was no answer. Fearing the worst, Dulcie Sommerlad immediately headed for the verandah, which her brother used as a bedroom. There, Eric Sommerlad lay on a bed, his head soaked in blood. The young farmer was not dead but critically wounded. Dulcie Sommerlad called the police and an ambulance rushed her brother to hospital, where he was admitted in a critical condition.

The murder weapon obviously was an axe, found leaning against the front of the house. It also was obvious that the brother and sister had been savagely hit with some considerable force, Miss Sommerlad dying immediately. It also was thought that her brother would not survive the axe attack. Police soon realised that farmhand John Trevor Kelly was missing, along with the Sommerlad utility. Police launched an immediate search for Kelly, 24, and notified police stationed in a wide radius of the murder scene. It was obvious that Kelly had made a 'run for it'.

Meanwhile, Kelly had driven from the northern New South Wales area to Brisbane. There, he rented himself a room in the suburb of Spring Hill. He was a wanted man, and knew it. He was too scared to venture from his room and the dragnet was so tight that he and the utility were spotted very early, police being given several leads. Queensland police took less than twenty-four hours to locate Kelly, the axe murderer soon telling a 'tale' of what happened at the farmhouse.

Kelly originally told police that Eric Sommerlad had sacked him on Friday, February 3, the sacking leading to the axe attack on Sommerlad that night. Kelly said he then attacked Miss Sommerlad in the hallway. However, Kelly later changed his account of the axings, declaring that he attacked Miss Sommerlad first. He said he made sexual overtures to Miss Sommerlad, who was engaged to be married to a local farmer, and was rejected. Miss Sommerlad called for her brother and Kelly struck her with his fists. He said he then went outside and when he returned he hit her with the axe because she was screaming. Kelly said he then attacked Sommerlad before fleeing.

Sommerlad proved doctors wrong by making a remarkable recovery from the savage axe blow to his head and later told police that he could tell them nothing of the attack. He said he was sleeping when attacked and could not give any description of the attacker. Significantly, he also denied that he had sacked Sommerlad on the Friday. This strongly suggested that Kelly's second account was the more accurate one, Kelly killing after being rejected by Miss Sommerlad.

Kelly had been drinking on the night of the murder and his plea was that of insanity. He also told the jury, 'I am sorry for what I have done'. However, Kelly was found guilty and sentenced to death.

This caused an uproar and an appeal to the State Full Court of Criminal Appeal failed to have the death penalty quashed. Kelly's next move was to ask the Full High Court of Australia for special leave to appeal. That was refused and Kelly's death penalty stood. Kelly's last chance was that State Cabinet would grant a stay of execution. Public meetings were called and a number of prominent New South Wales identities lent voice to the protests. However, Cabinet, under the leadership of Premier Alexander Mair, decided that Kelly should hang. The axe killer went to his death at the gallows in Long Bay jail on August 24, 1939.

THE DEADLY
MISTAKE

Many veteran Victorian police officers still shudder when they recall the infamous Shirley Collins murder of 1953. Shirley Collins, just 14, probably would still be alive today if it had not been for one tragic mistake. Instead, she suffered a terrible death at the hands of a monster. Worse, that monster has never been brought to justice for his savage crime. Police who worked on the Collins murder vowed they would get their man and there are plenty of police officers still desperate to nab the monster.

Shirley Collins, whose real name was Shirley Hughes, lived with Mr and Mrs Alfred Collins in the northern Melbourne suburb of Reservoir. Her real mother, Mrs Leila Hughes, shifted to Queensland and although Shirley kept in touch with her, she referred to Mrs Alfred Collins as her mother. A quiet, shy girl, Shirley took a job as a shop assistant in the city when old enough to leave school. An invitation from a store employee, Ronald Holmes, 21, to attend a party in Richmond on Saturday, September 12, 1953, was the first innocent step to tragedy.

Shirley, with Mrs Collins' blessing, accepted the invitation and Holmes arranged to meet the young girl at the Richmond station. Unfortunately, Shirley was confused about the meeting place, probably not realising that there are two rail stations bearing the name Richmond in Melbourne. Shirley, used to travelling to work in the city on the Reservoir line, passed through the West Richmond station each working day and obviously believed she had to meet Holmes at the West Richmond station, and not the Richmond station. That was her tragic mistake.

Naturally, Holmes waited at the Richmond station for Shirley, parking his car nearby. However, Shirley did not turn up and after a long wait Holmes went to the party believing that she had decided not to attend the party after all. However, Shirley had left her Reservoir home shortly after 7 p.m. She caught a train but what happened after she alighted from the train remains one of the biggest mysteries in Australian criminal history.

Shirley Collins was murdered that night but her body was not discovered until the following Tuesday morning. Incredibly, the girl was murdered some forty miles from Richmond, at the popular seaside resort of Mt Martha. The body was discovered by local elderly resident, Mr Lionel Evelyn-Liardet, who was out walking with his dog. Incredibly, other passers-by had seen the body in the driveway of a vacant holiday cottage but believed it was a girl suntanning. Meanwhile, Shirley's foster-mother had already alerted police over her daughter's disappearance. Shirley had been told to be home by midnight on the night of the party and Mrs Collins had notified a policeman neighbor at 3 a.m. that Shirley had not returned home. When Shirley did not arrive home after daybreak Mrs Collins officially notified police of Shirley's disappearance.

Police were shocked when they examined the body. It was a terrible sight, the girl being battered to death. Shirley had walked up the drive of the holiday cottage with her murderer and was hit over the head with three full bottles of beer. The murderer then smashed Shirley's face in with heavy slabs of concrete guttering. Her features were unrecognisable, her face smashed to pulp. The muderer also removed Shirley's panties, stockings and girdle, leaving the girl's skirt above her shoulders. Shirley was not sexually assaulted. The murder horrified Melbourne and police started a huge investigation. However, there were enormous obstacles.

The biggest problem was an accurate assessment of what happened after Shirley failed to meet Holmes. A light-coloured car was seen near West Richmond station around the time Shirley would have been waiting for Holmes. But what would induce a shy girl like Shirley to enter the car? Police could only speculate on that, with several theories being suggested. One suggestion was that Shirley knew the driver of the car (if the light-coloured car was the murderer's vehicle). Another theory was that the driver was a middle-aged or elderly man Shirley was led to trust because of her predicament. But what would have made her travel all the way to Mt Martha against her will, if that was the case? No theory proved conclusive and police were forced to reconstruct events as best they could, pieces of the jigsaw missing.

The police had few clues. However, they did know that the murderer travelled from Melbourne on the night of the murder. Police examined the labels from the shattered beer bottles and traced batch numbers to a large number of Melbourne city hotels, the beer being delivered to those hotels the day before the murder. Then, of course, there was the mysterious light-coloured car. But nothing really positive.

Police appealed to the public for help and went to extraordinary lengths in an attempt to close their files. They even used a model dressed in clothes identical to those worn by Shirley Collins the night she was murdered. Shirley was wearing a black and grey skirt, a yellow blouse and a black cardigan. The Melbourne Argus even ran a photograph of the model and the clothes, with a facial photograph of Shirley Collins superimposed to make the photograph appear as if it was a photo of Shirley taken the night she was murdered. This produced a few leads but did not solve the mystery. The unfortunate 14-year-old, on her first party outing, was murdered by a monster yet to be brought before the courts for a crime that horrified Melbourne.

THE
BOGLE-CHANDLER
MYSTERY

The Bogle-Chandler mystery might be out of context in a book on murder. But who knows how Dr Gilbert Bogle and Mrs Margaret Chandler died? Certainly, their deaths have baffled the New South Wales police force for more than forty years. In fact, the deaths are among Australia's greatest mysteries. How did they die? Were their deaths natural? Were they murdered, and if so, by whom? Those questions have been asked millions of times by thousands of people since the deaths on New Year's Day, 1963.

The bodies of Mrs Chandler and Dr Bogle were found early on New Year's Day in the Sydney suburb of Chatswood. The dead couple had been at a party given by a CSIRO officer in Waratah St, Chatswood. Most of the guests were from the scientific world and this included Dr Bogle, a brilliant physicist. It was not a wild New Year's Party by any stretch of the imagination and police ruled out the possibility of mass-poisoning, as other guests were not ill. The biggest pointer to total mystery was the placement and covering of the bodies.

Dr Bogle's body was found on its stomach, with jacket and trousers placed over the body. Someone must have placed the clothes over the body, one suggestion being that Mrs Chandler did this after seeing Dr Bogle ill. However, Mrs Chandler's body, discovered by police twenty metres from Dr Bogle's body, was covered by cardboard beer cartons. The body was naked except for a dress and petticoat around the waist. If Mrs Chandler had taken care of Dr Bogle in his illness, why did she cover herself with beer cartons, leaving herself virtually naked? Police were baffled. It was suggested that the two had died as a result of a suicide pact but that seemed the most unlikely theory of all. After all, they had met only once previously, neither had any serious worries and Dr Bogle was about to take up an important position in the United States. The dead couple were last seen alive when leaving the party at approximately 4.30 p.m. The bodies were discovered only a few hours later and rigor mortis had not set in.

Cause of death had to be established but that was a task beyond even the best forensic scientists in New South Wales. No wounds on either body were discovered and there were no puncture marks. The director of the NSW Department of Forensic Medicine, Dr John Laing, testified at the coroner's inquest in May, 1963, that the couple had died from acute circulatory failure but could not explain why the circulatory systems had failed. One of the most obvious reasons would have been a lethal injection but, despite repeated and painstaking examinations, no hypodermic marks were found on either body.

No poisonous substances were found in either body's internal organs.

Other tests were made, the baffled investigators even testing the bodies for radioactivity. These tests proved negative, as did all other tests. Chemical analysts were asked to investigate but these tests also proved negative. However, government analyst Mr Ernest Ogg did not rule out the possibility of chemical poisoning. However, he indicated that although 'I can see no prospect of this mystery being solved so far as chemical poisons are concerned' he also stated that there were thousands of new chemicals produced each year.

Even supposing that Dr Bogle and Mrs Chandler were poisoned, perhaps by a mystery gas or other sinister method, who killed them? There seemed no motive for their deaths. It was suggested that Mrs Chandler was interested in taking Dr Bogle as a lover but Mrs Chandler's husband, Mr Geoffrey Chandler, insisted that he was not jealous. Mr Chandler, a CSIRO officer, also left the party before his wife and Dr Bogle and later picked up his two children at his in-laws' home in Granville. Significantly, Mrs Chandler had not had sexual intercourse immediately before her mysterious death.

No theory has gone even halfway to explaining the Bogle-Chandler mystery, despite massive efforts by police and everyone connected with the strange case. Theories include death rays, gas pellets, CIA activities and even plain old rabbit poison. But no theory stands up to detailed examination and the mystery remains. In fact, was it murder at all?

THE EAST BRIGHTON STRANGLING

It seemed just another Sunday morning for plasterer Richard Hall as he he hopped into his truck to go to a job. However, Sunday, May 14, 1950, was to prove no ordinary day. Hall, as he drove down Glencairn Avenue, East Brighton, now a fashionable bayside Melbourne suburb, noticed a pair of shoes protruding from long grass. Hall stopped to investigate, although he could hardly have expected to know that he was about to discover the corpse of a murdered teenager. Hall saw the body facing downwards, with a neatly folded copy of a newspaper covering the back of the head. Hall rushed off immediately to telephone police from a nearby telephone box.

Several Glencairn Avenue residents saw the body but could not identify the girl, who had been beaten about the face and strangled. Even Hall could not recognise the dead girl, although he later realised that he knew her well. Police had a description of the dead girl broadcast over radio station 3DB. The description read '5 feet 8 inches tall, fair hair, brown eyes, well built, wearing brown short coat, grey velvet dress with a zip fastener down the front as far as the waist, a narrow gold belt, two gold tie strings on the neck of the dress, tan and white shoes with brown bow in front. She was also wearing a small gold wrist watch, and carrying a brown leather handbag and brown leather gloves.' Mr Roy F. Walters, who lived with his wife, daughter and two sons in Glencairn Avenue, heard the special broadcast and knew the identity of the dead girl. He could not go to identify the girl himself because he had been blinded by a bomb while serving with the Air Force during World War Two. Mr Walters sent his brother-in-law to identify the body, which proved tragic for the blinded former airman. The dead girl was his daughter Carmen, just 19. Carmen had not returned home on the Saturday night but Mr and Mrs Walters had assumed that their daughter was spending the weekend with friends.

Friends and neighbours, who knew Carmen Walters as a 'quiet, steady' girl, were shocked. Carmen worked as a porteress at the nearby Hampton railway station and was saving every penny she could earn so that she could travel to South Africa, and then on to Europe and Britain. Her death seemed senseless and police worked feverishly in an attempt to close their investigations. Bus driver Harry Richards told police that he saw Carmen Walters with a tall, thin man on his bus on the night Carmen was murdered. Mr Richards said that the couple had left the bus at the Glencairn Avenue stop at 9.35 p.m. That was the last time that Carmen Walters was seen alive and police wanted to interview the tall, thin man.

Meanwhile, Government analyst Mr H.G. Wignall examined the body in an attempt to trace the killer. Police took scrapings from beneath the dead girl's fingernails and the extent of the facial bruising convinced police that the killer was strongly built. Neighbour Mrs E. Neagle told police that she heard screams at about 9.45 p.m. on the night of the killing. 'They were nasty screams but I thought it was a neighbour's child who has nightmares,' Mrs Neagle told a newspaper reporter. Other neighbours reported hearing screams.

The best police clue in the early investigation was the description of the tall, thin man. Police were told that Carmen had been engaged to a tall, thin young man, and naturally, they wanted to interview him. A search was launched and a photograph of the young man was given to Melbourne newspapers. A report in the Melbourne Sun of May 16 gave this official description of the man: 'Age 24, about 6 foot, fair complexion and hair which has a tendency to stick up in front, medium features and good natural teeth. He was last seen wearing a light grey suit with a white pencil strip and an Air Servicemen's Association badge in the lapel, a light colored gabardine overcoat, black shoes, white shirt, red and blue square pattern tie. The man was a radar mechanic in the Air Force and saw service in Adelaide and Queensland.' The young man had disappeared but police were confident that they would be able to interview him sooner or later.

The hunt for the missing young man, named (slightly incorrectly) as Maurice Brewer in the Melbourne Age of May 17, was intensified. Meanwhile, the whole of Glencairn Avenue was in mourning for Carmen Walters. The quiet East Brighton neighbourhood was shattered and every resident in the avenue contributed to a wreath for the dead girl's funeral. A service was held in Middle Brighton and the body of Carmen Walters was cremated at the Springvale Crematorium. Two plain-clothes detectives attended the funeral, presumably in case the missing man turned up. A police lead then suggested that the missing man was in Gippsland and police rushed to eastern Victoria. However, police still were not certain. A taxi driver told them he drove a tall, thin man to Oakleigh railway station from Moorabbin on the night of the girl's death and a man of 'similar appearance' to the wanted Brewer was seen by a farmer at Yallourn. The man spent a night at a State Electricity workers' camp, borrowed a razor blade and disappeared into the bush. Police were becoming increasingly interested in the man missing in the bush.

The dead girl's former fiancee, Morris Sutton Ramsden Brewer, 24, of Reservoir, finally gave himself up on the night of May 17. He was taken to Brighton police station and then to the Russell Street headquarters before being charged with the murder of Carmen Walters. Brewer was charged at 3.45 on the morning of May 18. Brewer had been apprehended by Sergeant Edward Tye, of Yallourn police. Sergeant Tye had been called to a workers' camp, where Brewer was eating a meal after walking in from the bush. Brewer knew the area well, having worked at several farms in the district as a herd tester.

The Coroner's Inquest was held in July, 1950. The full text of a statement police alleged Brewer gave them was read by Senior Detective Cyril Currer. The alleged statement, an extraordinary account of a young man's anguish in love, reads:

> I first met Carmen on October 31, 1949 when I was doing a herd testing course at Burnley Primary Agricultural Department.
>
> She and I started the course on the same day. From the way she spoke and from her behaviour I knew right from the start that she was different from other girls I had met.
>
> I made it my business to try and find out more about her. We became very friendly and we visited each other's home.
>
> We became engaged in February, 1950. I was happy at this time. We intended getting married later this year—about October.
>
> While we were at the Agricultural School at Burnley, Carmen told me that she had been in Darwin for 18 months.
>
> Some time later she told me that she had not been in Darwin for 18 months but that she had been there for about six weeks.
>
> Other things she told me I also found to be untrue.
>
> I was concerned about Carmen telling me lies and I told her that I thought she was wilful and irresponsible.
>
> She told me that when we first met she never dreamed that our association would develop as it did.
>
> Carmen and I became engaged on a Friday.
>
> On the following Wednesday evening—I think it was March 1—my mother and father accompanied me to her home at 26 Glencairn Ave., East Brighton.
>
> After we had been there for a while Carmen disappeared for about 20 minutes.

When she returned I could see that something was on her mind. I suggested that she accompany me for a walk.

We went out and I asked her what was troubling her.

She said, 'There's nothing on my mind,' but her attitude seemed cool. We returned to the house.

As soon as she rejoined the others she addressed her mother in front of everybody in a disgusting manner.

She told them, 'Have you told Mrs Brewer yet of your dislike of the Hampton Hall for us to be married? Have you spoken about your dislike of Mr Clayton, who is not a reverend gentleman, officiating at our wedding?' Her mother was very upset.

I was astounded by Carmen's rudeness and I thought she was upset. I tried to comfort her as best I could.

I belong to the Plymouth Brethren and Carmen and I had agreed to be married at the Hampton Hall by Mr Clayton, who is a member of my faith. That night when I returned home I was greatly worried.

I tried to sleep it off.

The following morning I had a conversation with my father in the bathroom.

I told him that I had been upset previously about little incidents that had occurred between Carmen and me and that I didn't know what would happen if anything further happened to upset me.

After that the days went on.

Her behaviour towards me became cool and casual.

I could not understand it.

On Thursday, March 9, my parents were holidaying at Mount Dandenong.

That night I drove Carmen to where my parents were staying.

On the way to Mount Dandenong we had a discussion about our future life and she was very indefinite in her mind.

She seemed to be occupied by thoughts other than settling down. This worried me.

That night, at the cottage, Carmen appeared to be very uneasy. My mother left the room and I asked Carmen what was wrong. She wouldn't tell me for a while.

The alleged statement continued that she told him she had had an association with another man while in Darwin, then continued,

I was a bit dazed and upset about this and I told her that I couldn't see my way clear to go ahead with our engagement.

We talked for a while about it and I let it go at that.

I didn't get more than a few minutes sleep that night.

The following day (Thursday, March 9) father drove Carmen and me to Bayswater Railway Station and we caught the train to Melbourne. We had another discussion about the situation.

I was so upset that I couldn't go to work.

I was with Carmen that afternoon and I went with her to her doctor's at South Rd., Brighton Beach.

When I left her I went to my aunt's place, where I spent the night.

The following morning I had what seemed to be pressure from my temple at the back of my head.

My aunt got a doctor to see me.

I told him about the trouble I was having with Carmen.

He advised me to make a clean break of it.

I had an appointment to meet Carmen at 5 p.m. that day at the Flinders St. Station.

I met her there and told her as best I could, my own condition and that the only conclusion I could come to was to break it off.

She said, 'If you don't love me it's no use waiting.'

She gave me back the engagement ring.

I offered to take her home but she wouldn't hear of it.

I accompanied her to the Brighton train and went home.

I rang my aunt and told her what had happened.

I caught a train to Ferntree Gully and a bus to Olinda, where my father met me.

I told my mum and dad what had happened.

My father took me to Melbourne, where I saw a Dr Sinclair, who gave me a new lot of tablets.

We returned to the hills and stayed until the following Saturday. I did not get any better until March 19.

Then I had my first natural sleep.

On March 20 I was ill again and my father took me to the doctor who put me in Ratho Park Hospital, in Brighton.

I was there until April 15. A few days after I left hospital I went to Carmen. I saw her and her mother.

I went shopping with Carmen and had a further talk with her.

She told me that she had two personalities.

She told me, 'There are two me's.'

I returned to her home with her and left her there.

We parted on quite good terms.

That day she told me there was no one else that she would want to marry. I saw her twice again between then and last Saturday.

Last Friday (the day before her death) Carmen left a note under my door at home asking me to go with her to tea in town that night.

I saw her at the Hampton railway station at 1.30 p.m. that day.

I told her that I wasn't going to tea with her that night or any other night. She asked me if I'd take her on the following night (the Saturday).

I thought it over for a moment and told her that I didn't want to go, but, if we could get back early, I would go.

She particularly asked me if it would be possible to go to Mordialloc, and I agreed.

We made arrangements to meet under the clocks at 5.30 p.m. on Saturday. We met and I took a taxi to Mordialloc.

We had dinner and talked about ourselves.

After dinner Carmen wanted to go to the spot on the beach at Mordialloc where we had met on a previous occasion before I proposed to her.

We went to the beach and sat on a seat near the pier for about half an hour. We were talking things over there and she told me she was making plans to go travelling.

She asked me if we could make up our differences.

I told her there was no hope of that.

We went back to Mordialloc railway station, where I bought two tickets—one for myself from Mordialloc to Melbourne and one for her from Mordialloc to Moorabbin.

I told her that I would see her home.

When we got out at the station, there was no bus coming and we decided to start walking.

A bus came along after a while and we caught it.

We got off at Glencairn Ave.

Earlier that night Carmen had been blaming my parents for what had happened between us.

I'm very fond of my parents.

I didn't like her saying that about them.

We were walking along Glencairn Ave. and Carmen said to me, 'I have caused my parents a lot of worry and trouble in the past and you'll do the same.'

We were only a short distance from the corner when she said this, and I can't explain how I felt.

Everything seemed to clog up in my mind.

I either grabbed her by the throat with my hands and pushed her to the ground, or I pushed her down first and then grabbed her by the throat.

I had her by the throat on the ground and I held her there with my hand around her throat for some time.

I don't know just how long.

I got up then. Carmen was still lying on the grass.

I walked away and hired a taxi. I got out of the cab near Oakleigh railway gates and gave the driver a 10/- note.

I went into a lolly shop and asked for a glass of sarsparilla.

I think there was a dance hall near the shop.

A man came in and said something about beef sandwiches and a dance. After having a drink I went out and started walking towards Dandenong. A man came along and picked me up in his car.

He left me at a street he said was Box Hill Rd., and I then walked for a distance before being picked up in a milk truck.

This driver dropped me some miles on the Melbourne side of Drouin.

I walked on after that and another chap came along and gave me a lift on the pillion of his motor bike.

When we arrived at Drouin I tried to get something to eat, but I couldn't.

I asked some people in a shop the way to Jindivic, where I thought I might spend the night.

The people told me I would have to go back along the highway to get there and I decided not to go.

Then I saw a bike standing outside a shop in the main street and I took it and rode to Warragul.

I was exhausted.

I decided I needed a sleep.

I tried banging on hotel doors for a bed but I could get no answer.

I slept in a rail carriage. I awoke next morning at just daylight and I got a lift on a sand truck to Yallourn.

I was there just before 9 a.m. and I went to the Y.M.C.A. hut and a man there loaned me a book to read and I went into the reading room for a while.

Before lunch-time I left the reading room and walked over the bridge across the Latrobe River and into the bush behind a briquette factory.

I laid down in the bush and tried to sleep.

I could not sleep and I just walked around in the bush. I slept that night in the bush.

I stayed in the bush until about 3 p.m.

On Monday, when I came into Yallourn, I had a meal at a cafe and I was told I could sleep at the camp that night.

I spent that night in a hut at the camp with another man.

I went to the hut that night and I was dressed in a grey striped suit and a gabardine overcoat.

There were no blankets at the camp and I slept on a mattress and put another one over me.

The other man in the hut appeared to have been on a drinking bout. He had no clothes on him, so I put my overcoat over him.

The following morning I had a wash and shave and found a razor blade in the washroom.

I put the blade I found in a match box and took it into the bush with me and remained there until Tuesday afternoon.

I tried to cut a vein in my arm.

I had decided to commit suicide.

I made several cuts on my left arm with the razor but couldn't succeed in killing myself.

> Shortly after I arrived back at the camp I was approached by a
> policeman, who asked me to accompany him to the police station.

Brewer was committed for trial on a charge of having murdered
Carmen Walters. That trial was in the Melbourne Criminal Court in
September, 1950. Brewer pleaded not guilty on the grounds of
insanity. He told the court, in an unsworn statement from the dock,
'It seems I must have attacked her. I didn't know I was hurting her. I
only knew I could do nothing to cause worry to my parents. I don't
care what happens to me. I am only thinking of my parents and
hers.'

A great deal of the court's time was taken in hearing evidence
from medical experts, reporting on Brewer's mental state at the time
of Carmen Walters' death. Royal Melbourne Hospital honorary
psychologist Dr Edward Francis Campbell told the court that he
believed Brewer to be a latent paranoid schizophrenic. Dr Campbell
said, 'First, he came from a closely knit family. There were very close
emotional ties holding the members of the family and, in particular,
between the accused and his mother. The atmosphere in which the
accused had been brought up was a very religious one, highly
moralistic and indicated that his emotional reactions and emotional
growth had been rather repressed because of this.

'In my opinion, Brewer's capacity to transfer his affection from
his mother to some other woman is incomplete. Almost throughout
his life the accused tended to withdraw into himself. The relevant
term is "schizoid- characteristic". It is a tendency or preference to
withdraw from reality instead of having emotional contact with
interesting things going on around him. He preferred to live within
his own fantasy or imagination… In the event of his being subjected
to a similar set of circumstances, he would be likely to repeat the
same sort of reaction.'

Four doctors, including Dr Campbell, agreed that Brewer could
not have known what he was doing at the time of the crime. Brewer
even had a 'truth drug' treatment. Dr Ainsley Dixon Mears told the
court that under the drug Brewer continually referred to his love for
his mother. Dr Mears said, 'He spoke of some feeling of resentment
at times towards Carmen. I particularly examined him on this

question and his feelings towards her, and I believed it was a reaction to the circumstances.' Dr Mears also said, in reference to Brewer's feelings for his mother, 'It seemed that he thought she was some manifestation of God.'

Senior Government Medical Officer Dr Raymond Tennyson Allan told the court that he believed Brewer was aware of his act and knew it was wrong. Dr Allan, who interviewed Brewer for five hours at Pentridge, said that he was satisfied Brewer was a self-righteous man who had the capacity for telling untruths. However, when asked by Brewer's counsel, Mr R.V. Monahan, KC, if Brewer was suffering from an uncontrollable impulse at the time of the crime, Dr Allan replied, 'Yes.'

Mr Monahan, in summing up, told the jury that if there was any reasonable doubt that the prisoner was sane at the time of the offence —not at any other time—then the jury was obliged to give the prisoner the benefit of the doubt. Mr Monahan explained that the law allowed for a verdict of not guilty on the grounds of insanity and then reviewed evidence already given. Mr Monahan said, 'All the doctors, except Dr Allan, a Government medical officer, say Brewer is the very embodiment of truth. But because poor little Carmen Walters told him a few lies she turned out not to be the goddess he thought she was. What he then did was only in obedience to the law of self-preservation. He could not live with this conflict going on within him. It was resolved symbolically by the unconscious process of his mind. He was unable to reason and therefore, in the eyes of the law, he is not culpable. That is the case in a nutshell.'

Prosecutor Mr H.A. Winneke, KC (later to be Sir Henry Winneke, governor of Victoria) warned the jury, 'Don't think that because a man is abnormal or because he has some instability about his mind he may be called insane.' The jury took five-and-a-half hours to hand down its verdict, although much of that time was taken by the search for a book requested by the jury. The verdict was not guilty on the ground of insanity. Mr Justice Barry sentenced Brewer to be detained 'at the Governor's pleasure'. Brewer was released on parole from Pentridge on November 27, 1957, spending seven years in detention.

THE 'SON' WHO KILLED

Police, because of the very nature of their job, are not easily shocked. However, police at the Moonee Ponds police station, in Melbourne's northern suburbs, could not believe their ears when a man walked in on December 2, 1962, and claimed that he had a body in his car. Detective Ken Smith, of Moonee Ponds CIB, spoke to the young man and police then examined a car parked outside the police station. The body of a young woman was lying across the front seat. Police then went to a house in the nearby suburb of Niddrie and discovered the body of a younger woman. The dead women were sisters, and the man who had walked into the police station had been engaged to the older woman. Police had a twin killing on their hands but at least they did not have to launch a search for the killer.

The dead sisters were Lynette Ainsworth, 19, and Anthea Ainsworth, just 16 and still at school. The man who walked into the Moonee Ponds police station was taken to Russell Street headquarters for questioning. The man, Douglas Alfred Mauger, was charged with having murdered the two sisters. It was a tragic case. Mauger, 24, had moved into the Ainsworth family home two and a half years earlier and Mr Bernard Ainsworth, father of the dead girls, said he treated Mauger 'like a son'. Mr Ainsworth said he believed Mauger had been deprived as a youth and 'I wanted to give him the things he had missed'. Mauger and Lynette Ainsworth became engaged in November, 1961. Mauger moved into a pet shop business early the following year but that venture indirectly led to his troubles. The business failed and Mauger was declared bankrupt. He and Lynette broke off their engagement in October, 1962.

The engagement was an 'on-off' affair and the young couple made several attempts to reconcile their differences. However, it seemed they would never really get together again. At least, that is how it appeared to Mauger, and he was determined not to lose the girl he loved. The matter came to a head on the night of December 1 when Mauger watched his former fiancee talking to another young man at the Ainsworth home. It was an innocent enough conversation but it was the turning point for Mauger.

Mauger spoke to Lynette in her bedroom that night and told her that he did not want to lose her. But even then Lynette could not have known that Mauger would to go such extremes. Mauger loaded a .22 rifle, went into Lynette's bedroom again but did not pull the trigger. He just could not kill, not at that stage, anyway. Mauger, soon after nine o'clock the next morning, went into Anthea Ainsworth's bedroom and shot her in the body and then in the head. He then battered the girl about the head with a hammer. Mauger was convinced that Anthea had had something to do with his broken engagement. Mauger then drove to the Ainsworth garage business, picked up Lynette and drove her to an area near Anthea's school in Essendon. A struggle developed and Mauger shot Lynette five times in the head. Mauger then drove to Moonee Ponds police station.

Senior Detective John Baker later told the Criminal Court, at Mauger's trial for murder, that Mauger had 'poured out' his account of how he had killed the two Ainsworth girls. Senior Detective Baker said that Mauger took police to the Ainsworth house and showed them how he shot Anthea. Mauger also showed police his pet boxer dogs and fed his goldfish. Senior Detective Baker said that Mauger, in an interview at Russell Street police headquarters, said, 'I killed the girls in cold-blooded murder, being in the right frame of mind. I was not insane. I planned it the day before.' Senior Detective Baker also said that Mauger claimed he had intended to crash his car and shoot himself but realised he did not have the courage to suicide. Mauger then signed the interview and added in his own writing, 'Lyn I am sorry; pray for me.'

Mauger pleaded not guilty to two charges of murder, his counsel entering a plea of insanity on his behalf. Two doctors told the Criminal Court that they believed Mauger was psychopathic. Dr Jack Lewis Evans, superintendent at the Sunbury Mental Hospital, told the court that Mauger once had formed a suicide pact when he and a girl had been refused permission to marry. Dr Evans said Mauger and the girl had run away together in 1959 and made a suicide pact which was thwarted. Dr Leon Fennessy told the court that Mauger had thrown himself under a car when he had lost the affection of another girl, and had taken poison on two other occasions. Dr Fennessy, who also said Mauger was an epileptic and had a history of indiscriminate sexual behaviour, had told him, 'I always had an explosive temper. I just do my block. Once I do my block, that's it. I go mad. A doctor once told me when I was a kid I would kill someone by my temper one day.'

Dr Allen Bartholomew, superintendent of the Pentridge psychiatric clinic, said he had examined Mauger thirteen times. Dr Bartholomew also said that although Mauger was psychopathic, he would have realised that what he was doing at the time of the shootings was wrong.

The jury, after a one and a half hour retirement announced their verdict of 'guilty'. Mauger, asked if he wanted to say anything before sentence was passed, buttoned his coat, smiled and said 'no'. Mr Justice Monahan then sentenced Mauger to death. However, that sentence was not carried out. The State Executive Council, in September, 1963, commuted the sentence to fifty years imprisonment. The council ordered that Mauger be not eligible for parole until he had served forty years.

THE LAST MAN TO HANG

There have been few manhunts of such magnitude in Australian criminal history as the one that tracked down Pentridge escapees Ronald Ryan and Peter Walker over 17 days from December 19, 1965. The shooting and killing of prison guard George Hodson outraged Victorians and the media went into frenzy over the chase for Australia's most wanted criminals.

The case will forever hold a place in infamy as Ryan eventually was found guilty of the murder of Hodson and became the last man to be hanged in Australia. The execution was seen by hundreds of thousands of Australians as an outrage and by many close to the case as a travesty of justice and even as a political exercise.

Ronald Joseph Ryan was born in Melbourne on February 21, 1925, into a working class family. He had three sisters — Violet, Irma and Gloria — and a half-brother, George Thompson (by his mother Cecilia's first husband).

Father Jack Ryan could not find work and life was tough for the family. So much so that Cecilia Ryan could not cope and the Ryan children were put into homes, Ronald to the Salesian order's monastery at Sunbury and the girls to a convent in the inner Melbourne suburb of Abbotsford.

Ryan apparently was a good student, but ran away from the orphanage when he was just 14 years of age and headed north where he found work as a rail-cutter and general hand. He worked hard and long and, in 1943, returned to Melbourne. By now he was 18 years of age and had money in his pockets. Ryan took his sisters from the convent and, reunited with his mother, he became the family breadwinner.

He led a steady life for several years and, in 1948, married Dorothy George and settled down to raise a family — daughters Janice, Wendy and Rhonda. However, rail-splitting and timber-cutting did not enable Ryan to earn enough money to provide for his family as well as he would have wished and he finally attracted police attention when he passed forged cheques.

Ryan was 31 years of age when he was given a bond for these offences but, not long after, he again was caught passing bad cheques. Convicted, he was given a five-year bond and he again seemed to settle down.

However, three years later Ryan was arrested for theft but escaped from custody at the Melbourne City Watch House. Recaptured, he was sent to prison and, instead of settling down on release, drifted back into a life of crime and in 1964 was sent to Pentridge after a brief career as a safe-cracker.

Dorothy Ryan divorced her husband and re-married, but Ryan refused to concede that he had lost his family and set about planning his escape from Pentridge. After studying the sentry catwalks and measuring the thickness of the prison walls, he decided that Sunday, December 19, 1965, provided him with the perfect opportunity to escape. Ryan informed fellow prisoner Peter Walker of his plans and the 24-year-old agreed to join him in the bid for freedom.

That Sunday was selected because it was the day of the prison guards' Christmas party and the pair knew there was a skeleton staff on duty. Ryan gave Walker the go-ahead early in the afternoon and they scaled a wall to reach a catwalk. Ryan, with a piece of water pipe as a weapon and Walker behind him, came across prison guard Helmut Lange and grabbed an M1 rifle from a rack.

Lange, with the rifle pointed at him, opened a door to the outside while Ryan ejected a live round. Ryan demanded car keys from a passer-by and, when these weren't handed over, knocked the man down. The alarm by now had been raised and Ryan and Walker ran into busy Sydney Road, Coburg.

Ryan tried to hijack a passing car, but noticed that Walker was just about to be nabbed by guard Hodson. A shot rang out and Hodson fell dead on the tram tracks, while the escapees jumped into a car and fled from the scene.

Melbourne was abuzz with the escape and killing and, as police scoured the city, Ryan and Walker holed up in the house of a sympathiser in the seaside Melbourne suburb of Elwood.

Emboldened by their escape and desperately needing funds, they then held up a bank in the southern suburb of Ormond. By now, the media was in a frenzy and headlines blared every police comment or reported sighting of the outlaws. In fact, Ryan's mother at one stage appeared on television with an appeal for her son to give himself up.

Just five days after their escape, on Christmas Eve, their female sympathizer went to a party and brought home a companion. James Henderson. On meeting Ryan, the young man made the biggest mistake of his life in telling Walker that his companion looked a lot like the escaped criminal Ronald Ryan. Walker shot Henderson dead in a public toilet in Albert Park and he and Ryan were forced to go on the run.

They travelled to Sydney and moved into a flat in the seaside suburb of Coogee. However, Walker could not resist the opposite sex and, after making arrangements for a date, he and Ryan were caught in a police trap after 17 days on the run.

The pair was extradited to Melbourne and their trial opened on March 15, 1966, before Mr Justice Starke. The prosecution case relied on numerous eye-witnesses, whereas defence counsel Philip Opas QC was able to point to numerous instances of conflicting evidence.

For example, Opas used a leading mathematician to demonstrate that the shot which killed Hodson could not have been fired from ground level. Also, no fired bullet was ever found and, in fact, only one round was unaccounted for, yet Ryan had ejected that round. It begged the question of whether another weapon had been used in the slaying of Hodson.

Opas argued that Hodson's wound was caused by a shot from the prison guard tower. Later, in 1986 and well after Ryan's execution, a prison guard came forward to say that he might have accidentally fired the shot that killed Hodson and feared to say anything at the time in case he got into trouble. He also was convinced Ryan would never be hanged and that the death sentence would be commuted to life imprisonment.

Ryan, when he took the stand during his trial, was questioned by his defence counsel and the following is part of that evidence:

OPAS: Did you murder Prison Officer Hodson?

RYAN: Most emphatically not.

OPAS: Did you fire a shot at all on the nineteenth of December?

RYAN: I did not discharge that gun on the nineteenth of December.

Ryan also was asked about how he came into possession of the prison rifle.

OPAS: What did you grab the rifle for?

RYAN: So that it couldn't be used against me. I saw the cocking lever on the side of the rifle. Incidentally, I had never seen one of these M1.30s before, I had never handled one, and I pulled the cocking lever back to inject the shell into the rifle or see if there was one in there first. There were none in there, so I pushed the lever forward to inject one, to fit one, and pushed it in.

OPAS: What did you do that for?

RYAN: Oh, to bluff the warder (Lange), let him know that I meant business, to impress upon him that he had better do what I told him to. However, in pushing the lever forward I noticed that the extractors, I suppose you would call them, didn't close over the head of the shell, so I pulled the lever back to force it harder forward. In doing this I picked up another shell and forced it in behind the one which had first gone in. Consequently, my gun jammed.

OPAS: What happened next?

Ryan: Well then, I tested the gun and worked the lever and this all happened very quickly, of course, and I got the shell out; it tipped out on the floor, and I just let the lever go and this unfortunately picked up another shell, and again I was in the same predicament.

Opas later asked Ryan about prison guard Hodson.

OPAS: Did you see what happened to Hodson?

RYAN: No, I didn't see what happened to Hodson. I saw Hodson, who was chasing Walker; he was a pretty big fellow and very stout. He seemed to be just about at the end of his tether. He was pretty distressed, that was my impression, when he was chasing Peter. They ran from my sight behind this Plymouth (motor vehicle). I was approaching, not exactly from the rear but from the driver's side of the rear and consequently that car did obscure my vision of Hodson and Walker. In any case, I presume they were behind a car and I just lost sight of Peter and the officer.

OPAS: What happened with you? Did you hear a shot at any time?

RYAN: I couldn't swear that I heard a shot but I did hear two or three detonations, but this may have been pure auto-suggestion because I was expecting to be fired at by the guard at No. 2 Tower at any stage, but I would not swear that I heard any shots. They could have been shots or they could have been car doors slamming because quite a few people were jumping out of cars at this stage to, well, I assume to lend a hand to the officers.

Ryan, despite sometimes fierce cross-examination, did not deviate from his account of what had happened and there were many who believed he would be given the benefit of the doubt. However, the 12-man jury returned a 'guilty' verdict and Mr Justice Starke had no option but to pronounce the mandatory death sentence. Walker was sentenced to 12 years' imprisonment for manslaughter, with another 12 years for the killing of Henderson. He was released in 1983.

However, no one — least of all some of the jurors — expected the death sentence to be carried out. After all, there had been 36 reprieves since the previous execution in 1951. An appeal to the Victorian Court of Criminal Appeal was dismissed and Victorian Premier Sir Henry Bolte announced that Ryan, indeed, would hang.

At one stage Bolte, whose government was facing re-election, said: 'There is no possibility of the decision to hang Ryan being reversed. It is quite definite and final.' He was determined to make his point on law and order.

The Bolte government announced that the execution would take place on January 9, 1967, but this was rescheduled to after an appeal to the Privy Council in London. This appeal also failed and a new execution date was set, for February 3, 1967.

At 10 o'clock the night before the scheduled execution, a special meeting of the State Executive Council rejected Ryan's last minute appeal for mercy. Ryan's solicitor, Mr Ralph Freadman, said: 'We have just received a message from the Crown Solicitor, Mr Mornane, that the Queen, acting through the Governor-in-Council, has rejected the petition to exercise mercy. And that's the end of it.'

Ryan wrote letters to his family on prison toilet paper and said: 'With regard to my guilt I say only that I am innocent of intent and have a clear conscience in this matter.'

February 3 broke with the promise of a hot day as more than 3000 protestors, including Ryan's mother Cecilia, stood outside Pentridge as Ryan was hanged at 8am. His last words to the hangman were: 'God bless you, please make it quick.' At the same time, Cecilia Ryan told television journalist Dan Webb: 'He's a good boy, really.'

The remains of Ronald Joseph Ryan were buried in quicklime within the grounds of Pentridge.

THE 'DINKY' KILLING

Little Alan Cooper, just five years of age, liked riding his 'dinky' bike in a lane behind his house in the Sydney suburb of Crow's Nest. Alan was riding his 'dinky' on August 9, 1946, when approached by a youth who later took the little boy to a house in nearby Jenkins Street. The youth, 18-year-old Alexander William Tipping, took Alan into his bedroom and attacked him, apparently without motive. It was a senseless attack, leading to a charge of murder.

According to evidence at the trial in the Central Criminal Court, Tipping tried to choke the little boy, later 'bashing' with a flower pot and punching and kicking him. Little Alan did not die instantly and was rushed to the Misericordiae Hospital after Tipping himself rang police. Alan was found suffering from severe head injuries, under the Jenkins Street house.

Tipping at first told police that he heard moaning and groaning from under the house and when he investigated, discovered the badly injured boy. However, Tipping then stated, 'I'll tell you all about it—I done it. I bashed the kid. When I was lying on my bed I was thinking I would like to do something big and get away with it. I brought the little boy in from his 'dinky', sat him on the bed and tried to choke him. But he was too tough. I took him under the house, bashed him with a flower pot and went upstairs. I heard him still moaning, so I went down again and punched him. Then I rang the police.'

Tipping was committed for trial on a charge of murder. The jury could not agree on a verdict at the first trial, and a retrial was ordered. The jury at that trial handed down a verdict of 'insanity' and Tipping was detained at the 'governor's pleasure'.

Evidence was given at the inquest that Tipping had suffered from brain trouble from the age of three and that he had been examined by a number of specialists and psychiatrists. Four doctors told the court at Tipping's second trial that the youth had contracted encephalitis ('sleeping sickness') at the age of three. Child Welfare Clinic psychiatrist Dr Irene Sabire told the court that encephalitis was caused by an organism entering from the nasal passage and impairing brain tissue. Dr. Sabire also told the court that she feared that Tipping would be a 'menace to the community'. She said that she had been seeing Tipping for almost a year and that she had noticed a gradual impairment of his judgement and reasoning capacity. She also said she believed that a person in such a condition would not be able to distinguish between right and wrong.

Little Alan Cooper was not sexually assaulted and his death was tragic in the extreme, the killer having no motive.

TOO PRETTY TO HANG

Hanging in the nineteenth century was regarded almost as a public treat. Many hangings were carried out in public, spectators often fighting each other for positions near the gallows. Cases in which capital punishment might be the end result were big news, the broadsheets of the time devoting columns and columns of space to just about every detail mentioned in trials. The public was as interested in the fate of the accused as they were in the minute details of the crime. The public sweated on the jury's verdict and then the judge's sentence. Many criminals were hanged in the Australian colonies before Federation in 1901. However, the hanging of a woman was rare indeed. In fact, the first hanging of a woman in the colony of Victoria wasn't until 1863, and that created a real uproar. Many citizens claimed that it was morally wrong to hang a woman, while others claimed that the condemned woman was too pretty to hang. The gallows victim, Mrs Elizabeth Scott, became as famous as any bushranger waylaying goldfields coaches during this era. Mrs Scott was not only implicated in a horrible murder but was seen as the spider spinning a web for those who helped her. She was pretty and that was both her pride and her downfall.

Mrs Scott, an Englishwoman, was only 23 when she went to the gallows at the old Melbourne jail on November 11, 1863. She was found guilty of murdering her husband near the country hamlet of Devil's River earlier that year. Mrs Scott, a child bride, had been married to middle-aged Bob Scott for nine years before she finally decided that life would be better without him. By that time the Scotts ran a hotel near Devil's River. The hotel was a shanty where goldfield workers sought relief from the drudgery of their lives in the bush wilderness. Scott also sought relief from a bottle and became an habitual alcoholic. It was hardly a suitable life for an attractive 23-year-old woman who was only starting to enjoy life. Mrs Scott, behind her drunken husband's back, befriended two young men— local farmer David Dredge and half-caste Asian Julian Cross, who became slaves to Mrs Scott's every whim.

One of those whims was to get rid of Bob Scott, and that was done on the night of April 13, 1863. Cross and Dredge, on Mrs Scott's initiative, shot Scott in the head and tried to pass it off as suicide. However, the attempted cover-up was so clumsy that police immediately suspected murder. Dredge was so terrified that he made a statement that virtually led himself, Cross and Mrs Scott straight to the gallows.

Mrs Scott denied that she had anything to do with her husband's death but it was quite obvious that she had pushed both her friends into murder. Mrs Scott watched Dredge and Cross prepare for the murder and even gave them shots of brandy for Dutch courage. Yet that attitude of having nothing to do with the actual shooting was one of her big mistakes. She believed that she could only be charged with murder if she actually pulled the trigger. She was so wrong, the law knowing no such distinction. Her second big mistake was to believe that a woman wouldn't be hanged for murder in the colony of Victoria. She was counting on the fact that it had never happened before and no one would like to set such a precedent. Elizabeth Scott wrote her name into history by being the first woman hanged in Victoria. Years later Jean Lee made the same mistake and paid for murder with her own life. But that is another story.

BURIED UNDER CONCRETE

Mary Edson was a tall, extremely attractive young woman with dark brown bobbed hair in the fashion of the 1930s. She was twenty-two years of age, had a sixteen-month-old daughter and lived in the Adelaide suburb of Knoxville when she disappeared without trace on May 18, 1931.

Nextdoor neighbour Mrs Grace Lindsay was deeply puzzled and repeatedly asked the young woman's husband about the disappearance. Lawrence Edson (known to his friends as 'Lawrie'), a twenty-eight-year-old tram conductor, at first told Mrs Lindsay that his wife had run off with another man and that he had been left to care for their daughter, June. Mrs Lindsay thought this strange, although she knew that the Edsons had quarrelled many times over the previous months and that Mary Edson had adopted a 'beaten dog' attitude.

Other neighbours started gossiping, but Edson merely changed his story and told everyone that his wife had died. After all, he even had a letter which Mrs Edson's sister Dorothy Malycha was alleged to have received from an H. Wilson in Melbourne telling her of her sister's 'death' on June 19, 1931. He showed this letter to anyone who cared to read it as 'proof' that his wife had died. The letter read:

Dear Miss Malycha,

I regret that I have to send you very unpleasant advice, but your sister has been staying here for some time. She was to have gone to Europe three weeks ago, but was taken ill and could not go. The doctor wanted her to have an operation, but she refused, and getting worse, died on 19 June, a week after she should have sailed.

She had been living here under the name of Mrs May Matthews. She had a room here and the Mr Matthews who I thought was her husband used to come and take her out before she was taken ill. Before she died she gave me your address and asked me to let you know in case anything happened. She told me also about her husband and baby. She asked me to send you her brooch and wedding ring to give to her husband, and ask him to keep that for the baby; also to keep her photo and marriage ring she had left in her drawer, as June would like them when she grew up.

She begged her husband always to be good to little June. At the end she knew she was going to die, and said she was glad as she had nothing to live for. Her heart was broken.

She never told me her proper married name, but said she had a beautiful home near Adelaide and was very happy until last Christmas. She asked me not to send you my name and address, as it would only give her husband a chance to make inquiries as to her movements since she left home, and as some of his friends had been good to her it might only cause trouble between them.

I can assure you your poor sister did no wrong while she was here. She never went out at nights, only afternoons with Mr Matthews. She told me afterwards he wanted her to go away from Australia with him. He was very good to her to the end and arranged all about the funeral. I don't know what cemetery she was buried in. I have not seen Matthews since.

If neighbours had been suspicious before, they were now more determined than ever to get to the bottom of Mrs Edson's mysterious disappearance. They reported the matter to police, who went to Edson's home on July 23 to investigate. Edson, a former police officer, showed police the letter (another two letters allegedly from Melbourne had been burned) and then made a statement at the City Watchhouse about how his wife had left him in May and had then died in Melbourne.

Police were far from convinced and told Edson they would detain him until officers had had the opportunity to search his home and dig through his garden in Lestrange Street. Edson immediately stepped out of the room in which he was being questioned and on to a landing where he pulled an automatic pistol from his suit pocket and shot himself in the head. He died in hospital two hours later without regaining consciousness. Police were left with a riddle, but they knew that the threat of digging up Edson's garden had terrified him.

Naturally, police were convinced that Edson had buried his wife in the garden at their Knoxville home and rushed there to put their theory to the test. Neighbours had told them that Edson had been seen working feverishly in the tiny shed at the back of the garden. Edson, who had once kept a pet wallaby in the shed, had been seen taking grapevine cuttings there. The cuttings were still there when police investigated, but when they swept them clear they discovered freshly laid concrete.

Police used a pick to dig up the thin layer of concrete and found part of a woman's robe. They dug a little further and found a woman's body in a grave just fifteen centimetres deep. The body, after preliminary examination, was taken to the Adelaide morgue for identification. This horrendous responsibility fell on Mrs Edson's other sister, Miss Rose Malycha, who made a positive identification. Tragically, it was Miss Malycha's birthday.

Edson had obviously killed his wife and had suicided when threatened with the discovery of his wife's body. However, several questions remained. Who had written the letter allegedly sent from Melbourne? Why had Edson killed his wife? How had he killed her?

Police continued their investigations and discovered that at least the first half of the letter allegedly sent from Melbourne had been written by fourteen-year-old John McMahon, who had identified Edson from a newspaper photograph. McMahon told police that Edson had asked him to write a letter and had provided him with a fountain pen for the task. However, the boy said he stopped writing halfway through the letter as he had become suspicious. Police were never able to determine who finished the letter for Edson.

Meanwhile, Adelaide newspapers had a major sensation on their hands and pumped it for all it was worth. Newspaper reporters even tracked down Edson's first wife, even though few—if any—of the dead man's neighbours even suspected that he had been married twice. The first Mrs Edson told reporters that she had married Edson when she was just seventeen years of age and he was nineteen. 'Ours was a boy-girl marriage,' she said:

> We met at Lyndoch, where Edson was working. We lived at Lyndoch for some time and then in Adelaide.
>
> Lawrie had a passion for crime stories. He used to read Deadwood Dicks. He struck me several times and was cruel to me but, at the same time, I must say this for him—he could be very nice when he chose and had a nice manner. Laurie would flare up in a moment and work himself up into a terrific rage over the most trifling things. But he would cool down just as quickly, and be genuinely sorry for what he had done. His second wife was a sweet little thing. She came to see me several times.

The first Mrs Edson gave birth to a son in 1922 and Edson used to visit her often to pay maintenance after their divorce in 1928. He called on her late in June 1931, and told her that Mary had died in Melbourne. 'He seemed genuinely cut up about her death, but whether it was remorse or not I cannot say. I questioned him about it and he said that she left home on May 18 and died in Melbourne on June 19.'

Edson, who once told a neighbour that he would 'get rid' of his wife and think of a way to 'get away with it' obviously did not have much faith in his ability to fool the police. His parents received a letter from him soon after his suicide. He must have written the letter knowing that police would eventually unearth his wife's body and discover his hideous crime.

The letter read:

> To My Darling Parents,
>
> God bless you and give you strength to stand this blow. I was mad when I did what, by the time you get this, you will know all about.

> This will not be posted until I am dead [police found the letter among his belongings]. Try and forgive me. Oh, I am so unhappy. I would give anything to get Mary back again. Pray for me, and be brave and try and forget my insane acts. Your loving Laurie. I can't bear to leave June, but better suicide than the other disgrace.

This proved beyond doubt that Edson had killed his wife and had suicided rather than face a charge of murder.

An inquest into the deaths of Edson and his wife was held in Adelaide from July 29, 1931. The acting coroner, Mr F.C. Siekman, presided over a case which held South Australia spellbound and, naturally, everyone wanted to know the cause of Mrs Edson's death. There had been newspaper reports that the dead woman had suffered shocking internal injuries.

The clear inference from these reports was that Edson had bashed her to death.

However, Adelaide University's Professor J.B. Cleland, who had conducted the post-mortem, told the inquest that although there had been some bruising to the body, Mrs Edson had died of strangulation. The body had been dressed in a singlet and nightdress, with what appeared to be a pyjama coat wrapped around the neck. This was rolled into a band two or three times around the throat and tied loosely into a single knot.

Mr Siekman asked Professor Cleland if this pyjama coat might have been wrapped tightly around Mrs Edson 'during life'. The reply was: 'It might have been.' Professor Cleland added that there were no fractures of any kind and no sign of natural diseases. Forensic tests did not reveal any traces of poison in the organs taken from the body.

It seemed certain that Edson had strangled his wife in a rage, but why? This almost certainly will remain a mystery, but the inquest learned that the Edsons were far from being a happily married couple and neighbours told of rows and even death threats by Edson.

The nextdoor neighbour, Mrs Lindsay, told of how Mrs Edson had run into her house in February of that year screaming: 'Save me, save me.' Mrs Lindsay continued:

I asked her what was the matter and she replied: 'Oh, save me. He is going to murder me.' She was clad in an underskirt and was without shoes or stockings.

Edson came running in about two or three minutes later and when I tried to take Mrs Edson inside, Edson tried to grab hold of her. He said: 'If any of you do not stand back I will stick a bullet in you.'

Mrs Lindsay asked Edson to explain the reason for his outburst and he replied that he would teach his wife to 'stick her nose in my business'. Mrs Lindsay continued:

Edson went away but came back a few minutes later. He called out: 'I give you five minutes to come out. If you don't, I will go in and finish the baby, and then finish myself.' He went away and we sent for the police.

Edson came back again and called out that he would destroy the baby if his wife was not out within three minutes. We heard a shot shortly afterwards and thought he had murdered the child. He then came onto the verandah and shouted out that he would wait until the police came and then he would 'finish himself off.

I asked him if he had done anything to the baby and he replied that he had not. Then I told him that if he was agreeable we would take Mrs Edson, who was half-fainting, into her home. He promised on his word of honour that he would not harm his wife and that everything else would be all right if she came back to him at once.

They seemed to make up after that quarrel, but the next morning Mrs Edson came and showed me the bruises on her throat, which she said her husband had inflicted the previous night. Mrs Edson said: 'He threw me on the floor, kicked me, and tried to choke me. I felt the breath going out of my body and just had the presence of mind to kick him.'

Obviously, Mrs Edson had no such 'presence of mind' or luck when Edson attacked her on or around 18 May when he strangled her to death in, presumably, another fit of temper.

Mr Siekman did not have the slightest difficulty finding that Edson had strangled his wife to death on or about 18 May and then had committed suicide two months later.

Edson, tall, dark and hollow-cheeked, had a murderous temper and probably had killed his second wife in a rage. Or had he planned her death so that he would be free to marry another woman? An

Adelaide newspaper reported at the time of his death that he had recently given a young woman an engagement ring and had promised to marry her. The newspaper suggested that detectives had interviewed a woman at Reynella, but there was no mention of this at the inquest and this little mystery remains as one of Adelaide's most infamous murder-suicides.

THE DANCE OF DEATH

The band had just started playing an encore of 'Follow Yvette', a new and unfamiliar foxtrot. It was Perth's glittering social event of the year—the St John of God Hospital Ball at Government House. It was just past the witching hour on August 27, 1925, and as couples started gliding around the polished floor, a tall and beautiful young woman in a blue evening dress walked slowly but purposely towards one of the couples. She touched the man on the shoulder, but he brushed her aside with the sneering comment: 'Oh, go away! Can't you see I'm dancing?' The woman responded by pressing the trigger of a revolver she had hidden behind a handkerchief. The dashing young man in the dinner suit crashed to the floor, a crimson stain spreading across his white-starched shirt. Some women screamed, while others rushed to the scene to see what had happened. The young man had been mortally wounded, shot through the heart, and the woman who had killed him stood staring into space.

The shooting of Englishman Cyril Gidley by the woman he spurned became one of the most celebrated cases in Australian criminal history. Its Government House setting and its aura of melodrama created headlines around the country for months; the public devoured every word written about this sensational killing. The headlines in the now-defunct Perth Mirror the following day shrieked: 'BALLROOM HORROR!' The opening paragraphs of the report, overwritten as they were, at least captured the imagination:

> Perth's greatest ballroom shone brilliant with light and gaiety on Wednesday night, while hundreds of glad-hearted boys and girls and their elders danced and made merry to aid the benevolence of the Hospital of St John of God.
>
> They had 'chased the glowing hours with flying feet' and the grand ball was drawing to a happy close, the night had passed into early morn. It was one of those scenes on which the High Gods seem to smile.
>
> Then a shot hushed chatter, little startled cries, a scatter of dancers, a girl with a revolver, and a young man, with a blood-smeared face, dying on the floor.
>
> The High Gods had deserted their chosen. Terror was upon the gay hall. Mirth fled away into the shadows.
>
> The glory of the lights and the gaiety of the colours, the music and the laughter gave way to the awe that betokened the presence of the Dreadful Great. King Death had entered in!

A Mirror reporter, present at the ball, gave an eyewitness account, which was headlined: 'Mirror Man's Story'. It read:

> A newspaper man sees many strange things. In my newspaper experience I think I shall always vision this as the most terrific; the most terrible of the happenings I have been called upon to witness. How many of those who looked on that scene can tell a coherent story and say it is what he or she really saw? Many fragments can be pieced together from after-experiences, but they are not what one sees in a moment like this. And many who may try to visualise it find that many main features of this tragedy are a blank in their minds. Once I asked a soldier who won the VC what were his impressions in engaging three of the enemy as he had done single-handed. He replied that his most vivid recollection was a broken boot, which showed up as the last man fell. He could tell little else. And similarly most of those who saw the tragedy enacted on Wednesday night can give as ocular evidence little more than the few phrases which appealed differently to different minds. It was the third last dance—a foxtrot

called 'Follow Yvette' new to most of the dancers, and not as hilarious as many of the others of the evening had been.

I don't think anyone particularly noticed the tallish, slim girl in the radium blue frock who threaded her way through the dancers as the music was dying away and the crowd was demanding an encore. She made no display of her intentions, gave no sign of rage or hysteria. Near the centre of the hall slightly to the left, a well set-up young man, dark, nicely featured and attired in full evening dress, was standing chatting with his partner. Until then all the actions of the developing drama had been commonplace. She was noticed by only a few when she approached the man as he was standing there. The report of the revolver woke the dancers to the horror that had happened. Then a man was seen slipping to the floor. They hurried over, vaguely believing that there was a joke somewhere, that a cracker had been exploded or some stupid humourist was seeking to cause a stir. As I moved forward the few yards that separated me from the group I remember hearing a girl giggle and say 'What silly rot's on now?' Over the head of an elderly man and a thin wisp of a woman I saw what told me that it was not 'silly rot', but dreadful tragedy. For I glimpsed a fine figure of a young man there, surrounded by an increasing group of aghast people. Someone bent over him and felt his pulse. Then two young men lifted him up and I saw a dreadful smear of blood on his lips, increasing as I looked, to a trickle. His hand went with a sort of twitch to his face, and I saw too, then that the face was of a grey-green pallor that speaks of only one thing. His eyes were open, and there was an expression of wondering terror in them. The last semi-conscious thought that a dying brain had formed surely was there. They carried him to the side. 'This is no joke. There's the one who did it.' I recognised the voice of a friend of mine close beside me and he had a policeman by the arm. I looked where he pointed. Ten feet away from me, only a little aside from the group, was a girl. She was dainty, dressed in blue, and seemed naturally of that dancing throng. She had dark hair, and was pallid and dazed with a look of wonderment on her face that seemed to say: 'What have I done? What has happened?' She was unnaturally calm, almost trance-like.

Another witness, Frederick Crowder, said:

She was standing near one of the alcoves or arches on the western side. I was dancing and at one of the turns of the dance I noticed the girl coming across the floor, in between the dancers.

She was alone. As she was coming across, the music stopped. She made for a couple three or four yards further to the south than I was. With that the music resumed for an encore. I began to turn and lost sight of the girl for a second. With that a shot rang out. On looking up, I saw a gentleman put his hand to his forehead, stagger and fall. I went and knelt down at his side and helped carry him outside. The girl in blue was standing some four or five feet away from the gentleman. As I knelt by his side I heard her say: 'Well, I've got you now.' She had a revolver in her right hand, at the side of her dress. A policeman then arrived and I heard her say to the policeman, 'Get me out quickly and quietly.' We carried the gentleman out to the cloakroom where, after a few minutes, a doctor pronounced him dead.

The shooting brought the dance to an abrupt end and the band played 'God Save The King' as stunned revellers filed out of the ballroom. Perth had never seen anything like the shooting at Government House.

Audrey Campbell Jacob had shot her man dead and her photograph was splashed across the front page of just about every newspaper in Australia. Dark-haired, vivacious and pretty, Audrey Jacob would have been every young Australian's dream girl of the 1920s. But her man had done her wrong, and she had shot him down in front of a dancing throng of revellers. The Mirror also ran a huge photograph of the dead man, Cyril Gidley. The caption suggested that it was his favourite photograph of himself. The photograph showed him wearing a hat and bow tie; he was smoking a cigarette and looked precisely what one witness described him as: 'a gay Lothario'. Gidley certainly looked as if he could win, and break, hearts; he certainly had broken Audrey Jacob's heart.

When the policeman took Miss Jacob by the arm, she told him: 'It's all right; I know what I have done.' She was then placed in a chair before being taken to a nearby lock-up for questioning. Miss Jacob, a mere twenty years of age, was charged with the murder of twenty-five-year-old Gidley, who had arrived in Australia as fourth engineer on a British steamer in 1923. Although he had a family living in the north of England, he decided to leave his British ship to take employment as an engineer on a coastal vessel, the Kangaroo. It was during one of his many stops in the port of Fremantle that he had met the lovely and innocent Miss Jacob.

Gidley, blond and dashing, was a man of the world and Miss Jacob fell head over heels in love with him. In fact, she broke every rule of her convent upbringing to give herself—body and soul—to the man she loved. Although she had been engaged to another man, she broke this engagement off to suit Gidley and even left home so that she could see him whenever he was in port. However, Gidley obviously had a roving eye and there were other women in his life. His carefree attitude cost him his life.

Miss Jacob stood trial before Mr Justice Northmore just six weeks after the shooting. It was the cause célèbre of the year, if not the decade, and there were long queues outside the Criminal Court when Miss Jacob was due to give evidence. A newspaper report of the time said that Miss Jacob walked slowly but steadily to the witness box and made her oath in a low voice. After being sworn in, she told the court:

I was born in Western Australia and I am twenty years old. My father is clerk of courts at Fremantle and I have seven brothers and sisters. Until recently I lived with my parents. I was educated at a Roman Catholic Convent at Norseman until I was sixteen [her parents were Protestants]. Among other things I learnt painting, then a little over three years ago my father transferred to Fremantle, and we have lived there ever since. I have kept up my painting and I have sold 200 to 300 of my works. Through a cousin, who is on a mailboat, I met a Mr Claude Arundel, who is a ship's officer, and after a short acquaintance, became engaged to him in July 1924. I had known Cyril Gidley for over two years. I used to meet him sometimes when his boat was in port. Gidley was sixth engineer on the boat. When on shore that time Gidley asked me to break off my engagement with Mr Arundel and become engaged to him. I asked for time to consider it. The Kangaroo went to Singapore and when he returned Gidley again pressed his suit. When I realised he was serious I consented to marry him and our engagement was announced early in October. He had six weeks' leave then, and owing to a strike, was on shore for about four months altogether.

Miss Jacob also gave evidence that Gidley was 'the living embodiment of the Sheik', a clear reference to the movie hero created by Hollywood actor Rudolph Valentino. He had been meeting another woman and Miss Jacob decided to end the engagement. She gave him the engagement ring and he later told her he threw it into the sea. Miss Jacob had no intention of going to the St John of God ball, especially as she believed Gidley was on his way to Singapore aboard the Kangaroo. She might have broken off the engagement, but she was still grieving for her love. However, a friend (a Miss Josephine Humphries) talked her into going to the ball that fateful night.

Miss Jacob told the court:

> I had been feeling very unwell that morning with a sick headache, but at lunch time she [Miss Humphries] persuaded me to go with her. She had the costumes [Pierrot and Pierrette], which were put in my room. We arrived at the ballroom about 8.30 p.m. I danced with Miss Humphries all the evening. One or two gentlemen asked me to dance with them, but I refused. At about 9 o'clock I saw Cyril Gidley near the door [he was supposed to be on his way to Singapore]. As we passed his eyes and mine met, but he didn't recognise me.

Asked by the judge whether she saw Gidley again, she replied:

> Yes, I saw him frequently as I continued to dance with Miss Humphries, but he refused to recognise me. He passed me four or five times—more, in fact—but he was very cold. Sometimes he would look at me and put his chin up. Several times as he passed me he gave a bit of a sneer and then turned away and laughed. He was talking to a young lady in a heliotrope dress and laughing. She turned to run up the stairs and he ran after her and pulled her down. Then he looked up at me. I knew he only did it to annoy me.

Tremendously upset by Gidley's behaviour, Miss Jacob went home. She told the court:

> I was feeling very upset and ill, and my head was aching. I went to my room and I lay down on my bed. I cried for about half an hour, I think. I then started to undress. When I opened the drawer I saw a revolver [given to her by her previous fiancé, Claude Arundel, for protection] and then decided to end my life. So I started to dress again. I meant to go down to the foreshore to end my life. I didn't

put on the Pierrot costume because I didn't want to do it in a fancy dress. I picked up the first dress handy, which happened to be a blue costume hanging over the end of the bed …

I wrapped the revolver in a handkerchief and went out intending to go down to the foreshore. But on the Terrace [St George's Terrace] I changed my mind and decided to go to the Catholic Cathedral first and say my Rosary. I wanted to make my peace with God. I went inside the gates of the Cathedral where I knelt down. I had my beads and said my Rosary. After that I felt better, but my head was still queer and my heart was aching. I decided I would not do what I was going to do and determined to go home. I passed the ballroom on my way. They were still dancing. The thought came to me to go in and ask Cyril what was the matter. I went in, but I couldn't see him at first. I saw Miss Humphries and asked her to send Cyril to me on the balcony. After a time he came and stood under where I was and looked up at me. He then turned away with a nasty look. I felt that I must know what was causing him to treat me like this. When the dance stopped I went down to the floor and stepped forward to where he was standing. The music struck up again and he hurried towards his partner. I touched him with my left hand on the shoulder. He looked around and said: 'Excuse me, I am dancing.' Then something seemed to snap in my head. I don't remember any more. Everything seemed to be going round and round. When I came to my senses I was in a cell in the lock-up.

Miss Jacob's counsel, the brilliant Mr Arthur Haynes, then asked her a question which was critical to her defence. He asked: 'Did you have any intention of causing Cyril Gidley any harm?' Up to now it had all looked extremely bleak for Miss Jacob; after all, she had gone home from the ball, changed, packed a gun and had walked up to Gidley to shoot him dead. To all intents and purposes it had been a cold-blooded, premeditated murder. Everyone in the Criminal Court stared at Miss Jacob as she prepared to reply to this pivotal question. She replied: 'No, none whatsoever.' Mr Haynes: 'Ever threaten him or wish him any harm?' Miss Jacob: 'No. If I could I would undo what has been done.'

Miss Jacob, through the expert help of her skilled counsel, had sown the first seeds of doubt in the jury's collective mind. However, Miss Jacob then had to weave her way through the minefield of a one-hour cross-examination by prosecutor Mr Hubert Parker, who asked her about the revolver used to shoot Gidley. Mr Parker. 'I suppose you had some practice with it?'

Miss Jacob: 'I have never fired out a revolver in my life.'

Mr Parker: 'He had seduced you, used violence towards you ... within a month or six weeks of your engagement, yet you still desired to be engaged to him?'

Miss Jacob: 'Yes.'

In relation to the night of the shooting, Mr Parker asked: 'Why did you not walk down from the gallery to the lounge and ask him for an interview?'

Miss Jacob: 'Well, he was with a young lady.'

Mr Parker: 'But that didn't prevent you asking Miss Humphries to go into the lounge and deliver a message for you?'

Miss Jacob: 'No, but that was different.'

Mr Parker: 'But a little later on you did come down to speak to him in the crowded ballroom?'

Miss Jacob: 'I came down simply because he didn't come up. I wanted to ask him what was the matter – why he had changed so suddenly.'

Mr Parker 'Now show me how you held the revolver.'

Miss Jacob: 'I don't know exactly how I held it. Like this, I think.' Miss Jacob then wrapped a handkerchief around the revolver before putting it by her left side. She rearranged her hold on the revolver several times before adding: 'I don't remember exactly how I held it.'

Mr Parker: 'Show me how you pulled the trigger. Hold it up, please.'

The prosecution failed to shake Miss Jacob from her account of events and, in fact, she repeated that she could not recall most of the events directly relevant to the shooting of Gidley. Mr Haynes then asked her a few more questions before she left the witness box. Mr Haynes: 'You had forgiven him all his slights and snubs?'

Miss Jacob: 'Yes.'

Mr Haynes: 'Up to that moment you had forgiven him everything?'

Miss Jacob: 'Yes.'

Mr Haynes: 'So that when you walked downstairs you had no hurtful intentions?'

Miss Jacob: 'I merely wanted to ask him what was the matter.'

Mr Haynes: 'You had no intention of doing him any injury?'

Miss Jacob: 'None whatsoever.'

Mr Haynes: 'And just because he said "Excuse me, I am dancing" in a cold and off-handed manner, something went snap in your head?'

Miss Jacob: 'Yes, everything seemed to go around in a blaze.'

Mr Haynes : 'You had made your peace with your Creator and therefore would not harm anyone?'

Miss Jacob: 'That is absolutely true.'

Mr Haynes' questioning was masterly and everyone in court sympathised with the girl in the dock. It had been a ghastly incident and although Miss Jacob had originally been the subject of gossip and accusation, she was now regarded as a 'wronged woman' who never intended anyone any harm—despite the horrible nature of Gidley's death, which was detailed in court by the doctor who attended him just after the shooting.

Dr Sydney O'Neill told the court:

> I heard a shot fired. I looked around and saw a man lying on the floor about two yards from where I was standing. I walked over to him and took his hand. There was a small trace of blood coming from his mouth. I helped to carry him to the cloak room. As we were carrying him blood oozed from his nostrils. We laid him on the floor. I saw a little wound in the upper part of his left chest from which blood had emanated. He died within two minutes of being placed on the floor. He was unconscious all the time.

The post-mortem was carried out by the medical superintendent of the Perth Hospital, Dr D.S. McKenzie, who told the court that death was caused by haemorrhage following a bullet wound to the heart. Dr McKenzie said the bullet entered on the left side and traversed between the fourth and fifth ribs, passed through both lungs and was removed from the body beneath the skin on the right side of the chest. The bullet, in its course, passed through the aorta. Gidley did not stand a chance of survival.

Mr Haynes told the jury that Miss Jacob's life would be 'forfeited' if she was found guilty and he therefore made an impassioned plea for what he described as 'fair play', insisting that the girl had no intention of killing, or even harming, Gidley. The fact that she was carrying a revolver was purely accidental and, in fact, the shooting itself was accidental. Haynes needed all his powers of persuasion as the Crown at first appeared to have an open-shut case. The jury retired, but less than three hours later, at precisely 8.45 pm on October 9, 1925, it returned to announce its verdict. Miss Jacob braced herself as the foreman announced: 'Not guilty.' Miss Jacob collapsed in the dock and was led away by her mother, Mrs Jessie Jacob, and a doctor. The crowd in the Criminal Court cheered the verdict and many rushed outside to announce the news to the world. It was an enormously popular decision and the excellent work of her defence counsel, Mr Haynes, had proved critical.

There was no doubt that the public—and, probably, the jury—believed that Gidley had inadvertently caused his own death. Evidence presented at Miss Jacob's trial painted a picture of a cruel, arrogant womaniser. He had treated Miss Jacob harshly and paid the extreme penalty. Incredibly, Gidley posed for a photograph just twelve hours before he was shot dead. He had made an appointment with a Perth photographer and was photographed in full evening suit—the same evening suit he wore at Government House that night. He left the photographic studio at 7 pm and headed straight for the ball, and to his death. The photograph was not developed until the following day, but was later published in the Perth Mirror along with a photograph of a wreath of flowers at his funeral. The flowers, sent anonymously, were forwarded by messenger and carried a card which read: 'From one who will never forget'. The newspaper caption read: 'Can anyone identify the writing?'

Miss Jacob left Perth almost immediately after her acquittal and, presumably, made a new life for herself under another name in another state. She had had more than her share of the public spotlight, in a case which gripped a nation and mesmerised the city of Perth.

Paul Denyer in Barwon Prison trying to gain permission to have a sex change.

*Reginald Wingfield Spence Brown after
being sentenced to life imprisonment
for the murder of Bronia Armstrong*
MY CONSCIENCE IS CLEAR - Page 36

*Thomas Ley, the former
NSW Minister for Justice*
THE CHALK-PIT MURDER - Page 33

Bronia Armstrong, victim in the Brisbane Arcade murder
MY CONSCIENCE IS CLEAR - Page 36

Andrew Kilpatrick
THE BODY IN THE BARWON
- Page 52

The car used in the Body in the Barwon case

Donald Maxfield
THE BODY IN THE BARWON - Page 52

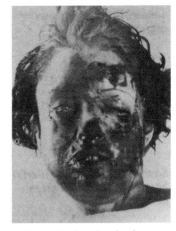

The Pyjama Girl as she looked before her death, and right, after death
THE PYJAMA GIRL - Page 117

Police search for clues
THE PYJAMA GIRL - Page 117

The culvert in which the Pyjama Girl's body was dumped
THE PYJAMA GIRL - Page 117

Antonio Agostini
THE PYJAMA GIRL - Page 117

Shirley Collins in the clothes
she was wearing the night
she was killed
THE DEADLY MISTAKE - Page 200

Charles le Gallion Jnr (left) and Charles le Gallion Snr (right)
A BONZER KID - Page 73

John Kelly is led away by police after his arrest in the Sommerlad case
AXED TO DEATH - Page 197

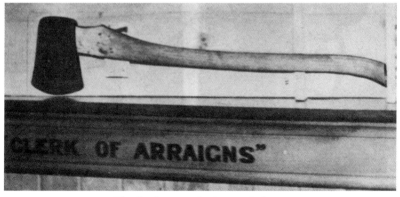

The death axe in the Sommerlad case
AXED TO DEATH - Page 197

The fireplace in the Deeming cottage in Windsor
THE BODY BEHIND THE FIREPLACE - Page 166

The Deeming cottage in Windsor, Victoria
THE BODY BEHIND THE FIREPLACE - Page 166

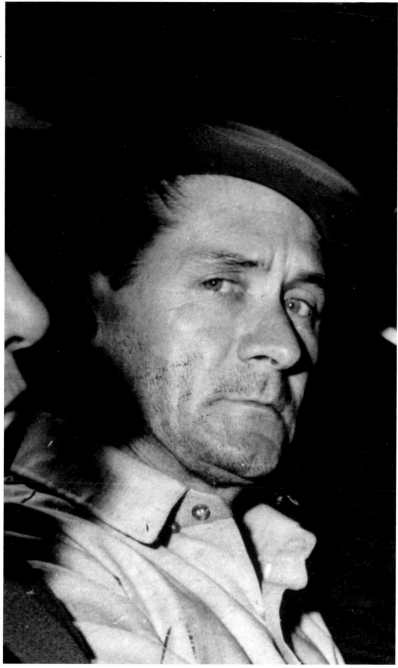

Ronald Ryan heading for Mascot in a police car
THE LAST MAN TO HANG - Page 221

Morris Sutton Brewer   Carmen Walters

THE EAST BRIGHTON STRANGLING - Page 206

The funeral of Carmen Walters

THE EAST BRIGHTON STRANGLING - Page 206

*Miss Gladys Hosking, third
victim in the Brown-out Killings*
THE BROWN OUT KILLINGS
- Page 171

Eddie Leonski
THE BROWN-OUT KILLINGS - Page 171

*Police look for clues in Royal Park after the body of Miss Gladys
Hosking is discovered. It was the last of the Leonski killings*
THE BROWN-OUT KILLINGS - Page 171

Herbert Jenner tries to cover his face as he is led into court for the Sherry murder trial
THE PAYROLL KILLING - Page 290

A crowd gathers at the scene of the Sherry killing
THE PAYROLL KILLING - Page 290

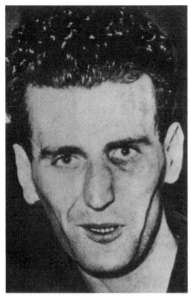

John Balaban

The scene of the Balaban horror. Verna Manie jumped from the window marked 'X'

Zora Kusic, one of Balaban's victims

The tin shack in which John Balaban killed Zora Kusic

Imre Mallach
THE HEADLESS BODY - Page 268

The Lewis farmhouse at Jerilderie. Mr and Mrs Mick Lewis
were shot to death over an insurance fraud
THE HOUSE OF HORRORS - Page 360

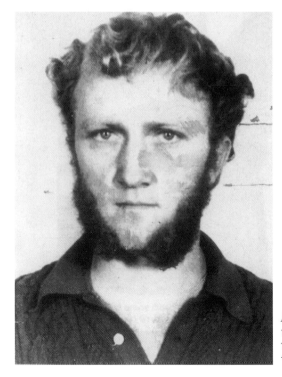

Mick Lewis, one of the
victims
THE HOUSE OF HORRORS
- Page 360

Samuel Borg
THE SEALED ROOM MURDER
- Page 65

William Krope and his mother after their court ordeal
THE KROPE CASE - Page 304

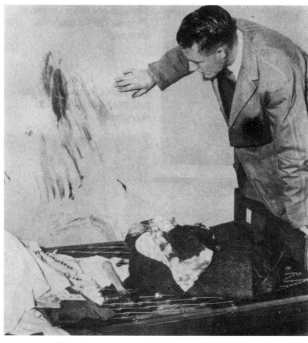

A forensic expert examines bloodstains near where Samuel Borg's body was found
THE SEALED ROOM MURDER - Page 65

Convicted murderer Ivan Milat is led by police to East Maitland Court
THE BACKPACKER MURDERS - Page 1

The loft off Chapel Street, Prahran, where Theresa Crowe's body was found
THE 'DISGUSTING' MONSTER - Page 5

DEATH AMONG THE TOMBSTONES

Joan Norris, eleven years of age, was a charming, pleasant girl who liked to help her mother with the household chores. Early on the evening of 12 June 1946, Joan's mother asked her to run down the street to buy some bread for her stepfather's breakfast. Joan skipped out of the house on the simplest of errands and her mother never saw her alive again.

As Joan was a punctual girl, her mother contacted police as soon as she realised that her daughter was missing, and one of the biggest Sydney searches for years was launched in an effort to find the missing girl. Police and volunteers searched through the night, but dared not think of the worst. However, their nightmares turned to reality early the next morning when Joan's mutilated body was found among mossy old tombstones at a disused Camperdown cemetery. Joan was lying on her back, with a piece of her own singlet knotted around her throat. Police were horrified and described it as one of the most brutal attacks they had seen.

The cemetery, badly overgrown and dotted with rotting tombstones, was—strangely enough—a favourite playground for local children. However, children were terrified of going anywhere near the cemetery at night and police suspected that Joan had been taken into the cemetery through one of many holes in the surrounding fence. Joan's body was found in a hollow about fifty metres from the entrance. There was no lighting where the body was discovered.

An examination by the Government medical officer revealed that Joan had been dead for about ten hours when her body was found. She had been strangled to death and there were marks on the body that were so severe the killer was described as a 'degenerate of the worst type'. Meanwhile, police retraced Joan's movements from the time she left her home in Enmore Road, Newtown. Apart from trying to buy the bread her mother wanted, she had called in to the home of her second cousin, Mrs Hazel Geary, in King Street, Newtown. Mrs Geary directed the girl to a local milkbar, but also told the girl to get home as soon as she could as it was already dark.

Joan was also seen in a hamburger shop and there were reports that she had been seen in a telephone box with a man wearing a military greatcoat. He was described as being twenty-seven or twenty-eight years of age, of medium height and build and wearing a light-coloured open neck shirt and grey trousers. The phone booth was outside the cemetery and police believed this lead was vital. Police, naturally, inspected the phone booth and discovered that its light had been smashed only recently as there was glass scattered around the floor. Police now worked on the theory that the killer had taken Joan to the phone booth and knocked her unconscious, but had killed her at the cemetery.

Police were painstaking in their efforts and had a huge squad of men working on the case. They even had special slides made for presentation at local cinemas in their effort to gain the break they needed. An advertising agency wrote to the CIB offering twenty-five pounds towards a reward fund and the New South Wales Government posted a £1000 reward for information leading to the conviction of Joan's killer.

Meanwhile, Joan's funeral was one of the biggest in the Newtown area for many years. The crowd was so dense three hours before the funeral that police had to redirect traffic. Tragically, Joan's mother later collapsed at the graveside and was carried unconscious to a nearby car. Police became more determined than ever to find the killer and set up a special 'hotline', which took more than 2000 calls from the public.

The police also had to deal with cranks, one man even walking into a police station to confess killing Joan. He obviously needed psychiatric help and was absolutely innocent. Joan's mother received numerous anonymous letters, which police branded as 'irresponsible'. One letter criticised Mrs Norris for having sent her daughter on an errand at night. Another letter was written in ink in block letters on paper torn from an exercise book. It read: 'Your girl never knew she was in the company of a man right up to the last. I can speak like a woman, and I was dressed like a woman. You say you would like to be with me for two minutes. Well, you will have the pleasure one day but I think it will take about half an hour with ease to fix you up.' Another letter was signed 'From A Spiritualist' and another was from a Brisbane hypnotist who suggested that if Mrs Norris allowed herself to be hypnotised her subconscious mind would throw some light on the case. The letter from 'A Spiritualist' included a picture of a man hanging from a gallows and advised Mrs Norris that the man police were looking for was a fifty-year-old businessman with greying dark hair, blue eyes and a full face.

Police maintained their massive efforts and interviewed more than 160 sex offenders. They examined a pair of bloodstained trousers found in a house in Glebe and even rushed to Thornton, near West Maitland in northern New South Wales, following a report of an attempted assault on a nine-year-old girl two months after Joan's death.

The inquest into Joan's death was held in November 1946, and Detective-Sergeant Denis Hughes told the coroner that police believed the dead girl must have known her killer. Mrs Norris, who broke down during the inquest, said she did not believe her daughter would approach anyone she did not know.

Joan might have known her killer, but after so many years police still cannot identify the killer.

THE LONELY
HEARTS TOMB

Veronica Dienhoff—known to her friends as 'Ronnie'—was a slim, attractive, forty-five year old who lived in a neat-as-a-pin flat in the inner eastern Melbourne suburb of Armadale. She worked as a secretary and, to help with the mortgage payments, also had a part-time job as a restaurant waitress. Life seemed full for Ronnie Deinhoff, except that she was lonely; so lonely, in fact, that she contacted a Melbourne dating agency in an effort to find a partner. Ronnie had been married three times—the first time at just sixteen years of age—and had four grown-up children. All three marriages had failed, but Ronnie seemed determined to find Mr Right. And why not? Ronnie, who had been born in Czechoslovakia and had migrated to Australia as a child, had succeeded in every other regard and had even won a brave fight against breast cancer. Determined to find lasting happiness, she had reached out for that happiness through a now-defunct Melbourne 'lonely hearts' service.

Wolfgang Hindenberg, a thirty-year-old who worked at a Dandenong engineering firm, was also seeking happiness and had contacted the same club. Ronnie and Hindenberg were 'paired', but Ronnie was never told that her new 'friend' had a history of violent behaviour and, in fact, had once been charged with the attempted murder of a policeman. That was in 1982 when police had been called to a domestic dispute between Hindenberg and his then wife. Police shot Hindenberg in both legs after he tried to stab a police officer in the stomach. Hindenberg was placed on a good behaviour bond on condition that he receive psychiatric treatment.

Ronnie started dating Hindenberg in 1985, but soon became aware of his violent nature. In fact, she became terrified of Hindenberg and avoided his company at all costs and even changed her telephone number to avoid his calls. Then, on November 28, 1985, Ronnie failed to keep a luncheon date with a friend. Police were called and, on December 3, Ronnie's unfed cat and two mould-encrusted coffee cups were found in her empty flat. Police also found money, clothing and Ronnie's spectacles. She had disappeared and newspaper reports suggested a police report later recommended that the case be investigated by the Homicide Squad. However, this recommendation was rejected because of insufficient evidence, even though Hindenberg had been seen at Ronnie's flat only days before her disappearance. Besides, Hindenberg had left his employment on November 22 and never returned. Ronnie and Hindenberg were both reported as 'missing'.

Police later issued a description of Hindenberg's car, a white four-wheel drive which had seen service as an ambulance. It was a unique vehicle, but although it had been seen in the street where Ronnie lived just before her disappearance, it then vanished from the streets altogether—for more than six years.

Then, on February 6, 1992, the distinctive white vehicle was found entangled in bush off a country track near Rubicon, 130 kilometres east of Melbourne. The vehicle—registration number CAR218—was found fifty metres off a logging track in the Cathedral Ranges State Park. The badly decomposed bodies of Hindenberg and Ronnie Dienhoff were found on a mattress in the back of the vehicle, which had been a bush tomb for more than six years. A hose had been connected to the exhaust pipe.

Immediately after the bodies had been found, the Homicide Squad's Detective Senior-Sergeant Paul Hollowood said: 'Let's just say that it looks like a mystery has been solved.'

POISON AT THE
PARSONAGE

Despite popular belief, death by poisoning has become relatively rare in the twentieth century and any murder trial with the merest whiff of poison in the evidence is certain to create headlines. The killer's most preferred poison is arsenic for several reasons: it is an innocent-looking white powder and is virtually tasteless—just the thing for slipping into a victim's tea or mixed with butter for the cucumber sandwiches. And, until a century ago, it was the perfect poison as it was impossible to trace in the body.

However, all that changed in the nineteenth century when English chemist James Marsh devised a method to detect and measure the amount of arsenic in human organs. Marsh's techniques have been refined over the last century, but his work put the use of arsenic as a murder weapon out of fashion. The accurate measurement of arsenic in corpses helped create enormous interest in a number of murder cases, including a sensational one in Victoria in 1928.

Parson's wife Ethel Constance Griggs died of arsenic poisoning in the tiny Gippsland farming town of Omeo (400 kilometres west of Melbourne) on January 3, 1928. Within weeks Mrs Griggs' death was the subject of considerable speculation, not only in Gippsland but also in Melbourne. Had Mrs Griggs been murdered, or had she committed suicide? These questions were debated by two juries, even though it at first appeared that Mrs Griggs had died of natural causes.

Mrs Griggs was the unhappy wife of Omeo's Methodist parson, Ronald Geeves Griggs, a man who had been destined for the cloth. A member of one of Tasmania's most prominent Methodist families, Griggs wore his religion like a tie pin and it was always on show. A moody loner with a youthful face and prominent ears, Griggs had been born in 1900 and had always been what his friends and neighbours had described as 'pious'. Even war service with the AIF in France had failed to dilute his strict religious beliefs and, in fact, he decided to give his life to the Methodist church after an incident in a French cafe.

Griggs was with a group of Australian soldiers when one of them took Christ's name in vain. Griggs, in recalling the incident, said:

> A girl turned around and said, 'Don't talk like that about that Man. That Man loves the likes of us'. The thing impressed me. I stopped the girl and expressed my wonder at her speech. She whipped around on me and said, 'Why should you wonder? What are you doing for Christ more than I am?' I wandered into the night outside, thinking deeply. I found myself at last beneath a roadside crucifix. Suddenly I saw the Cross and, kneeling down, cried out that if I could be used I would give my life to Christ's service.

Having been 'called by Christ', Griggs started studying for the Methodist ministry as soon as he returned to Australia and, at the same time, started courting Ethel White, the daughter of a Tasmanian farmer. Griggs had known Ethel from childhood, but it seems extremely doubtful that he ever really loved the unfortunate girl. Indeed, it could be argued that Griggs needed a wife to help him achieve his ambition of becoming a minister and that Ethel White was as good a choice as any. After all, she came from a good family, was reasonably well educated and was religious. It did not matter that she was no beauty queen.

Griggs courted Ethel, and on completion of his theological studies at Queen's College, Melbourne they were married. That was in 1926, shortly before the Methodist Church appointed him licentiate (a preacher yet to be ordained) at Omeo. Griggs, then twenty-six, and his wife, twenty, moved into the tidy weatherboard parsonage with little thought that within two years their names would be known in every household in Victoria.

Griggs settled into his duties without any great relish, although he was known to give fiery sermons, especially when it came to sins of the flesh. To all intents and purposes he was the very epitomy of what Australians would call a 'wowser'. He frowned on gaiety and admonished his flock for the slightest departure from the straight and narrow. After all, he would argue, as small as the eye of a needle was the entrance to heaven. But, to continue the Biblical analogy, Griggs was a camel with a considerable hump and his private life in Omeo would have made it impossible for him to enter the kingdom of heaven without considerable forgiveness from the Almighty. Griggs, in fact, became an adulterer and, in consequence, the grossest of hypocrites.

Although the Griggs' marriage was not an outwardly happy one, there was little reason to suspect that Griggs would fall prey to the sins of the flesh which he denounced with such vigour from the pulpit. However, soon after his arrival in Omeo he became infatuated with twenty-year-old farmer's daughter Lottie Condon, a vivacious and attractive churchgoer. Griggs and the pretty Miss Condon were often seen together, invariably with the parson riding his motorcycle and the girl as sidecar passenger. At first there was no hint that Mrs Griggs objected to the friendship and she even invited Miss Condon to stay at the parsonage for the final week of 1926. However, Mrs Griggs soon detected small signs of familiarity and affection and at the end of the week ordered the girl out of the parsonage, ending her outburst by describing Miss Condon as 'a hussy'.

Naturally, Mrs Griggs asked her husband if he had committed adultery. The parson was shocked and insisted that there had been no impropriety. He almost certainly was telling the truth, but Mrs Griggs obviously had a crystal ball and it was not long before Griggs and the delectable Miss Condon became lovers. He even stayed over at her father's farmhouse, and although the lovers slept in different rooms, Miss Condon was not averse to sneaking along passage-ways in the early hours of the morning. She would creep back to her own room before dawn and sit at the breakfast table as if butter would not melt in her mouth.

This clandestine relationship lasted for several months, the lovers becoming progressively open. They were often seen kissing and cuddling in the bush surrounding Omeo and Miss Condon seemed to be a permanent passenger in the cycle sidecar as the parson did his rounds. To make matters worse, Mrs Griggs learned that she was pregnant. It gave her no comfort to see her husband in almost constant company with Miss Condon. Then, to bring matters to a head, Griggs followed his lover to the New South Wales town of Wagga Wagga when Miss Condon went there for a couple of months in 192 7.

Mrs Griggs gave birth to a girl and she hoped that her husband would end the affair with Miss Condon for the sake of his baby daughter. It had the opposite effect and Griggs was unnaturally cool towards his baby. In fact, he even convinced Mrs Griggs that she and the baby go for a holiday to see her family in Tasmania. Mrs Griggs agreed, only for the parson to have an inexplicable change of heart. He tracked his wife down in Melbourne and convinced her to return with the baby to Omeo. That was in May 192 7, but Griggs still had no intention of ending the affair with Miss Condon.

Finally, Mrs Griggs could take no more and told her husband that she wanted a divorce. Griggs' advice was for her to 'think it over', and Mrs Griggs finally took her holiday in Tasmania. She was absent for almost six months, returning on December 31, 1927. She was in perfect health, but died of 'illness' within three days of her return. Only Griggs was left to tell of what happened to his wife between the time she arrived back at the parsonage late on the evening of December 31 and when she died on January 3.

According to Griggs, his wife complained of being ill almost as soon as she arrived back at the parsonage. She vomited and Griggs later prepared her a snack—bread and butter, a cheese sandwich and a pot of tea. Mrs Griggs ate some biscuits she brought to the table herself, according to Griggs. She drank some of the tea and ate half a sandwich before declaring emphatically that she would not drink any more of 'that tea'. However, she poured a little of the tea into a saucer and gave it to the baby, without any ill effect.

Griggs made his wife a cup of tea next morning, but Mrs Griggs could not drink it all. He called for the doctor that afternoon, but a prescription medicine had no effect. Mrs Griggs' condition worsened and she could take only sips of soda water. Soaked in sweat and in agonising pain, Mrs Griggs eventually went into delirium and the doctor was called twice more over a lengthy period. At one o'clock on the morning of January 3, Griggs knocked on the door of neighbour Herbert Mitchell to ask him if he could have a look at his wife. 'I can't tell if she's dead,' Griggs told Mitchell. 'She may be in a very heavy sleep. The only way I know is to put a mirror to her lips.' Mitchell did just that, but the mirror remained dry; Mrs Griggs was dead. This was confirmed by the doctor, who was at the deathbed within minutes.

Griggs asked the doctor: 'Will you give a death certificate?' The doctor, who concluded that the trip from Tasmania and a prolonged vomiting attack had been too much for Mrs Griggs' heart, said he could see no reason why he should not sign the certificate, to which Griggs replied: 'I should not like to think of her body being cut up [for an autopsy].'

Mrs Griggs was buried without the slightest police suspicion, but the swish of gossiping Gippsland tongues was heard in Melbourne. Both the police and the Methodist hierarchy became increasingly interested in the mysterious death of Mrs Griggs. The Methodist Church acted first by asking Griggs to attend a special committee meeting. There had been persistent rumours that Griggs had been having an affair with Miss Condon, and even the girl's father wanted to know the truth. Griggs told him: 'Upon my God, I swear there is nothing but friendship between her and me.' Griggs, despite adding the sin of a blatant lie to his greater sin of adultery, convinced the girl's father that there had never been an affair. Griggs also told the special committee that he had 'clean hands'.

Meanwhile, Detective Sergeant Daniel Mulfahey, a vastly experienced police officer, was sent to Omeo to investigate the mystery surrounding Mrs Griggs' sudden death. He decided that the first step in his investigation would be to ask Miss Condon if she had been having an affair with Griggs. To Mulfahey's surprise, the girl did not hesitate in telling him that she and Griggs had been lovers for some time. 'He promised to marry me,' she confessed.

Mulfahey next confronted Griggs, who was stunned by Miss Condon's frank admission. Griggs went into a state of shock when told that substantial traces of arsenic had been found in Mrs Griggs' body upon exhumation. Griggs was charged with his wife's murder and stood trial at the Gippsland town of Sale, not far from Omeo. The most damning evidence was the fifteen and a half grams of arsenic found in his wife's body.

Mrs Griggs' body, on exhumation, became the subject of scientific testing for arsenic poisoning. The examination was conducted by State pathologist Dr C.M. Mollison, while portions of the body were tested chemically by government analyst Mr C.A. Taylor for traces of arsenic. Arsenic, apart from being virtually tasteless, can be administered with lethal results through several doses. However, two grams is recognised as being a fatal dose. The amount of arsenic found in Mrs Griggs' body would have killed several oxes.

Although the prosecution had no difficulty proving that Mrs Griggs died of arsenic poisoning, it was another matter to prove that Griggs had deliberately poisoned his wife. The prosecution proved that Griggs had access to poison (at Mr John Condon's farm), but there was no proof that he had put arsenic in Mrs Griggs' tea or food. On the other hand, police could not find even a trace of arsenic at the parsonage. This was a critical point as Griggs claimed that his wife had suicided. He told the court that Mrs Griggs had once tried to throw herself on to a fire. The problem with the suicide theory was that there was no trace of any arsenic at the parsonage and it would have been impossible for Mrs Griggs, on her deathbed, to remove the poison from the parsonage.

Griggs finally admitted at the trial that he had been having an affair with Miss Condon, but steadfastly denied killing his wife. The evidence was conflicting and the jury, after a long deliberation, finally admitted that it could not agree on a verdict. Ten jury members were in favour of convicting Griggs, but two jury members disagreed. Consequently, a second trial was ordered.

This was held in Melbourne, far from those gossiping Gippsland tongues. However, by now the case was hogging the newspaper headlines and crowds packed the Criminal Court for the sensational retrial. Prosecutor, Mr C.H. Book, told the jury:

> There are two divisions in this case. Firstly, you have to be satisfied that this woman was murdered. To do that, you must be convinced that she met her death by arsenic poisoning. Secondly, you have to decide that, if she was poisoned, whether you are satisfied beyond reasonable doubt that the accused administered the poison.
>
> You should have no doubt on the first matter. You have evidence that almost as soon as the woman returned home [from Tasmania] she showed signs of arsenic poisoning. This unfortunate woman showed signs of sickness shortly after the tea prepared by her husband. The question for you is—are you reasonably satisfied that she died of poison administered by her husband?
>
> This is a case of what is called 'circumstantial evidence'. Nobody is called to say 'I saw Griggs poison his wife'. Nearly all cases of this kind depend on circumstantial evidence. It is frequently said that witnesses may lie, but the circumstances cannot lie. It is your duty to draw a reasonable inference from the circumstances.
>
> One of the reasonable inferences you may draw is that the accused poisoned his wife. I suggest that this is the only reasonable inference which is open to you.
>
> There are only three possible ways in which the arsenic could have got into Mrs Griggs' body. The first is by accident. The second that she took it herself. The third, that her husband administered it to her. The first two suggestions, when you come to consider them, are so fanciful that they should be ruled out of your mind.

Mr Book entirely dismissed the possibility of an accident and then tackled the question of suicide, raised by the defence. Mr Book told the jury:

> It is said she [Mrs Griggs] was jealous of Lottie Condon and that, because of this, she made away with herself. You will consider whether there have been any facts proved to you to show that she had any motive for committing suicide.
>
> What sort of woman was she? You have the facts that she was a good woman, and religious. A woman of that kind must have an exceedingly strong motive before she would go to the extreme of doing away with herself. And what is the motive? Her husband's relations with this woman? It seems she was jealous of his familiarity with her, but Griggs says he never told his wife he was unfaithful and that, as far as she knew, that was a secret between himself and Lottie Condon.
>
> Do you think that this woman, with her little baby of which no doubt she was intensely fond, would leave her mother in Tasmania, where she had been staying for months, and come across the water to destroy her life and leave her baby there?
>
> I suggest, if Mrs Griggs had any idea of doing away with herself, she would do it somewhere where her baby would be looked after by her own people. Do you think she would return to this unfaithful husband and the woman and leave the baby with them?
>
> The whole of the evidence shows that, when she returned, she was happy and bright. Griggs himself said the same thing. They had no quarrel. She went around the house saying it had not changed much in six months, asked him to admire the baby and kissed him. There was no suggestion about 'I have come back for my things. I am leaving tomorrow'.

Mr Book then told the jury that the final, and fatal, dose of poison was administered some time between 9 pm and midnight, just hours before Mrs Griggs' death. 'The accused was the only person who could have administered it,' Mr Book thundered.

Griggs' defence counsel, Mr G.A. Maxwell KC, admitted that the accused had sinned, but that his sin was one of adultery and not one of murder. Mr Maxwell also suggested to the jury that Griggs was on trial partly because of his honesty. He explained that Griggs admitted that he had made the tea and sandwich for his wife and it would have been 'the easiest thing in the world' to tell the police that his wife had made her own supper. Mr Maxwell continued:

> When his wife became ill Griggs called the doctor. What more could he do? The doctor examined Mrs Griggs and prescribed medicines and powders, which Griggs obtained from the chemist. He called in his neighbour and acted in a way in which you would expect an innocent man to act.

> Griggs admits his wife was sick immediately after taking the tea he prepared for her. Don't you think if he were guilty that would be the last thing he would admit? It is inconsistent with the idea that he was the poisoner. At a time when it is said there were unmistakable symptoms of poison he calls in a neighbour and the doctor. Is that what a poisoner would do?

> I ask you to say that not only is Griggs' conduct consistent with innocence, but that it points strongly against the theory of guilt.

> The Crown says that because of his infatuation for Lottie Condon the wife is an obstacle, and that the only way to remove her is by cold-blooded murder. They say that because Griggs wanted to marry Lottie Condon, and the alternative would have been giving up his position in the church, he killed his wife. Our duty is to show you how inherently improbable is the Crown contention of murder.

Mr Maxwell, in respect to the suicide theory, argued that this was entirely plausible. He said:

> She [Mrs Griggs] returned home knowing it was impossible to stay there, and knowing that she must go back to her people and admit that her married life was a mistake and that she had been supplanted by another woman. Might she not say to herself: 'I would rather go out altogether?' It may seem a small reason for suicide, but is it not commonplace for people to say: 'Just imagine So and So taking his life for that reason?'

Of the mistake theory dismissed out of hand by the defence, Mr Maxwell said that it was entirely possible that the chemist had made a mistake with his prescription. 'Just consider for a moment the possibility of mistake by the chemist,' he said:

> There were three grains of carbonate of soda in each powder [in the doctor's prescription]. Bicarbonate of soda is a white powder like arsenic. We are told arsenic is always kept in a cupboard by itself ... but suppose that he [the chemist] had used the arsenic

powder and instead of putting it back in the poisons cupboard he had left it among other powders. Thinking he is handling bicarbonate of soda, he takes a bottle and instead he puts in arsenic.

There was a crowd of 400 in the Criminal Court for Mr Justice Macfarlane's summing up. Griggs, according to newspaper reports of the time, sat back and 'listened intently' to every word.

After telling the jury to forget anything they might have heard about this case outside court, the trial judge said: 'Before you can find him [Griggs] guilty you must be satisfied beyond all reasonable doubt that he killed her intentionally. In this case you may take it your duty is to find: "Did Griggs kill his wife intentionally? It is narrowed down further, did Griggs kill his wife by administering or causing her to take arsenic?"'

The judge then warned the jury not to be influenced by Griggs' admission of adultery. He said:

It would be improper for you to approach the case with the idea – here is a man carrying on with this girl. It is very convenient for him to get rid of his wife. That would be an improper and dangerous way to approach this case. I am suggesting these matters to you, for Griggs does not stand before you charged with adultery or leading a double life … the proper manner to set your mind in approaching this case is to inquire how this woman met her death.

Mr Justice Macfarlane also referred to a letter Griggs had written to his mother-in-law in Tasmania. The judge said:

One cannot help feeling a certain amount of indignation, perhaps disgust, when one reads the letter written to the deceased's mother under these circumstances. Holding feelings of resentment and disgust with Griggs' conduct is very bad, and unless one watches one's judgment very closely, they may warp your judgment of these matters entering upon the case.

The letter, written to Mrs White on 5 January 1928, read:

Dear Mother, I think you will understand when I say I cannot write very much right now. You will realise just how hard it is. It seems to me it has all been a dream that I will wake up sometime and find your dear girl still with me.

Perhaps you would like me to tell you everything from the start. I could not say very much in the wire [informing Mrs White of her daughter's death], and I did not like sending it, but you had to know. I had the parsonage all clean and sweet for Ethel's homecoming, the tea set in the kitchen, hot water ready etc. and the day seemed as if it would never pass.

It was an exceedingly hot day. The motor arrived about 9 o'clock and after our little girl had been put to bed she [Ethel] had a bath and we had tea.

Afterwards she was just a little bit sick, but I thought it was the heat and the excitement. She did not eat very much and about halfway through she was sick again. She felt ill, so I got her to bed and she lay there, while I finished off my work for the Sunday, watching me.

She went to sleep about 7 o'clock. She woke up and from then on she was very sick. All night, between the sickness she went to sleep, but by morning she seemed a lot better and had a cup of tea. She could not keep that down, so I thought it best that she should have nothing but soda water. The baby was splendid. About church time she dropped off to sleep and at 1 o'clock appeared to have recovered. I thought that she had better have nothing to eat.

I did not like leaving her, but I had service twenty miles away and started. I went back as quickly as I could. She was sitting up in bed, playing with baby, and said she had had a good sleep and felt better, but was still feeling sick. I gave her a cup of tea and after that she seemed to get bad again.

So I went for the doctor. He seemed to think that it was nothing but heat and excitement, gave her medicine, and said he would call in again in the morning. She was bad all night; sick every half-hour. So at daybreak I went again for the doctor. He did what he could, got her easy, and came back again about 10. She seemed much better.

About 2 o'clock on Monday afternoon the change came, and she was bad, indeed, no pain but sickness and, of course, she was intensely weak. The doctor was away and would not be back until six. Neighbours came in and we did what we could but, although we managed to stop the sickness, she became delirious from weakness. At 6 the doctor came again. She seemed better again, but he said he would come back at 10 and give her something to give her rest. He did and between 6 and 10 she was still very sick and very weak, but was in no pain and was quite conscious.

The doctor gave her an injection and as she was falling asleep she said, 'How long will I sleep, doctor?' He said: 'Till midday tomorrow and you will wake up happy and well.' His words, or part of them, proved true. About 11 she seemed sound asleep. So I lay down and, as I had been up two nights—never even had my collar off—I was feeling done.

I was asleep for two hours and went in to look at her, and she had gone, apparently only a few minutes before. The doctor was up for 10 minutes, but it was true. She had never spoken or moved, and knew nothing of pain or weariness or anything. He said the heart had just stopped beating and she would know or feel nothing. It was really a beautiful way to go. She just fell asleep and woke up in heaven.

Apart from two days of sickness and weakness there was no pain, and there was nothing to indicate anything serious. She simply fell asleep, and there heard the call. I cannot realise it even yet. We had planned such a lot for the new year, but it was not to be. Who shall say that it is not better?

The little baby is indeed wonderful, and has found her way right into my heart. I will not know how to part with her.

Ethel is now lying in a beautiful part of the Omeo resting place. The funeral was conducted by the Presbyterian and Church of England ministers [Griggs wanted to conduct the service himself, but was talked out of it]. It has been a shock to the whole town. Father and mother will arrive tomorrow night.

There, mother dear, I cannot say anything more now. After I hear from you I will write again. This seems to have bound me all the closer to you. Please write just when you can. May God give you strength and grace to see His hand in it all.

I feel too stunned to realise it all. I have not known how to write this, but I have tried to tell you all. If you have any wishes—anything at all—let me know, and I will do my very best to fulfil them.

Goodnight, mother dear, you are still that to me. Goodnight and God bless you all. Love from Ronald.

Despite his scathing attack on this sanctimonious letter (Griggs had been seen arm in arm with Lottie Condon shortly after Ethel Griggs' funeral), Mr Justice Macfarlane then most fairly analysed the case for the Crown and that of the defence before asking the jury to consider its verdict. Griggs looked intently at members of the jury as they filed out of the courtroom. He was composed and at ease with himself.

However, he looked distressed when the jury returned six hours and twenty minutes later. He gripped a rail as he turned his head to hear the jury foreman. A Methodist minister, the Reverend Knuckey, collapsed as the foreman announced the verdict—'Not guilty'. Griggs' ordeal was over.

Griggs, of course, wanted to marry Miss Condon. After all, the girl's father said he would stand by the parson. However, that was when Griggs denied there had been an affair. His courtroom admission of adultery changed all that and Mr John Condon shifted his family to New South Wales. Griggs never saw his beloved Lottie again.

Although Griggs was found not guilty of murdering his wife, his life was almost beyond repair. He tried to enter the Presbyterian Ministry in South Australia under a false name but, after being uncovered, faded from public record, presumably under another assumed name. Griggs might have been found not guilty of poisoning his wife, but his own life had been poisoned and the mystery of Ethel Griggs' death has gone with her to her grave.

THE HEADLESS
BODY

The condemned and abandoned cottage in Greeves Street, Fitzroy, was the perfect hiding place for ten-year-old Edward Irvine, who was playing 'cowboys and Indians' with his friends from the George Street State School on February 26, 1964. The grey building, which had no front garden, had had its windows covered by corrugated iron for several months. However, Edward discovered a way to get into the cottage—much to his eventual horror.

Little Edward stared wide-eyed at what he saw and rushed to tell his friend, nine-year-old Terry Karvalis, who immediately rushed to have a look at Edward's discovery. The boys, who both lived in nearby Napier Street, went home to tell their parents that they had seen parts of a man's body. However, their parents chastised the boys for returning home late from school. The boys, not wanting to get deeper into trouble, kept their secret to themselves until the following morning, when they met a teacher on their way to school. They blurted out the details of what they had seen and the teacher sensibly contacted the police.

Detective Sergeant Tom White and two uniformed constables went to the boarded-up cottage and took only seconds to find the 'body' the boys had described. The head of the Homicide Squad,

Detective Inspector Jack Matthews, was immediately called for an investigation into a death which made splash headlines in Melbourne for days. The two schoolboys had made one of the grisliest discoveries in years as the 'body' was in two parts—the chest and shoulders, and the pelvic part of the torso. The middle part of the torso was missing, as were the limbs and head.

Forensic examination soon revealed that the body parts were from a middle-aged man used to hard work and that he was of solid build, but relatively short. A pair of trousers, size 36, was found near the torso parts in the abandoned house. The dark grey trousers had the name 'Molack' marked on one pocket; this was to prove a vital clue in the identification of the 'body'.

Meanwhile, police launched a massive search for the rest of the body. They were convinced that the two torso parts had been dumped in the house as there was no blood in the surrounding area and, besides, the parts seemed drained of blood. Detective Inspector Matthews was convinced that the dismemberment of the man's body had occurred some distance from the abandoned cottage.

Ironically, two other boys made the next gruesome discovery, just twenty-four hours after Edward Irvine had stumbled on to the two torso parts. John Garoni, fourteen, and Terry Kennedy, fifteen, were riding their bikes around a lot in Gore Street, Fitzroy, when Kennedy hit a bump and fell off his bike.

He reached out and was horrified. He literally had stumbled on to two arms (one with a watch on the wrist), thigh sections and a missing part of the abdomen. Police knew immediately that they were locking together parts of a human jigsaw, with the head, part of one arm, part of a leg and part of the torso still missing. Meanwhile, forensic tests revealed that the unidentified man had been dead only forty-eight hours before Edward Irvine had made the initial discovery. At least the trail was still 'hot' for Detective Inspector Matthews and his investigating team.

There were suggestions that there was a 'mad killer at large' and police were baffled. Meanwhile, the major breakthrough in the investigation came when a reader of the Melbourne Herald responded to a report on the front page of the February 27 edition that the name 'Molack' had been found on a pocket of the trousers found at the abandoned cottage. The caller told police that a man named Mallach who fitted the description of the dead man lived in Richmond. Police went to a house in Elm Grove, Richmond, and fingerprints taken at the house fitted those of the dismembered corpse. There was no doubt that the dead man was a thirty-two-year-old process worker named Imre 'Jimmy' Mallach, who had not turned up for work for several days.

The dead man's head and right arm were finally found twenty-four hours later in grass at a reserve off Alfred Crescent, North Fitzroy. The jigsaw was all but complete, even if parts of the body had been scattered over more than a mile.

Mallach, a naturalised Australian, had been born in Hungary and migrated to Australia in 1957 after fleeing Hungary during the 1956 uprising. Friends described him as a 'quiet and likeable' man who kept very much to himself. He lived by himself, but his landlord told police that the dead man had only recently separated from his 'wife'.

On February 29, 1964 police charged thirty-seven-year-old Mrs Vilma Broda with the murder of her estranged de facto husband, who was the father of her three daughters, aged three, two and ten months. Police impounded a bloodstained couch and carpet taken from Mrs Broda's Gore Street, Fitzroy home. Mrs Broda, a factory machinist, wept as the City Court was told that there had been 'ill-feeling' between herself and Mallach.

It was alleged that Mallach arrived at Mrs Broda's home early on the morning of February 25 and that there had been an argument. It was also alleged that Mrs Broda struck Mallach several times on the head with a hammer. She went to work, but Mallach had not moved by the time she returned. It was further alleged that Mrs Broda dissected the body with razors and a knife and dumped the parts in several areas of Fitzroy.

Mrs Broda stood trial in October 1964, and told the Criminal Court that Mallach had treated her and her three daughters so 'badly' that she had left him (Mrs Broda had lost contact with her legal husband some years earlier). She said that Mallach went to her home late on the evening of February 24. Mrs Broda claimed that Mallach was heavily affected by drink and took three pounds from her. He returned several hours later, at two in the morning, and demanded more money after losing at cards. Mallach stayed for several hours and Mrs Broda claimed that he then blocked every effort she made to take her children to a creche so that she could go to work. She fought with him and hit him on the head with a hammer.

Mr Justice Adam warned the jury not to let the fact that Mrs Broda had dissected the body influence their verdict. He told the jury members that if they found provocation or excessive use of force was used in self-defence, they could return a verdict of manslaughter. Mrs Broda, he added, was entitled to an acquittal if they found she acted in reasonable self-defence or if they were not satisfied beyond reasonable measure she had committed a crime.

The jury found Mrs Broda not guilty of both murder and manslaughter and she walked away a free woman, to disappear from the public spotlight and to get on with her life with her three daughters.

DEATH AT THE CRICKET

It would be impossible to describe a more typical Australian summer scene. It was Wednesday, February 13, 1952. The sun was shining, cicadas were singing in chorus and the flannelled fools were at their game of cricket. The match was between South-East and Upper-North at the Railway Oval, ten minutes from the city streets of Adelaide, as part of South Australia's Country Week. South-East batsman George Kay was about to play a shot from the bowling of Les Patroney when the handful of spectators noticed that the fieldsman at point, Captain Arthur Francis Henderson, thirty-one, had fallen to the ground.

They at first thought that Henderson, who had served in the Middle East and New Guinea in World War II, was skylarking. However, they soon noticed blood pumping from a wound over his heart. Captain Henderson was dead. Almost immediately spectators heard the crack of a rifle and another fieldsman, twenty-two-year-old builder Ron Reed, fell with a severe wound to his arm. A bullet had severed an artery.

Cricketers then made a dash for the pavilion as further shots whistled through the air from the tree-lined eastern end of the ground. Witnesses saw a small, dark-haired man running in a crouched position from one tree to another and then watched in horror as the man held the rifle in a firing position and aimed a shot at a pedestrian. Incredibly, the pedestrian seemed unaware of what was happening, even after the shot had been fired. A bullet thudded into the ground just in front of him, setting alight long grass. The pedestrian paused, looked at the grass, and kept walking.

A witness, assistant groundsman Arthur Blight, said:

> I saw the man go behind a peppercorn tree in the adjoining parklands. He crouched down and appeared to take aim at something. Then I saw a man walking along a pathway about thirty yards from the gunman. Suddenly, a shot was fired. The pedestrian stopped in his stride, looked and then walked on.

Meanwhile, one of the spectators had telephoned the police, who were at the oval within minutes. Detective Brian Giles and Constables Laurie Lenton and Jack Zeunert and police from the nearby Thebarton station tracked the rifle-wielding maniac. Detective Giles, showing remarkable courage, decided to confront the gunman. He abandoned his crouched position and walked straight up to the gunman—one hundred metres, ninety metres, eighty metres, seventy metres … he kept walking until he was within sixty metres of the gunman and the barrel of a .303 rifle.

The gunman lifted the rifle and aimed it at Giles' heart, but not even this deterred the detective. 'Don't come any further. Go away. I am all right. I am going to the police,' the gunman shouted.

Giles shouted in reply: 'Come along then. I will take you to the police station in a car.'

'Will I get good meals there? And a nice bed?'

'Yes. You will. Now will you come over here and talk things over?'

'No. I will cut my throat.'

The gunman did not have time to carry out his threat as he was still pointing the rifle at Giles when he was tackled from behind by a police constable and overpowered. He was immediately disarmed and police found a bullet in the breach of the rifle and another six in the magazine. Police found another seven rounds in the gunman's pockets.

The arrested man was twenty-four-year-old Lebanese migrant Elias Gaha, a former patient at two Melbourne mental institutions. Gaha appeared to have an inferiority complex and was convinced that Australians looked down on him. Doctors said he was suffering from a mental disorder known as paraphrenia. He had spent some time at the Royal Park Receiving Home and then the Kew Mental Hospital in 1951 before being paroled in his brother's care.

Gaha moved to Adelaide and got a job as a railway cleaner. He lived at the South Australian Railway Hostel, North Adelaide, and workmates described him as a quiet, apparently inoffensive young man. However, he bought the rifle only days before the tragedy and it seemed obvious that Gaha wanted to avenge what he considered to be the superior attitude of Australians.

Gaha was charged with the murder of Captain Henderson, the father of three young children, but did not stand trial. He was sent for medical examination at the Parkside Mental Hospital, where doctors certified him as insane.

The mad gunman was later deported to Lebanon, with Detective Giles as one of his escorts. Detective Giles, for his courage in confronting Gaha, was awarded the George Medal.

Tragically, both Henderson and Reed (who made a full recovery from his wound) were last-minute replacements in the Upper North team. Even more tragically, the Country Week match in which they were playing was a last-minute replacement for a match abandoned because of the death of King George VI.

Such is fate.

THE MUTILATING
MONSTER

Peter Norris Dupas was just 15 years of age when he first came to the attention of the Victoria Police. Dressed in his school uniform, he visited a neighbour and asked to borrow a knife. He then started slashing her before breaking down in tears and then explaining to police that he did not know what he was doing.

Dupas was put on probation but, despite being given psychiatric treatment, he was found guilty of rape in 1973 and sentenced to nine years' jail. However, he was released after five years, only to almost immediately re-offend and was sentenced to a further five years' jail.

Although a report in his file noted that Dupas was a 'disturbed, immature and dangerous man' he was freed again in 1985. Then, just a month later, he raped a 21-year-old woman at a Rye beach. This time he was jailed for 12 years, with a 10-year minimum. Released in 1992, he held a woman at knifepoint in a toilet block at Lake Eppalock and was sentenced to a further two years and nine months in jail.

A serial sexual offender, he was convicted in 2000 of the murder of 28-year-old psychotherapist Nicole Patterson, whose mutilated body was found at her Northcote home on April 19, 1999. Both

Miss Patterson's breasts had been removed, but never found. She had been stabbed 27 times

Dupas was sentenced to life imprisonment, with no possibility of parole for this murder, but then faced another charge of murder, of 40-year-old prostitute Margaret Maher, whose mutilated body was found by fossickers in long grass at Somerton on October 3, 1997. Significantly, her left breast had been removed and stuffed into her mouth.

Police believed that the body of Maher, who had plied her trade along the Hume Highway just north of Melbourne, had been dumped after her death elsewhere. A black glove was found near the body and evidence was given at Dupas' trial for the murder of Maher that it could be linked to him.

Fornesic scientist Dr Henry Roberts told the Victorian Supreme Court there was strong evidence that DNA taken from the woolen glove came from Dupas and at least one other other person. He also said that a DNA test revealed that the glove was more that 450,000 times more likely to have come from Dupas and another person than from two other randomly selected Caucasian people in the state of Victoria.

Dr Roberts added in the trial before Justice Stephen Kaye: 'In my opinion it (the test) provides very strong evidence the DNA came from Dupas and at least one other unknown person.'

Dupas, 52, pleaded not guilty, but the jury took less than a day to announce its verdict. As the guilty verdict was announced, a relative of Dupas' other victim, Nicole Patterson, shouted 'Yeah'. Dupas, however, described his trial as a 'kangaroo court'.

Meanwhile, police said they would review at least two other unsolved cases in which they believe Dupas was involved, one being the murder of 25-year-old Mersina Halvagis, who was killed in the Fawkner Cemetery in November, 1997, when she was visiting her grandmother's grave. Halvagis, a quiet, reserved young woman who was very close to her family, was stabbed to death.

Police also believe Dupas could be connected to the death of 95-year-old Kathleen Downes in a Brunswick nursing home in

December, 1997. Mrs Downes was stabbed to death and, significantly, the murders of Maher, Halvagis and Downes all occurred in Melbourne's northern suburbs, where Dupas lived (in Pascoe Vale) over just three months.

Dupas, short, bespectacled and podgy, was sentenced to a second term of life imprisonment. Australians therefore can be thankful the Mutilating Monster will never be released.

SHIVERS AT THE GRAVE

It is doubtful if any man in Australian legal history was found guilty of murder and executed on such flimsy circumstantial evidence as John Healey, who was hanged in Melbourne on November 30, 1847, after police noted he had shivered when standing on the grave of the man he was supposed to have killed.

The body of a man named James Ritchie was found in Gippsland earlier that year. He had been brutally battered around the head and police constables were able to establish that the dead man had been drinking with Healey, a woman named Hannah Wilson and two men named Savage and Francis. Suspicion fell on Healey because he had blood stains on his shirt and trousers. Police also found a bloodstained axe in a shed attached to a house where he had spent the night with Hannah Wilson. However, Wilson insisted that the axe had been used to decapitate a goose.

Police seemed determined to charge Healey with Ritchie's murder as they had heard that the two men had often quarrelled and, in fact, Healey had once threatened to kill Ritchie. Police did not seem interested in Hannah Wilson's information that Healey had once rescued the drunken Ritchie when he fell off his horse.

The police took Healey to a cemetery one moonlit night and made him stand directly over Ritchie's grave. They noted that Healey appeared to shiver and took this as a sign of guilt.

However, the police needed further 'proof' and decided to accept the offer of an anonymous volunteer who suggested that he could get a confession from Healey. The volunteer was locked in a cell with Healey at the Melbourne jail and struck up a conversation. He told Healey: 'If you did that murder and don't confess it and die like a man, the sight of God you will never have.'

Healey allegedly replied: 'Well, I did it, and I'm willing to die for it.' That comment was enough for the police and Healey was charged with Ritchie's murder and sent to trial. He was found guilty and, when sentenced to death, protested his innocence. He was marched to the gallows still protesting his innocence when publicly executed.

Healey possibly was innocent and the evidence presented at his trial would not even be considered today. Besides, several witnesses claimed that Healey was so drunk on the night of Ritchie's murder that they had to put him to bed.

Healey's companions, Savage and Francis, were never charged with murder, even though they were arrested with Healey. Significantly, when Ritchie's body was found, the body of his dead dog was laying across its dead master's chest; its throat had been cut. Francis, during his short time in jail, was seen treating himself for a wound on his arm. He dressed the wound with butter from his prison meals and told the police that he had been bitten by Ritchie's dog.

The police argued at Healey's trial that Ritchie's dog had been killed in spite. But was it? Was it possible that the drunken Francis, after being bitten by the dog, killed it and its master? Or had the dog, in loyalty to its master, defended Ritchie from Francis' axe blows? And was Hannah Wilson implicated in the crime? No one will ever know, but it is possible that an innocent man was publicly executed in Melbourne in 1847.

DOCTOR DEATH

To all intents and purposes, Dr George Cranstoun was a pillar of society in the Melbourne bayside suburb of Hampton. He lived in an extremely comfortable Queen Anne villa in Station Street, just fifty metres from the Hampton railway station, and had a thriving practice. His wife regularly attended the local Congregational Church and their five children went to Sunday School.

Dr Cranstoun, forty-five, was a pharmacist until he graduated in medicine at the University of Melbourne in 1914; he practised in Gippsland for several years before establishing the practice in Hampton. He was well liked and another Hampton medical practitioner, Dr Garnet Leary, said he had 'never met a more charming personality'. He added: 'Everyone who met him liked him.'

However, Dr Leary shared one of Dr Cranstoun's darkest secrets as just a month after the former pharmacist opened his practice in Hampton, Dr Leary had to treat him for an over-injection of morphia. Dr Cranstoun was unconscious for sixteen hours, but then made a full recovery, only to continue his drug addiction.

Dr Leary could not possibly have known what Dr Cranstoun's drug addiction would lead to, and on the morning of August 14, 1922 Melbourne newspapers trumpeted what they described as the worst domestic tragedy in the history of Victoria. Dr Cranstoun had killed three of his children and a servant and had tried to kill his wife and their other two children before suiciding. The victims were servant Gladys Baylis, twenty-two, John Cranstoun, fifteen, Robert Cranstoun, ten, and Colin Cranstoun, eight. Mrs Cranstoun and daughters Margaret, thirteen, and Belle, six, survived Dr Cranstoun's deadly attacks by hypodermic needle.

The discovery of the family tragedy which shocked Victoria was made by one of Dr Cranstoun's patients, whose baby was having treatment by the Hampton doctor. She telephoned for an appointment, but there was no answer. The woman then rang the telephone exchange and an operator told her there was no problem with the telephone line. She then decided to make a personal call and arrived at the Cranstoun house at approximately 10.30 am.

The woman rang the doorbell, but again there was no answer. However, the hall light was on and she could hear the telephone ringing in the house. In exasperation, she lifted the letterbox slot and saw the pyjama-clad Dr Cranstoun lying in the hall. The woman yelled out to local butcher Alexander Dick, who was driving past the Cranstoun house, and he and the woman entered the house. They then called the Sandringham police, who arrived within minutes along with Dr Leary.

They discovered a hypodermic needle on the hall floor near Dr Cranstoun, who was still alive. Fearing the worst for the rest of the family, police rushed to the other rooms. They found John, Robert and Colin Cranstoun and Miss Baylis dead, but Mrs Cranstoun and her two daughters were still alive. In fact, little Margaret Cranstoun was still conscious, despite being desperately ill. Dick asked Margaret if she recognised him and she replied: 'Yes, you are Mr Dick.' He then asked her what happened and the thirteen-year-old girl said: 'We are sick. We got an injection last night.'

Mrs Cranstoun was found in an extremely distressed condition in her bedroom. She was fully dressed, but in great pain as she groaned: 'Oh George, oh George.' Miss Baylis' body was discovered in her room and apparently she had died only minutes before the house was entered. She was fully dressed. Colin and Robert Cranstoun were found dead in their room and had been dead for several hours.

Dr and Mrs Cranstoun were rushed by ambulance to the Melbourne Hospital (now the Royal Melbourne) and the two girls by taxi, but Dr Cranstoun died shortly after 4 pm. He lapsed into unconsciousness before he could be questioned. However, Margaret was interviewed by police and she told them: 'I think my father gave me an injection last night. I think he did the others, too.'

Senior-Detective F.J. Piggott, in charge of the investigation, found a fully charged hypodermic needle in Dr Cranstoun's house and also a broken glass tube marked 'strychnine' in one of Dr Cranstoun's trouser pockets. There were four other tubes of strychnine on the drug table. One of them was open.

Strychnine is used medicinally as a stimulant, despite being extremely lethal in large doses. It is absorbed rapidly into the bloodstream and affects the central nervous system. Breathing becomes extremely difficult and there are convulsions before death.

Police also found an addressed unstamped envelope on Dr Cranstoun's desk in his consulting room. Dated August 13, 1922, it read: 'It may make it easier for you if I formally acknowledge that I owe you 110 pounds for money lent to me and interest. I have felt for some time that I should have given you a P.N. for the amount, and if you think the same we can fix it up next time we meet.' Police did not release the name of the intended recipient.

Dr Cranstoun obviously was heavily in debt and this was confirmed by the discovery of a number of race programs and form guides in his surgery. It also was learned that Dr Cranstoun had attended the Caulfield races the previous Saturday and was, in fact, a keen race-goer.

Mrs Cranstoun and her two daughters eventually made a full recovery from their poisonings by injection, but Melburnians were shocked when they read that fifteen-year-old John Cranstoun had struggled vigorously before being lethally injected. His room was a mess, with books thrown around the room, chairs disarranged and a vase broken. There was a puncture mark on his left wrist and he must have fought with all his strength to fight off his deranged father. Tragically, Dr Cranstoun had seen the headmaster at John's school, the Hampton State and Higher Elementary School, to check on his son's progress only days before the tragedy; Dr Cranstoun was told that John was doing well.

The doctor, so revered in the Hampton community, had taken not only his own life, but the lives of four innocent people, including his three sons.

ASHES DOWN THE SHAFT

Outback boring contractor James Patrick Callaghan thought he had committed the perfect murder in 1940. He was convinced that it would be impossible to find the body, let alone press a charge of murder.

Callaghan employed an old swaggy, Bill Groves, to work on artesian bores on the Boorara Station in far western Queensland. It was hot, dirty work and the nearest 'civilisation' was hours away at Cunnamulla, where Groves sometimes went to slake his fierce thirst. Groves was something of a grizzler and would bend anyone's ear at any time about one complaint or another. His latest complaint, in July 1940, was that he had been 'diddled' by his boss, Callaghan. Groves complained that he had been underpaid and that he would have to do something about it.

No one in Cunnamulla took Groves' complaints seriously and the old man headed back to the Boorara Station to continue his work with Callaghan. He threw his swag on to his back and marched into the dusty red outback. Groves was never seen alive again.

Meanwhile, Groves had complained to the Australian Workers' Union about not being paid for his work at Boorara Station. He told the union that he was owed more than 100 pounds and the union decided to investigate on behalf of their comrade. However, Groves did not reply to the union's letters and it was decided to send a representative to the Boorara Station.

Callaghan was surprised to see the union man, but told him that Groves had left the camp several weeks earlier with two men in a utility. Callaghan suggested that Groves was heading for Charleville. However, Groves had not been seen at Charleville for months and the union official became suspicious, especially as Groves had been owed a considerable amount in wages.

The union called in the police and Detectives Jack Mahoney and Frank Bischoff headed for the outback in an effort to solve the mysterious disappearance of the old grizzler. Callaghan, to their surprise, welcomed them to his camp and then told the two detectives about how he had been glad to see the last of Groves, whom he described as 'quarrelsome'.

Callaghan was so convincing that most police officers would have closed the files. However, Detectives Mahoney and Bischoff decided to make a thorough search of the camp. They began by raking over every old fire within kilometres. They dug up suspicious mounds and even sifted through the sunburnt red soil for the slightest trace of Groves or any of his belongings.

The search proved fruitless, until they found shreds of old clothing in a bore several days after they had started their search.

The detectives had been pumping the bore at about thirty metres, but decided to go much deeper and asked Callaghan if he had a sand pump. Callaghan was horrified and explained to the detectives that the bore was for drinking water and that he certainly would never have dumped a body there, even if he had killed the old man.

Mahoney and Bischoff were unimpressed and pumped down to more than 300 metres. They carefully collected all the sand and soil in a wooden frame and painstakingly sifted through every load. They were rewarded with the discovery of what appeared to be minute fragments of bone and ashes. However, the most important discovery was a pair of metal buckles.

The detectives, experienced bushmen, realised that the buckles were from overalls worn by outback working men and soon learned that Groves had bought a pair of these overalls at the Eulo general store, the closest hamlet to Boorara Station. They were now convinced that Callaghan had killed his quarrelsome worker, had burned the body beyond recognition and had dumped it down the bore.

They told Callaghan of their suspicions and arrested him, when he broke down and confessed to disposing of the body. However, Callaghan insisted that he had not meant to kill the old man and that he had acted in self-defence. He claimed that Groves had accused him of withholding his wages and had then attacked him. Callaghan said he defended himself and had struck Groves a fatal blow. He told the detectives he then panicked and lit a massive funeral pyre to dispose of the body. Callaghan stoked the fire for hours to generate enormous heat and then pounded the dead man's bones on an anvil to reduce them to mere fragments before dropping all the remains down the bore.

The fragments of bone collected by Detectives Mahoney and Bischoff were examined by the Queensland Government Pathologist, who identified them as human. The buckles helped identify Groves as the victim and Callaghan was convicted of murder and sentenced to life imprisonment.

BURIED UNDER GRASS

Little Svetlana Zetovic, just six years of age, was a strikingly pretty girl with beautiful straw-coloured hair. She lived with her parents and eight-year-old brother Danny in the western Sydney suburb of Guildford and attended the Granville South Public School. Svetlana's mother worked during the day and her father worked at nights. The Zetovic family was typical of Sydney's western suburbs—hard working and determined to reap the rewards of their labour. The family had migrated from Yugoslavia in 1970 and, by 1974, had settled into a quiet routine. Mrs Barbara Zetovic would care for the children at night and Mr Adam Zetovic, being a night-worker, was always at home when the children returned from school. However, Svetlana did not return from school on November 7, 1974. Her father might have been at home, but Svetlana had last been seen playing in a park after school. She went missing in just ten minutes, between 3.40 and 3.50 pm.

Mrs Zetovic returned home from work and knew immediately that her daughter was missing and contacted police. Mrs Zetovic told them that little Lana was a creature of habit and always met her at the front gate of their home. Police, fearing the worst, immediately launched a massive search for the missing girl. More

287

than 200 police officers, cadets and volunteers scoured the neighbourhood and even combed through nearby bushland at Duck Creek, which runs into the Parramatta River. The chief of the CIB, Detective-Superintendent F. Bradstreet, told the media: 'We need all the help we can get to find her.' A Yugoslav police officer even broadcast a special plea for help and told listeners that Lana had been wearing her blue and white striped school uniform, long white socks and black shoes. Mr and Mrs Zetovic waited in anguish for any sighting of their daughter, despairing with every passing hour.

The search was two days old when the police made the discovery they hoped they would never make. They found Lana's body under a pile of grass clippings, rags and rubble in the backyard of a house just three doors from the Zetovic home. Lana had been choked, stabbed through the heart and sexually assaulted. Police charged forty-five-year-old labourer Noel Edward Holden with the murder of the six-year-old girl.

The entire state of New South Wales was outraged, and when Holden appeared in Fairfield Court several days later, police and court officials had to lock the doors as more than 100 people packed into the courtroom to get a glimpse of the small and slightly built prisoner. Some of those who did get into the courtroom hissed and booed as Holden was led in and a police constable several times had to shout 'SILENCE'. Holden, handcuffed and surrounded by three detectives and six uniformed police officers, was led into the courtroom from a side door. Another nine police officers linked arms to prevent gallery spectators moving to the centre of the courtroom. Outside, several other police officers kept crowds from the door. However, the hearing was disturbed by people banging on the courtroom doors in an effort to get inside. The police prosecutor, Sergeant N. Short, told magistrate Mr D. Hughes that a record of interview had been taken and that police opposed bail. He said:

> The allegations will be that at about 3.50 pm on 7 November Lana was either abducted or enticed from her home by Holden. She went into his house and we allege she was later sexually assaulted and murdered. We say Holden attempted to hide

Lana's body in his backyard by covering it with grass clippings. He lives only three doors from the dead girl's home ... we allege she had visited Holden's house before to see his horse.

Holden was remanded without bail.

At Holden's committal hearing at the Glebe City Court, Constable R. Schell said he had been helping in the search for Lana when he went to Holden's house and, after looking through a shed, pushed some grass clippings aside and discovered Lana's body. Detective-Sergeant J. Sharpe told the court he then interviewed Holden, who told him: 'I'm sorry, I knew you'd find her. Are you going to take her home? I didn't know what to do. She wanted to go home and cried. I wanted to keep her. I made her sleep here.'

Police chemist Inspector J. Goulding told the court that tests he had made showed that hairs taken from the girl's body and from Holden's trousers were the same 'beyond reasonable doubt'. The Government Medical Officer at the Liverpool District Hospital, Dr Bruce Carlyle, told the court that Lana had died from a stab wound to the heart, but there had also been signs of strangulation by hand. He said a knife taken from Holden's house could have caused the stab wound. Magistrate Mr J. Dunn SM found a prima facie case of murder established against Holden, who then stood trial at the Central Criminal Court before Mr Justice Isaacs and jury.

Holden pleaded not guilty but the jury deliberated for a mere ninety minutes before announcing its verdict—guilty. Mr Justice Isaacs, in sentencing Holden to life imprisonment, described the murder of little Lana Zetovic as 'a horrible crime'. Indeed it was.

THE PAYROLL
KILLING

Killings during armed robberies have been, thankfully, relatively rare in Australia. Even in desperate times few criminals have resorted to being killer bandits. There have been no marauding, killing 'Bonnie and Clyde' gangs in Australian criminal history, although one armed robbery in Melbourne in 1938 not only resulted in the death of an innocent man, but outraged a nation.

Brothers Frederick and Clarence Sherry had started a small shoe-making business in the inner Melbourne suburb of Abbotsford in 1924. Despite the Great Depression the business flourished and, by 1938, the Sherry Shoe Company had more than thirty employees. This, of course, meant a substantial payroll in an era before pay cheques or, indeed, armed security services. On the other hand, Melbourne was a much quieter, more peaceful city in those days and armed robbery was not an everyday event. The Sherry brothers were confident that they would be able to draw the wages from their bank and deliver it to their employees with little trouble. That view changed dramatically in March 1938, when two masked men tried to hijack the Sherry wages. One of the men drove a car alongside the Sherry car and the other masked man leant out of a window and pointed a pistol at Clarence Sherry. 'Hand over your money,' the bandit shouted as he pointed the gun. Clarence Sherry responded by speeding away from the bandit's car and reported the incident to police. For several months the Sherrys had a police escort for the collection of the weekly wages.

Time passed and the brothers felt that the attempted hold-up had been a one-off incident. After all, Melbourne was not Chicago. They decided to discontinue using the police escort. It proved to be a fatal mistake for forty-six-year-old Frederick Sherry, a father of six. On September 1, 1938, Sherry and company secretary Henry Thomas drove to the Northcote branch of the Commercial Bank and withdrew more than 600 pounds. Thomas stuffed the notes into his coat pocket, but threw a large bag of coins into a bag. Sherry and Thomas left the bank and were confronted by a youth. However, neither was aware that there would be another hold-up. Sherry and Thomas got into their small brown car and were followed by a blue tourer with two men in the front.

Sherry drove his car down High Street and around a curve along a railway line into Queen's Parade, not far from his factory. The blue tourer pulled alongside and Sherry and Thomas saw two men with handkerchiefs pulled over their faces. The two shoe factory men must have thought they were caught in some weird Hollywood drama, with the men in the car playing the baddies in a Western movie. However, this was no make-believe incident and the man driving the blue tourer forced Sherry to pull over. The two men jumped from their car and ran over to Sherry and Thomas shouting: 'Hand over the bag.' One of the men was pointing a pistol at the front window at Sherry. Thomas, desperately seeking help, leant over and pressed his hand on the horn to attract attention from passers-by. The man holding the pistol lost his patience and fired a shot which pierced the window glass and cut Thomas about the face. Sherry bravely grabbed the gunman's hand and struggled for several seconds, then opened his car door and ran down the street.

The gunman followed him and, when Sherry fell over, shot him through the heart from almost point-blank range. The bandit turned to a gathering crowd and warned them to keep away. He then rushed to the blue tourer before turning on Thomas and ordering him to hand over the bag. Thomas, a gun in front of his face, obliged and the two gunmen tore off in the blue tourer.

Sherry had been fatally wounded. He had struggled a few paces forward after being shot, but collapsed on the pavement, blood spurting from the wound in his chest. The blue tourer headed for the northern suburbs and was later found abandoned—and incinerated —near the Ivanhoe police station. The gunmen had torched the car in an effort to destroy clues. Police soon learned that the car had been stolen several weeks earlier and had been garaged specifically for this hold-up. Police also had a fairly good idea of the identity of the two gunmen and made their move just five days after the hold-up killing.

Selwyn Wallace, twenty-two years of age, admitted to police that he had been involved in the hold-up, but insisted he had not been responsible for the shooting of the unfortunate Sherry. Police desperately wanted to apprehend Wallace's partner in crime, but were tipped off (not by Wallace) that the man they wanted had gone to Queensland. Victorian detectives finally tracked the man down in Sydney. Labourer Herbert Jenner, twenty-three years of age, was spotted by Detective-Sergeant Davis and Detective Rosewarne at the Homebush railway station. Davis covered the wanted man with a revolver and said: 'Put up your hands; I want you for stealing a car in Melbourne.' Jenner immediately insisted that there had been some mistake and even tried to convince the detectives that it was a case of mistaken identity. However, there was no mistake and Jenner and his mate Wallace were charged with the murder of Frederick Sherry.

Jenner and Wallace stood trial before Mr justice Gavan Duffy in the Criminal Court just three months after the shooting. One of the first witnesses was Government pathologist Dr C.H. Mollison, who carried out the post-mortem examination on Sherry's body. Dr Mollison told the court that Sherry had been killed by a bullet which had entered the left side of the chest, passed slightly downward, wounding the heart and both lungs, and stopped between the ribs on the right side. He said Sherry could not have lived more than two minutes after he had been shot. Significantly, there were no burn marks on Sherry's clothing. This indicated that the revolver had been fired at least several centimetres from Sherry. Clarence Sherry then told the court in evidence that he believed he had seen at least one of the two gunmen—Jenner—previously. Asked when, he replied: 'At the previous hold-up. That is the only time I can think of.'

Another witness, Aubrey Herschell, told the court that he was the owner of the blue tourer used in the fatal hold-up. He said he had lent it to a man named Harder in July that year and had not seen it again until he was asked to examine it at police headquarters the day after the hold-up. Walter Harder then told the court that the car had been stolen from his property. The Government analyst, Mr Charles Taylor, told the court that he had examined the car, a Plymouth (registration number 201-685) soon after the shooting and had noted a mark on the front door of the driver's side, just below the window. Mr Taylor said this mark could have been made by a bullet. There was also a small hole at the front of the car on the driver's side and Mr Taylor said he was satisfied that this mark had been made by a bullet and there were small spots of human blood on the windscreen and the dash.

The trial evidence later became extremely tangled, mainly because both gunmen had been wearing masks during the hold-up. No less than eleven witnesses gave evidence, but no one was certain who had fired the fatal shot. Earlier, defence counsel Dr T.C. Brennan KC (for Jenner) told the jury that the Crown view was that 'it was a case where there was concert between the two prisoners.' He added:

> The Crown said that they had put their heads together to commit the crime, and it did not matter which one of them fired the fatal shot. But when dealing with the case the important thing to consider is what agreement had been at the back of it. If it had been agreed between the prisoners that they should go out on this robbery and should use violence to the extent that was required to be successful, then both of them would be guilty of murder. But we say that in this case the position falls short of that. The onus is on

the Crown to prove every essential element in the case, and that includes also the state of mind.

Wallace's counsel, Mr W.A. Fazio, told the jury that his client had nothing to do with the killing, that there was no question of 'concert' and no evidence to show that Wallace intended to commit murder. He said:

> It is not part of my duty to put the blame on to anyone else—and I don't want to do that. But the Crown says: 'Two men did this and we don't care who fired that fatal shot.' But I suggest that that is what is going to trouble you. If it is shown that there were two men, and one of them did not do it, then the other did. I want you to pardon me for saying that, and thus making an attack on Jenner. But I must put it to you that the man who fired the fatal shot was not Wallace.

The Crown prosecutor, Mr C.H. Book KC, warned the jury not to be swayed by the attempts of counsel for the defence to 'harrow their feelings' and urged the jury members to put their feelings to one side. He said:

> If you talk about sympathy for these two young men at all you have to remember that on their own admissions they put their heads together to commit the very serious crime of robbery at least, and the Crown suggests that, in view of the fatal result of the crime they planned and carried out, they are guilty not merely of robbery, but of murder. Both counsel for the defence concluded their addresses by holding out to you that you should convict of manslaughter. The Crown does not put this case to you as one of manslaughter, but one of murder. I am sure that if you are satisfied that murder was committed here, this is a case of murder or nothing. Consider the nature of this crime, because I suggest that it is very important in considering the proposition that I put to you in the opening of this case—that it really does not matter which man fired the shot; they would both be guilty of murder. It is put by the Crown that having regard to everything that happened, there must have been a common purpose sufficiently strong to enable both these men to be guilty of the crime with which they are charged. The nature of that common purpose is that they made up their minds to commit a desperate crime. They went there armed, with the idea that if they were resisted—no doubt they hoped it would not become necessary—the revolvers would be used. If you are

satisfied about that, you need not bother about which one of them fired the shot ... If two men set out on that sort of enterprise in broad daylight in the city of Melbourne to steal a payroll, do you think they can have overlooked the possibility of resistance? All the circumstances of the case show that this was a crime that was carried out by two men and was carefully prepared. on the point of law, there is nothing to choose between the two men. It was a cruel and callous murder. Can you have any doubt that both these men are guilty of the crime with which they are charged?

Mr Justice Duffy, in his summing up, examined this perplexing question of responsibility when he told the jury:

I think you are going to have a very difficult task to decide on the evidence which of the two men pulled the trigger. Except for the doctrine of common purpose, it would be necessary for the jury to make up their minds as to whose hand had pulled the trigger, and if they could not satisfy themselves beyond reasonable doubt which of the two men had done so, they would have to find them both not guilty. But there is another way of looking at it. While, as a rule, the only man who is guilty of murder is the man who does the actual killing, there are other cases in which a man who does not do the killing may be guilty of murder. For instance, if someone hires another person to commit a murder, he would himself be guilty. Or, to come closer to home, when two men set out to rob with a common purpose and to shoot if it is necessary to achieve their purpose or for some other reason and, if in pursuit of that common purpose, one of them does grevous bodily harm, each of those persons is guilty of murder—the one who has not pulled the trigger as much as the one who has.

It obviously was an extremely difficult task for the jury and its problems were highlighted when it returned a verdict of guilty against Jenner and a verdict of being guilty of being an accessory after the fact against Wallace. However, the judge had to point out to the jury that the verdict it had made against Wallace was impossible under law as the prisoner had been charged with murder and not with being an accessory. The jury therefore had to decide again and, when it returned, it announced a verdict of guilty of murder against Wallace. However, the jury gave strong recommendations of mercy for both men because of their relative youth.

Mr Justice Duffy asked both men in turn if they wanted to comment before he passed sentence. Jenner, obviously shaken by the jury's decision, said:

> Well, Your Honour, deliberate perjury has been permitted in this case. If I had been given a trial in the lower court I would have had a chance to see the statements that had been made against me and to have known of the lies that have been told about me. I had to face this trial not knowing much that I would have known if I had had a preliminary trial. I would have had the evidence to show that I did not fire the shot that killed Mr Sherry and did not have a gun.

Wallace asked the judge: 'I want to ask Your Honour is the jury, at first having returned a verdict of accessory after the fact, which must mean that they must have had in their minds that I was not guilty of murder, but after being advised to retire and consider their verdict, is it right they they should now come back with a verdict against me of guilty of murder?'

Mr Justice Duffy replied: 'I pointed out to the jury that they should not return such a verdict because you were not charged with being an accessory after the fact. I told the jury that they must consider whether you were guilty of murder, guilty of manslaughter or not guilty. Having reconsidered their verdict they have found you guilty of murder.'

Wallace was distraught, especially as he had insisted all along that he had not agreed to violence of any kind in the hold-up and had not pulled the trigger. Jenner made similar claims, but whereas Wallace made an unsworn statement, Jenner made no statement. Wallace, in his statement during the trial, said:

> I took part in this affair but I did not agree with anybody to use firearms or any such weapon, and I did not kill Mr Sherry. I drove the car and I was the man who was identified by witnesses as the driver of the car just before and just after the hold-up. All I did at the scene was shortly after the Ford car stopped, was to get out and run across to the sedan. I tried to open the back door with a view to getting the bag containing the money. I could not open the back door, so I smashed the window and grabbed a bag, but it was the linen laundry bag, and I dropped it again. I then ran back to the Ford car, got in and started the engine, which had stopped. Shortly

after that my companions [there were suggestions at the trial that a mysterious and unnamed third man had been involved] got into the car and I drove away. I did not threaten or struggle with anybody or shoot at anybody who was there. I could not have done any more than I have told you in the time that I was on the scene. As a result of a conversation I had I believe that Mr Sherry was shot in a struggle ... I did not fire a shot.

Mr Justice Duffy then sentenced both men to death, but told the jury that their recommendation to mercy would be conveyed to the Executive Council. Both sentences were commuted to life imprisonment, with no benefit of remissions. Both men spent almost twenty years in maximum security at Pentridge before Jenner was transferred to the Corriemungle prison camp in western Victoria and Wallace was transferred to the French Island prison farm in 1958. Then, in October 1959, both men were released from prison after the State Executive Council had exercised the Royal prerogative for their release on a recommendation of the Parole Board. They were free men, twenty-one years after Frederick Sherry was shot dead in a bungled hold-up.

Interestingly, the British legal system faced a similar set of circumstances in 1952 when two youths were tried for the murder of a policeman at Croydon, just outside London. Christopher Craig and Derek Bentley broke into a factory and, when confronted by police, an officer was shot dead. Craig had been armed with a revolver and, when Bentley yelled out to 'let him have it, Chris', this was interpreted as telling his companion to shoot. However, there was another interpretation—that Bentley was telling Craig to hand over the revolver. Regardless, both youths were found guilty of murder because of a precedent set in a case twelve years earlier in which it was determined that if a police officer is killed in a crime with 'common design' it does not matter who does the actual killing. Craig, because he was just sixteen years of age, was sentenced to be detained, but nineteen-year-old Bentley was sentenced to death. Despite an appeal, Bentley was executed on 28 January 1953, even though he had not pulled the trigger in the killing of Police

Constable Sidney Miles. Craig, who had pulled the trigger, was released from prison in 1963.

In this case, there was no doubt who had pulled the trigger. One youth was executed and another—the one who actually had killed the police officer—is now a free man. At least Wallace and Jenner served identical sentences and Australia was spared the controversy of a case like the infamous Croydon shooting and its consequences.

A SUBURBAN
TRAGEDY

It was a quiet, peaceful morning in the inner western Melbourne suburb of Moonee Ponds in March 1935. For little Allan Carl Richter, just nine years of age, it should have been just another day at school. Big brother Leonard, thirteen years of age, went to school as usual, but Allan complained of a minor illness and his father allowed him to stay at home.

Allan spent the morning with his mother and grandmother, but neighbours heard piercing screams from the Richter laundry just before noon. A neighbour rushed to investigate and found the grandmother, invalid pensioner Mrs Mary Egan, in a terrible state of confusion. She told the neighbour that Mrs Alma Richter had confessed to killing her son. The neighbour immediately called police, who found Allan's body in a pool of blood in the laundry shed at the back of the house. He had been hit several times across the neck and head with an axe and he had all but been decapitated. The bloodstained axe was found in the laundry shed. Mrs Richter was sobbing uncontrollably in her bedroom, where she was interviewed and charged with murder.

At the inquest into Allan's death, before Deputy Coroner Mr Haser PM, Mr John Richter said that for several months his wife had been approaching a nervous breakdown. He said she had suffered from delusions and was worried that 'something terrible' would happen to her sons. Mrs Richter had been having medical treatment, but her husband never suspected that she would have such a tragic and total mental breakdown. Neighbours told Mr Hauser that Mrs Richter had been a devoted mother and was particularly house-proud. Her actions were inexplicably out of character.

Mr Hauser found that Allan Richter had died from injuries inflicted by his mother at a time when she 'was of unsound mind'. Mrs Richter was later placed in a mental hospital. It had been a suburban tragedy of the saddest proportions.

THE GRIEVING SON

To all intents and purposes, Sef Gonzales was the epitome of a heartbroken young man dealing with a tragedy of monumental proportions. The fresh-faced Gonzales gave an emotional eulogy at the funeral of his parents and sister in singing 'One Sweet Day' made famous by Mariah Carey and Boys II Men. It went:

> Sorry I never told you
> All I wanted to say
> Now it's too late to hold you
> 'Cause you've flown away, so far away ...
> And I know you're shining down from me from heaven
> Like so many friends I have lost along the way.
> And I know eventually well be together –
> One Sweet Day

Gonzales was the ultimate hypocrite because he had killed parents Teddy and Mary-Loiva and 18-year-old sister Clodine at the family's home in the quiet north-west Sydney suburb of North Ryde on July 10, 2001.

The Gonzales family had migrated to Australia from the Philippines after an earthquake had destroyed a hotel the family had built. Sef, just 10 years of age, was trapped by debris on a staircase, but father Ted pulled him to safety.

Despite having his life saved by his father, Sef resented the strict discipline imposed on him and, besides, there was the question of the $1 million he would inherit if his parents died. The 21-year-old Sef Gonzales therefore tried to poison his family with seeds he had bought on the internet. His mother was admitted to hospital, but recovered, so Sef waited just two weeks before setting in motion another plan.

This time he stabbed his family to death and blamed it on a mystery intruder. Sef Gonzales even painted the words 'f ... off Asians' on a kitchen wall to divert attention from himself.

Police were suspicious from the start, but Gonzales appeared to have the perfect alibi as he told police he was having dinner with friends at the time his family had been slaughtered.

Gonzales, after making out that he had found the bodies of his three family members, called police and told them: 'Somebody shot my parents, I think. They're all bleeding; they're on the floor.'

Police: 'What suburb are you in?'

Gonzales: 'They're not breathing. What do I do?'

Police: 'What suburb are you in?'

Gonzales: 'North Ryde?'

Police at a press conference later said: 'Young Sef and his family have cooperated with the investigators at this stage, and we're satisfied with the explanation so far.'

Then, when the dinner alibi turned out to be a lie, Gonzales said he was having sex at a brothel at the time and had made up the story about having dinner because his mother would have been horrified at the thought of him going to a brothel.

Police then broke through his tissue of lies bit by bit, starting with disproving Gonzales' claim that he had been to the brothel. It turned out that the particular prostitute Gonzales referred to was not at the brothel at the time he suggested.

Police dogs were unable to pick up the scent of any intruder and traces of the paint used to daub the wall were found on one of Gonzales' jumpers. Also, he claimed to have hugged members of his family after he had found their bodies, but no trace of these signs of affection could be found on his clothes.

Meanwhile, Gonzales visited his father's accountant just three days after the family tragedy and paid deposits on luxury motor vehicles. He moved into an apartment, sold his parents' car and generally lived it up.

Gonzales was charged with three counts of murder 11 months after the slayings and he eventually pleaded not guilty before a six-week trial in the Supreme Court of NSW. Crown prosecutor Mark Tedeschi told the jury: 'Feeling his life unravel, Sef set in train a plan to murder his parents and his sister.'

The court was told that when police seized Gonzales' computer they found reference to internet sites such as 'How to Kill' and 'White Man Killer'. The jury took just four and a half hours to find Gonzales guilty and, as the decision was announced, his aunt, Annia Paraan, broke down and muttered 'Thank you'.

She said later: 'I think justice has been done, but it would have been easier to accept if it were another person. It's just so hard to accept.'

THE KROPE CASE

It is difficult to imagine a more sensational case than the one involving the family of a reigning Miss Australia beauty queen, Gloria Krope, in December 1977. The death of Miss Krope's father, Frederick Krope, in the quiet north Melbourne suburb of Glenroy made newspaper headlines around Australia for many months. The news of Frederick Krope's death was broken in the December 22, 1977 edition of the now-defunct afternoon paper, the Herald. The newspaper ran a huge photograph of Miss Krope in her Miss Australia regalia, including crown and mitre. The news was headlined: '17 rifle shots kill Miss Australia's father'. The report also carried a photograph of the Krope home, where Frederick Krope was shot to death in a hail of bullets. The home, in Sims Crescent, could have been any humble home in any Melbourne suburb—small, neat and unpretentious. However, it had not been a happy home for the Krope family.

Frederick Krope met his future wife, Josephine, in Yugoslavia in 1947; they were married eighteen months later and decided to migrate to Australia in late 1951. The Kropes settled in Melbourne and, in May 1954, Rosemary, the first of their three children, was born. Gloria was born eighteen months later and William in May 1957. The family moved into the Sims Crescent house in July 1955. Krope worked as a fitter and turner, but his wages from this job were supplemented by sales from small metal production items made in the family garage. Frederick Krope was an obsessive gambler and the family's financial fortunes fluctuated from week to week, from one race meeting to another. To make matters worse, Krope had a violent temper and would fly into a rage at the slightest provocation. He was, in fact, a family bully and his wife and three children lived in fear of him. He also used to watch his own daughters through a peephole he had made for himself to the family bathroom.

The Krope family lived with this for years, with Mrs Krope the unifying force in a terrified household. There might have been some happy times, but there were also bitterly miserable times when Frederick Krope would have the members of his family trembling in fear. He beat his wife and children, although Mrs Krope usually took the full weight of her husband's attacks, often to save her children. Frederick Krope once kicked his wife in the back, injuring her so badly that she was forced to wear a steel brace for several months.

It was against this background that young William Krope, just twenty years of age, became involved in tragedy. He could no longer tolerate the situation and late on the evening of Wednesday, December 31, 1977, he shot his father dead with a .22 Ruger semi-automatic. William had waited inside the house with the gun cocked and ready to fire as soon as his father walked through the back door. Earlier, William had been disturbed in the garage whilst trying to get his father's gun. As he waited for his father to enter the house, William believed it was a case of kill or be killed and was convinced that his father was carrying a gun. Frederick Krope eventually walked through the door and was shot repeatedly.

Both Mrs Krope and Rosemary were in the house at the time of the shooting (Gloria was no longer living at home) and immediately rushed in to see what had happened. They saw Frederick Krope dead on the floor in a pool of blood. Mrs Krope then walked to the telephone and called the police. William gave himself up and told police exactly what had happened. The police immediately inspected the body and noted that Frederick Krope was lying face down. There were numerous bullet wounds, including several to the head. Police also found a number of .22 calibre cartridges in the entrance foyer and surrounding area. According to Senior Constable Wayne Pinner, he asked William what had happened that night and to make a brief statement. William told the police:

> It happened about half an hour ago about 11.15 pm. I fired about seventeen or eighteen shots into him from my Ruger .22 rifle. It's a 1022 model with a revolving magazine. I hit him in the neck with the first shot then continued to fire the rifle at him. After the rifle was empty I refilled the magazine from a box of bullets I had on the bed. I waited until he came into the house from being out in the garage. While he was outside in the garage I got the rifle from behind my wardrobe in the bedroom. When I got the rifle it was empty and the magazine was on the shelf behind the stereo with the bullets. I loaded the magazine and put it in the gun and then I waited for him in the lounge room … standing up beside the wall cabinet in the lounge, then I heard the back door and he came through with a torch and I fired a shot at him and he fell in the doorway of the dining room and the hall and then I stood at his feet and fired the other nine shots into him lying on the floor. I stepped across him and went to the bedroom after I fired the rest of the shots and reloaded the magazine with another ten bullets and then I stood at the doorway between his bedroom and the hall, and shot him seven more times in the head and shoulders. The reason I shot him with the extra bullets was because he was still moving after the first lot and I didn't want to take any chances. After everything had happened I put the rifle on the buffet and then tried to contact the police. My mother actually rang the police, trying to cover up for me. When he came in the back door I knew it was him because my sister [Rosemary] was in the bedroom and my mother was in the kitchen. The light was on. The light in the lounge and dining room was not on and I did not shoot the first time until I could see him quite clearly and he was about 10 feet from me. The main reason things happened today was that my mother and father were arguing over me and that triggered it off. But the whole thing has been going on for a number of years with the whole family.

The amazing piece of information from this interview with Senior Constable Pinner was that it was painfully evident that Mrs Krope was prepared to take the blame for her son's actions, just as she often had in the past. William, however, showed tremendous courage and character to brush this offer of assumed responsibility aside. William then explained to police that he had bought the death rifle only two weeks earlier and said:

> When I bought the rifle I bought it with the intention of protecting my family—that is, the rest of my family—against my father because he is very unpredictable. Last year he told me to leave home. I was in the bedroom packing my bags when he came in with a shifting spanner in his hand and started waving it about, and now this time he was starting to fall into the same pattern. Over the last six months he has become more and more violent towards me and the family, only verbal and not physical. The reason I went away from home last year was because he drove me out. I took a flat but things got too much with things going on at home and me living in a flat, but I couldn't cope and tried to commit suicide. When I left home on that occasion I had intentions of killing him then before he kicked me out, but I thought that if I got away from him it would be all right. But it wasn't. When I first shot him I just let all the fear and tenseness out.

William later made a statement to detectives. This statement was not only signed, but was also recorded and played a significant part in his subsequent trial.

Detectives asked William more than 100 questions and he answered all as succinctly as possible, hiding nothing. He then signed the statement, which was countersigned by Detective Senior Constable R.S. Wilson. William was then taken to the Russell Street police headquarters to await his first appearance in court for the killing of his father.

The inquest into Frederick Krope's death ended on April 11, 1978, and Coroners H.W. Pascoe and B.M. Gillman, SMs, found that Krope had 'died from the effects of multiple bullet wounds unlawfully, maliciously and feloniously inflicted by his son, William'. This meant that William had to stand trial on a charge of murder. Then, just a little more than two months later, Australian newspapers had a feast on yet another twist in the Krope case. Mrs Krope was charged with conspiracy to murder her husband and inciting to murder. However, the drama did not end there as Rosemary later tried to commit suicide by taking an overdose of medication. She survived, but all members of the Krope family, including Gloria, were suffering from extreme distress.

Mrs Krope and her son stood trial together, the case opening before Mr justice Jenkinson on August 1, 1978. Both pleaded not guilty to all charges. The prosecutor, Mr Len Flanagan, told the court that it had been a 'cold, callous and premeditated crime'. The word 'premeditated' has extreme significance as, indeed, it has for all cases of murder. For any person to be found guilty of murder under the Common Law system the prosecution must prove what generally is termed as 'malice aforethought'. The legal term is 'mens rea', which is Latin for 'guilty mind'. However, the problem often arises: what precisely is 'guilty mind'? What is the definition of 'guilty mind'? These questions have plagued lawyers and jurors for many, many years and there have been numerous interpretations, depending on circumstances such as state of mental health, state of sobriety, etc.

Mr Flanagan continued:

> William Krope stalked his father around the backyard and finally shot him in the hallway of the house. The victim has been described as a man who was cruel, sadistic and hard on his family, but his conduct did not justify the son killing his father, nor his wife egging on her son to do the killing ... The killing of Frederick Krope was initiated by his wife's words and actions. She knew her son resented his father, and had recently bought a .22 rifle.

Mr Flanagan pointed out that William had bought a rifle for $146 only days before the shooting, that he had hidden the gun in his room, that Mrs Krope had argued with her husband on the day of his killing over spending money for Christmas and that Mrs Krope had told police she had decided that day that she would kill her husband and had even told her son of her intention. The prosecution obviously was trying to build its case of 'malice aforethought' or 'mens rea'.

The prosecution called a number of witnesses, including Victorian Government pathologist Dr James McNamara, who gave expert medical evidence. He told the court that Frederick Krope's body had taken 'approximately' twenty-four bullets. Mr Flanagan asked him: 'Would you tell us what the injuries were and where they were, please?' Dr McNamara replied, in some detail:

There were multiple gunshot wounds, bruises and abrasions, these being mainly in the left flank. That is the left side of the body, and in the head region as under. A two-inch area of abrasion above the right eye; half-inch gunshot wound in the inner canthus of the right eye-just here [pointing to his own eye]; bruising of the inner canthus of the left eye; half-inch abrasion above the nose; half-inch abrasion just below the bridge of the nose just here [pointing to his own face by way of indication]. A quarter-inch gunshot wound just above the left upper lip; a quarter-inch gunshot wound on the right-hand side of the neck; a two-inch bruise on the right-hand side of the neck; a half-inch gunshot wound in the right shoulder anteriorly, which means in the front; a two-inch bruise over the right collarbone in the midline, from whence a bullet was recovered. A one and a half inch abrasion on the anterior aspect of the left lower leg, under the knee, and it is not shown on the photographs provided to me. There were three quarter-inch gunshot wounds in the left flank in the mid-axillary line. A half-inch gunshot wound on the right-hand side of the head above the right ear, and another gunshot wound behind the left ear; multiple gunshot wounds to the back of the head, mainly to the right-hand side. A two-inch graze abrasion consistent with a gunshot wound over the left-hand side of the head. Five gunshot wounds over the back of the right shoulder; a four-inch abrasion mark consistent with a gunshot wound on the back of the left shoulder; a gunshot wound on the left-hand side of the back below the left scapula [pointing to his own shoulder blade]; a gunshot wound over the left buttock; abrasion to the right buttock.

Internal examination: Heart was of normal size with normal valves and normal myocardium or muscle tissue. The coronary vessels, or blood vessels, that supply the heart, showed some thickening. There were gunshot wounds in the left and right lobes of the lungs; two bullets were lying loose in the chest cavity, and underlying the gunshot wounds on the left-hand side of the chest there were fractured ribs. All these organs below the chest—the abdominal organs were normal. Skull and brain: there were multiple fractures of the skull, and some bullets were recovered from the cranial cavity, the inside of the head. The brain was completely lacerated and torn apart and haemorrhagic, a lot of bleeding.

There was no doubting the full effect of what Dr McNamara told the court: Frederick Krope's injuries were massive.

There were several sensations in the ten-day trial, one of the first occurring on the fifth day when the defence counsel, the silver-haired and extremely eloquent Mr Frank Galbally (for William Krope) and Mr John Walker (for Mrs Krope), requested that the jury inspect the Krope home. This was an essential part of the defence as the jurors, who went to the Krope home by bus and were given a police guard when they inspected the house, were able to see first-hand at least part of what had taken place at Sims Crescent over many years. The jurors were shown the partly repaired peephole Frederick Krope had used to the bathroom.

Another sensation was when Mr Galbally called Gloria Krope, the reigning Miss Australia, to the witness box. Gloria, twenty-two years of age and, naturally, extremely attractive, told the court that she 'could not tolerate living under the same roof' as her father and had therefore decided to leave home. She added that her father 'was very cruel, very threatening and most of the time that I lived under the roof I lived in fear'. Mr Galbally asked her if she had ever seen her father use violence towards any member of the family, and she replied 'yes'. She also told the court that her father had been abusive to William's friends and recalled how he had once thrown a china plate or bowl at her mother. 'It frightened the whole family,' she said.

Finally, there was the unsworn statement to the court by William. He said:

> What I did on that night when my father was killed was a result of years of fear and it's true I grew to hate my father. That's because I was terrified of him for as long as I can remember and he never showed me any love but only made me frightened of him. I can't remember exactly what happened when I was very young but two things stick out in my memory of my life. It's as though there was always two sides at home, my mum, sisters and me, and on the other side my father. My mum, sisters and I always got on well and we love one another very, very much. My mum has been the most wonderful mum. She has always loved and looked after me and my sisters. She has been through hell with my father, she has been treated and abused like a dog. I couldn't love my father the

way he treated my mum, sisters and myself. It wasn't just that he was always using physical violence, but it was the fear that he caused just being there, saying the things he said and the cruel things he used to do. I never saw him kiss any one of us. My mother told us that he kicked and punched her and that she thought he had tried to kill her. I remember him chasing me around the yard with a stick when I was very young. I remember him hitting me at different times with a belt and other things when I was young and once when I ran to my mum he kicked me and started to hit her because she was trying to protect me. On one occasion he came into the lounge room where I was and sat at the table. He abused my mum and told me to do something, but I didn't obey. He then jumped up and kicked me in the side with all his force. I was sitting down in front of the fireplace. My mum had to pull me away from him—this was early in my life. On many occasions he would scare us kids. He would always say there was someone under the house and on some occasions he would make noises under the floorboards.

William continued with the horrific details of family life under Frederick Krope:

From an early age I have heard my father calling my mother a bitch and a slut and yelling at her. He used to terrify us with stories of how he killed people during the war and at times he had us in tears of fright and I've seen Rosemary run out of the house. From the time I first went to school my mother was working. As I was growing up at school I wasn't treated like the other boys. I wasn't allowed to bring them home or go out and play with them, except when he wasn't there I did it.

I once remember when I was about ten playing with the boy up the road. My father called me home and belted me with a machine belt. I could barely walk afterwards. I couldn't bend my legs for a while because the skin on the back of my legs was red raw. From then on I was terrified of him. Instead of letting me play with my friends I used to have to work in the garage—in the garden and the garage. One of the other things that made me terrified of my father is this. He used to gamble a lot. He was always looking at the racing papers and betting. He never seemed to have any money to give Mum or us. At Christmas he would give us a present like an orange and perhaps ten or twenty cents. We would look for toys and never found them, except when my mum gave us them. He frightened me into working after school and at the weekends and during the holidays.

William also spoke of how he was ashamed of himself because of the way his father treated him:

He [his father] had this workshop at home; it's the one I had to work in all my spare time. He used to make all sorts of things and sell them. He told me one of the reasons he wanted me working at Gadsdens [a manufacturing company where his father also worked] was to help him steal materials from there to work on in the garage. He used to make things like grape presses and cake dishes and other things. He had quite a big business at home and there is a book with all the names of people he used to sell these things to which will prove how big his business was. My mum has this book I think. I asked him why I had to work on weekends and he told me he was gambling and would win a fortune. He was always saying he would win a fortune. He'd say to me on Friday nights, 'Don't make any plans for the weekend, you've a lot of work to do.' I was losing all my mates. Even when I'd left home, before I tried to kill myself [he had slashed his wrists], I had to go fishing and other things on my own because I had no friends left. I was very lonely …

My father used to gamble a lot at cards. I've seen him playing in the lunch hour at work. He had a guillotine machine in the garage for cutting card decks. It was obvious he was doing this to cheat. He had several decks with different alterations to each; one would give him four aces or four kings and that. He told me he used to rotate the decks so no one would know anything. He used to steal sheet metal from Gadsdens and make various items for a number of cake shops around Melbourne, like dishes to put cakes on and things. This is why I am ashamed of myself, because I was forced to do this work on stolen material. If I'd told Gadsdens or anyone else what he was doing he would have killed me. I was frightened of him because I knew he was doing those criminal things and that he must have been mixing with that sort of person because he often said he had plenty of friends that could fix anyone at Gadsdens or anyone else, if anyone told on him.

William also explained why he thought his father was so dangerous:

One of the reasons I thought my father was so dangerous was because he always had a weapon close at hand. He used to carry a large club about two feet long in his car. He also carried a switch-blade knife in his bag. He also had a rifle in the garage and Mum told me he had been doing something to it and she wondered whether we should get rid of it. We thought that if we moved it he would know and we were terrified of what he would do. I thought he was the sort of person who would easily kill us in our sleep and that he could easily kill himself. He told us that his three brothers had committed suicide.

William then told of his father's foul mood on the day of the shooting. He said, in the unsworn statement:

The day he died he was in one of the worst moods I had ever seen. I'd heard my mother asking for extra money for Christmas and I heard him say, 'Not for you bloody bastards.' I heard Mum pleading with him, saying we could have a nice, peaceful Christmas and that she might be able to get Gloria to come home, and him saying things like 'not a bloody cent' and 'get that bastard to work or I'll have him crawling on the ground like a rat'. I heard my mother pleading with him but he just got in a rage. I heard him telling my mother she was a stupid bitch and if she wanted money to get out and work for it and get me to work …

He came home again about 7 pm and my mother gave him his meal, which he ate on his own. He was listening to the wireless and he was using the phone for his betting. He seemed to be in the same bad mood as earlier. I heard him abuse Mum because I hadn't helped her in the garage. He was going on about how useless we all were to him and saying things like as far as we were all concerned we were finished. When I was watching the TV my mother was in the kitchen. I went out on a couple of occasions and put my arm around her, and tried to comfort her and brighten her up. She was still cooking because she said she had to have something to do to keep her mind off things. When I was with her in the kitchen my father came out, gave us one of his mad, threatening looks and said something like: 'I'll figure something out for you.' I was sure he was going to do something to us that night. I thought of his gun and how I could get it away from him. I couldn't bring it in through the house as he would have seen me. That's why I took the flywire off my window, to get out and bring the gun in through the window and hide it in my room. I did this and went to the garage to get his gun to take back.

When I was in the garage I got the gun out of the trunk and just then my father was coming with the torch. I left the gun and walked straight out and ran into the house in fear and got my gun, and got out the window as I knew once he had seen me with his gun, that would be it. I would be finished. When I got out the back I saw him through the window in the garage where the rifle had been and I thought he was getting it. I got terrified and ran back into the house and hid in the lounge. I heard my father come in from the garage into the house. The lounge light was off and the TV room dimly lit. I was absolutely terrified of him and all the fear I had of him over the past times took control of me and I was just certain that he was going to kill me—Mum and me and Rosemary. I believed he had the gun and I thought I had to kill him first. I was that frightened and I shot him. At that time in my mind there was nothing else I could do to save us. I don't know what made me shoot him so often, it must have been fear. I've no clear memory of how often I did it. I was so panicky. I'd often thought over the years that if he attacked me or Mum I would have to kill him. This is the sort of thing that had been going through my mind for years because of his threats and cruelty towards us.

One of the most poignant moments in this statement was when William said: 'No one could believe what we've been through and what sort of a man he was. If you had lived in that house with us and him for even only a week you would have known what fear was and how it was with us all the time. I believe that he was truly mad.'

Mrs Krope made an unsworn statement the following day in court. Earlier, Mr Justice Jenkinson had told the jury that there was insufficient evidence to press the charge of 'inciting to murder' against Mrs Krope and the jury automatically returned a verdict of 'not guilty'. However, she still faced a charge of conspiracy to murder and in her unsworn statement she told of how the entire family had been terrified of Frederick Krope. She said:

I have lived in terror and fear from day to day and more over the last year when he seemed to be getting madder and crueller. The violence of this man and fear and threats we lived under are perhaps hard for you to understand. Many times early on I wanted to go to the police about him but he always threatened if I did it would be worse for me and the children. Once when he knocked me to the floor and kicked me in the back my spine was injured and

I was in a steel brace for six months and even now the X-rays still show the damage to my spine, which has now left me with permanent pain. Another time he threw a plate at me in front of the children which hit me in the face. Another time he punched me on the jaw and broke it.

He was so unpredictable, and what happened that night was a terrible shock, even though we knew how mad he was. When Bill [William] said '[the deceased] is coming in with a gun', I nearly died inside myself. I froze up. I didn't know what I could do, and you cannot imagine how I felt when I heard the first shot and then it's all a bit of a blur. I came around really expecting to see Bill dead and [the deceased] with the gun and I was prepared to die, but it was Bill shooting and he was in a state I have never seen him in before. By this time too many shots were fired, it was all too late, and my world came to an end. I thought I must give to the children the future. I rung the police and I told them I had shot him, but Bill would not let me do it. He was still trembling and I was trying to tell him that he and Rosemary must keep up the payments on the house but he didn't seem to listen. He went outside. I knew the police would arrive and I thought then that it was silly to try and take the blame because I didn't think Bill had done anything wrong anyway, but I was still terribly worried. From then on it was a nightmare, even though the police were very good.

The jury, on August 14, retired to consider its verdict. The jurors did not return for seven hours. Their verdict? Not guilty on all charges. Both Mrs Krope and her son William had been acquitted. William, wearing a wide-lapelled, pinstriped suit, and his mother embraced each other before being escorted by friends from the court. Their nightmare was well and truly over and they were at peace to continue their lives without the terror generated by a husband who paid the extreme penalty for his gross behaviour. The Krope family showed remarkable courage and unity during the trial and the 'not guilty' decisions were enormously popular with the Australian public. There were times during the trial when women sobbed in court and there were deafening silences as William and his mother detailed the litany of day to day horror of life with Frederick Krope. Gloria Krope, the beautiful and elegant Miss Australia, later became a highly successful business executive courageously casting aside the horror of her early life in Glenroy and the tragic events of 1977.

THE BATTERED
BRIDE

Pretty Mona Beacher was radiant as she prepared for her 'marriage' to James Turner. Unwittingly, she was also preparing for her death at the hands of her young husband, who used the wedding ceremony as the first step in an elaborate plan to free himself of the entanglements of love.

The young couple were married at the Catholic Church in the Newcastle suburb of Tighes Hill on the afternoon of Friday, 15 May 1925. Mona and Jim told everyone, including the bride's parents, they would be honeymooning in Melbourne. In reality, they headed straight for their newly rented home at Lake Macquarie, an extremely popular honeymoon destination in the years between the two World Wars. Jim convinced Mona that this would give them even greater privacy and would also help them settle into married life not far from where he worked in Newcastle.

Mona booked the cottage, on a six-month rental agreement, through an advertisement in a Newcastle newspaper. The cottage owners, Mr and Mrs Arthur Williams, lived in Newcastle but used the cottage as a holiday home and were delighted to rent it to the young couple. Although Mona made the initial inspection and agreement, Jim Turner made a follow-up inspection and was delighted with his fiancée's choice. He even ordered groceries from a nearby shop and asked a newsagent to deliver daily newspapers.

Williams, being a good landlord, was keen to see how his new tenants settled and made three calls on the honeymooners. He noted on the first two visits that bread, milk and newspapers had been delivered as ordered, but were untouched on the cottage porch. On the third visit, there was an extra day's delivery of milk, bread and a newspaper—again untouched. Williams, deeply puzzled, knocked several times on the front door—with no reply. Williams found both the front and back doors locked and no sign of either Jim or Mona. He decided to enter the cottage through the front bedroom window.

Williams managed to prise open the window and then lifted the blind to discover the naked body of the young woman who had rented the cottage. Williams knew immediately that the girl was dead, as there was blood splattered over much of the tiny bedroom, which resembled a slaughterhouse. Besides, there was a gaping hole in the young woman's neck and there were several horrendous head wounds. An autopsy later revealed that the woman's throat had been slashed by a knife and that she had been battered about the head by a hammer. Williams almost tripped over himself in his haste to tell the local police constable of his gruesome discovery.

Constable Bill Thompson made a brief inspection of the murder scene and, to his credit, immediately called for expert assistance from Newcastle police. Inspector John Ramsay, who led the investigation, questioned Williams about the macabre discovery and was told that the dead woman had identified herself only as a 'Miss Anderson' and had not even given her Christian name. Inspector Ramsay at first did not suspect 'Miss Anderson' had used an assumed name. However, a thorough examination of the cottage convinced him that every effort had been made to prevent anyone identifying the body.

The burnt fragments of the dead woman's dresses were found under the kitchen stove and a broom handle had been used to poke underclothes up a narrow chimney. The murderer had removed or destroyed as many manufacturer's tags and labels as necessary.

Inspector Ramsay convinced himself that even identifying the body would take an eternity—until one of his officers sifted the ash from under the stove and discovered small fragments of rosary beads. This was a vital clue as police were able to narrow their inquiries of recent weddings to Catholic churches. Although there was no record of a woman named Anderson marrying a man named Turner, Inspector Ramsay was by this time convinced that these were false names.

The second clue was a tiny brooch from the clothes stuffed up the chimney. The murderer could not have known that the dead woman's Christian name of Mona had been engraved on the back of the brooch. Finally, the police discovered the name Mona Beacher on a sheet of ballad music—'Deep Seas'— in a bundle brought to the cottage by the honeymooners. Police therefore concluded that the dead woman was a Mona Beacher and that she had married at a Catholic Church on May 15 (they found a newspaper dated May 16 inside the cottage). Police also reasoned that she had been killed either late on the night of Saturday, May 16, or early the following morning.

Police contacted Mona Beacher's parents in Newcastle, but were told that the young woman was on her honeymoon in Melbourne. In fact, they showed police a telegram they had received from their daughter. The telegram had been sent from the Sydney suburb of Strathfield and it read: 'ARRIVED SAFE AND SOUND. ARTHUR HAS THREE WEEKS' HOLIDAY AS WEDDING PRESENT. GOING TO MELBOURNE WEDNESDAY. LOVE MONA.'

Besides, they were told, she had not married anyone named James Turner but, in fact, had married her long-standing boyfriend Arthur Oates, a warehouse worker. Naturally, police wanted to interview Oates but were told at the warehouse that there was no one named Oates on the payroll. The police were just about to turn away when the foreman told them that there was an employee named Arthur Oakes and that he had been on sick leave since May 15.

Oakes immediately became a wanted man and police issued a state-wide description, although in hindsight this was not necessary. Oakes, in fact, was apprehended on the evening of May 24 at his own home in Tighes Hill. Both he and his wife were ready for bed. Oakes at first denied any knowledge of Mona Beacher or of the honeymoon cottage at Lake Macquarie, but the evidence was so overwhelming that he was charged with the murder of Mona Beacher.

Oakes told the jury and the Chief justice of New South Wales, Sir Philip Street, that Mona Beacher knew that he was married but insisted on the marriage ceremony even though she knew it would be bigamous. Oakes also claimed that he drank wine before going to bed on the evening of May 16 and found his 'wife' dead next to him when he awoke the following morning. He panicked and then tried to prevent any identification of the body. The jury, of course, took little time to dismiss this defence and Oakes was found guilty and sentenced to death. The NSW Executive Council commuted this sentence to one of life imprisonment.

The jury obviously believed that Oakes' crime had been planned well in advance and that he had gone to extraordinary lengths to lay a false trail and to prevent identification of the dead woman. There were assumed names, a deliberately misleading telegram and the inexplicable and illogically explained discovery of a horrendously mutilated body in Oakes' bed. And had Mona Beacher really known that Oakes was already married? If not, this would have been the obvious motive for murder. Alternatively, Oakes might have murdered her in a rage during a drunken row at the cottage. No one will ever know and Mona Beacher took the mystery with her to her grave.

THE LIMBS IN THE YARRA

It was described in Melbourne newspaper headlines of the time as a 'Ghastly Discovery'. It was March 29, 1937, and Melbourne buzzed with excitement for several weeks over the finding of a woman's severed arms and legs in the Yarra River.

Two boys were playing on the banks of the river near the Morell Bridge, Richmond, when they noticed something floating in the water near a stormwater drain. The boys investigated and were horrified when they noticed a human leg protruding from a sugar bag. They ran screaming for help and hailed down passing motorist Mr Elvin Heyre, who took one look at the decomposed contents of the sugar bag and drove to the city, where he stopped traffic policeman Constable J. Wardle, who pulled the bag and its grizzly contents from the water.

The bag contained two arms and two legs and an immediate inspection revealed that the dismemberment had been expertly done with an extremely sharp instrument. The arms has been amputated at the shoulder joints and the two legs at the knee. Police took the limbs to the city morgue where they were examined by the Government pathologist, Dr R.J. Wright-Smith.

Police had no idea whether they would find the head or torso, and this made their task of identification almost entirely reliant on Dr Wright-Smith's work. Dr Wright-Smith's preliminary investigation revealed that the limbs were from a woman aged between thirty and forty years. Dr Wright-Smith also concluded that she was well nourished and probably had dark hair. She would have been only 157 centimetres (5 ft 2 in) in height and had four vaccination marks at the top of her right arm.

The pathologist told detectives working on the case that the woman had been dead about three weeks and that the body had been dismembered about a week after death. Dr Wright-Smith said the body had been drained of blood and this in itself made his task extremely difficult. However, the doctor was able to remove a 'glove' of skin from the right hand for fingerprinting. The left hand was far too badly decomposed for possible fingerprinting and police relied enormously on whether there would be prints on file to match those taken from the human glove. The task proved fruitless.

The sugar bag in which the limbs had been placed did not contain any other item and police could not find any traces of clothing along the Yarra. Their only other clue was a small scar at the back of one finger, but this also failed to lead to the identification of the dead woman and police became extremely frustrated. They were convinced there had been a murder, but could not even determine how the woman had died or even identify her.

Police also found it difficult to determine precisely where the bag and its nauseating cargo had been dumped into the Yarra. There were three possibilities. The bag could have been washed downstream from well up the Yarra, it could have been washed upstream by the river's tidal flow or it could have been washed into the river from a stormwater drain by heavy rain just days before the boys' discovery.

Police dragged the Yarra and hauled in only the corpses of cats, dogs and rats. Detectives also cruised up and down the Yarra, using grappling hooks to haul in anything and everything they thought might help their investigations. They did not find a single clue, let alone the missing head or torso.

Police also faced the possibility that there would not even be an inquest. In the infamous 'Shark Arm Case' in Sydney in which an aquarium shark disgorged a human arm, the New South Wales Supreme Court's Mr Justice Halse Rogers, on June 24, 1935, directed that there could be no inquest as there was no body. The question raised was: 'How much of a body constitutes a body?'

An inquest into the shark arm case was held and the arm was identified through fingerprinting as belonging to ex-boxer James Smith, who had been missing for two weeks before the arm was disgorged. Police charged Sydney underworld figure Patrick Brady with the murder of Smith, but the defence insisted that there was no proof that Smith was dead. Brady was acquitted (see 'The Shark Arm Case' in this book).

The Yarra River case was referred to the Melbourne City coroner, Mr Tingate PM, who said he would have to study the judgment made in the shark arm case. However, the Victorian Coroners Act of 1928 gave power to the Supreme Court, on the application of a law officer, to order that an inquest be held. Section 10 (3) of this Act stated: 'Upon such inquest, if the case is one of death, it shall not be necessary, unless the Court or judge otherwise orders, to view the body, but save as aforesaid the inquest shall be held in like manner in all respects as any other inquest under this act.' Obviously, the Yarra case did involve a death as Dr Wright-Smith had concluded that the amputations had occurred 'after death'.

Mr Tingate gave police as much time as possible to solve the mystery of the limbs in the Yarra. However, an inquest was finally held at the city morgue on June 3, 1937, and although police evidence was presented, it was impossible to identify the body or the cause of death. It was the first time in Victorian legal history that an inquest was held without either the head or torso being 'viewed' by the coroner. Mr Tingate had no option but to adjourn the inquest indefinitely and the mystery remains. Who was the dead woman and how did she die? Also, what happened to the head and torso? And will this mystery ever be solved?

POOR CHRISTOPHER ROBIN

Little Christopher Robin Weltman was looking forward to his first camping experience. He was just seven years of age and the YMCA holiday camp at Loftia Park in the Adelaide Hills would provide him with his first experience of the bush. However, Christopher, a mild asthmatic, disappeared from the camp on the evening of January 12, 1977.

The blond-haired boy's disappearance created headlines throughout Australia, although there were hopes that Christopher had merely lost his way in the scrub surrounding the camp. He had told friends that he was going to look for dinosaur bones and was last seen wandering down a track very close to the main camp site.

More than 200 police and volunteers took part in the search for Christopher, a quietly spoken boy who often said that he wanted to be a policeman when he grew up. Tragically, Christopher's body was found by a volunteer on the afternoon of January 13, just twenty hours after the boy had last been seen. The body was found a mere fifty metres from the camp lavatory block and only 100 metres from the but Christopher shared with other children.

Christopher had been bashed around the head and there was blood around his nose. There was a trail of blood from a nearby track and police correctly assumed that the little boy had been attacked on the track and that his body had been dragged into the scrub. Half a house brick was found close to the body and, significantly, forensic tests revealed that there were traces of blood and organic material attached to it. Christopher had been hit on the top left side of the head with the brick. There were no indications of a struggle and there was no evidence of a sexual attack.

Police immediately started questioning the seventy-three children at the camp and, by the end of the week, had charged a twelve-year-old boy with Christopher's murder. Meanwhile, poor Christopher Robin was buried following a service at Black Forest. His mother, Mrs Teresa Dato, had been involved in a motor accident four days after her son's killing and was released from hospital (suffering shock and a badly bruised arm) only hours before the funeral. The boy's father, former prison warder Mr David Weltman, attended the funeral with his former wife.

The twelve-year-old boy faced the South Australian Supreme Court in July 1977. The boy, in an unsworn statement to the jury of seven men and five women, said that he had hit Christopher with the brick because he was angry with him telling other children at the camp that he had 'done a poo near a car'. The psychiatrist in charge at the adolescent unit at the Enfield Hospital, Dr J.G. Govan, said that when he asked the boy if Christopher had deserved to be bashed, he replied: 'At the time he did, but not now.' Dr Govan asked the boy why not now and he replied: 'Because I killed him.' Dr Govan told the court that the twelve-year-old seemed to gain 'unusual pleasure' from violence on television. He also told the court that the boy had once poured tomato sauce over himself and pretended that he had a sharp stick in his chest. Dr Govan said he interpreted this 'as a demonstration of his [the boy's] preoccupation with death'. He added that the boy's whole history was one of grave anti-social conduct.

Medical evidence was given that Christopher had been struck at least three times to the head and shoulders and that a bruise mark on his chest had matched the pattern of the twelve-year-old boy's shoes.

The jury took only forty minutes to find the boy guilty of Christopher's murder. Justice Mitchell then said that under the South Australian juvenile Crimes Act she could only impose the one sentence, for the boy to be 'detained during the Governor's pleasure'. Justice Mitchell then refused an application by the Adelaide Advertiser to publish the boy's name. 'I hope that by the time he is released he will be sufficiently rehabilitated and the public will not be in any danger,' she said.

There was a sad sequel to the case of poor Christopher Robin when, in 1979, Theresa Dato armed herself with a knife and went to a reform home to 'get the stinking animal who killed my son'. Mrs Dato, mother of a six-year-old daughter, caught a cab to the McNally Training Centre at 2.45 a.m. on April 16 and told staff she wanted to 'see someone'. Police were called and Mrs Dato was disarmed and arrested.

This tragic sequel unfolded in the Adelaide Magistrates' Court when Mrs Dato pleaded guilty to carrying an offensive weapon. The court was told that Mrs Dato had twice had mental breakdowns and had taken sleeping tablets on the night she caught the taxi to the training centre. She had been thinking of 'my little boy', the court was told. However, the sleeping tablets had no effect and Mrs Dato later found herself digging in a cemetery before catching the cab to the training centre. She could give no explanation of why she was in the cemetery, or why she was digging.

Magistrate Mr I.C. Grieve convicted Mrs Dato and released her on a $250, two-year good behaviour bond. Poor Christopher Robin's soul might have been at rest, but his mother's grief was a perpetual torment to her.

THE BOILED BODY

Old Bill Oliver was a well-known and well-loved character in outback New South Wales. Everyone had a kind word to say about him and he often helped friends in need. However, the local mailman noticed that Old Bill had not been collecting his letters from early January 1926. Although Old Bill was something of a nomad bushman, the mailman decided to report him missing as the mail had accumulated over several weeks and Old Bill had never been missing for more than a few days at a time.

Police made a thorough search of the bush country around the tiny hamlet of Wanaaring, but there was no sign of the old bushman. The search dragged on until police came across the ruins of an old camp at Yanterbangee. Police noticed a mound at the camp and decided to dig. Within minutes they had dug up human remains wrapped in an old coat. The body's skull had been smashed in and police were convinced that it was Old Bill's body and that he had been murdered.

The first task was to identify the remains, but this proved difficult as Old Bill's killer had boiled the body before burying it. In fact, the killer had even stripped flesh from the old man's skull in an effort to hinder identification. Besides, the body had been in the makeshift grave for more than a month and was badly decomposed. Flesh had been torn from every limb and every effort was made to foil medical experts. However, forensic pathologists were still able to determine the body's sex, approximate age and physical characteristics. There was no doubt that it was Old Bill's body.

Meanwhile, one of Old Bill's cheques had been cashed at Wilcannia and his mail had been collected on a forged order form. Finally, a Wilcannia garage had received a letter instructing it to sell Old Bill's car and to give the proceeds to a man named Walter Harney, who immediately became the number one suspect. Police apprehended him and found Old Bill's watch, spirit level, chain and several documents in his possession. Police also learned that Harney had tried to raise money in Broken Hill on land deeds owned by Old Bill.

Harney, thirty years of age, was committed for trial on a charge of having murdered Old Bill on about January 14, 1926. The case was heard in Broken Hill before Judge Bevan and a jury. However, the jury failed to agree and a second trail was ordered. Harney was found guilty of murder at the second trial and his prior convictions were then read to the court.

Harney, who often used the alias of Walter Nelson, had been born in South Africa and was described in newspaper reports of his trial as a 'Boer'. He was sent to a South African reformatory when he was just fifteen years of age and later sailed for England on condition that should he return to South Africa he would report to legal authorities.

Harney apparently found it difficult to stay out of trouble and was convicted of larceny in England. However, he was extremely lucky as he was released as a first offender because the English authorities did not know of his prior convictions in South Africa. Harney decided to move to Australia and arrived at Sydney in 1917, landing in trouble almost immediately. He was convicted for unlawful possession, but in 1919 shifted to Newcastle after marrying an Australian girl.

Marriage failed to settle Harney and his crimes went from petty to serious. He next found himself in trouble in 1920 when he shot a Newcastle taxi driver and robbed him of his watch and chain and one pound and five shillings in cash. The taxi driver was left seriously injured on the roadside and was fortunate to survive the shooting. Harney was sentenced to seven years' jail for the shooting, but was released on licence (probation) in 1924. He then held a number of jobs around Australia before he and his wife found employment as married help on an outback station near Wilcannia.

Harney, meanwhile, had failed to report to prison officials and, at the time of Old Bill's killing, was a wanted man. Harney obviously was a hardened criminal and the mutilation of Old Bill's body after fracturing his skull with a blow to the head shocked the whole of Australia.

Judge Bevan asked Harney, after he had been found guilty of Old Bill's murder, if he wanted to say anything before sentence was passed and he replied: 'All I can say is that I am not guilty of the murder. I am quite satisfied with the judge's summing up and I thank the Crown for supplying me with Mr Davoren [defence counsel] for what he has done for me, and the manner in which he has conducted the defence.'

Judge Bevan then told Harney:

> You have been found guilty of a most bloodthirsty murder, and of the murder of a man who had been most kind to you. I agree with the verdict of the jury that the murder could only have been committed with a view to gain … If you have a spark of humanity in you, you must show some remorse for your cold-blooded crime.

Judge Bevan then passed the death sentence. Harney was duly executed, and few mourned his death.

THE SHARK ARM CASE

Brothers Ron and Bert Hobson wanted a star attraction for their aquarium at the seaside Sydney suburb of Coogee. They decided that what they needed was a shark—a big shark. They therefore set up lines off Maroubra on April 17, 1935, and waited. Within twenty-four hours they had hooked a monster of the seas—a four-metre tiger shark, so big that it had to be lifted from the sea by block and tackle. The shark, which had gorged itself on a smaller shark in the moments leading up to its capture, was soon on display at the Hobson aquarium.

Just one week later, on Anzac Day, a young man named Narcisse Young was watching the huge shark circling the aquarium pool. Young noticed that the shark seemed distressed and appeared to be making what he described as 'coughing movements'. The shark then shuddered hugely and disgorged an object and considerable brownish liquid. The shark had vomited up a human arm.

The arm, severed from the shoulder, had a rope knotted with a clove hitch around its wrist. The arm was tattooed, with the figures of two boxers outlined in red and blue. This tattoo convinced police that identification would be relatively easy but, just to make sure, police scientists took a 'human glove' from the hand. The fingerprints from this 'glove' proved beyond doubt that the arm was from a well-known criminal named James Smith.

The problem facing police was whether Smith was dead or alive. The discovery of the arm was not proof in itself that Smith was dead, although medical specialists advised the police that it was highly unlikely Smith would be found alive. Naturally, the case captured public imagination and newspapers of the time ran column after column of information regarding the 'Shark Arm Case'. However, police ran into a brick wall in their investigations, despite every attempt to solve the mystery.

Police finally learned that Smith had been holidaying near Port Hacking with a man named Patrick Brady, a shearer and a noted forger. Police were convinced that Smith, who ran an SP book in Sydney, had been involved in criminal activities and had been 'silenced'. Their star witness was a boat-builder named Reginald Holmes, who had told them about a dealing with Smith over a forged cheque. In an alleged statement to police, Holmes claimed that Brady had told him: 'I had a row with Smith and I have done for him. Any squeak out of you and you will also get yours. If I'm not able to get you, one of my cobbers will.' Holmes is alleged to have asked Brady about the body and was told: 'They won't get that. I dumped that in a tin trunk outside Port Hacking. You might as well know the lot, because then I know who squealed if anything comes out, and if the police ever take me, you will get yours.'

On 17 May 1935 Brady was charged with Smith's murder. Then, just three days later, there was another sensation when police were asked to intercept a motor launch which had been running out of control on Sydney Harbour. They investigated, boarded the boat and found Holmes at the helm with a bullet wound to his head. The wound was not serious and Holmes later told police that he had tried to commit suicide.

An inquest was ordered into the shark arm case and Holmes' evidence would have been critical—except that he was shot dead in a car near the Sydney Harbour Bridge less than twelve hours before the opening of the inquest on 12 June. Holmes had left his home at nearby McMahon's Point and, soon after, a wharf labourer heard three shots. Holmes had been shot three times, in a circle around his heart. Two men were later charged with his murder, but were acquitted. There was also the almost unbelievable theory that Holmes had paid someone to kill him. If this was true, it was a most unusual suicide.

The inquest was conducted by the Sydney City coroner, Mr Oram, with the Chief Government medical officer, Dr A.A. Palmer, giving evidence that the arm had not been severed by a surgeon. 'It was very roughly done,' he said. The arm was well preserved, with the skin edge at the shoulder revealing a sharp cut which Dr Palmer insisted could only have been made by a knife. Asked how the arm could have been so well preserved after being in a shark's stomach for at least a week, Dr Palmer admitted that he was unable to give an answer. His only possible explanation was that the shark's gastric secretions might have been affected and added that it was 'a million to one chance that this one shark in all the sea should have been the only one to be brought ashore alive'.

Although Brady's counsel, Mr Clive Evatt, insisted that there could be no charge of murder against his client simply because there was no body, Brady faced trial at the Sydney Central Criminal Court on 9 September. The trial was before Mr Justice Jordan and jury and, after the prosecution presented its witnesses, there was a tremendous shock when Mr Evatt insisted that the case should not continue as there was insufficient evidence.

Mr Justice Jordan adjourned the case and, when he returned, said:

> The case is one in which the evidence is circumstantial, and in any such case it is well established that the jury is not entitled to convict unless there is no other reasonable explanation of the evidence than that the accused is guilty. In such cases, if there is a reasonable explanation of evidence which is consistent with innocence, the jury must acquit.
>
> Now, in the present case, I think, there is no doubt that there is plenty of matter of suspicion on the evidence put before the court in the past two days. But the clear opinion I have formed is that,

upon settled principles, a conviction upon the evidence could not
be allowed to stand. I have no alternative but to direct an acquittal,
and I direct an acquittal.

Brady was a free man.

The shark arm case almost certainly will never be solved,
especially as Brady died in August 1965 aged seventy-one. He
insisted to the very end that he was innocent. However, it does seem
certain that Smith was murdered by a person or persons unknown,
with his body stuffed into a sea trunk and dumped offshore. The
most plausible explanation for the disgorged arm is that the trunk
was not big enough to take the entire body, so the left arm was
hacked off and tied to the side of the trunk. The huge tiger shark
later hooked at Maroubra gobbled up the arm with glee, ripping it
from the trunk, but with the rope still attached to the wrist. It
certainly was a 'one in a million' chance that the shark was captured
and that it disgorged the arm to present the world with a gruesome
mystery.

DEATH OF A HERO

Constable Joseph Delaney, of the Victorian mounted police, was one of the most highly respected members of the Swan Hill community. A tall man, Constable Delaney dispensed justice along the Murray River with tremendous authority and the backing of a thankful rural community. In fact, Constable Delaney was regarded as something of a hero as he had been awarded the Military Medal in France in World War I. He and another soldier were engaged in laying wires at Villers Bretonneux when they were surprised by the enemy. The other soldier was shot, but Delaney completed his task and then carried his mate to the safety of the trenches.

Police had been called to a farmhouse at Tyntynder, about twelve kilometres from Swan Hill, on August 28, 1923. There had been a break-in during the absence of the owner, Mr William Crick. Police suspected a young farmhand from a neighbouring property had taken advantage of Mr Crick's absence and he was questioned over the break-in. However, Constable Delaney decided to interview the suspect himself on 30 August. He went straight to the house where the youth was living and, once inside, noticed a movement from behind a door. The police officer was then shot in the chest from almost point-blank range.

The youth was seen running out of the house and neighbours who went to investigate found Constable Delaney lying in a pool of

335

blood. He was still alive and conscious and told the men who found him what had happened. One man stayed with the wounded police officer while the other jumped on Constable Delaney's horse to notify other police.

A police officer and a doctor arrived two hours later. Their vehicle had been bogged in a quagmire several kilometres from the Crick farmhouse and they ran the last few hundred metres to the house, fearing they would be too late. However, Constable Delaney was still alive and arrangements were made to have him transported to Swan Hill, where he arrived several hours later. Officials at the Swan Hill Public Hospital reported that the policeman's condition was 'serious'.

Meanwhile, police officers scoured the countryside for any sign of the youth who had shot Constable Delaney and finally tracked him down to a farmhouse several kilometres from the scene of the shooting. Later, at the Swan Hill police station, fifteen-year-old Frederick Smith, a ward of the state, was charged with having shot Constable Delaney with intent to murder.

Doctors at the Swan Hill Public Hospital knew that Constable Delaney was dying, but one last effort was made to save his life. The police surgeon, Mr G.A. Syme (together with police commissioner Mr A.N. Nicholson), was flown to Swan Hill, where he performed an emergency operation. The Chief Secretary, Mr Baird, had given instructions that every effort be made in the attempt to save Constable Delaney's life.

However, the sad news of Constable Delaney's death was announced on the morning of September 4. He had died at 4 a.m. despite every medical attention. The whole of Swan Hill went into deep mourning and arrangements were made for memorial services and a hero's funeral. It was decided to bury Constable Delaney at his birthplace of Greta, near Benalla, but Swan Hill was determined to give him a fitting farewell.

A huge crowd attended a special late morning service at the Swan Hill Catholic Church and the Swan Hill Municipal Band then led a procession to the railway station. Three police officers and three returned servicemen carried Constable Delaney's coffin, which was covered by the Union Jack. Every available returned serviceman marched behind the coffin in tribute to their fallen comrade and residents lined the streets in one of the most heart-rending scenes in Swan Hill history. Buglers sounded 'The Last Post' as the train pulled out of the station.

Constable Delaney's coffin arrived at Benalla the following day and was carried from the station by uniformed police officers and transported to Greta. 'He was a courageous and efficient officer,' Mr Nicholson said in tribute. 'I deeply regret his death as he was one of the most promising young men in the force.'

Smith finally faced trial in Bendigo for the murder of Constable Delaney. The court was told that Smith had been hiding behind a bedroom door when Constable Delaney entered the house. Smith ordered the policeman to 'put up' his hands, but Constable Delaney 'rushed' Smith, who put the gun to his shoulder and pulled the trigger. Smith, in a voluntary statement, admitted these facts, but denied them when giving evidence from the witness box and claimed that the shooting had been an accident.

He was found guilty of the lesser charge of manslaughter and Mr Justice McArthur indicated in no uncertain terms that he believed Smith had lied to the court. He told Smith:

> You have added to the offence by telling lies in the witness box. The jury did not find you guilty of the grave charge [murder], but of manslaughter. For that you must be adequately punished. The Court must declare that the promiscuous firing of guns—whether by young or old—has to be put down with a firm hand. I intend to inflict a sentence upon you that in my opinion is well deserved, and one which I hope will act as a deterrent to others—young or old—who may be inclined to launch out upon a career of crime.

Mr Justice McArthur sentenced Smith to five years' imprisonment and a private whipping of at least ten lashes of the birch.

THE KILLER POET

Mabel Elizabeth James was an attractive young woman with curly blonde hair. She was a country girl living in Melbourne and, like many country girls of the 1920s, was shy and reserved. She had left her home in Maryborough to look for work in the city, and secured a position as a housemaid at the St Ive's Guest House, Toorak Road, South Yarra. Poor Mabel James, just twenty years of age when she accepted the position, was not to know that her job would lead to her death at the hands of a crazed suitor.

One of her workmates was Cecil Ronald Leet, who had spent several years in the navy. He was a houseman at the guest house and fell instantly and hopelessly in love with Mabel. His infatuation was so intense that he drove Mabel to despair. He peppered her with declarations of love and wrote her passionate poems and letters. In short, he became a nuisance and Mabel did not know how to reject his overtures.

This situation lasted for more than two years, until Leet resigned his position and went looking for work in rural New South Wales. He secured a job in 1927 as a boundary rider on a sheep farm, but continued to bombard poor Mabel with letters and poems. Mabel, despite her naivety, did not give Leet the slightest encouragement and, in fact, did her best to dampen his passion. However, she made one small, but grave, error. After receiving yet another letter from

Leet she replied and signed off with 'your sincere friend, Mabel James'. Leet, twenty-six, was beside himself with joy. Here, at last, was a sign from the woman he loved that, at least, there was some reciprocal affection. He clutched at this tiny straw, resigned his position and headed for Melbourne.

Leet then confronted Mabel in a Melbourne street on July 19, 1927, and repeated his declarations of love. Mabel, who was with workmate Jessie Kelty, again rejected his overtures and firmly refused to allow Leet to walk her back to the guest house where she lived. Leet, however, followed the two girls to the tram stop and watched them disappear into the night. It was not the last Mabel would see of the eccentric Leet.

Next evening Mabel was still trying to recover from the shock of seeing Leet and asked her friend Jessie to walk with her to her quarters at the back of the guest house. The two young women walked through the shadows in silence and, when they had reached Mabel's room, were relieved that there had been no sign of Leet. Mabel then tried to turn the key in her doorlock, only to drop the key. She bent to pick it up and saw Leet leap at her from nearby bushes. He was carrying a rifle. Leet grabbed both young women, but Jessie wriggled free; Leet then shot Mabel in the leg. The screams and the rifle shot alerted other workers, and pantry maid Mrs Mavis Woods rushed out into the walkway alongside the staff bungalows. 'Help me, help me,' Mabel cried as she struggled to break free. Mrs Woods bravely grabbed hold of Mabel, but was shot in the shoulder for her trouble.

Leet saw his chance and fired at Mabel's head, killing the woman he loved with such maniacal passion. Leet then turned the gun on himself, putting a bullet through his brain. He died just minutes after an ambulance delivered him to the Alfred Hospital.

Detective-Sergeant Holden and Detective Lyon, who rushed to the murder-suicide scene, reasoned that Leet had been driven by uncontrollable infatuation. They found scraps of paper in Leet's pockets and experts finally deciphered a weird and unnerving series of symbols telling of how Leet judged Mabel's reactions to him. The poet killer, who used to spend long hours poring over love poems written by the giants of literature, had clearly planned the murder as he had bought the murder weapon only the day before he killed Mabel.

One of Leet's letters to Mabel read:

My dear Mabel,

It is a happy moment when I think of you, and a happier one when I look forward to the time when I shall meet you again and realise that each day and each month you are building into your life the essence of nobility, that you know the meaning of life, the preciousness of time and your responsibilities, so that in later life you can bring into your happiness the consciousness of having upheld the dignity of your sweet young womanhood.

Do be true to your higher self. Spurn everything that will tempt you to even a wrong thought, and much more a wrong action. Love the true and the beautiful. Serve your teachers and your parents with determination and steadfastness. And be assured of my deepest regard for you. Ron.

This was followed by a poem:

'Remember him thou leav'st behind,
Whose heart is warmly bound to thee;
Close as the tend'rest links can bind
A heart as warm as heart could be.'

Another letter, after a telephone conversation with Mabel read: 'The sound of your voice today sent a longing thrill through my feelings … You can never conceive how deep my regard of you is and so I have your whole interests at heart. My whole thoughts are centred in you. I think of you everlastingly, day and night, until the tears well in my eyes.' Leet signed off 'God bless you, Chere Ange, Fraternally, Ron.'

The son of an Edinburgh University graduate, Leet was well educated himself. However, he was a loner and shunned friendship. He sought only Mabel James' friendship, and when he was rejected once and for all he snapped. Melbourne City coroner Mr Berriman found that Cecil Leet was of 'unsound mind' when he killed Mabel James.

A BEER BOTTLE THROUGH THE HEART

Maureen Bradley, fourteen years of age, was not the type of girl to run away from home. She had regular habits and, before she disappeared on her way home from her Sydney school on the afternoon of December 3, 1971, she had telephoned her mother from Hornsby railway station to say that she would not be long. It was the last time Mrs Bradley heard her daughter's voice.

Despite every effort and one of the biggest searches in Sydney for many years, no sign of Maureen Bradley was found over the following ten days. Police arranged with Sydney television stations to show acted replays of the girl's last movements from Hornsby to her home in the northern suburb of Mt Kuring-gai, and Maureen's photo was printed in all the daily newspapers. She was blonde, pretty—and dead.

Maureen's naked body was eventually found in a disused septic tank at McKell Park, Brooklyn, ten days after her disappearance. She had been stabbed in the heart with a broken beer bottle. The public was outraged and the New South Wales Government offered a reward of $100,000 for the capture of Maureen's killer.

Police eventually made an arrest on January 16, 1972, when a twenty-year-old man was charged with the attempted rape of a woman at the northern suburb of Cowan. The arrest ended a six-week investigation into a murder which shocked Sydney.

Labourer Bruce Kenneth McKenzie faced trial at the Central Criminal Court on June 5 that year and the court was told McKenzie had confessed to murder. Detective-Sergeant Albert MacDonald told the court that he interviewed McKenzie immediately after the arrest and said that McKenzie at first denied killing Maureen. However, the detective said that McKenzie eventually said: 'All right, I did it.'

Detective-Sergeant MacDonald said McKenzie told him he had waited near a bush track as Maureen was coming home from school. He then grabbed her by the neck, dragged her to his car and locked her in the boot before driving her to Brooklyn, about fourteen kilometres away. He then backed the car into the bush at Brooklyn and, with the girl's neck locked in his arms, marched her to the septic tank. There, with one hand on her throat, he made her undress and indecently assaulted her.

The detective told the court that McKenzie said he heard someone shout 'hey' and thought someone had seen him. McKenzie picked up a beer bottle, smashed it and drove it twice into Maureen's chest, piercing her heart. He then threw the body, clothing and school bag into the septic tank.

Detective-Sergeant Noel C. Morey told the court that McKenzie took him to the scene of the crime and demonstrated how he had held Maureen in a headlock and stabbed her with the beer bottle. The senior defence counsel, Mr H. Purcell, then asked Mr Justice Slattery for a short adjournment so that he could talk to McKenzie. On resumption, the indictment was re-read and McKenzie changed his plea from not guilty to guilty.

The case had been in progress just four hours and Mr Justice Slattery addressed the jury for only a few minutes before asking it to retire. He told jury members that there had been no evidence to reduce McKenzie's guilt and the jury took just ten minutes to make its decision.

McKenzie, a single man who lived with his mother and sisters at Cowan, was sentenced to life imprisonment. When asked by Mr Justice Slattery if he had anything to say, he replied: 'I am sorry for the trouble I have caused the girl's family and my own and I just wish to do what is right in the future.'

THE PICNIC PARTY
KILLER

It was a perfect summer's day, ideal for a bush picnic. Sunday, February 10, 1924, dawned hot and still and Mr and Mrs Charles McGrath made early preparations for the picnic they would hold on the banks of the Jingellic Creek, a small tributary of the Murray River. A number of country neighbours had been invited to the picnic, just 200 metres from the McGrath homestead. Guests were asked to assemble at the picnic site from about 1 o'clock.

Dairy farmer Mr Charles Barber and his wife Ruth were the first to arrive, followed by Mr and Mrs McGrath, tobacco grower Mr Richard King, butter factory manager Mr David Shephard and his wife and child, farmer Charles Gainer and his wife and eight-year-old George Pointz. The group ate a lazy luncheon under the willows draping the Jingellic Creek, unaware that someone on the opposite bank of the creek had been watching every mouthful, every gesture, every movement.

Barber decided at 2.30 p.m. that it was time for the men to go for a walk. They were only 100 metres from the women and children when there was a loud cracking noise from the opposite bank. One of the men yelled 'Oh, oh' and fell to the ground. It was King, who was seriously wounded in the chest. The men looked up and saw a man in a black hat taking aim for a second shot. Barber immediately recognised the man as his farmhand, Claude Valentine Batson, regarded as one of the best shots in southern New South Wales.

The men were sitting ducks as Batson fired the second shot, which hit Gainer in the right knee. They started running back towards the picnic site, only for Batson to spray the area with bullets. Shephard took a bullet through the body as Barber shouted to the women and children to take cover.

It was a desperate situation, but Barber realised that the best hope of avoiding a major catastrophe was to get help. Barber, showing great courage, ran to a horse, mounted it and took off in a cloud of dust. Meanwhile, former army major McGrath decided that Batson had to be shot down. He made a dash for his homestead, but was hit four times by bullets—twice in the back. McGrath, critically wounded but with a gun in his hand, scrambled back to the creek bank. However, Batson had disappeared into the bush. He had fired more than thirty rounds from his rifle and had left four men wounded.

Barber's daring ride for help alerted the entire Murray region that a 'madman' was on the loose. The problem was that trying to find Batson would be like trying to find the proverbial needle in the haystack. He was an expert bushman and was heavily armed. However, a massive manhunt was launched immediately and more than 100 police and volunteers scoured the bush.

The shooting incident took a tragic turn the following morning when Shephard died in hospital. This made the search party even more determined to take Batson, dead or alive. An extra thirty armed police from southern New South Wales and northern Victoria joined the manhunt in searing temperatures. The searchers had several sightings of Batson, but the wanted man was far too clever and bush-wise to walk into any trap. The twenty-three-year-old farmhand had spent his entire life in the bush and knew every rabbit track, every gully, every source of food in the area.

The problem for Batson was that the Murray area was in the grip of a heatwave and he could hold out for only so long. To avoid more than 100 police and volunteers in such ferociously hot conditions would take more than local knowledge and willpower. The man in charge of what was one of Australia's biggest manhunts, Detective George Cleaver, knew that sooner or later Batson would be captured, or shot. However, Batson was extremely dangerous and the police did not want any further tragedies.

On the second day of the manhunt, Batson was confronted by two police officers at an orchard near Lankeys Creek. Sergeants John O'Connor and Charles Morris ordered Batson to throw up his hands. There was an exchange of fire and a shot from Sergeant Morris' revolver ripped through the right sleeve of Batson's shirt. Batson ran for his life and escaped.

Batson managed to avoid his hunters for five days. At one stage he had swum the Murray naked, leaving his rifle and ammunition behind a tree in the bush. He then backtracked to the Barber farm, stole clothes and left a note which read: 'C. Batson has taken a dose of cyanide. It tastes lovely too. I left my rifle and cartridges down near Drummoyne's cowshed on the other side of the river. Goodbye Mother, CVB.'

Batson obviously wanted his pursuers to believe that he had committed suicide. However, he could not have known that cyanide would have killed him instantly and he would not have been able to write a letter after taking the poison.

Finally, on February 15 he walked up to two men on a dairy farm just out of Jingellic. Farmhands Robert Emerson and William Hore knew Batson well and were stunned when the weary killer, wearing riding breeches, a blue coat and a tweed cap, said: 'Good-day, what do you think of it? Where are the police?' Emerson told Batson he did not know anything about the police or a manhunt. He even gave Batson some milk. The killer then produced a tin which he said contained cyanide, but Emerson did not believe him and convinced Batson to go to the farmhouse. Emerson asked him: 'What did you do it for?'

Batson replied: 'I was driven to it. I hope they put me on trial. I will tell them something.' Minutes later Batson was arrested by two police officers who had been called to the farmhouse. The manhunt was over.

Batson faced charges at the Albury Police Court just ten days after his capture. Barber told the court that he had employed Batson for six years and had had no trouble with him. Mrs Barber told the court that Batson had often helped her with household chores, 'such as cutting wood and drying dishes'. However, she added that Batson showed his dislike when Richard King helped with any of the chores. Significantly, Batson asked Emerson just before the arrest whether King was dead. When Emerson told him that King was still alive, Batson replied: 'I will not rest until I get him.'

Several theories were put forward to explain Batson's attack on the picnickers. It was suggested that he had been disappointed in love and also that he had suffered a mental breakdown following his failure to produce a successful rabbit poison he had been working on for several years. There was also his obvious dislike of King, who had never done him any harm. Barber told a newspaper reporter during the manhunt that Batson was a 'madly jealous man'.

New South Wales Government Medical Officer Dr Cleaver Woods told the Albury Police Court that he had examined Batson at the Albury police station on February 16. He said Batson was weak physically because of his exposure to the bush, but 'answered questions freely and intelligently'. Dr Woods concluded that Batson's mentality was normal. He added that Batson's behaviour at Albury jail had been 'exemplary'.

The wounded men—King, McGrath and Gainer—were too ill to give evidence in court, which was adjourned to hear their evidence from hospital. None of these men could explain why Batson had fired on them. Gainer even told the court he had never met Batson. Gainer, who had been shot through the right knee, made a full recovery. King was the most severely wounded, a bullet passing through one lung, his stomach and part of his liver. His life had been in danger but he, too, made a full recovery.

Batson was committed for trial on one charge of murder and three charges of felonious wounding with intent to murder.

However, he never stood trial as he was committed to a mental institution. Batson obviously had had a mental breakdown, but there was nothing in the days leading up to the picnic ambush to suggest that he would run amok with a rifle.

No one will ever know why he shot at innocent picnickers.

THE CHILD BRIDE

Orma and Donald Warner were married as teenagers, with pretty, dark-haired Orma little more than a child bride. She was just seventeen years of age when she married nineteen-year-old timber mill worker Donald in early 1951. Neither was to know that they would be married for just five months.

Farmer Athol Lyon was driving past the Warners' weatherboard and fibro house near Casino, on the north coast of New South Wales, at about 9.45 p.m. on July 15, 1951, when he noticed that the house was ablaze. There was nothing he could do, as the flames had already taken hold. Police were called and were shocked to find two charred bodies in the ashes of the huge blaze. Even more horrifying, police also found the remains of a couple of rifles, a revolver and two shotgun cartridges. They immediately sensed that the newlyweds had been shot to death and the house then torched.

A post-mortem quickly revealed that both Orma and Donald Warner had taken gunshot wounds to the body. There were numerous pellets in both bodies and, as proof that the house had been torched, police found the charred remains of three kerosene tins. Someone had blasted the young couple to death and had then set fire to their home. But who?

Police did not have to question too many locals as there were persistent rumours that Orma had been nervous of a local stock inspector. However, twenty-nine-year-old William Henry Abbott had had an impeccable record during World War II and had even been awarded the Distinguished Conduct Medal for his courage. He was married, with his wife pregnant with their first child.

Police learned that Donald Warner had complained to Abbott about 'pestering' his wife and that the newlywed husband had spoken about getting Abbott shifted from the district in his job. That was just three days before the deaths of Donald and Orma Warner, and police, naturally, were now suspicious of Abbott, despite his fine war record.

Abbott was unable to give police an alibi and when detectives found a shotgun at his home they knew they were close to breaking the case. Ballistic tests proved that the shotgun found in the Abbott home had been used to shoot the Warners. Finally, police found bloodstained clothes at Abbott's home and although he at first insisted that the blood was from cattle, police suspected otherwise. Abbott was charged with murder and two days later made a statement to police.

Abbott, in the statement, said he went to the Warner home to 'have it out' with Donald Warner. He added:

> Don and Orma came up the back steps. I stepped out and asked Don what he had in mind when he was talking to me at the sawmill [regarding his 'pestering Orma']. He didn't answer, but told Orma to go inside. He said he didn't want me hanging about. He stepped out on the verandah and told me if I didn't clear out he'd clout me.
>
> I knew I could handle him and I pulled off my pullover. He swung a punch at me, but missed. I always hit them in the body. I don't hit them on the jaw and hurt my hands. I knew too much about the game for that. I planted one in his belly and he went down. I can't hit a man when he's down and I waited for him to get up. When Don got up he seemed to dive and stumble to where the gun was leaning on the verandah. I thought he was grabbing for it and I grabbed for it, too. I think we both got it. I don't know whether I fired it or not, but it went off and it hit Don between the hip and the short rib. Orma ran out screaming.

I can still hear her screaming. We got Don on his feet and helped him into the bedroom. I didn't know whether to get a doctor or try to patch him up. We were striking matches and looking at his wound. I told Orma to go and get a light, and I went out to the kitchen with her and we got some water and rag to bandage him. On the way I picked up my gun—I don't know why. When we got back to the bedroom Don was standing up. I thought he was coming at me, and I jerked my gun. I think I fired it automatically.

Orma was in front of me, carrying a lamp, and it crashed down on the floor. Then there was no light at all. I heard a thud. It must have been Orma hitting the floor. I reloaded in the dark, then switched on a torch I had picked up in the kitchen. Don was standing up and I thought he was coming at me. I fired and he went down again. Then I shone the torch on Orma.

I could see that she was dead. You only had to look at her to see that. She had taken the charge in the stomach. I didn't know what to do then. I thought I would burn the place down to cover it up. I didn't want to take any chances that Orma might be alive and suffer in the fire, so I pulled out my revolver and shot her in the head. I ran around and set fire to the place. I went and got kerosene and splashed it everywhere. Then I poured it on the bedspread. I remember Orma talking about buying it. Then I set fire to the bedspread and cleared out.

Abbott, at his trial before Mr Justice McClemens and jury, repudiated this confession and insisted that police had threatened to 'bash' him. However, Abbott was found guilty and sentenced to death. However, this sentence was later commuted to one of life imprisonment.

THE EVIL COUPLE

If Valmae Fae Beck was an unattractive woman, her husband Barrie John Watts was even less appealing. While Beck was dumpy with a pot belly, Watts was a curly-haired, shrivelled creature with rodent-like features. They might have been opposites in appearance, but shared sexual fantasies.

Watts dreamed of raping and killing a young virgin, while Beck was more than willing to satisfy this sick and evil fantasy. They put their plan into operation on November 27, 1987, with Watts telling his wife of one year: 'Today is the day. It's on.'

Beck and Watts, like spiders in a web, waited in their car on Queensland's Sunshine Coast for a victim. Tragically, pretty, blonde 12-year-old Sian Kingi was riding her bike at Tewantin when the evil couple called her over to their car to ask her if she had seen a poodle.

They abducted Kingi, with Watts grabbing her from behind and, with her arms bound and mouth taped, was taken to a nearby forest where Watts raped her while Beck watched. Watts then stabbed the innocent young girl a dozen times before slashing her throat and then strangling her with his wife's belt.

Watts' list had been satisfied and, almost unbelievably, he and his wicked wife went home and had a bath before watching television and then going to bed. The discovery of Kingi's body outraged

Queensland and, when Watts and Beck eventually were brought to justice a lynch mob greeted them, with some people carrying banners and placards which read 'Hang Them'.

Although Beck and Watts had separate trials, both were sentenced to life imprisonment. During the sentencing of Beck, Justice Jack Kelly said: 'No decent person could not feel revulsion at what you did — and a woman with children of your own (she had six children from previous marriages).' He also described the woman prepared to watch an innocent girl raped and killed just to pelase her husband's sick fantasies as 'callous and cruel'.

Incredibly, Beck gave evidence at her trial that Kingi 'never cried, never shed a tear, she never uttered a peep, she just did everything we told her'. Watts was described at his trial as 'a thoroughly evil man devoid of any sense of morality'.

Even more amazingly, Beck later claimed she was not as evil as she had been painted and had even become a born-again Christian. She said: 'I am not a repeat serious crime offender. I have no sex or violence offences on my record.'

Although she made an appeal to have a lower security rating, this move failed. However, Beck insisted that she had found God and would be applying for parole, much to the horror of little Sian's parents, Barry and Lynda Kingi.

There therefore was outrage in Queensland in 2000 when Beck, (who changed her surname to Cramb) applied for work release, home detention and parole. The application was denied, but a friend said that everyone deserved forgiveness and added: 'If I had a daughter, I hope I would be big enough to try and forgive her, but I probably wouldn't. She was a victim of an obsessive love relationship with her husband.'

Queensland Premier Peter Beattie, when told that Beck was seeking parole described the murder of Kingi as 'shocking' and added: 'Just because someone applies for parole does not necessarily mean they will get it.'

SPIRIT VOICES

Anyone walking past the Turner home in the quiet east Melbourne suburb of Glen Iris would have rated it one of the prettiest in the neighbourhood. A white weatherboard cottage with a neat picket fence, it could have been a setting for domestic bliss. Instead, the home in Tooronga Road became a slaughterhouse on April 30, 1934.

Boilermaker David Turner left for work early on that morning, leaving his wife May at home with their two children. When Turner returned home just after 6 p.m. the house was in total darkness and the key was missing from its usual hiding place. Turner sensed something was wrong, he later said:

> I went to the back door, but it was locked. I rattled it, but no one answered. I went to the front gate and stood for five minutes looking down the street. Soon after, I heard footsteps in the passage. I walked to the front door, which I had found opened about an inch. I opened the door and found the passage in darkness. As I switched on the passage light I saw my wife walk through the hall curtains. She did not speak. When I got to the end of the passage I felt for the light switch, but before I found it I heard a thud. I switched on the light and saw my wife lying on the floor, which was covered in blood.
>
> I ran straight out of the house to a neighbour, who returned with me. I lifted my wife's head, but she did not speak. My neighbour

> then asked me to look for the children. I did so and then found my
> elder child, Martha, in bed with the clothes up to her neck. I saw
> that she had injuries to the head. I did not see the younger child,
> Eliza, at all. When the doctor arrived he told me that my younger
> child was dead on my bed. I had not noticed her before.

The two children, ten-year-old Martha and eight-year-old Eliza, died from their horrific head injuries. Their mother, thirty-five-year-old Mrs May Turner, had bashed their heads in with an axe. Mrs Turner herself was very seriously injured, with an extremely deep wound to the throat; her wrists had also been slashed. A bloodstained axe and a razor were found by her side. Mrs Turner was rushed to the Alfred Hospital, but died of her wounds the following day.

An inquest into the Glen Iris tragedy was held the following month, with the Alfred Hospital's Dr Eric Langley telling the coroner, Mr McLean PM, that he had asked Mrs Turner who had attacked her. The dying woman, whose vocal cords had been severed, was unable to answer, but wrote a note for the doctor. Mr McLean was handed this note, but refused to release its contents. Later, Constable M. Murphy told the inquest that he had found an exercise book in the Turner home. One note read: 'After being followed all day I wish to die with my children.' Another note said 'spirit voices' had been speaking to Mrs Turner every day.

Turner told the inquest that he and his wife had migrated to Australia from Scotland eight years earlier and that his wife's mother had died in a mental institution. He also told the inquest that his wife had become increasingly morbid and fascinated with spiritualism. Turner said his wife regularly attended spiritualist meetings and 'constantly pondered over life and death beyond the grave'. He also said that he and his wife had attended a dance at nearby Hawthorn just two nights before the tragedy, but had had to return home early when Mrs Turner started making strange comments. He said this pattern of behaviour continued into the next day, with 'several strange remarks'. These included: 'Everyone is against me ... you have been out in the backyard waving to people in the front.' Turner said his wife had been seeing three different doctors and was extremely worried about her health.

Turner, who had been working part time as a gardener, denied having an argument with his wife on the day of the tragedy and, in fact, was 'terribly shaken' by what had happened on April 30. The coroner found that Martha and Eliza Turner had died of injuries inflicted by their mother 'while of unsound mind' and that Mrs Turner had died as the result of self-inflicted wounds.

DEATH OF A
PROSTITUTE

Prostitution, by its very nature, is an extremely dangerous profession and police files around the world are crammed with cases involving the killing of prostitutes. Of course, the most infamous examples are Jack the Ripper and his modern counterpart, the Yorkshire Ripper. Jack the Ripper's identity, of course, is still a mystery, despite almost countless theories and hypotheses. The Yorkshire Ripper, Peter Sutcliffe, began a reign of terror in 1975 that lasted until 1981. Sutcliffe was charged with the murder of thirteen women, mostly prostitutes; he had mutilated their bodies. Sutcliffe pleaded not guilty on the grounds of diminished responsibility, but was found guilty of murder and sentenced to life imprisonment. Thankfully, no Australian city has had to endure the agony and terror of a Ripper-type killer, but there have been serial killers and prostitute murders are far from rare.

One of Australia's most baffling prostitute killings was in 1934 and police have never been able to solve the crime. Almost certainly, the bludgeoning to death of pretty, vivacious Jean McKenzie in a St Kilda flat will never be solved, despite every police effort over a number of years. McKenzie, twenty-four years of age and elegantly slim and well dressed, was not your average streetwalker. She loved the good life and appeared to live in a fantasy world in which princes came to the rescue of fair young maidens. McKenzie was waiting for her prince to arrive on a white stallion when, one dark wintry Melbourne night in 1934, she was killed in the most brutal of circumstances.

McKenzie was at home in her St Kilda flat on the night of June 7 when there was a knock at the door. Her landlord, Henry Bloom, later heard McKenzie arguing with a man for more than an hour, but could not catch the words. Earlier, a tall, fair-haired man in an overcoat had been seen entering McKenzie's ground floor bed-sit. The row later died and Bloom saw the tall man leave McKenzie's flat and walk through the front garden. He thought no more of the row until the next morning when there was no sign of McKenzie. Bloom's wife investigated and, when she opened the door to McKenzie's flat, found the young woman dead in the hallway. McKenzie's head had been battered in by a huge piece of wood taken from the fireplace. It was an horrific sight, with McKenzie dressed only in a white singlet. There was blood everywhere and it was obvious McKenzie had struggled with her killer. Furniture had been knocked over and clothing was strewn around the room. Police also disclosed that the killer had washed his hands before leaving the flat. He was obviously a cool customer and the nature of the crime suggested to police that McKenzie had been executed.

The first problem police faced was in the identification of the dead woman as there were few clues in the flat. Police fingerprinted the body and discovered that the dead woman was, in fact, a woman who had been apprehended three years earlier after approaching men in Melbourne's red-light district of St Kilda. Police made a positive identification of Jean McKenzie, but they were lucky as the woman had used a number of aliases in an obvious attempt to hide her identity. Police reasoned that McKenzie was afraid of someone and was trying to lose herself in the seedier parts of St Kilda. One theory was that McKenzie had been bashed to death by a pimp, but police were unable to prove this.

Police, in fact, interviewed hundreds of people in the St Kilda area. They questioned prostitutes and pimps and discreetly pulled over respectable men walking or driving through the red-light district. However, all their questions and investigations proved fruitless, even though there were a number of suspects. In fact, police twice thought they were close to solving the murder riddle, but both times the 'suspect' had a firm alibi.

An inquest into the death of Jean McKenzie was held at the Coroner's Court five months after the killing, but police were forced to admit that they did not have enough evidence to identify the killer. The coroner had no alternative but to return a finding of murder against a 'person unknown'. That person is still unknown to police although the case was re-opened several times over a number of years. It is now likely that the woman's killer has gone to the grave with his secret.

THE HOUSE OF HORRORS

Mick Lewis was what was known in rural areas of Australia as a 'gun shearer'. In fact, he was so good at his job that his workmates nicknamed him 'Trickey Mickey' and he often sheared more than 200 sheep a day. Mick worked hard, and played hard. He had a big thirst and loved a gamble. In fact, it was said that if he had had a good win on the horses he would sometimes have his pockets stuffed with notes. Lewis, twenty-five, was married to a typical country girl, Sue Lewis, twenty-seven, who had a much quieter personality and was devoted to her two children, five-year-old Tania and three-year-old Michael. In October 1978, the Lewis family was living near the southern New South Wales town of Jerilderie, in an old rented homestead picturesquely named 'Summerfield'. It was a typical Australian country homestead, with a high-pitched corrugated iron roof and a surround verandah. Early in its days it must have been something of a mansion; in 1978 it became the house of horrors.

On the morning of Tuesday, October 3, 1978, telephonist Mrs Nola Evans was asked if she could check the Lewis' telephone line at 'Summerfield'. A switchboard operator in the nearby town of Hay had been trying to connect a call, but a little girl kept answering the telephone. Mrs Evans rang the number and a sad little voice told her that her 'mummy and daddy' were asleep. Mrs Evans later said: 'I then asked her if she had tried to wake him [the father] and she said "I've tried to, but he just won't wake up." I then asked her to wait and went to another switch-board and rang the Jerilderie police. I talked to her for half an hour until the police arrived and came on the line.'

The police officers, Sergeant Paul Payne and Senior Constable Ken Waterhouse, walked straight into a ghastly scene—they found Lewis dead in the kitchen, his head in a pool of blood. The police officers moved further into the house and turned their noses up at a foul odour from the main bedroom. They walked in and discovered Sue Lewis' decomposing and maggot-infested body in a double bed. The Lewis children, grubby but unharmed, had been caring for themselves in the house where their parents had been killed and left to rot. Little Tania had looked after her brother by feeding him milk and biscuits. She had also turned the heater up at night to keep them warm. They were convinced that their parents were 'asleep'. Mrs Evans said that Tania had told her the two children had entertained themselves by watching television.

Police at first believed that Lewis had been bashed around the head, although they were convinced his wife had been shot in the head. They had found a spent .22 cartridge in the bedroom where her body was found, but had not found any bullet wound in her husband's head. They were also puzzled by the different condition of the bodies. Lewis' body showed little sign of decomposition, while his wife's body was in a terrible state of putrefaction. Lewis had been killed in the kitchen, but his wife had apparently been killed while she was in bed. It was discovered that Mrs Lewis' electric blanket was turned on to the 'high' position and this explained the high level of decomposition. Police were stunned by what they saw in this house of horrors, and newspapers in Melbourne and Sydney quickly described the murders as 'executions'.

There seemed no doubt that the Lewises had been executed, but what had been the motive? Police at first thought that Lewis might have had a successful punting spree and then been robbed. However, this theory was quickly discounted as the murders appeared to have been extremely well planned and executed. Meanwhile, police launched one of the most painstaking murder investigations in Australian criminal history, interviewing every Jerilderie resident in the search for clues. It later was disclosed that more than 2000 people were asked to help with even the smallest scrap of information. Police took weeks to piece the information together, and were eventually rewarded for all their interviews and forensic investigations.

Careful examination of the house of horrors turned up the first clue, which was a small tear in a flywire door to the kitchen. It was precisely the same size as a .22 bullet and a post-mortem examination of Lewis' body showed that he had died of a single gunshot wound to the head, behind the right ear. A post-mortem examination of Mrs Lewis' body revealed that she had been shot twice in the head.

Police therefore reasoned that Lewis had been shot where he stood in the kitchen, through the flywire door. The killer had then entered the house and had shot Mrs Lewis twice as she lay in bed. Lewis had been preparing a meal when shot and an omelette and bacon rashers were still in the oven; another omelette and a frypan lay upturned on the floor next to his body. He had presumably cooked one omelette and was preparing another when shot.

The time of death also puzzled police as Lewis had telephoned his mother late on the evening of September 30. It was therefore assumed that the Lewises had been killed shortly after Lewis had called his mother. Police believed that the killer had waited for an opportunity to kill the shearer and his wife and had shot them dead in an act of cold-blooded brutality. Meanwhile, police launched a massive search for the .22 rifle which had been used to kill the Lewises and soldiers from an engineering unit were even called in from the Puckapunyal Army base near Seymour, Victoria. They used mine detectors in an effort to find the weapon, without success.

Forensic tests on the .22 calibre cartridge and a bullet taken from Lewis' skull revealed that the murder weapon was an Australian-made Fieldman rifle. This information proved vital, as the Melbourne manufacturer was able to narrow it down to a batch of 750. Police also pricked their ears at local gossip which suggested that Lewis had been planning to 'write off' his car so that he could collect $5000 in insurance money. A Jerilderie panelbeater told police Lewis was planning to 'stack up' the car.

This information also proved vital, and another link in the chain of evidence was forged when police questioned people listed in the Lewis telephone directory. One of those listed was a Shepparton painting contractor and part-time insurance representative, John Fairley, who had previously arranged motor insurance for Lewis. When police discovered that one of Fairley's friends had lent him a .22 Fieldman rifle to 'shoot a couple of bunnies', they were convinced they were close to solving the gruesome double murder. Raymond Rafferty told police he had lent Fairley the rifle only days before the Jerilderie couple were murdered. Fairley was a forty-year-old immigrant who had been in Australia for eighteen years and had five children, aged between nineteen and two years.

Fairley pleaded guilty at his Central Criminal Court trial before Mr Justice Yeldham. Detective-Sergeant Donald Worsley told the court that earlier Lewis had paid Fairley $295 as part-payment on a premium for his car. However, Fairley had kept the money and Lewis' car was therefore not insured. Lewis contacted Fairley to say that he was planning to deliberately wreck his car so that he could claim the insurance money. Fairley tried to talk him out of this, for obvious reasons, but Lewis crashed the car and had expected to collect money from the insurance company. Fairley then decided that the only solution was to kill Mick and Sue Lewis. He borrowed the rifle and shot Lewis dead before walking into the old homestead to kill Sue Lewis.

Fairley, when questioned by police, showed them a spot two metres from the kitchen door. It was from there that he had shot Lewis dead. Fairley told police he had then stepped into the house and noticed that there was a light on in the bedroom. He looked in and saw Sue Lewis on her side in the bed. He walked to the side of the bed and fired one shot. He thought she was getting up, so decided to shoot again. Asked if he saw the children in the house, Fairley replied: 'No, they must have been asleep—I just left them.'

Fairley, who had never previously been in trouble with the police, was sentenced to two terms of life imprisonment for what can only be described as one of the most ruthlessly cold-blooded killings in modern Australian criminal history. He killed a young couple, the parents of two small children, in a drastic attempt to camouflage the tracks he made in a small-time insurance fraud.

Little Tania and Michael Lewis, who lived side by jowl with death in the house of horrors, went to live with their mother's parents in Deniliquin. Their parents' killer was brought to justice only because of the determination and dedication of the police investigating team. Detective-Sergeant Worsley, who headed the team, was later presented with a special prize for the most outstanding phase of police duty in 1978. He said that police had had wonderful co-operation from the townspeople of Jerilderie. 'After six weeks of investigation we had very little to go on,' he said. 'Then two or three clues fell into place and we knew we were very close to finding the murderer.'

'COOKED IN A WOK'

Kyung Bup Lee was a Korean national who arrived in Australia from Japan in 1984 seeking a better life. He spent about three years in Queensland, but drove his car to Victoria in 1987 convinced that he would find permanent work in Melbourne. Lee re-registered the car in January 1988, and immediately started his search for work. Meanwhile, he used his car—a 1980 Toyota station wagon—as a mobile home, sleeping and changing in it until he could find himself a more comfortable and far more conventional home. Lee spent some summer months picking fruit in Victoria but, on May 3, found the home he so desperately needed, be it ever so humble. Lee, forty-three years of age, immediately contacted a Melbourne service organisation to say that he had found accommodation at a South Melbourne warehouse. Lee was not to know that he had made an appointment with death. In fact, he was stabbed to death the following day—May 4.

Police were not aware of any crime until a woman found a severed penis in the women's toilets at the Flinders Street railway station. It was an horrific experience for the unfortunate woman, but police at first did not know what to make of it. It could have meant anything from murder to self mutilation. However, the gruesome discovery sparked prompt and efficient investigation and, at a later date, police found a scrotum on tram lines in South

Melbourne. The break police needed in this strange and mystifying case came from a most unusual source—the New Zealand Customs Department, which had intercepted an intriguing letter. It was from a man who had boasted to friends in New Zealand that he had 'done in a Korean' and then explained in detail how he had committed the crime.

Police went to a South Melbourne warehouse to question the writer of the letter and walked straight into a chamber of horrors. The man they wanted to question had dismembered a human body. Police found pieces of flesh in a cooking wok, a pile of bones and burnt pieces of body under railway sleepers. They also found numerous weapons, including a blood-stained hunting knife and a rod with a screwdriver attached to it. The disused warehouse had been home to a number of vagrants over several years, even though there was no electricity or running water. Police found flagons of water at the warehouse.

New Zealander David William Philip, thirty-two years of age, was remanded in custody and a committal hearing at the Hawthorn Magistrate's Court was told that he had killed Lee and then had cut off the Korean's genitals. Philip, the court was also told, had stripped parts of Lee's thighs before cooking the meat in a wok and then eating it. Philip then burned the rest of the body on a fire stoked by railway sleepers. Philip sat motionless as these nauseating details were presented. Magistrate Miss Christine Thornton found there was sufficient evidence for Philip to stand trial on a charge of murdering the unfortunate Korean.

Philip stood trial at the Supreme Court and the jury heard that he had stabbed Lee in the stomach and then had cut his victim's throat before severing the genitals and slicing flesh from the thighs. In a statement, Philip allegedly told police he had killed Lee because he was: 'Getting slacked off about this lopsided world where the Asians have everything, you know.' Earlier, at the committal hearing, Philip was alleged to have said he killed Lee because he was 'short of meat'. Philip, who had re-enacted the murder for police, was obviously suffering from a mental disorder.

Mr Justice O'Bryan told the jury not to be angry at the 'horrifying aspects of the case'. He told the jury to bring down a verdict which took into account the paranoid schizophrenia which made Philip legally insane. The jury took just twenty minutes to announce its verdict—not guilty on the grounds of insanity. Philip earlier had been declared insane and, after the verdict, Mr Justice O'Bryan ordered that Philip be detained at the Arandale Hospital, Ararat.

The circumstances surrounding the case might have been horrific and gruesome in the extreme, but it was also a very sad case of mental disorder involving the plight of homeless men. Although Lee was believed to have had parents and a wife in Japan, he was regarded as a loner. He was killed in the most tragic of circumstances. Philip was also a loner, who arrived in Australia four years before he killed Lee. The word 'cannibalism' was used in at least one headline on this case, but absolutely no comparison could be made with other infamous cases worldwide or even the fictional Hanibal the Cannibal of 'Silence of the Lambs' fame. Indeed, cannibalism is extremely rare and has been reported in modern times mainly in circumstances involving near starvation. One of the most infamous cannibalism cases was that involving child killer Albert Fish in New York in 1934. Fish confessed to killing a ten-year-old girl and then cooking her with carrots and onions over a period of nine days. He was executed (by electric chair) in January 1936. There was also the case which horrified the world after Milwaukee police discovered severed heads in a refrigerator at the apartment of one Jeffrey Dahmer. Dahmer confessed to murder and cannibalism.

DEATH AT SEA

Murders have been committed in every imaginable situation and place. There have been killings in pubs, in alleys, in theatres and even at sea. The most infamous case involving murder on the high seas was the James Camb case, in which a ship's steward was convicted of the murder of a young woman, an actress named Eileen Gibson, on a liner sailing between Cape Town and Southampton in 1947.

Gibson went missing on board the Durban Castle, and her body was never found. Camb had been seen with the unfortunate Miss Gibson the night she went missing and was charged with her murder. He was found guilty of killing Miss Gibson, largely on medical evidence that saliva, blood and urine stains found on cabin sheets were consistent with strangulation. Camb admitted pushing the woman through a port-hole, but insisted that she had had a fit during sexual intercourse. He told the court at his trial: 'I hoped to give the impression that she had fallen overboard.' Camb was sentenced to death, but as capital punishment was under review at the time, this sentence was never passed and he was released from jail in 1959.

There is at least one documented case of murder aboard ship in Australian criminal history. It was a sad case involving two naval ratings who quarrelled aboard HMAS Brisbane in 1924. The vessel was anchored off Garden Island, Sydney, on April 19 when the body of seventeen-year-old seaman David Rich, from the western Melbourne suburb of Yarraville, was found in his hammock. His head had been battered in and his throat had been slashed. Police were called immediately and, meanwhile, the ship's officers called for a muster. All hands were accounted for, except one. The missing seaman was an assistant cook, George Brown, from Brisbane. A search for Brown resulted in the discovery of a second death aboard HMAS Brisbane: Brown's body was found hanging in a refrigerator chamber.

Brown had obviously killed Rich before suiciding, but police were unable to determine a precise motive, although ratings did tell police and naval officers that Brown had often quarrelled with his shipmates. Brown had bashed in Rich's forehead with a hammer, which was later found under the seventeen-year-old's hammock. Rich had joined the navy in search of adventure, but was killed by a shipmate in a cruel and vicious attack barely months after embarking on his chosen career at sea.

FAMILY TRAGEDIES

The saddest murder cases police are asked to investigate are those involving children. Even sadder are the cases involving a number of children, killed by their own parents. There are several such cases in this book and, unfortunately, they have been relatively common through the years. Today's Australians often feel that such family tragedies reflect the pressures of the modern era. However, two cases from as far apart as Western Australia and Tasmania from many years ago indicate that family murder-suicides are not a modern phenomenon.

The first of these two cases occurred in the tiny township of Don, near Devonport, Tasmania, on February 26, 1929. A farmer noticed smoke coming from the home of the Archer family. It was early morning and the flames had already turned the timber house into an inferno. Neighbours stood helpless as the flames devoured the building and its contents. Later, after the flames had died to an ember, it was discovered that the entire Archer family of husband, wife and five children had died in the flames. Seven charred bodies were found in the ruins of the homestead. Andrew Thomas Archer, forty-nine, had shot himself in the head and his body was found on the floor, resting on a shotgun. Olive Archer, also forty-nine, had died in her bed, alongside her ten-month-old daughter Nilma. The bodies of the other children, Lexie (eleven), Phyllis (eight), Murray (six) and Trevor (five), were found in another bedroom. All bodies were charred beyond recognition, but it was presumed that Andrew Archer had shot his family dead before setting the house alight and then turning the gun on himself. A note found outside the house in a leather bag was the final proof. It was written by Andrew Archer, known as Tom, and said simply: 'The bag and contents is from Tom. Goodbye.' The word 'goodbye' trailed off and was unfinished. It was also learned that Archer had consulted a doctor two years earlier about fears that he would have 'mental trouble'.

Just over two years later, in a quiet Perth suburb, Australia was rocked by yet another family tragedy. Roderick Davies, his wife Dorothy and five children had been living on a dole of two pounds and nine shillings (about $4.90) a week. Davies, thirty-six, had been unemployed for months, but no one knew that this had depressed him to the point of suicide. On August 21, 1931, neighbour Samuel Knifton found a note on the back door of the three-bedroom Davies home in the suburb of Carlisle. The note read: 'Mr Knifton, please open the door.' Knifton believed the note was part of an elaborate joke, but once he stepped inside the house he realised that the note had been a pointer to death. Mrs Davies, thirty-five, was dead in a bed in the kitchen, a bullet wound through her head. Next to her, sitting in a chair, was the body of her husband. He also had a bullet wound in the head, and a revolver in his right hand.

Knifton did not want to see any more and rushed to the police, who discovered the bodies of the five Davies children—Rita (fourteen), Robert (twelve), Dorothy (ten), John (six) and Alfred (five months)—in two of the house's three bedrooms. The bodies of John, Rita and baby Alfred were in one room, with the bodies of Dorothy and Robert on stretchers in another room. All had bullet wounds to the head and there were no signs of a struggle. Detectives concluded that Mr and Mrs Davies had made a suicide pact, with Davies shooting the children and then his wife before turning the gun on himself. Mrs Davies' body had been found in bed in the kitchen, but the bed had previously been on the back porch. Detectives reasoned that Mr and Mrs Davies had dragged the bed into the kitchen and that Mr Davies had sat by his wife's side before killing her and then himself. Police also believed that the children had been drugged before each was shot in the head.

Police found nineteen discharged cartridges in the house but, strangely, not one neighbour had heard a single shot. The nearest house might have been more than fifteen metres away, but the shots which wiped out an entire family exploded without comment. The Davies family had lived together and had died together. The house had been well stocked with food, but the Great Depression had taken its toll on Mr Davies' mental health and pride. Sadly, it was fourteen-year-old Rita's birthday the day she and her family died.

THE TRAGIC LITTLE DIGGER

Alfred Bye was as harmless as a fly, and not much bigger. He stood just 160 centimetres (5 ft 3 in) and could have ridden as a lightweight jockey at just 45 kilograms (7 stone). In fact, Bye once worked as a stablehand at Flemington for James Scobie, who had trained 1927 Melbourne Cup winner Trivalve. However, it was just one of many jobs Bye had during an almost nomadic existence between the two great wars.

Bye was born in the Victorian town of Yan Yean in 1899, the fifth in a family of ten children. His father was a railway ganger and the family shifted homes in the Gippsland area several times. Bye had never had a settled childhood and seemed to be dogged by bad luck. He was just four years of age when a horse kicked him in the head, leaving him with permanent hearing damage in his left ear. Bye was also knocked unconscious at ten years of age when struck on the head by a stone during schoolboy skylarking.

Teachers considered him 'backwards' and the tiny youngster never made it past the third grade at primary school. He left school at fourteen years of age, barely able to read and write. He was living in Melbourne's western suburbs when he left school and found himself a number of jobs in the area, first as a hand at a rope factory and then as bottle washer and at a rubber works in Footscray. Bye might have been a humble labourer, but always had a job and never gave anyone the slightest trouble.

Bye enrolled in the AIF in 1917 and served on the Western Front until gassed by the Germans and repatriated to a hospital in England. On return to Australia, he worked as a labourer with the Victorian railways in Footscray and then bought an allotment on King Island under the soldier settlement scheme. However, bad luck continued to dog Bye and a fire destroyed his crops and his home. He was forced to return to the Victorian mainland, almost penniless and in desperate need of a change of luck.

Job followed job (including his work as a stablehand with Scobie), but his luck seemed to turn when, in 1930, he met the girl of his dreams. Bye was working in the Western District when he met Amelia Ogier and they became engaged to be married. Bye at last seemed likely to settle down, until his fiancée learned of his liking for a bet. Miss Ogier wanted Bye to save his wages for married life, but Bye seemed intent on playing the punt. The wedding was called off and Bye and Miss Ogier parted, apparently on good terms, in 1933.

Bye again drifted from job to job and, in 1939, enlisted in the Second AIF for service in the Home Defence Force. He was stationed at Bacchus Marsh in 1941 when he literally bumped into Miss Ogier in a Melbourne street. He had not seen his former fiancée for eight years, but the flame of love had never died. He tracked her down to her home in Elsternwick and then pestered her to resume their courtship. Miss Ogier politely refused.

When Bye saw Miss Ogier for the first time in eight years she was with another soldier, Gallipoli veteran Thomas Edward Walker, who also had re-enlisted for service in the Home Defence Force. Bye saw Walker as a rival for Miss Ogier's affection and he begged her to stop seeing her new boyfriend. Then, on September 27, 1941, Bye again saw Miss Ogier with Walker. They were with Miss Ogier's two young nieces and were walking along Swanston Street on their way to the Princess Theatre.

Bye walked up behind Miss Ogier, tapped her on the shoulder and drew her to one side. However, Walker was about to turn when Bye tried to strike him from behind. Miss Ogier stood between them and separated the two soldiers. Walker, angry with Bye's behaviour, told his tiny rival in love that he would see him later. However, Miss Ogier warned Walker that Bye 'might have a razor'. Bye had once thrown her to the ground near her home in Elsternwick and she had seen a flash of steel in his right hand. Walker told Miss Ogier: 'He can't strike me a blow from behind and get away with it.'

Walker then took Miss Ogier and her nieces to the theatre at the Spring Street end of Bourke Street but, after five minutes, stood up and said he was going outside for a 'smoke'. That was the last Miss Ogier saw of Walker. He was stabbed to death several minutes after he left the theatre.

A pedestrian walking through the Treasury Gardens late on the evening of September 27 found Walker lying in a pool of blood in the middle of a public pathway leading from Gisborne Street to Gipps Street. The area, with its trees and tall shrubs, was badly lit—the perfect setting for a murder. Police were in the Treasury Gardens within minutes of the discovery of the body.

The police officers, led by Detective Sergeants Lyon and McGuffie, quickly determined that the dead man had prepared himself for a fight. His army jacket, bearing the 1915 Gallipoli ribbon, was underneath the body, but did not show the slightest trace of a knife mark. The dead man had obviously removed his jacket, presumably for a fight. Police noticed a fifteen-metre trail of blood and correctly assumed that the dead man had been mortally wounded and had then staggered back to the jacket he had earlier removed.

Police also ruled out robbery as the motive as eighteen shillings and sixpence in coins were found in the dead man's pockets, along with six shillings and eight pence scattered around the body. Police knew with some degree of certainty that the dead man had prepared himself for a fight, but had not counted on his fellow combatant carrying a knife.

Police were able to identify the body very early in their investigation, and medical examination showed that Walker had been stabbed sixteen times. It was a vicious attack, especially as there was a gaping wound in Walker's back. True, there were also stab wounds in Walker's chest, but Walker had obviously been attacked from behind and the attacker had stabbed him repeatedly in considerable rage and fury. The murder weapon, a sheath knife, was found near the body.

Investigations revealed that Walker had been born in Scotland, but had served in the First AIF with the famous Light Horse Brigade. Until re-enlisting, Walker had operated a small grocery and confectionery business in the country town of Skipton.

Of course, it did not take police long to learn the name of Walker's killer and an arrest was made within twenty-four hours. Bye, forty-two years of age, was charged with the murder of the forty-five-year-old Walker and, at the City Court, was refused bail. The inquest was held on October 20 and the City Coroner, Mr Tingate, found that Bye had murdered Walker. He committed him for trial.

Bye, at the Criminal Court, denied that he had killed Walker in a jealous rage. Pleading not guilty before Mr Justice Gavan Duffy and a jury, Bye agreed that he and Walker had gone to the Treasury Gardens. He said that Walker seemed hostile and took off his jacket in preparation for a fight. Bye said he told Walker: 'Why should two old Diggers fight?' He added:

> With that Walker let fly and hit me on the jaw. Before I could do anything he made a further flying leap at me. His weight knocked me on the broad of my back to the ground.
>
> He had me by the throat with his two hands and had his knees into my body. His thumbs were pushing into my windpipe … I could not move or call out. I had a knife in my right-hand trouser pocket. I reached to get it out and, as I did so, Walker suddenly rolled on to it and it was forced into his back.

Bye showed the jury how he and Walker had then struggled for the knife, claiming that both he and Walker had their hands on it. Bye told the court:

I did not realise at the time that the knife was getting Walker. He kept putting it back toward him and I was pulling it toward myself but he, being stronger in the arms than me, forced my hand with the knife in it toward his body.

I realised Walker was wounded, but I did not think it was serious. I did not think the knife had gone in very far and until I had seen the photos of the wounds in his body I did not know he had been got that many times.

When I got the knife from Walker's grip Walker started to call out 'help'. He called two or three times. I got up on my feet, picked up my coat and walked away. I threw the knife away and afterwards stopped to put on my coat.

I walked into Collins Street, caught a tram to Spencer Street where I found out that the Bacchus Marsh train left at 11.25.

Bye then told the court how he had washed blood from his trousers at a horse trough in Spencer Street and later returned to the city, where he had supper before catching the train to Bacchus Marsh. Police apprehended him the following evening. However, Bye told police that Walker was alive when he left him.

It was almost an open and shut case for police, but the most incriminating evidence was the murder weapon. Bye claimed he had bought it months before Walker's death. However, his explanation for carrying the weapon on the evening of Walker's death was feeble. Bye tried to convince the jury that he was carrying the knife so that he could get a box for it and send it to a farmer friend in Gippsland. The problem with this explanation was that the knife was unsheathed and Bye had been carrying it point upward in his trouser pocket. Police alleged that Walker had been attacked from behind as he was placing his jacket on the ground.

Bye's trial lasted two days, but the jury took a mere forty-five minutes to make its decision—guilty. Bye was asked if he wanted to say anything before sentence was passed and replied that he had not intended to murder Walker, but had drawn the knife to defend himself. Bye was then sentenced to death.

Bye, despite being a bit of a knockabout, had never previously been in trouble with the police. Relatives said he was regarded as harmless and one of his sisters told a newspaper reporter that her brother had 'never done anything bad'. She added: 'I do not remember him ever getting into fights or quarrelling and I do not think he deserves the awful fate they are sending him to.'

Labor members of Parliament, including John Cain Snr, intervened with Premier Dunstan for remission of Bye's death sentence. A memorandum submitted to the Governor-in-Council by Bye's solicitor, Mr J. Barnett, declared:

> As to the crime of which he has been found guilty, I desire to submit that it was not a premeditated crime. The whole of the evidence points, I would submit, against the conclusion that he plotted it in advance and towards the conclusion that his meeting in Swanston Street with the deceased man on the night of 27 September was accidental. It seems very clear that it was the deceased man who suggested the appointment for a fight and I would submit that the verdict of the jury is consistent with the crime having been committed in a sudden passion.

> I understand that since the date of his sentence, Bye had a seizure or fit at the jail. I am informed by his sisters that he has had such a seizure or fit on one previous occasion, shortly after he left school and at a time when he was working at Miller's rope works at Yarraville.

> Some inkling of his backwardness of the accused may be gauged from the fact that, although he was found guilty and sentenced to death on Wednesday, 19 November 1941, he did not realise the nature of the sentence passed on him. On Saturday, 22 November he asked his counsel [Mr Murray McInerney] what sentence he had received, and whether he had been sentenced to imprisonment for life. Mr McInerney then had the task of explaining to him that the sentence which had been imposed on him was a sentence of death.

> Although the accused has been found guilty of the crime of murder he is not, I submit, of the criminal type. For forty-two years he has led a sober, respectable life. I would urge that that fact should be borne in mind when considering his lawless act on the night of 27 September.

> On his behalf, and for the reasons set out above, I humbly ask that clemency be extended to him and that the sentence be commuted.

The Executive Council approved of the State Cabinet decision not to alter the sentence and Alfred Bye, as harmless as a fly for all but one minute of his life, had his execution set for 8 am on Monday, December 22, 1941.

BLOOD AND BONES

The discovery of a body, no matter how gruesome the circumstances, does not automatically mean there has been a murder. Police are often presented with the question: suicide or murder? The highly publicised discovery of blackened human bones in 1931 set New South Wales police one of their greatest suicide-or-murder riddles.

Farmer Bernard Cunningham was mustering sheep near Bungendore, about ten kilometres from Canberra, on November 21, 1931, when his dogs yapped and ran into a hollow. Cunningham went to investigate and came across the remains of a huge log fire. He at first thought it was a swaggy's camping site, until he noticed the dogs tugging on bones at the bottom of the ashes. Cunningham bent over, retrieved a bone from one of his dogs mouth and immediately recognised it as human.

Cunningham called police and Detective-Sergeant Tom McRae and a team of investigating officers rushed to the scene. They verified that the blackened bones were human and started sifting ashes. Police worked in relay, sifting and re-sifting, looking for even the tiniest clue. Their task looked hopeless, especially when hours of work netted them just a handful of objects, including the molten remains of a gold watch, a belt buckle, a few teeth, a button, several coins and the barrel of a small calibre rifle.

Meanwhile, forensic experts told police that the human remains were male and that death had occurred on or around October 27—more than three weeks before Cunningham's dogs had tugged at the bones. This was about all police had to work on as the clues sifted from the ashes seemed virtually useless. Police therefore decided to re-sift the ashes—yet again. This time police found a small key. More importantly, it carried a code number which police were unable to read with the naked eye. The key was sent to police laboratories in Sydney and tests showed that the number on the key read 784 MV12774. This proved to be vital in the eventual identification of the body.

However, the question remained—suicide or murder? Police at this stage were convinced it was murder as most of the bones were found *under* the logs used in the fire, which appeared to have been stoked. If it had been murder, the killer could have beaten the victim to death or even shot him before building a fire around and on top of the body. If it had been suicide, the dead man would have had to shoot himself and then have an accomplice stoke the fire for him. The suicide theory seemed totally implausable and Detective-Sergeant McRae treated it as a murder investigation.

Police at first believed it would be near impossible to track down the owner of the tiny key found in the ashes. However, painfully slow investigations revealed that the key was manufactured in Britain.

Undeterred, police called in Scotland Yard to help determine the key batch and where it had been sent. Scotland Yard provided McRae and his team with the breakthrough they needed as the key was one of a batch sent to a Sydney lock manufacturer in 1929.

Police eventually traced key number 784 MV12774 to the Sydney YMCA, which had given it to a young man for his locker. It had been issued to twenty-one-year-old Sidney James Morrison, captain of the club's basketball team. Significantly, Morrison had not been seen since early October. Police, convinced that the remains at Bungendore were Morrison's, asked Professor A.N. Birkett of the Sydney University's Anatomy Department to make a study of the bones. Professor Birkett reported that the body was that of a young man of approximately 182 centimetres (6 ft) and well built—precisely Morrison's physical description. Police were now certain that the dead man was the missing Morrison. But again the question remained: suicide or murder?

The old murder theory lost credence when McRae started questioning Morrison's friends and relatives. He learned that Morrison had resigned his job as a clerk on October 6, 1931, and had told friends he was going to the bush to prospect for gold. It seemed out of character for Morrison but, even more disturbing, McRae was told that Morrison had been having psychiatric treatment. It seemed Morrison had an inferiority complex and kept telling his relatives that he lacked personality. He once told his sister, Mrs Lily Evans: 'I feel so useless I wouldn't care if I died tomorrow.'

Police again turned to the suicide theory and suggested that Morrison had lit the huge fire before shooting himself so that he would fall back into the flames. This theory gained favour when police investigations proved that Morrison had bought the rifle at a well-known Sydney sports store at the time of his resignation from work. It therefore appeared that Morrison might have planned a bizarre suicide.

The problem with this theory was that there were logs found *across* Morrison's blackened bones and traces of blood were found on dry branches several metres from the fire. And what about the tyre marks? Who had driven a car to and from the death scene? Were the tyre marks even relevant? Could they have been made by someone rabbiting in previous weeks?

Police painstakingly continued their investigations, but could not trace Morrison's movements over the last weeks of his life. The only sighting of him in the two weeks before his death was by an old prospector who had seen him with two men in a car about thirty kilometres from the death scene. Police were never able to trace these men.

An inquest was held into Morrison's death but the coroner returned an open finding. The mystery remains: suicide, or murder?

RELEASED TO KILL AGAIN

When wharf labourer George Bromell found the bodies of an entire family in a small, weatherboard shack in the inner Melbourne suburb of Richmond on May 30, 1934, he could hardly have suspected that he would be unlocking the door to one of the greatest controversies of the era.

Bromell had not seen his wharf workmate and neighbour Frank O'Brien for several days and decided to enlist the help of another neighbour to break into the house in Bosisto Street. Bromell feared the worst as O'Brien had been severely depressed and had told his mate that he did not have enough money to buy food for his wife and three small children. However, Bromell was not prepared for the ghastly scenes he saw in O'Brien's house. O'Brien, fifty-nine, his wife Rose, thirty-nine, and their three children were dead—their throats slashed.

All of the bodies were found in the tiny bedroom at the front of the house. The bodies of O'Brien and his wife were fully dressed in their double bed and the bodies of the three tiny children—Owen, three, Joan, two, and Marie, nine months—were found in their bloodstained cots. The scene was heart-rending. O'Brien had obviously wiped out his family in desperation over his fear that he was not able to support them. He left a suicide note which, in part, read:

> I began to lose interest in everything since coming to this hovel, with no conveniences, no copper, no washing troughs, not even a decent bath ... dear, patient, unselfish Rose, always cheerful and self-sacrificing, has tried to keep a smiling face in spite of bad times. She has been a one hundred per cent wife and mother, and deserves the best in life. I soon will not be able to continue work and you know what that means to them all.

Bromell told police that O'Brien had been working only part time on the wharves and this looked like ending because of the financial depression wracking the country. O'Brien, at best, could earn only two pounds a week and had told Bromell the week before he killed his family and then suicided that he had only seven shillings and threepence to his name, and no job prospects. He had complained to Bromell that there was not enough food for the family. However, police found meat, a loaf of bread and milk in the O'Brien home. Later, Government pathologist Dr C.H. Mollison said there was no sign of malnutrition in any of the bodies.

Melburnians were still coming to grips with head-lines shrieking 'RICHMOND TRAGEDY' and 'A GHASTLY TRAGEDY' when the O'Brien case took a dramatic turn. The Melbourne Herald, on June 1, broke the news that O'Brien appeared to have been the same man who had killed his wife ten years earlier. The Herald report suggested that a photograph of O'Brien's body had been taken at the city morgue and that officials from the Mont Park Mental Home had 'expressed the belief that he was identical' to the man who had killed his wife.

Fingerprints were taken of the dead man and these later matched those on police files. O'Brien therefore was the man who had killed his wife ten years earlier, and the slaying of his family and his subsequent suicide opened a very nasty can of worms for Victorian government officials. The Inspector General for the Insane, Dr W.E. Jones, admitted that O'Brien had been charged with murder in 1924 and had been committed to an asylum (Mont Park) during the Governor's pleasure. O'Brien had been found to be suffering from transitory confusional insanity. He was a highly educated man and, according to reports, his mental and physical condition improved dramatically at Mont Park.

O'Brien, in fact, had been a school teacher who was found not guilty of the murder of his wife at Mildura in 1924 because of insanity. He was released from Mont Park three years and eight months after being committed, on the approval of the Attorney-General, the condition being that he reported monthly to Dr Jones.

O'Brien's release was on the instigation of one of his brothers, who wrote to the Chief Secretary stating that Dr Jones had advised that if some person would undertake the responsibility of providing for O'Brien's future, his release 'might reasonably be granted'.

Dr Jones had previously pointed out that the Lunacy Act did not permit a 'criminal lunatic' to be allowed out on probation and that, as far as he was concerned, O'Brien would need to be discharged and suggested a discharge might be granted provided there was a personal guarantee for O'Brien's future welfare. O'Brien was released by the order of the Chief Secretary (Mr Slater) in November 1927.

At the inquest into the deaths of the O'Briens, the Coroner (Mr McLean PM) was told that Rose O'Brien herself had been a patient at Mont Park, but was 'perfectly normal' after her marriage to O'Brien.

However, the big sensation of the inquest was provided by the medical superintendent of Mont Park, Dr John Catarinich, who said he had made a report on O'Brien in September 1924 at the request of the Law Department. This report, in part said:

> Patient Frank O'Brien is at present, and has been since admission here, sane. There is, however, present a lack of emotional reaction, which, to some extent, may be due to no conscious memory of the crime committed. He has had more than one attack of insanity, and he is, therefore, very likely to relapse.
>
> Under no circumstances would I suggest O'Brien ever again live with his children [from his first marriage], nor do I consider it safe to give O'Brien his liberty, even with restrictions.

Yet O'Brien *was* released, only to kill again in horrific circumstances.

The pressure at the inquest was directed at Dr Jones, and Mr McLean PM asked him: 'Is there no record of O'Brien's condition on the days when he reported?'

Dr Jones replied: 'No.'

Coroner: 'Is there any system in the department about these things?'

Dr Jones: 'No, this is an unusual case.'

Coroner: 'Then there is no provision to ensure that the released patient shall report? Surely the responsibility is upon you, as the only person who could notify the Law Department?'

Dr Jones: 'That is so, but I was not aware of the legal obligation to make that report. I was not aware of that section of the Crimes Act.'

Coroner: 'But it must have occurred to you that these conditions are not mere words, and that means for their enforcement must exist?'

Dr Jones: 'Had I known of it, I would not have considered it necessary to make him report for the rest of his life.'

Coroner: 'You know that after he was discharged that he lived in Richmond?'

Dr Jones: 'Yes, but we did not know he had married again. He had been warned not to.'

Coroner: 'I presume you would regard any measure taken to prevent a recurrence of his homicidal act as a paramount importance?'

Dr Jones: 'Yes.'

Coroner: 'Do you think now, seeing that his material welfare was so important, that you should have communicated with the brother who promised to look after him?'

Dr Jones: 'I was under the impression that he was in touch with his brother. O'Brien was quite sensible.'

Coroner: 'Have you any doubt that the previous verdict of insanity was correct?'

Dr Jones: 'I could only accept what I was told, namely that he had committed a murder under mental stress.'

Mr McLean was scathing in his criticism of Dr Jones at the end of the inquest. Mr McLean found that O'Brien's family had died from wounds inflicted by O'Brien, who was of 'unsound mind' before suiciding. This, of course, was stating the obvious, but Mr McLean then directed his attention towards Dr Jones when he said:

> In my opinion, the public is entitled to expect that when a person has been found not guilty of murder on the grounds of insanity, and has been committed to custody during the Governor's pleasure, ample precaution is taken to guard against any repetition of the homicidal act. While the authorities of the Mont Park Mental Hospital had shown themselves fully seized of their responsibilities in regard to O'Brien, subsequent events had shown that there had been a relaxation of responsibility on the part of the Director of Mental Hygiene [Dr Jones]. It was curious that the conditions of O'Brien's release advised by the Superintendent of the Hospital [Dr Catarinich] had not been enforced.
>
> It was a remarkable omission on the part of Dr Jones that he was not aware of his powers under the Crimes Act. Had O'Brien reported from time to time after his release, as he might have been made to do, the recurrence of the symptoms might have been observed, and the tragedy might possibly have been averted.

DEATH AT THE
CHURCH FETE

Arthur Head, sixteen years of age, was a youth with a future. He had just graduated with honours in the Leaving Certificate from Coburg High School, Victoria, and was only two months into his chosen career of teaching at the Moreland State School. He regularly attended Bible classes at the Coburg Presbyterian Church and in all ways was regarded as forthright, honest and destined for a brilliant career.

Head had helped organise stalls at the church fete in 1931 and was with several of his friends when a gang of youths pelted them with tomatoes late on the evening of Thursday, March 26. Insults were hurled back and forth and two of the church group ran out of the church grounds (on the corner of Sydney Road and Munro Street) to remonstrate with the tomato throwers. A police constable was also called, but the whole affair was forgotten within minutes—at least, by the church group.

Later, around midnight, Head and three companions—sixteen-year-old Gordon Andrews, sixteen-year-old Allen Beaver and fourteen-year-old Oswald Beaver—left to walk home together. However, they had not gone far before they came across an older group of youths. Then, at the corner of Harding and Fowler Streets, one of the youths punched Head to the ground; he had been struck to the back of the head. The others scattered, although Andrews also took a blow to the head.

Andrews, after outrunning his pursuers, climbed a fence and asked the occupants of the house if he could make a telephone call to the police. There was no phone in the house, so he was directed to a neighbour's house, where he failed to make contact because the telephone party line was in use at the time. Andrews decided to go back to where he and his friends had been attacked and was shocked to see Head unconscious on the roadway. There was blood coming from his ears and mouth. Head was rushed to the Melbourne Hospital but died four hours after being admitted. Four youths—Leslie Lewis (seventeen), Allan Ward (eighteen), Richard Jackson (nineteen) and Ralph Fuller (nineteen)—were later charged at the City Watchhouse with Head's murder.

The inquest into Head's death was held before the coroner, Mr D. Grant PM, who was told that one of the group of youths had jumped forward to punch Head on the back of the head. Andrews told the coroner that he believed Ward had struck the blow. Senior-Detective O'Keeffe said that Ward had made a statement accounting for his movements, but denying he had struck Head. However, Detective-Sergeant O'Keeffe said Ward later told him this statement was not true and then made a second statement in which he said he would have 'first hit' at the church youths as they walked down the street. The statement, in part, read:

> When we were opposite a vacant block of land Lewis, who was ahead of us, hit one of the four young men. They all started to run and we ran after them. When I got within striking distance of one of them, I hit him on the right cheek. He hit me in the eye as he swung his right hand round and then fell forward in a crumpled position. I saw him trying to get up; he was moaning. I then ran away.

The four youths were sent for trial and faced the Chief justice, Sir William Irvine, and jury in the Criminal Court in May 1931. Ward, who told the court he had not known Head, said in evidence:

> We walked down at the back of them [the youths from the church] and we seemed to be overtaking them. We were walking, not

running. Nothing important was said by any of us as we were walking along towards Harding Street. When we got near the council yards Lewis was about ten or fifteen paces ahead of us, and singing. I saw him strike one of the chaps in front of us. I think it was Head he struck. With that the other chaps who were with Head started to run. I then heard Fuller say 'I'll have a hit if I am getting hurt.' I then struck Head on the right cheek with my fist. He had just started to run and he staggered before I struck him. Head then hit me a blow across the left eye as he was falling to the footpath. He started to rise again, and he was moaning. Across the other side of the street I saw some people and I thought they would come to his assistance. I got frightened and ran away. I did not do anything beyond striking Head with my fist. I was wearing dancing pumps that night.

The Government pathologist, Dr C.H. Mollison, told the court that Head had taken at least seven blows to the head and that there had been a fracture of the skull. Dr Mollison, under cross-examination, said it was possible the injuries might have been caused by Head falling and hitting his head on the footpath on one side, and then falling on the other side and further injuring himself. Head's father, Mr Arthur Head, said that when he saw his son after the attack he could barely recognise him 'as he was so knocked about'.

The Chief justice, in his summing up, told the jury that 'the mere fact of the existence of the lust for violence may account for this unprovoked and savage attack on Head'. Earlier, he had launched a virulent attack on what he described as 'moving pictures' and their effect on youth. He said:

You will naturally look for a motive for the attack. If you accept Ward's evidence, he did not know Head and had no malice against him. The very nature of the savage attack would be, in itself, sufficient to justify a jury in believing there must have been some personal motive. But that must not be taken too far. It happens that there is growing among us a number of youths—I am afraid an increasing number of youths—who are becoming interested in violence for its own sake.

I do not desire to say anything against the influence of film pictures in general, but I have no hesitation in saying that one particular class of those pictures is responsible for inculcating and fostering a kind of adventure that takes the form of violence. And as long as that particular class of exhibition is permitted to go on unrestrained, you may expect to find increasing numbers of youths indulging in violence.

The Chief Justice also warned the jury that statements alleged to have been made outside the court by the accused youths were not evidence against any person but the person who made them. He said:

> The outstanding feature of this case is that this young man [Head] came to his death by extreme violence. That violence took place in connection with an assault upon him and his three companions by the four prisoners.
>
> But you are not to allow that general fact to divert your mind from the case made against each. Each youth is entitled to say you must not confuse him with the others until a charge is proved against him. Each of these accused is charged with murder. Such a charge enables the jury, if it is not satisfied beyond reasonable doubt that murder was committed, to find manslaughter. I have already intimated that as regards Jackson, Fuller and Lewis, the evidence is not sufficient to establish murder. I intimated at the same time that there was evidence fit to go before the jury on a charge of murder against Ward.

The Chief Justice then explained to the jury the meaning of a charge of murder—that where an accused person had been shown to have intended to inflict grievous bodily harm, more or less to disable a man permanently or disfigure him, but had actually killed him, then that was murder. The Chief Justice said that, as regards Ward, there was no evidence that he deliberately intended to kill Head, but there was evidence that the jury had to consider, either that he intended to injure Head permanently and that death resulted, or that he knew that what he was doing was dangerous to life and recklessly persisted in it. He then said:

> The evidence against Ward, so far as it goes, is consistent with the possibility that one blow only was struck by Ward, and that blow with his fist. It appears clear that immediately after the first blow struck by Ward, or at the same time, the other three boys accompanying Head ran away and were followed by the other three who were with Ward. Ward was left alone with Head. According to his own account he did nothing more than run away.

The time which elapsed between when Ward ran away and when he struck that blow might have been very short.

As to what took place in that period we have no direct evidence except that of Ward himself. The record of what took place in that short period was marked on the body of Head. You have heard the evidence of the Government pathologist [Dr Mollison]. He told how there were at least seven distinct blows on the head, a fracture of the skull, blood flowing from the nostrils and ears, and death following in four hours. It is possible those injuries might have resulted from Head falling and hitting his head on the footpath on one side, and then falling on the other side and further injuring himself. That was put to Dr Mollison and he said it was not impossible, provided you accepted the theory of two falls. If you regard it as so highly improbable that Head first fell on one side and then, in a similar way, on the other side, then you have to consider how those injuries were caused.

The case against Fuller, Jackson and Lewis stands on a much, much lower level. In the first place, none of them, it is admitted, struck the fatal blow or blows. But that does not mean that, in taking the part they did, they cannot be guilty of manslaughter. There are all kinds of degrees of manslaughter, some of which are nearly as bad as murder, while others are comparatively mild in their degree of guilt.

The jury was in retirement for three hours and thirty minutes. The foreman then announced that the jury had found Ward and Lewis guilty of manslaughter, but Fuller and Jackson not guilty. The jury added a recommendation of mercy and the Chief Justice sentenced both Ward and Lewis to four years' imprisonment, with twenty strokes of the birch each. He told them: 'You have narrowly escaped conviction for an even greater offence. In cases such as this the protection of the community must override all other questions and all sentimental suggestions.'

THE DEATH WALK

Sunday, October 11, 1964, had been a quiet, pleasant day for the Ganino family in the northern Melbourne suburb of Fawkner. It had been like many Sundays, spent in quiet relaxation and family activities. Dominic Ganino, 15, had spent the morning at Mass and Communion, then spending the afternoon looking for bits and pieces of motor cars at a nearby rubbish tip. He returned home in time for an early dinner and washed up the dishes for his mother.

Dominic, a student at Fawkner Technical School, did not feel like watching television with his brother and sister after dinner but elected to take his dog Lassie for a walk. It was still a pleasant spring day and Dominic could not have known that his day would end in death. He stepped into Sydney Road, immediately outside his home, without a worry in the world.

Dominic did not return from his walk and his parents became worried almost immediately. It was unlike Dominic to stay away for long without telling his parents. When it became obvious he was not with friends or relatives, the family contacted police. A description of Dominic was flashed to police patrols soon after 10 p.m. and Dominic Ganino officially became a missing person.

What now particularly worried Dominic's family and police was that the boy's dog had returned home by herself soon after 7 p.m. An intensive police search the next day failed to find any trace of the missing boy.

Two weeks later, on Monday, October 26, a security officer at the Ford motor works (six kilometres from the Ganino house) was searching swamp country behind the works. He was looking for hollow logs, and eventually spotted what he might have been after. However, Mr Alexander McCann also discovered the body of Dominic Ganino under a tree trunk.

The face was immersed in about ten inches (16cm) of water and the boy's clothing was disarranged. Dominic had been murdered and police immediately launched a massive investigation.

Forensic examination later showed that Dominic had died of asphyxiation due to strangling. However, the post mortem also showed that that boy had been homosexually raped. Dominic obviously had struggled with his attacker but because the body was not discovered until two weeks after his disappearance, the trail to the killer was cold.

Police had few clues. There were footprints and car tracks near where the body had been found but they were too old to be of much use. A blue comb also was found near the body, but this also proved to be a negative clue.

Police decided that the public had to help in inquiries and thousands of people in the Fawkner and Broadmeadows area were questioned and interviewed. In fact, police launched a doorknock campaign, speaking to everyone in the neighborhood. Residents were asked if they had seen the boy on the night he was murdered.

Dominic had been wearing dark jeans, a check shirt and a grey school pullover. He was just 5 ft 3 in (160cm), was slightly built and dark. Several sightings were given, the most useful being by a 14-year-old neighbour, who told police that he had seen Dominic in Sydney Road but on the opposite side of his home, Dominic obviously crossing busy Sydney Road.

It seemed that the whole Italian community of Melbourne mourned the death of Dominic Ganino. His funeral, on November 5, was a mass display of grief, with hundreds of schoolmates, friends, relatives and sympathizers moving from St Matthew's Church, North Fawkner, to the Fawkner Cemetery.

Dominic's killer was still free. Police continued their investigations, convinced that someone had abducted the boy and driven him to the lonely swamp country at the back of Ford. One theory was that the killer offered to give Dominic driving lessons 'away from the traffic'. The boy was interested in cars and desperately wanted to learn to drive.

Although police never arrested anyone over Dominic's killing, it has been alleged that a notorious paedophile Catholic church worker might have been implicated. Robert Charles Blunden, known as 'Bert', was living at the St Matthew's presbytery at the time of Dominic's death and was known to have been abusing children and young men.

Police interviewed Blunden soon after Dominic's murder, but had no information at that time of his sexual activities. Indeed, they knew nothing of this until a victim stepped forward in 1996.

Blunden was 79 years of age and in poor health when police were told of his background and, in 1997, he was jailed for four years after pleading guilty in the Melbourne County Court to 27 charges of indecent assault and buggery between 1964-70.

Significantly, Blunden used a ruse of offering boys a lift on the pretext that he would give them driving lessons. But, although questioned by police in 1996 about Dominic's death, Blunden refused to make any admissions.

Blunden died in 1998 at 81 years of age.

THE INCINERATED CORPSE

The most obvious problem for murderers in their attempt to avoid detection is usually the body, known legally as the 'corpus delecti'. Forensic science is so advanced that the body can yield countless clues, from basic identification to time of death and even obscure causes of death. Many killers therefore try to dispose of the body to either prevent an investigation altogether, to divert suspicion or to deny police access to vital information.

It has long been a common misconception that there can be no charge of murder without a body. The most obvious method of disposal is secret burial, but there have also been cases of victims' bodies being dissolved in acid baths (the infamous George Haigh used this method in England in 1949), dismemberment or even burning. Several cases of dismemberment are outlined in this book, along with several cases in which funeral pyres have been used to dispose of the body. However, none of these cases caused more public interest than the incineration of a farmer's corpse on a New Zealand farm in 1933.

Several farmers living at Ruawaro, a tiny dot on the map 100 kilometres from Auckland, sniffed the cool twilight air on October 15, 1933 and could clearly smell smoke coming from a neighbour,

William Bayly's, paddock. They took no notice as farmers often burnt off rubbish and even incinerated dead sheep or cattle. It was just another day in the quiet rural valley on New Zealand's north island.

However, farmer Bert Stevens thought it strange the next morning that one of his neighbours, Samuel Lakey, had not milked his cows. Lakey, who had been born in England and had fought in the New Zealand army in World War I, was a meticulous man and Stevens correctly reasoned that there was 'something wrong' at the small Lakey farm. He investigated and found the body of Mrs Christobel Lakey face down in a duck pond. The body had been covered by hessian sacks and the dead woman's husband was missing. Police were called and were at the farm within minutes.

Lakey's disappearance puzzled police as he was known to be devoted to his wife and there had not even been a hint of trouble at the farm. However, it did appear at first glance that Lakey had killed his wife. Police, in searching the farmhouse, noticed that Lakey's clothes and shoes were missing, along with a shotgun and a small-bore rifle. Police reasoned that Lakey might have killed his wife and had disappeared, perhaps with another woman.

However, police soon discounted this theory because the shoes taken from the house were not Lakey's, but those of a neighbour who had left them there. It looked more and more likely that whoever had killed Mrs Lakey had faked her husband's disappearance. Besides, police were extremely suspicious of Lakey's neighbour, the slightly built, balding Bayly, who had been a key figure in an inquiry into the death of his seventeen-year-old cousin Elsie Walker in 1929.

Police decided that whoever had killed Mrs Lakey had also killed her husband. The big problem was that there was no sign of Lakey, who appeared to have vanished from the face of the earth. Meanwhile, forensic pathologists determined that Mrs Lakey had drowned. It appeared that she had been knocked unconscious and that her killer had then held her head under the duck-pond water.

An army of volunteers scoured the local countryside for any sign of Lakey, without result. This convinced the investigating police that Lakey had also been killed. But where was the body? Police explored every possibility, but paid particular attention when told that there had been a large fire at Bayly's property on the evening of Lakey's disappearance. Police decided to concentrate their search on Bayly's property—and they did not do it in half measures. More than sixty police officers camped in a dozen tents in the area surrounding the Bayly farmhouse. They turned over every sod, looked under every log and looked into every nook and cranny. They were convinced they would find Lakey's body.

Earlier, police had noticed bloodstains on a wooden fence at the Lakey farmhouse. They theorised that Lakey had gone to his wife's defence and had been shot for his trouble. The blood was not Mrs Lakey's and it was fresh. Further investigations revealed bloodstains on cart wheels and a tray owned by Bayly. Police became increasingly convinced that Bayly had killed Mr and Mrs Lakey and had then lifted Lakey's body onto his cart for disposal on his own property.

Police were meticulous in their efforts and were rewarded by a number of finds. The first was the discovery of a shotgun and a rifle in a swampy part of Bayly's property. Both were positively identified as Lakey's. Police also found several of Lakey's personal possessions, including a uniquely designed cigarette lighter, along with fragments of human bone. These discoveries gave the investigating officers renewed hope, but further evidence had to be obtained to charge Bayly with murder.

The most significant finds were in the two halves of a 44-gallon drum found on different parts of the Bayly property. These drums contained bone fragments which police were convinced were from Lakey's body. However, police were still not satisfied as the bones had been reduced almost to ashes and it would have had to have been a ferocious fire to dispose of a human body with such near perfection.

Police decided to incinerate both a calf and a sheep in similar drums. They were burned separately and both carcases were reduced to fragments of bone and ashes. Importantly, forensic investigators lined both drums with sheets of corrugated iron. After all, the drum halves on Bayly's property had been lined with corrugated iron, presumably to maintain great heat in the reduction of the body to ashes.

The drum lining was particularly incriminating and when police found a hank of Lakey's greying red hair and pieces of burnt material, they charged Bayly with the murder of his neighbours. They had not found Lakey's body, but they were convinced they had enough evidence to put before a jury.

Bayly went on trial in the Supreme Court in Auckland on May 21, 1934, and the prosecution, led by Mr V.R. Meredith, was as meticulous as the police in trying to prove that Bayly had killed his neighbours. Mr Meredith detailed every piece of evidence, including bloodstains found at the Bayly milking sheds. Fragments of timber had been sliced from the shed and covered with oil stains. The prosecution claimed that Bayly had taken Lakey's body by cart to his property and had then set about to remove all traces of his neighbour. Bayly had even tried to remove bloodstains from the milking shed timber. However, he had found it impossible to dispose of the entire body as fragments of bone had been found in the drums, in his orchard and even in his flower garden. Bayly could hardly argue that it was 'blood and bone' fertiliser.

The evidence, despite the lack of a body, seemed overwhelming. However, there was one huge problem for the prosecution. There simply was no apparent motive for the murder of Mr and Mrs Lakey. The presumption of a neighbours' dispute was not good enough and Bayly's defence counsel, Mr E.H. Northcroft, made much of this. Mr Northcroft also tried desperately to convince the jury that the evidence against his client was largely circumstantial. However, forensic evidence proved beyond doubt that the bone fragments found at Bayly's farm were from a well-built, middle-aged man. Lakey was powerfully built and was thirty-seven years of age. Besides, police had found Lakey's cigarette lighter and guns on Bayly's property.

During the ten-day trial, a large part of Lakey's scalp was produced in court and this must have had a devastating effect on

Bayly's chances of acquittal. It was a gruesome sight and the jury must have noticed Bayly temporarily lose his composure during one of the trial's most dramatic moments.

Mr Northcroft suggested to the jury that Bayly had not been involved in the deaths of his neighbours. He also suggested that if a third person had discovered the bodies, that person would not have had a hope of convincing police he was innocent and, to distance himself from the deaths, could be forgiven for disposing of one of the bodies.

The jury retired at 11.15 am on June 23, 1934, but this was overshadowed by the collapse of Bayly's wife Phyllis, mother of their two boys, aged five and three. Most observers believed the jury would deliberate only briefly and were not surprised when it returned just before 12.30 p.m. It had taken the jury just over an hour to find Bayly guilty of both murders. Judge Sir Alexander Herdman had no option but to sentence Bayly to death by hanging. Bayly, as inscrutable as ever, made no comment and did not even show the slightest sign of agitation as he was led from the dock.

Bayly's execution was set for July 20, 1934, at Auckland Prison. There were few who believed in his pleas of innocence and the grizzly incineration of his neighbour's body had shocked the whole of New Zealand. Bayly, with the hangman's noose about to be placed around his neck, was asked if he would like to say anything. A man who chose his words carefully, Bayly obviously had been expecting this and replied slowly but firmly.

> I would like to say that I am entirely innocent. The circumstantial evidence might appear to be entirely against me, but there is no tittle of truth in the circumstantial evidence which has been produced against me. If I had received the treatment outside which I have received in this place [prison] I would never be here today. Everybody has done all they could for me, and I do not think anyone who has helped me here could have done more.

Bayly then paused and was asked: 'Is that all?'

'Just a minute, just a minute,' Bayly said in a rare display of emotion. 'I don't think I can say more, but I do repeat that I am innocent. A fair and dispassionate study of my evidence is as much against my accusers as it is against me. I don't think there is any more I can say.' Bayly's last words were to the prison chaplain, the Reverend George Moreton. 'Thank you,' he said, and was hanged.

A GANGLAND MURDER

Australia, unfortunately, has had more than its share of gangland killings. Sydney, in the post-war era of the 1940s and 50s, saw numerous killings as gangsters fought over lucrative prostitution and gambling interests. Melbourne also had its criminal gangs and the Depression era of the 1930s saw a spate of vicious attacks and several gangland killings during the heyday of the two-up rackets. However, there was nothing in Sydney or Melbourne criminal annals to match the sheer audacity of what happened in a dark, narrow Melbourne street in 1933.

Well-known criminal James John, who lived in the tough inner suburb of Collingwood, was a gambler and stand-over man with few friends and many enemies. He lived by night and regularly attended Melbourne's illegal gambling dens. John, twenty-five years of age, had been at a club in the city early on the morning of September 22, 1933, and decided to walk to his lodgings through the Exhibition Gardens. He was with a group of men, but two of them left John and another man, Jack Chrisfield, at the top of Nicholson Street. John and Chrisfield kept walking through the dimly lit streets of grimy Fitzroy when they noticed a cream-coloured car about 100 metres behind them. The car appeared to be cruising behind them and every time the two men stopped, the car stopped. John and Chrisfield therefore decided to 'lose' themselves in a narrow, tree-lined street which offered them plenty of cover in case there was trouble.

The two men walked into Gore Street and watched in horror as they saw the car's headlight beams turn the corner in their direction. The car moved to within metres of the two men, but Chrisfield decided that discretion was the better part of valour and stepped aside. John was left alone as a man jumped out of the car from the front passenger seat and, with a handkerchief over his face, started firing at him. John had no chance of escape and was riddled with bullets, the gunman even pumping three bullets into John as he lay in the gutter. Chrisfield watched in horror as the gunman climbed back into the car and the driver sped away.

Police were called to the scene, but John was in a critical condition and died under examination at the Melbourne Hospital. Later, at the inquest into his death, the Government pathologist, Dr C.H. Mollison, said that John had been shot fives times. One bullet had pierced his right side and had passed through the chest and liver, another had passed through the middle of his back, the third had lodged in the middle of his back, the fourth had entered the left buttock and the fifth bullet had entered the right buttock.

There was absolutely no doubt that John had been the victim of a gangland killing, but by whom? Chrisfield told coroner Mr Grant PM that he had been unable to identify the gunman or the driver of the car. Chrisfield said that after the shooting he ran over to the wounded John and asked him if he had been hurt. It was asking the obvious, but John replied: 'Yes, get me help quick.' Chrisfield turned around and saw a group of people running into the street from their homes and asked them to telephone police.

However, Chrisfield knew very well that he had to be extremely careful about what information he gave to police and the coroner. When asked at the inquest if he knew whether John had any enemies, he replied: 'I do not know.' Police already had a suspect, well-known criminal James Robert Walker, and Chrisfield was asked if Walker looked like the gunman. Chrisfield did not hesitate in saying 'no'.

Meanwhile, police had been trying to link John's killing with the shooting and wounding of another Melbourne underworld identity two nights earlier. Then, twenty-five-year-old Daniel Hossack had been slightly wounded in the left buttock. Gunsmith William Allan told the inquest into John's death that he had made an examination of the bullets fired at both John and Hossack and was certain that they were fired from the same .25 calibre pistol. Allan said the gun barrel had not only been dirty, but was rusted.

The inquest was then told that salesman Henry Mitchell had made a statement alleging that Walker and a man named Bert Adams had approached him at the Mentone racecourse on September 23, (the day after John's killing) and had asked him if he wanted to earn 100 pounds. Mitchell asked: 'What do I have to do?'

He alleged in the statement that Adams pulled a gun from his pocket and said: 'Get rid of this gun.'

Mitchell was terrified, especially when Adams told him: 'If you don't, I'll fix you.' Mitchell said he then agreed to hide the gun, but Adams asked for another 'favour', in the form of an alibi for Walker. Adams wanted Mitchell to say that he had seen Walker, in Adams' company, on a bus from St Kilda at 2.45 a.m. on 22 September—precisely the time the gunman had ambushed John. Mitchell told the inquest he then went to the State Secretary's Department and made his statement to detectives. However, Mitchell insisted at the inquest that he had not told the truth in the statement. He had changed his mind about giving evidence incriminating Walker and the coroner had no option but to find that John had 'died at the Melbourne Hospital as the result of bullet wounds maliciously inflicted at Gore Street, Fitzroy, by a man whose identity has not been determined'. Mr Grant then ordered a warrant be issued for the arrest of the unknown murderer.

Police had been stymied by the underworld code of silence and were convinced that Walker had killed John in a gangland feud. Walker, one of the most infamous criminals of his era, was given a life sentence in 1953 for the shotgun death of a man in St Kilda. Just one year later he shot himself dead during an attempted escape from Pentridge. He left behind a series of notes in exercise books. It was a chronicle of crime and the notes included a confession to the killing of John. He wrote that he confronted John that dark night in 1933 with 'an ice-cold rod in my right hand'. Police were able to close their files on John's killing, even though they had always known that Walker was the gunman in the cream car.

THIRD TIME 'LUCKY'

It is not unusual for a criminal jury to disagree and for a retrial to be ordered. In fact, there have been many such cases, not only in Australia and New Zealand, but around the world. However, it is most unusual for anyone to face three trials on the one charge—especially a murder charge—as forty-eight-year-old Walter James Henderson did in Melbourne in 1932.

Henderson had been a farmer at Lake Boga, but had shifted to the Melbourne suburb of Albert Park at the suggestion of his mother, Mrs Sarah Jane Henderson, early in 1932. The home Mrs Henderson found for herself and her son was in St Vincent's Place, now one of Melbourne's most fashionable streets. It is a tree-lined avenue of magnificent terrace houses, but in 1932 it was not regarded as anything more than an average residential street. The Henderson home in St Vincent's Place reflected the family's quiet, conservative tastes; it was pleasantly furnished in the style of the period and was a more than comfortable residence for Mrs Henderson and her middle-aged son. It was also close to the home of Mrs Henderson's daughter in Kerferd Road, Albert Park.

Henderson, who had been married but was living apart from his wife, was at home early on the afternoon of July 27, 1932, when he found his mother seriously injured at the foot of the stairs. Henderson called to nextdoor neighbour Mrs Elizabeth Meurillian for help. 'Get a doctor, quick,' he told her. 'My mother has fallen downstairs.' Henderson, in a statement made to police later that day, said:

> Mother and I were in the kitchen when a man called to see a room. Mother took him upstairs and later let him out the front door. I heard a thud and mother called 'my boy'. I found her lying at the foot of the stairs and I carried her to a chair in the kitchen, and went to the neighbours. I did not see any wounds on her head when I picked her up.

Police were suspicious at the outset, especially as they had found a broken, bloodstained hammer in the St Vincent's Place house. There was blood everywhere, with pieces of cloth scattered about the floor. Mrs Henderson was still alive when her son found her at the foot of the one-flight stairs, but died at the Homeopathic Hospital shortly after her admission. The sixty-three-year-old woman had suffered horrific head injuries.

An inquest was held three weeks later into Mrs Henderson's death and the Government pathologist, Dr C.H. Mollison, told the coroner, Mr D. Grant, that there were five lacerations to the left side of Mrs Henderson's head and a laceration to the brain. The skull, amazingly, was not fractured. Dr Mollison said the injuries could not have been caused by a fall down the stairs, but could have been caused by hammer blows. The Government analytical chemist, Mr Harold Wignell, told the coroner that a bloodstain on the carpet at the foot of the stairs appeared to have been diffused by the rubbing of blood while it was still moist and that hairs had been found on the hammer by police.

Detective Daniel Webster told the coroner that Henderson, in the statement made to him, said: 'I last used my hammer when I broke it putting up some trellis for my mother.' Henderson could not explain the bloodstains on the hammer. Detective Webster asked Henderson if there were any insurance policies on his mother's life and the reply was 'yes'. However, Henderson said his mother had made a will leaving everything to her daughter. He also said that his mother had told him she had changed her mind and that she would make another will, which would include him. There were three small policies on Mrs Henderson's life—one for 100 pounds for accident and two for smaller amounts for death or maturity at seventy-five years.

The coroner was also told that Henderson, who was wearing overalls on the afternoon of his mother's death, had been covered in blood. He was distraught and frothing at the mouth. The coroner committed Henderson for trial on a charge of murder. Bail was refused.

Henderson faced the charge in the Criminal Court before Mr justice Mann and a jury. Henderson's defence counsel, Mr J.V. Barry, suggested to the court that the hairs found on the bloodstained hammer were from a dog or a Persian cat and not from the head of the dead woman. Mr Wignell said he had taken hairs from a dog at the home of Mrs Henderson's daughter and had compared them with those found on the hammer. He was adamant that they were different. However, he admitted that he had not examined hair from a Persian cat. Mr Barry asked: 'The hair of a slate-grey Persian cat would be similar to human hair?'

Mr Wignell replied: 'It would be much finer than human hair, and I think its colour would be different.'

However, Dr Mollison changed his mind and admitted to the court that he did not believe that the hammer produced in court could have killed Mrs Henderson. He said that the dead woman's skull, although unusually thick, could not have resisted a blow from such a heavy instrument and would show at least some fracture. The defence therefore had found a chink in the Crown's case against Henderson.

Constable J. Brown, of the St Kilda Road Police Station, told the court that he had found the bloodstained hammer handle under clothes pegs in a box in the scullery. He said it appeared to have been recently broken, with the head missing. The head, also bloodstained, was later found hidden in a bag in another box. Significantly, Constable Brown said a Persian cat had been tied to a rope in the box in which the hammer handle had been found. Senior-Constable A. McKerral then told the court that the bag under which the hammer had been found had been used as a sleeping mat by the Persian cat and this, of course, was another chink in the Crown case.

The Crown alleged that Henderson killed his mother with the claw hammer in a fit of temper. Mr Book said that in this case there was no suggestion of premeditation and that, therefore, the motive was relatively unimportant. He suggested that mother and son might have fought over money or Henderson's matrimonial affairs, as he had married a second time (he was later charged with bigamy) without telling his mother until shortly before her death. Mr Book insisted that if Mrs Henderson had fallen down the stairs, as Henderson claimed, there would have been blood and hairs on the stairs, and there was no sign of either. Also, there were no bruises on Mrs Henderson's body.

Mr Justice Mann told the jury that evidence of motive was expected in a charge of murder, but in this case there was 'an utter absence of any such evidence' and that the finding of Mrs Henderson's insurance policies amounted to nothing. However, Mr Justice Mann said:

> The most significant evidence is the finding of the broken hammer handle, thickly smeared with blood and bearing on its surface human hair ... and it must not be forgotten that Henderson's hands and clothes were covered with blood and that the accused was moving in different parts of the house where there was a great deal of blood. The question is: Can you [the jury] find anything that is reasonably consistent with the innocence of the accused that would explain the finding of the hammer in the condition in which it was found? If you can, the accused is entitled to the benefit of any reasonable doubt.

The jury deliberated for more than five hours before sending a message to the judge that it could not agree upon a verdict. 'It would be a pity for this trial to be gone through again simply because you are unable to keep your minds open and prolong your discussion,' Mr Justice Mann told the jury members on recalling them to court. 'You will never get any further if you take up sides. It is the duty of every juryman to try and understand and appreciate the point of view of those who differ from him. I hope that you will call to mind what a disagreement in this case will mean.' The jury retired again, only to return just an hour later to announce that it was still unable to agree. Mr Justice Mann discharged the jury and remanded Henderson for retrial at the Criminal Court from October 17.

The retrial was before Mr justice Wasley and jury and the evidence presented by both Crown and defence was almost identical to the evidence given at the first trial. Henderson, clearly but with emotion cracking his voice, told the court: 'I did nothing that could have caused her [his mother's] death.'

Mr Barry, again defending Henderson, asked: 'On what terms were you with your mother?'

Henderson replied: 'On the best of terms. I was her only son.'

Mr Justice Walsey, in his summing up, told the jury that if Henderson, in a dispute with his mother, had had a hammer in his hand and had made a blow at her or thrown it at her, the jury 'might well say that it was not murder'. However, he said the jury would find it difficult to return a verdict of manslaughter as there had been multiple blows to Mrs Henderson's head and it would be difficult to 'escape the conclusion that the blows were struck deliberately'. Mr Justice Wasley refused to speculate on whether it was possible for Mrs Henderson to have fallen down the stairs, as suggested by Henderson's defence counsel. The jury retired at 1.25 p.m. on October 20 and returned six hours later to say it could not agree on a verdict. Henderson was remanded for trial at the Criminal Court the following month.

Henderson's third trial was before Mr Justice Macfarlane and jury, with most of the same evidence paraded yet again. By this time the Melbourne public had tired of the mother-son case and little of the evidence was reported. After all, the public had read it all before. There was very, very little new evidence at the third trial and it really was a question of whether a jury finally could reach a decision.

The third trial lasted three days and, in his summing up, Mr Justice Macfarlane told the jury that it had been the responsibility of the Crown to prove that Mrs Henderson had died in the way alleged by the Crown. Henderson again gave evidence and said that he had heard his mother fall and merely had gone to her aid, hence the blood on his clothing. Two highly qualified doctors again gave evidence that Mrs Henderson's injuries could have been caused by falling down the stairs. Significantly, Mr Justice Macfarlane asked the jury if it believed a guilty man would seek help 'before he had finished the job'. He also suggested that if Henderson had been the 'cool, calculating scoundrel' portrayed by the Crown, 'would he have been so foolish as to have left the two broken pieces of the hammer in such conspicuous places?'

The jury retired at 5.45 p.m. on November 23 and returned three hours later. Its verdict? Not guilty. Henderson, despite his marathon ordeal, walked away a free man.

THE GATTON
MURDERS

There are, in Australian criminal history, several murder cases which have gained worldwide notoriety. These include the Pyjama Girl Case of 1934 (the pyjama-clad body of Linda Agostini's body was found in a culvert near Albury and was unidentified for ten years) and the kidnap-murder of schoolboy Graeme Thorne by Stephen Bradley in 1960. However, the Gatton murders, as they are universally known, have fascinated amateur criminologists for almost a decade and the case has continually defied even the most painstaking investigation.

The Christmas period in Queensland in 1898 was one of the hottest on record. The inland area west of Brisbane was baked mercilessly under a flaming orange sun and drought ravaged even the best crop and grazing districts. The area around the tiny town of Gatton (population 450), fifty kilometres east of Toowoomba, resembled a dustbowl and only the truly hardy ventured into the midday sun. However, Christmas was Christmas, drought or no drought, and the large Murphy family celebrated as if the drought was about to break and there would soon be prosperity for all. Daniel and Mary Murphy, as Irish as the shamrock, had ten children—six sons and four daughters. Only one of their children, Polly, was married. Daniel and Mary Murphy had been born in Ireland, but had established themselves at Blackfellow's Creek, where they became relatively prosperous and well known in the Gatton district.

Michael Murphy, a twenty-nine-year-old police sergeant, and his sisters Norah, twenty-seven, and Ellen, eighteen, had been to the Mt Sylvia races on Boxing Day and had decided to attend a dance at Gatton that night. They returned home for a meal before Michael hitched family horse Tom to a sulky and drove his sisters to the dance at the Divisional Board's Hall in Gatton. The three Murphys passed their brother Patrick, who was on horseback, at about 8.15 p.m. and arrived at the hall just after 9 p.m. However, there was no sign of activity and the dance was eventually cancelled because there were not enough women. The Murphys turned around to go home and again ran into their brother Patrick, who chatted with his brother and two sisters for several minutes. The four met only about one and a half kilometres from an area known as Moran's Paddock and Patrick Murphy never saw his brother or two sisters alive again. It had been a brilliantly bright evening, but three of the Murphy clan met gruesome deaths under starlight.

The alarm was raised early the next morning when there was no sign of Michael, Norah or Ellen at the Murphy farm. Mrs Murphy sensed something was wrong and William McNeil, married to Polly and staying with the Murphys over the Christmas period, saddled a horse and rode to Gatton. He was shocked when told that the three missing Murphys had headed towards home before 10 o'clock the previous night. McNeil decided to retrace their route to Gatton, an easy task as the Murphy sulky had a wobbly wheel which left a distinctive mark on the dust road out of tiny Gatton. He followed the wheel marks to a sliprail at Moran's Paddock, three kilometres out of Gatton, and decided to investigate.

McNeil at first believed that the track would lead to a farmhouse. He was also convinced that the sulky or the horse had broken down and that his three in-laws had decided to stay there overnight. He certainly was not prepared for what he found just one minute's ride into the paddock. McNeil discovered the bodies of the three Murphys; the horse had also been killed, shot through the head.

The bodies of Michael and Ellen were back to back, with the dead horse nearby. Norah's body was about eight metres away behind a large gum tree. McNeil, at a Magisterial Inquiry in January 1899, said in evidence that he noticed ants crawling over Norah's face. He said: 'Her jacket was pulled up to her shoulders and her stays were exposed. Her skirts were on but the hooks were undone at the back. They also were slightly pulled up at the back.' It was obvious that both the Murphy girls had been sexually violated. Their hands had been tied behind their backs and their heads had been battered with extreme savagery. Norah Murphy had a leather strap from the sulky knotted around her throat and Michael Murphy, it was later proven, had been shot in the head.

McNeil quickly mounted his horse and rode back to Gatton at full gallop to tell authorities what had happened at Moran's Paddock. McNeil raced into the hamlet and asked publican Charles Gilbert: 'Where is the police station? The three Murphys are lying dead in a paddock. There must have been some accident, as the horse is dead, too.'

Gilbert directed McNeil, who was a stranger to the area, to the police station where he blurted out the details of his discovery to Sergeant William Arrell, the officer in charge. Arrell then accompanied McNeil back to Moran's Paddock. Meanwhile, news of the three deaths spread like oil on water and most of Gatton's inhabitants raced for Moran's Paddock, just minutes behind McNeil and Sergeant Arrell. McNeil, with Arrell standing alongside him, then made a full identification of the bodies before riding back to the Murphy farm to break the tragic news to the rest of the family.

Sergeant Arrell then rode back into town to telegram high-ranking police officers of the triple tragedy and by the time he arrived back at Moran's Paddock it was overrun by ghoulish sightseers. He ordered them away from the murder scene, but they refused, despite every protestation. Finally, Mrs Murphy asked for the bodies to be removed and they were transported to the Brian

Boru Hotel in Gatton, where the Government medical officer for Ipswich, Dr William von Lossberg, conducted post-mortem examinations.

Dr von Lossberg noted that Ellen's face and body were smeared with blood and that the brain protruded from the right side of the head. There were fingernail marks on the body and abrasions on both hands. The skull had been severely fractured and the doctor concluded that the teenage girl had been bashed several times over the head by a heavy, blunt instrument. The girl had been sexually assaulted as there were traces of semen in the vagina.

Norah Murphy had been savagely beaten about the face and the strap around her neck was so tight that it had stopped circulation to the brain. In fact, it was so tight that it cut into her flesh and could barely be seen. There was a cut (made by a knife) near the right eye and there were fingernail marks on her breasts, arms and hands. Dr von Lossberg also determined that there were fingernail marks on the dead woman's vagina and anus. She had also been raped. The doctor also examined a piece of wood retrieved from the murder scene and said that he had found traces of blood, hair and brain on it. It undoubtedly was the murder weapon. Dr von Lossberg suggested that both women had been hit when they were in a standing position and had been raped before they had had their heads bashed by the heavy piece of timber.

The post-mortem examination on Michael Murphy's body was not so straightforward. Dr von Lossberg noted that there was a bloody wound behind the right ear. He washed the blood away and, noting a gaping hole, was convinced he would find a bullet in the dead man's skull. The doctor probed with his fingers, but stopped to wash his hands in disinfectant after pricking a finger on a sharp piece of bone. On resumption of his probing, he felt his hand go numb and realised that he had been poisoned. He asked a local chemist to continue the probe, but no bullet was found. Dr von Lossberg's blood poisoning caused him more than three months of illness, but also a considerable amount of anguish.

Dr von Lossberg finally determined that Michael Murphy had also been bashed around the head by the heavy piece of timber, but said that this was after death. He believed that Michael Murphy had been shot in the head, but as he was unable to find the bullet he said that the wound must have been made by a stick. The fact that he could not find an exit wound helped him form this theory. However, police later ordered an exhumation of all three bodies and before dawn on January 4, 1899, the Government medical officer, Dr Charles Wray, arrived from Brisbane. The second post-mortem found the bullet in Michael Murphy's skull.

Finally, police were able to piece together the events of that moonlit night of December 26. They theorised that the Murphys had been ambushed and that Michael Murphy had been forced at gunpoint to drive into Moran's Paddock and then tie his sisters' hands before he had his own hands tied. The Murphy sisters were then raped and bashed to death, with Michael Murphy shot through the brain. The killer then vanished.

So who killed the Murphys? Police, of course, had their suspects, including a known criminal who had been in the Garton area at the time of the killings. In fact, police concentrated their efforts on this suspect, who had recently been released from jail after having served a sentence for a sexual offence. The suspect, Richard Burgess, was even remanded for eight days, but had to be released as police had no real evidence against him. Burgess even made a statement detailing his movements over Christmas and Boxing Days. Police investigated further, but almost every move was corroborated by witnesses, including a Presbyterian minister. Police even took the extraordinary step of warning police around Australia to 'keep an eye' on Burgess and he boasted in later years that he was, in fact, the Gatton murderer. The evidence, however, suggests otherwise and Burgess was almost certainly boasting to impress the gullible. He died many years later in Western Australia.

The other suspect was a young man named Thomas Day, who was working in the Gatton area at the time of the tragedy. Day, an army deserter, was seen washing bloodstains from his clothes soon after the murder of the three Murphys. He had also been seen near Moran's Paddock at night at least twice before that fateful evening of December 26, 1898. However, police concentrated their efforts on Burgess, virtually neglecting evidence involving Day. It was possible, therefore, that Day, who was reported to have been killed in the Boer War, could have been the killer.

Police were unable to solve the Gatton murders and a Police Inquiry Commission into police operations in Queensland, which took particular note of the Gatton mystery, noted in November 1899:

> We are of the opinion that sufficiently exhaustive investigation and inquiry were not made in every instance as regards suspects.
>
> Taking all the facts before us in connection with the action of the police in reference to both the Gatton and Oxley [another infamous case] murders, we feel bound to say that there was a lack of cohesion and efficient organisation to enable them to cope with serious crimes in such a manner as the people of the Colony [Queensland] are entitled to expect.
>
> On the other hand we feel constrained to acknowledge that great mystery surrounds the Gatton murders, and it does not follow that if the police had been in the highest state of efficiency that the murderer or murderers would have been discovered. That there was inertness and dilatoriness at the outset cannot be gainsaid, but after the matter was fairly taken in hand the officers and men acted individually with zeal.

Queensland police have never closed their files on the Gatton murders, even after almost a century. However, there are several interesting footnotes to one of Australian crime's greatest mysteries, in relation to the medical evidence and a death-bed confession.

First, the medical evidence and the fact that semen was found in Ellen Murphy's vagina. At the time, there was no way medical experts could group semen. However, seminal fluid can now be grouped and suspects can be eliminated through this process. It would have been extremely interesting to see whether Burgess and/or Day would have been eliminated from suspicion had modern methods been available in 1898. The Gatton murders today might not be such mysteries.

As to the death-bed confession, it was reported in New South Wales in 1973 that a ninety-five-year-old man had told two elderly sisters that he was the Gatton murderer. The women, knowing that the old man was dying, decided not to inform police until he had died. They then went to police at Murwillumbah and said after the man had seen a television documentary on the Gatton murders he had decided to confess to his crimes. He even told the sisters where he had hidden the revolver used to shoot Michael Murphy and the horse.

The sisters, Mrs Margaret Rutherford and Mrs Violet Russell, were convinced the old man was genuine in his confession. Mrs Russell, who had known the man for more than twenty-five years, said she knew that he had lived a tough and brutal life. Also, she insisted that the old man, known as 'Pop', gave extremely intricate details of the case and could not have gleaned this information from newspapers as he could not read or write. Police, naturally, investigated the 'confession' but were unable to shed any light on the mystery. The old man had told the sisters he had hidden the gun under a gum tree in Moran's Paddock, but police found that it was impossible even to search for the gun as Gatton had grown and spread enormously over the intervening years.

The old man's 'confession', if true, would eliminate Burgess and Day as the suspects. Burgess died many years earlier in Western Australia, and although Day would have been about ninety-five years of age in 1973 (he was about twenty-one or twenty-two years of age in 1898), he was a highly educated young man. In fact, police once saw him reading a book beyond the comprehension of most rural workers. Besides, police investigated 'Pop's' death-bed confession and discovered several discrepancies. It can be assumed with some certainty that the old man, despite his confession, was not the Gatton murderer.

Queensland police, from time to time, examine public claims about the murders and, in 1962, investigated claims by a woman that she knew the identity of the killer. She 'named' the Gatton murderer, but her information was proved incorrect. It now seems

certain the Gatton murders will remain one of Australia's greatest
mysteries.

GATHER YE ROSEBUDS

Elderly widow Mrs Elizabeth Little was devoted to her grown-up family of a son and two daughters. She lived with one of her children, veterinary surgeon George, on the family's eighty-acre farm near the tiny Victorian township of Stratford. Mrs Little was well known in the district as her father had been a successful Gippsland grazier. The family was well liked and respected by the entire community. It was a happy family and, on the afternoon of October 16, 1930, Mrs Little collected roses from her garden for a visit to one of her daughters. Sadly, Mrs Little, who was not in the best of health, was never able to deliver the roses as she was strangled to death in the middle of her preparations for her visit.

The alarm was raised by fifteen-year-old farmhand Daphne O'Brien, who told Sale police that she had been attacked by another farmhand, eighteen-year-old Herbert Donovan, who had rushed into the farmhouse and demanded to know where Mrs Little had kept her money. Miss O'Brien told police that Donovan then went into a bedroom and took three five pound notes from a bag before attacking her and then forcing her to harness Mr Little's horse to a buggy. He drove off in a cloud of dust and Miss O'Brien called police.

Mrs Little's body was found in a cowshed on the property. Her hands were tied behind her back by a cow halter and her legs were also tied. There were facial wounds, but police were unable to tell at first how Mrs Little had died. Their immediate concern was to apprehend Donovan, who had abandoned the horse and buggy outside a house in Sale. Police believed he had caught a late afternoon train to Melbourne and police throughout the state were given his description. Police also gave Melbourne newspapers a photograph of the wanted youth. The photograph showed Donovan in work clothes, with a baggy wide-brimmed hat and his hands deep in his trouser pockets. The official police description of Donovan was: 'Aged 18, 5 ft 10 in in height, ruddy, sunburnt complexion, slight build, dressed in soiled double-breasted blue suit.'

The first break in the hunt for Donovan was when a taxi driver told police he had driven a young man answering Donovan's description to Melbourne. The driver, Norman Buntine, told police that he found the young man sitting in his cab outside the Star Hotel in Sale at 5.15 p.m. on the day of Mrs Little's death. The young man asked Buntine to drive him to Melbourne and explained that he wanted to visit his sick sister. Buntine told him that the charge would be one shilling a mile, but the youth made no objection to this expense. However, the young man later asked Buntine to pull over at Berwick so that he could hitch a ride by truck to the city. A truck driver, Eric Craig, told police that he had taken the young man to the Dandenong railway station. Police assumed that Donovan had caught a train to the city from there.

Police launched a massive manhunt in Melbourne and at one stage three police groups were investigating three 'sightings' of the wanted Donovan. One woman had reported that she had seen Donovan in the suburb of Melbourne and another report suggested that Donovan had been seen leaving a Footscray hotel. Police were also stationed at Spencer Street railway station in case Donovan tried to catch a train interstate. Police also kept a close watch on the Prahran home of Donovan's parents.

Two police officers, Constables E. Lanigan and T. Rochford, were patrolling Nicholson Street, Carlton, on the morning of October 18—two days after the killing-when they noticed a dishevelled young man coming out of the Exhibition Gardens. Constable Lanigan turned to his colleague and said: 'That chap looks like Donovan.' They watched the youth for several minutes before apprehending him and taking him to police headquarters. Donovan, who admitted his identity, was kept under surveillance until questioned by senior detectives and charged with murder after making a statement confessing to the crime.

Donovan, in the statement, said he knew that Mrs Little kept money in the house and he was determined to steal it. After lunch on October 16 he went to a paddock on Mrs Little's property and put a mare into a loose box. He then told Mrs Little that the mare had girth gall and asked her to have a look. It was a ruse to get Mrs Little on her own and, according to the statement, Donovan then swung a handkerchief around Mrs Little's mouth as she bent to examine the mare. Donovan claimed he had not intended hurting Mrs Little, but she had screamed and fallen to the ground. He struggled with her and then knelt over her and pushed the handkerchief into her mouth. He then tied her hands behind her back and struck her over the head with a pair of pincers before running back to the house and stealing the fifteen pounds. Evidence was given at both the inquest into Mrs Little's death and at Donovan's trial at the Criminal Court, Sale, that Mrs Little had been struck six times around the head, but had died of asphyxiation caused by the handkerchief in her mouth.

Donovan was found guilty of murder and, on November 26, 1930, was sentenced to death by hanging. However, this sentence was later commuted to one of life imprisonment. Donovan had murdered a frail old widow for just fifteen pounds.

THE HAUNTED HOTEL

Those Australians who lived through the Great Depression never want to see a return to soup kitchens, bread queues and the general malaise of hundreds and thousands of workers desperate for any kind of job. Men rolled up their swags and tramped from town to town in search of work and 'dossed' where they could, under gum trees, along railway cuttings and even in abandoned buildings. They were the 'squatters' of the 1930s.

The derelict Windsor Castle Hotel in the old gold-mining town of Dunolly in central Victoria was the near-perfect 'doss' house. Its walls might have been cracked, its timber flooring might have been uprooted in places and many of its windows broken, but it was 'home' to a colony of tramps. In October 1938 at least five men were living there, despite the lack of running water or anything resembling comforts. It was little more than a roof over the head and some Dunolly residents claimed the hotel, which was de-licensed in 1914, was haunted.

Those living at the derelict hotel included pensioners Frederick Douglas, Charles Bunney and Robert Gray and a younger man named Thomas Johnson. On Monday, October 3, 1938, sixty-one-year-old Bunney (a World War I veteran) and seventy-three-year-old

Gray were seen alive for the last time. The following day, Douglas suggested to Johnson that 'something's happened to Bunney. Then, on the Thursday, he made a search for the old Digger and found a trail of blood on a landing outside one of the rooms. However, the door to the room was padlocked and, in a state of near panic, Douglas ran to a young local to ask him to climb a wall to peep through the room's window.

The young man climbed up to the window and, peering through the dust and gloom, was able to see what appeared to be two men lying on the floor. He yelled out to the men in the room, but there was not the slightest movement from them. Police were called immediately and, when the door was broken down, found the bodies of Bunney and Gray. Both men had been bludgeoned to death by an axe, which was still in a corner of the room. The wounds were horrific, with both men having their skulls split wide open.

Police soon deduced that Bunney had been killed on the landing and had then been dragged into the room where it was discovered. Bunney had taken one savage blow to the head and police found his bloodstained felt hat on the landing. He had obviously been wearing the hat when attacked as it had a five centimetre gash across its crown. Gray was killed in the room and had taken two heavy blows to the head

The axe, covered in blood, was the most obvious clue and suspicion fell first on its owner, fellow 'squatter' Lancelot Cazneau. However, Cazneau told police he had lent the axe to Johnson and, further, that Johnson had tried to borrow money from several men. Suspicion then fell on Johnson, who had disappeared.

Police immediately launched a manhunt for Johnson, but were still in the process of distributing his description when he walked into a police station at Dandenong, on the other side of Melbourne, and confessed. He told police that he was asleep at the old hotel when Gray woke him up by hammering at some floorboards. Johnson said he picked up the axe and smashed the old man over the head. Bunney, who went to investigate, copped the same vicious

424

treatment. Police were stunned by Johnson's frankness and charged him with the murder of both men.

Johnson, forty, stood trial at Ballarat before Mr Justice Lowe and a jury. The trial opened on December 13, 1938, and the court was packed as Johnson, wearing a dark brown suit, was led to the dock. The Crown, through Mr M. Cussen, told the court that Gray and Bunney were last seen alive by a postman at 5.15 p.m. on Monday, October 3, and that their bodies were found on Thursday, October 6. The Crown also told the court that Johnson, who came from a respectable working-class family, had made a statement to police at Dandenong even though he was warned he was not obliged to say anything.

Johnson, in the statement, told how he had hit both men over the head with the axe and had then padlocked the door. He stayed at the hotel over the next two nights before walking to Maryborough and then hitching a ride to Melbourne and walking to Dandenong. Johnson's only explanation for attacking his fellow residents with the axe was that he had lost his temper and that he had killed Bunney to prevent him being a witness to Gray's murder.

Although Johnson was extraordinarily honest in admitting to killing Gray and Bunney, he used this as an attempt to prove that he could not be held responsible for his actions as he had killed in a fit of rage. However, the Crown tried to prove that there was no diminished responsibility and that Johnson had killed for financial gain. Witnesses told the court that Johnson had been penniless on the day of the murders, but had been seen changing a ten shilling note the next day. The licensee of the Railway Hotel at Dunolly, Mrs Elizabeth Whelan, told the court that Johnson walked into the hotel late on the Monday evening and gave her a one pound note to purchase a bottle of wine. Even more incriminating, the court was told that Gray had received a pension payment of six pounds only shortly before he was killed and Johnson had asked Gray about it.

The jury found Johnson guilty and he was sentenced to death. However, the case provoked considerable public debate and the Victorian government was urged to have Johnson undergo psychiatric examination in an effort to have the sentence commuted to one of life imprisonment. However, the government refused to intervene and Johnson was hanged at Pentridge at 8 a.m. on January 23, 1939.

THE BLACK NEGLIGÉE

The 1950s, despite the emergence of rock 'n' roll and the bodgies and widgies who danced to the beat of this different drum, were conservative years. The family unit was considered almost sacred and it just was not done for couples to live with each other before marriage, let alone have children.

Eileen Joan Moriarty, a twenty-three-year-old nurse, was not the typical Australian woman of the era. She had had a child in Western Australia before moving to Sydney and then to Tasmania to seek a new life for herself, during this time she had at least a couple of lovers. Miss Moriarty's daughter was eight months old in 1959 and was 'boarded out' in Hobart while her mother lived at Wingfield House, part of the Royal Hobart Hospital complex. It was in the Apple Isle that Miss Moriarty met a most unusual man.

Graham Alan Stewart, a twenty-four-year-old Tasmanian, was an amateur hypnotist whose hobby was the occult. Stewart, a slim dark man with a goatee beard, carried business cards which suggested he specialised in the hypnotic treatment of nervous disorders. He also performed in nightclubs and decorated his flat with occult signs and symbols. His flat, in north Hobart, had an attic which had a mysterious black circle, with accompanying symbols, painted on the floor. A red light, which blinked on and off, was rigged to the ceiling to highlight the circle and symbols. It was suggested that Stewart regularly held midnight black magic meetings.

Stewart met the pretty, dark-haired Miss Moriarty in 1958 and soon fell in love with her. However, this love was not entirely reciprocated, despite Stewart's best endeavours. He made many approaches, but although Miss Moriarty 'liked' Stewart, she was wary of his unusual appearance and pursuits. Finally, on April 8, 1959, Stewart proposed marriage and—strangely—Miss Moriarty accepted. Stewart prepared a marriage application, which Miss Moriarty signed. The couple was to have been married the following day, but for some unknown reason Miss Moriarty changed her mind and fixed another wedding date—April 23. Stewart made preparations for the wedding, but he was left at the altar. Miss Moriarty had returned to a former lover.

Stewart, infuriated, went on a shopping spree. He bought himself a black-handled stiletto and a black negligee before renting a luxury apartment at the seaside suburb of Sandy Bay. He contacted Miss Moriarty, who then failed to turn up for work at the hospital. The police were contacted three days later and an officer from the Hobart Missing Persons Bureau investigated the girl's disappearance. Sergeant Lloyd Bennett quickly learned that Miss Moriarty had been seeing Stewart and that the amateur hypnotist had rented the apartment in Sandy Bay. He went to the apartment to investigate, but found it locked from the inside. He returned with a team of detectives, who entered the first-floor flat by climbing a ladder and entering through an unlocked window. They walked in on a scene far worse than they could have imagined. Miss Moriarty and Stewart lay dead in a huge pool of blood on a double bed, the girl's body covered only by the black negligee Stewart had bought on his shopping spree; Stewart was dressed in only a shirt. The stiletto he had bought was at his side and police determined that Stewart had stabbed Miss Moriarty and then had thrust the knife deep into his own heart. Miss Moriarty had been repeatedly, and furiously, stabbed in the chest and her death was no accident.

Police reconstructed the crime and suggested that Stewart called on Miss Moriarty at the hospital at the end of her work shift and took her to the Sandy Bay apartment. Police also suggested that Stewart gave Miss Moriarty the black negligee as a present and, after she had tried it on, he asked her to marry him. He then killed her in fury when she rejected his marriage proposal yet again. He thrust the stiletto into her chest time and time again before driving it through his own heart. Stewart, in buying the stiletto, obviously planned to kill Miss Moriarty. But what if she had accepted the marriage proposal? Stewart, a man who loved the mysterious, left this mystery with his own death.

DEATH AT THE VICARAGE

Parishioners at St Saviour's Anglican Church, Collingwood, loved their vicar, the Reverend Harold Cecil. He truly was a man of the people and worked tirelessly for the many poor in his parish. The quietly spoken, bespectacled Reverend Cecil tended his flock like the best of shepherds and even went without to help the more unfortunate. He lived an extremely modest life at the vicarage facing Smith Street, in one of Melbourne's toughest neighbourhoods. However, there had been persistent rumours that the Reverend Cecil was a very wealthy man and that he had a fortune hidden at the vicarage.

The rumours were only partly true as although the Reverend Cecil had invested wisely in a farming venture in the 1920s, there was very little money at the vicarage, let alone a fortune in hidden gold. However, every petty thief in the neighbourhood in 1935 knew that the Reverend Cecil was making his annual Christmas appeal and that there had been a number of donations.

Of course, the Collingwood parish was a poor parish and the donations amounted to no more than thirty-five pounds in cash and cheques. But they were desperate times and the Reverend Cecil should have been more careful when he opened his door to a stranger on December 12, 1935. The Reverend Cecil's body was discovered by church officials the next day.

The Reverend Cecil had been bashed over the head by a heavy object. The autopsy revealed seventeen separate wounds to the head, with a number of other cuts and abrasions to the body. Robbery was the obvious motive as the vicar's wallet was missing, the pockets had been torn from his trousers and two watches (on chains) and a gold chain were missing. One of the watches was of an unusual design and police reasoned that if the murderer tried to 'hock' it they would make an early arrest. The only significant clue at the ransacked vicarage was a signed notice-of-marriage certificate dated December 12. It was almost certain that the killer had used the notification of marriage as an excuse to get into the vicarage. The certificate had been signed Francis Edward Loyne or Layne.

Next day police found a blood-splattered spanner wedged between the brick chimney and the weatherboards at the old vicarage. A pattern on the spanner matched perfectly with the Reverend Cecil's head wounds. The murder weapon and the notice-of-marriage certificate were to become vital clues in the apprehension of the Reverend Cecil's brutal killer.

However, police investigations ran into a dead-end, even though the signature on the notice-of-marriage certificate was photographed and printed in Mel-bourne newspapers. Police even checked with signatures at Pentridge in the hope that they would be able to match one with the one on the certificate, to no immediate avail.

The investigation stalled for several weeks, until a detective recalled that a petty criminal had once signed the Pentridge jail record as Frank Lane. Police kept a close eye on twenty-nine-year-old Edward Cornelius, who often used the name Frank Lane as an alias. Besides, a South Yarra jeweller had bought the Reverend Cecil's missing gold chain from a young man whose description fitted Cornelius's. More importantly, the handwriting on the receipt book was similar to the signature on the wedding certificate at the vicarage.

Another jeweller bought a missing gold watchchain from a man answering Cornelius's description and, finally, a South Yarra second-hand dealer recalled selling the death spanner to a young man for nine-pence.

Cornelius was arrested at his home in East Melbourne on February 12, 1936. He had been released from Pentridge only a short time before the vicarage murder. He had served three years for housebreaking and handwriting experts determined that there were striking similarities in the jail signature and the one on the notice-of-marriage certificate.

Cornelius broke down under police questioning and confessed to the murder of the Reverend Cecil. He told police that he went to the vicarage to ask about a wedding certificate purely as an excuse to prepare for a future housebreaking. He signed the name Francis Edward Loyne on the certificate the Reverend Cecil handed to him, and then left.

Cornelius walked down Smith Street to Victoria Parade before remembering that the vicar had not closed the front door. Cornelius retraced his steps, found the front door still open and walked into the vicarage. The Reverend Cecil was in the kitchen, so Cornelius decided to rifle the study drawers as quietly as he could. He said:

> I'd gone through a couple of drawers in the desk looking for money. The next thing I knew someone grabbed me from behind and a struggle took place. A voice said: 'What are you after?'
>
> He began to get the better of me. I then struck him several times on the head with the spanner, which was partly covered by a brown paper bag. After I hit him two or three times he fell on the couch and partly on to the floor.
>
> I went to close the front door. I still had the spanner in my hand. The vicar must have come in because he was right in the passage behind me. He made another grab at me, saying. 'You can't get away.' I hit him on the head with the spanner a couple of times. He fell in the doorway.
>
> I found myself in the dining room. I saw myself in a mirror and saw blood on my face. I then picked up a water jug from a table and washed my hands and face. I wiped my hands on a pyjama coat.

The fact that Cornelius had armed himself with a spanner and that the Reverend Cecil had taken seventeen savage blows to the head told against the killer. Besides, his horrific crime netted him just ten pounds. He was found guilty and sentenced to death. Cornelius spent much of his time in the exercise yard at Pentridge with another condemned killer, Arnold Sodeman, who had been found guilty of strangling a six-year-old girl at Leongatha. Both men appealed against their sentences, unsuccessfully, and both were hanged at Pentridge.

THE KILLER GI

Every Australian who lived through World War II and experienced the influx of American troops would be only too familiar with the now-hackneyed expression 'over-paid, over-sexed and over here'. There were Americans in every bar and restaurant and on almost every corner of every Sydney, Melbourne and Brisbane city street.

One of the Americans, paratrooper Private Avelino Fernandez, was looking for a 'good time' in Brisbane on June 19, 1944. He and a few of his GI mates ate steaks at a restaurant and then went on a pub crawl before deciding to eat again at Nick's Cafe, Elizabeth Street. They stayed there most of the afternoon and were joined by two women after one of the Americans went out and returned with two quart bottles of whisky.

One of the women was thirty-four-year-old Doris Roberts, who had caught Fernandez' eye. She rose to leave the cafe, but was followed by the amorous GI. Roberts and Fernandez fell over each other as they walked down the stairs and into an alleyway. Hours later, Roberts' battered body was found in the laneway.

The Director of the Laboratory in the Queensland State Health Department, Dr E.H. Derrick, examined the body and found that there were a number of abrasions to the face and neck. The lower jaw was broken in two places and there was a quantity of blood in the left cavity surrounding the lung. He said that Roberts had died of haemorrhage, shock and asphyxiation. She had choked on her own blood and would have been in a state of shock in the moments before death.

Police had little trouble tracing Fernandez as a number of people had seen the paratrooper with Roberts at Nick's Cafe. Besides, Fernandez had had treatment for a cut hand at the American Red Cross. The officer in charge of the investigation, Detective Sergeant C.E. Risch, told a United States Court Martial on July 21 that Fernandez admitted bashing Roberts in the laneway off Elizabeth Street. 'I beat the hell out of her,' Fernandez is alleged to have confessed to the detective. 'I kicked her all over. I was real mad. If she is dead that's where she ought to be. I struck her in the face. I knocked her down. She got up and I struck her again. I kicked her in the stomach and I would do it again.'

Risch told the Court Martial that he and an American provost sergeant named Trask asked Fernandez why he had bashed the woman after he had had intercourse with her. He replied: 'Because she made me look cheap. She asked for money.' Fernandez, under cross-examination, admitted that he had been a boxer in the United States and that he had punched Roberts. However, he said he could not remember kicking her. He added: 'If they say I did kick her then I guess I must have done so.'

The Trial Judge Advocate asked Fernandez: 'How was she when you left her?'

Fernandez replied: 'She was still breathing.'

Fernandez told the Court Martial that he had five pounds when he started on the pub crawl, but had just a few shillings left when Roberts asked him for money. He also said that he objected to Roberts trying to kiss him as he thought she might have been 'a coloured woman'. He added that he would not have hit Roberts, believed to have been part-Aborigine, if she had been white. 'She should have asked for money before we went into the alleyway,' he said and added that he had been 'rolled' twice in the United States and that he thought Roberts might have been planning to rob him.

Private Ressie Goff, one of the Americans on the pub crawl with Fernandez, told the Court Martial that he looked into the laneway and heard a noise 'as if someone was choking' and saw what he took to be a man and a woman lying on the ground. Private Goff said he later saw Fernandez' hand wrapped in a khaki handkerchief. Fernandez told him the woman had 'passed out'.

Another witness, civilian William McEncroe, told the Court Martial that he was in the vicinity on the night of Roberts' death and saw a soldier shoving a woman along the road towards the laneway. He then heard a scream from the laneway, but did not intervene because he believed it to be a drunken argument. Fernandez admitted that he had struck Roberts, but had not intended to kill her. He also told the Court Martial that he had never previously been in trouble. Fernandez had left school at an early age and sold newspapers for a living before being taught sheet metal work in the United States. He had enlisted on February 3, 1942 and soon after had had paratrooper training. The Court Martial was also told that Fernandez had a wife in the United States.

The court took just a few minutes to find Fernandez guilty of murder, but deliberated a further hour and a half on the question of penalty. The Court Martial president told Fernandez: 'You are found guilty and are sentenced to be hanged by the neck till you are dead.' Fernandez did not even blink as sentence was passed; he turned and marched off with his military police escort.

There was considerable doubt as to whether Fernandez would be hanged as capital punishment had been abolished in Queensland in 1922. The Queensland government refused to provide the American Army with a scaffold for the hanging, so the Americans transported Fernandez to Oro Bay, New Guinea, where he was hanged on November 21, 1944.

THE WRONG BODY

William Griffenhagen was a quiet young man who desperately wanted to get married to his sweetheart and settle down on his bush allotment eight kilometres from the old Victorian mining city of Bendigo. He lived in a but on the property with his uncle, James Pattison, a well-known local prospector. Griffenhagen, twenty-six, spent most of his time clearing his land of scrub. Pattison, sixty-eight, was a dedicated fossicker, living in the hope that he would one day come across a nugget as big as his fist.

Both men were seen on Sunday, October 1, 1933, but Griffenhagen's friends became worried when they had not seen him for several days after that date. Police were informed and two constables went to Griffenhagen's hut, only to find it had been severely damaged by fire. Inside, the constables found a huge pile of ashes in the centre of the log and mud hut. There, under the charred and fallen corrugated iron roof, they found a body. But was it that of Griffenhagen or his uncle?

The local police informed the CID and Detective Bill Sloan took charge of the investigation. His first task was to sift the ashes for clues to enable him to identify the body. Police found a pair of badly damaged spectacles, a ring, a watch, a rabbit trap and several misshapen household items. The ring was an obvious clue and several people identified it as belonging to the old man. The spectacles, however, puzzled police and locals. Neither Griffenhagen nor his uncle wore glasses. Besides, the old man had only one eye.

It was impossible to identify the body as it had been reduced to a blackened skeleton. The discovery of the ring therefore assumed critical importance and, because of its identification as Pattison's, police assumed that the human ashes found in the but were the remains of the old man.

Pattison was buried with all due ceremony, but locals questioned the identification. This prompted Detective Sloan to investigate further, especially as there was no sign of Griffenhagen. Had he, too, been murdered? If so, where was his body? Was robbery the motive? Had the old man found a nugget and had Griffenhagen murdered him for financial gain? Or had someone murdered both men? There were many, many questions to be answered, but Detective Sloan first had to positively identify the body found in the burnt-out bush hut.

Detective Sloan made further exhaustive inquiries and police and fifty volunteers scoured the surrounding countryside. They also re-sifted the ashes taken from the hut. This was a considerable job as police reasoned that the body had been placed under a massive pyre of logs, generating fantastically intense heat. However, the re-sifting revealed further clues, including the metal buckle from a belt worn by Griffenhagen. Police also found three brass caps from a shotgun cartridge.

Police were by this time more convinced than ever that there had been a case of mistaken identity and that locals had attended the funeral of a man who might well be alive. Sloan's investigations then revealed that Griffenhagen did, in fact, wear glasses and that he had bought them in Echuca. This was not common knowledge as the young man tried to keep it a secret. However, at least two locals had seen him wearing spectacles.

Police also learned from a Bendigo jeweller that Griffenhagen had had a ring repaired only two months earlier. The jeweller identified the ring originally thought to have been Pattison's.

These findings dramatically altered the course of the investigation. Police were now convinced that the ashes were those of Griffenhagen.

The final proof, if it was needed, was that Pattison wore false teeth—and no false teeth had been found in the ashes sifted by police, even though they would have survived the fire. But if the body was that of Griffenhagen, where was Pattison? The solving of one mystery merely revealed another.

Eventually, on November 9, Axedale bee-keeper Fred Bennett discovered a man's body in scrub along the banks of the Mosquito River, several kilometres from the Griffenhagen hut. The body was positively identified as that of Pattison. The body was badly decomposed, but the thumb and forefinger of the right hand were missing and Pattison had lost these digits in an accident many years ago. A suicide note revealed that he had shot himself. But why? Had he killed his nephew in a rage? Had he then taken his own life in remorse? Pattison, in his suicide note, made no mention of his nephew.

That might have been the end of the 'Wrong Body' case if it had not been for a strange confession several months later by a young man who claimed to be Griffenhagen. The young man walked into the Swan Hill police station and told the wife of the senior constable that he was 'wanted for murder'. Mrs J. McDougall tried to detain the young man, but he rushed out of the police station and said: 'I cannot wait any longer; I have to do myself in.'

The man claiming to be Griffenhagen went straight to the flooded Murray River, boarded a motor launch and jumped into the river mid-stream. However, police discounted the possibility that the young man who drowned himself in the Murray was, in fact, Griffenhagen. Although the drowned man was about the same age, there was a big difference in height and build as Griffenhagen was tall and powerfully built, whereas the man claiming to be Griffenhagen was of medium high and slightly built.

Griffenhagen was almost certainly shot by his uncle, who then turned his nephew's hut into a funeral pyre. But why? And who was the mysterious young man who drowned himself in the Murray River? These are mysteries unlikely to ever be solved.